Rick Steves'

SCANDINAVIA

2005

D1051743

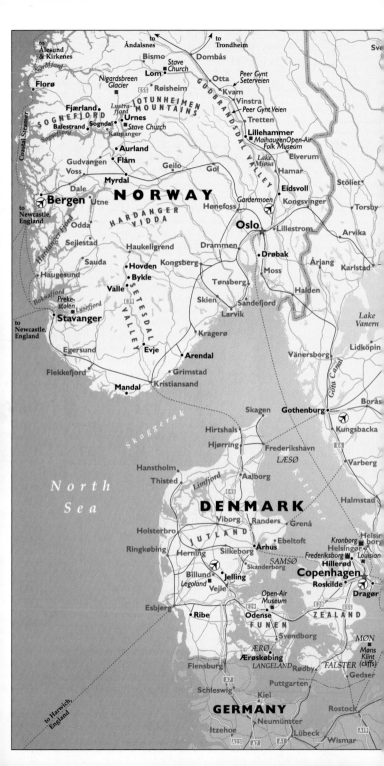

to Boden and Narvik

Tampere

Gulf of Bothnia

FINLAND

Pori

Lahti

Rauma

Porvoo

Mora

Helsinki ✈

Rättvik

Gävle

Naantali • **Turku**

DALARNA

Falun

ÅLAND

Borlänge

Mariehamn

Hanko

Gulf of Finland

lipstad

Tallinn ★

Uppsala

Arlanda Airport ✈

ESTONIA

Örebro

Västerås

Sigtuna

Vaxholm

Inset (slightly reduced)

Drottningholm ▮

Millesgården ■

HIIUMAA

☆ **Stockholm**

Nynäshamn

SAAREMAA

Norrköping

E4

Nyköping

Canal

Göta Canal

Lake Vättern

Söderköping

GOTSKA SANDÖN

Linköping

kovde

to Riga, Latvia

Västervik

•**Visby** *GOTLAND*

nköping

Vimmerby

•Ljugarn

SWEDEN

•**Byxelkrok**

LATVIA

Oskarshamn

•Burgsvik

GLASS

Orrefors Glass ■

Alvesta

Växjö

ÖLAND

Kalmar

Baltic Sea

COUNTRY

•Eketorp

Hässleholm

Karlskrona

Kristianstad

to Gdynia, Poland

lmö

Ystad

lleborg

•**Rønne**

BORNHOLM (Denmark)

ssnitz

RÜGEN

ralsund

Kolobrzeg

Koszalin

Swinoujscie

to Berlin

POLAND

LEGEND

⟨A24⟩	Freeway
———	Major Rail Line
✈	Airport
Bergen	Recommended location*
Skovde	Just passing through**
■	Ruin, Museum, other Point of Interest
▮	Castle/Monument/Palace

* Black locations are places of interest to tourists, sized by importance.

** Gray locations are places of little or no interest to tourists and are sized by population.

0 km   50   100 km

0 mi   50   100 mi

Rick Steves'

SCANDINAVIA

2005

AVALON
TRAVEL

CONTENTS

Top Destinations in Scandinavia

INTRODUCTION

Scandinavia—known for its stunning natural beauty, fun-loving cities, trend-setting design, progressive politics, high latitudes, and even higher taxes—is one of Europe's most enjoyable and most interesting corners. A visit here connects you with immigrant roots, modern European values, and the great outdoors like none other. You'll gasp at breathtaking fjords, glide on a cruise ship among picturesque islands, and marvel at the efficiency and livability of its big cities. Yes, Scandinavia is expensive. But, delightfully, the best time to visit—midsummer—is also the cheapest.

This book breaks Scandinavia into its top big-city, small-town, and rural destinations. It gives you all the information and opinions necessary to wring the maximum value out of your limited time and money. If you plan a month or less in Scandinavia, this lean and mean little book is all you need.

Experiencing the culture, people, and natural wonders of Scandinavia economically and hassle-free has been my goal for more than 25 years of traveling, guiding tours, and travel writing. With this book, I pass on to you the lessons I've learned, updated for 2005.

Rick Steves' Scandinavia is your smiling Swede, your Nordic navigator, and a tour guide in your pocket. This book is balanced to include a comfortable mix of exciting capital cities and cozy small towns. It covers the predictable biggies and mixes in a healthy dose of Back Door intimacy. Along with seeing Tivoli Gardens, Hans Christian Andersen's house, and *The Little Mermaid,* you'll take a bike tour of a sleepy, remote Danish isle, dock at a time-passed fjord village, and wander among eerie, prehistoric monoliths in Sweden. And for a breezy look at the Baltics, I've added Tallinn, Estonia.

To save time, maximize diversity, and avoid tourist burnout, I've been very selective. We won't cruise both the Geirangerfjord and Sognefjord. Instead, we'll see just the better of the two—Sognefjord.

The best is, of course, only my opinion. But after spending half my life researching Europe, I've developed a sixth sense for what travelers enjoy.

This Information is Accurate and Up-to-Date

Most publishers of guidebooks that cover a country from top to bottom can afford an update only every two or three years, and even then, the research is often by letter or e-mail. Since this book is selective, covering only the places that I think make the best month of sightseeing, it's easy to update it in person every year. The information in this book is accurate as of mid-2004, but even with an annual update, things change. Still, if you're traveling with the current edition of this book, I guarantee you're using the most up-to-date information available in print. For the latest, see www.ricksteves .com/update. Also at my Web site, check our Graffiti Wall (select "Rick Steves' Guidebooks," then "Scandinavia") for a huge, valuable list of reports and experiences—good and bad—from fellow travelers.

Use this year's edition. If you're packing an old book, you'll understand the seriousness of your mistake...in Europe. Your trip costs about $10 per waking hour. Your time is valuable. This guidebook saves lots of time.

About This Book

This book is organized by destinations. Each of these destinations is a mini-vacation on its own, filled with exciting sights and homey, affordable places to stay. In each chapter, you'll find:

Planning Your Time, a suggested schedule with thoughts on how best to use your limited time.

Orientation, including tourist information, city transportation, and an easy-to-read map designed to make the text clear and your arrival smooth.

Sights with ratings: ▲▲▲—Don't miss; **▲▲**—Try hard to see; **▲**—Worthwhile if you can make it; no rating—Worth knowing about.

Sleeping and Eating, with addresses and phone numbers of my favorite budget hotels and restaurants.

Transportation Connections, including train information and route tips for drivers, with recommended roadside attractions along the way.

The **appendix** is a traveler's tool kit, with telephone tips, a climate chart, public transportation routes, and a list of festivals.

Browse through this book, choose your favorite destinations, and link them up. Then have a great trip! You won't waste time on mediocre sights because, unlike other guidebook authors, I cover only the best. Since lousy, expensive hotels are a major financial pitfall, I've worked hard to assemble the best accommodations values for each stop. You'll travel like a temporary local, getting the absolute most out of every mile, minute, and dollar. As you travel the route I know and love, I'm happy you'll be meeting some of my favorite Scandinavian people.

PLANNING

Trip Costs

Five components make up the cost of your trip: airfare, surface transportation, room and board, sightseeing/entertainment, and shopping/miscellaneous.

Airfare: Don't try to sort through the mess. Get and use a good travel agent. A basic round-trip United States–Copenhagen flight will cost $900–1,200 (even cheaper in winter), depending on where you fly from and when. Always consider saving time and money in Europe by flying "open-jaw" (for instance, flying into Copenhagen and out of Bergen).

Surface Transportation: For a three-week whirlwind trip of all my recommended destinations, allow $550 per person for public transportation (second-class 21-day Scanrail pass and extra boat rides) or $700 per person (based on 2 people sharing car and gas) for a three-week car rental, tolls, gas, and insurance. Car rental is usually cheapest if arranged from the United States. Consider flying. Hopping on a plane to zip from Tallinn (Estonia) to Copenhagen (Denmark) in an hour can be a fine move.

Room and Board: You can eat and sleep well in Scandinavia for $100 a day for room and board. A $100-a-day budget allows $10 for lunch, $20 for dinner, and $70 for lodging (based on 2 people splitting the cost of a $140 double room that includes breakfast). Students and tightwads do it on $40 ($20 a bed, $20 for groceries and snacks). But budget sleeping and eating requires the skills and information covered in this book (and in much more depth in my book, *Rick Steves' Europe Through the Back Door*).

Sightseeing and Entertainment: In big cities, figure $5–12 per major sight (Oslo's *Kon-Tiki* Museum-$6, Copenhagen's Tivoli-$11), $3 for minor ones (climbing towers), and $25 for splurge experiences (e.g., folk concerts, bus tours, and fjord cruises). The major cities have cards giving you a 24-hour free run of the public transit system and entrance to all the sights for about $33/day. An overall average of $20 per day works for most people. Don't skimp here. After all, this category directly powers most of the experiences all the other expenses are designed to make possible.

Shopping and Miscellaneous: While Scandinavia is expensive, transportation passes, groceries, alternative accommodations, and admissions are affordable (about what you'd pay in England or Italy). The great scenery is free. When things are expensive, remind yourself you're not getting less for your travel dollar. Up here there simply aren't any lousy or cheap alternatives to classy, cozy, sleek Scandinavia.

Scandinavia's Best Three-Week Trip (By Car)

Day	Plan	Sleep in
1	Arrive in Copenhagen	Copenhagen
2	Copenhagen	Copenhagen
3	Copenhagen	Copenhagen
4	North Zealand, into Sweden	Växjö
5	Växjö, Kalmar, Glass Country	Kalmar
6	Kalmar to Stockholm	Stockholm
7	Stockholm	Stockholm
8	Stockholm	boat to Helsinki
9	Helsinki	boat to Stockholm
10	Uppsala to Oslo	Oslo
11	Oslo	Oslo
12	Oslo	Oslo
13	Lillehammer, Gudbrandsdal Valley	Jotunheimen or Sogndal
14	Jotunheimen Country	Sogndal or Aurland
15	Sognefjord, Norway in a Nutshell	Bergen
16	Bergen	Bergen
17	Long drive south, Setesdal	Kristiansand
18	Jutland, Århus, Legoland	Århus/Billund
19	Jutland to Ærø	Ærøskøbing
20	Ærø	Ærøskøbing
21	Odense, Roskilde	Copenhagen

Flying home from Bergen (with a likely transfer in Copenhagen) can be wonderfully efficient; if you opt for this, you can see Jutland and Ærø sights from Copenhagen near the beginning of your trip. Otherwise, it's about 20 hours by train from Bergen to Copenhagen via Oslo.

Electronic sensors flush youth-hostel toilets and breakfasts are all-you-can-eat. And, since every kroner you spend is about half taxes, you're subsidizing the cradle-to-grave good lives of Europe's wealthiest people.

Shopping can brutalize your budget in Scandinavia. Good budget travelers find that this category has little to do with assembling a trip full of lifelong and wonderful memories. (But if you're a dedicated shopper, see "VAT Refunds for Shoppers," page 13.) This book will help you save a shipload of money and days of headaches. Read it carefully. Many of the skills and tricks that are effective in Copenhagen work in Oslo and Stockholm as well.

When to Go

Summer is a great time to go. Scandinavia bustles and glistens under the July and August sun; it's the height of the tourist season, when all

the sightseeing attractions are open and in full swing. In many cases, things don't kick into gear until midsummer—around June 20—when Scandinavian schools let out. Most local industries take July off, and the British and central Europeans tend to visit Scandinavia in August. You'll notice crowds during these times, but up here "crowds" mean fun and action rather than congestion. Things quiet down when the local kids go back to school around August 20.

"Shoulder-season" travel—in late May, early June, and September—lacks the vitality of summer but offers good weather and minimal crowds.

Winter is a bad time to explore Scandinavia. Like a bear, Scandinavia's metabolism goes down and many sights and accommodations are closed or open on a limited schedule. Business travelers drive hotel prices way up. Winter weather can be cold and dreary, and nighttime will draw the shades on your sightseeing well before dinner.

Scandinavia's Best
Three-Week Trip (By Train)

Day	Plan	Sleep in
1	Arrive in Copenhagen	Copenhagen
2	Copenhagen	Copenhagen
3	Copenhagen	Copenhagen
4	Roskilde, Odense, Ærø	Ærøskøbing
5	Ærø	Ærøskøbing
6	Ærø to Kalmar	Kalmar
7	Kalmar	Kalmar
8	Kalmar, early train to Stockholm	Stockholm
9	Stockholm	Stockholm
10	Stockholm, night boat	boat
11	Helsinki	Helsinki
12	Helsinki, jet boat to Tallinn	Tallinn
13	Tallinn, night boat to Stockholm	Stockholm
14	Stockholm, afternoon train to Oslo	Oslo
15	Oslo	Oslo
16	Oslo	Oslo
17	Train to Aurland	Aurland
18	Aurland to Bergen via fjord cruise	Bergen
19	Bergen	Bergen
20	Free day: more fjords, Århus, resting, or whatever	
21	Trip over	

If you want to see Legoland and the Bog Man (in Århus), visit Jutland from Odense (closer) or Copenhagen.

Sightseeing Priorities

Depending on the length of your trip, and taking geographic proximity into account, here are my recommended priorities:

4 days:	Copenhagen, Stockholm (connected by a 5-hour express train)
6 days, add:	Oslo
8 days, add:	Norway in a Nutshell fjord trip, Bergen
10 days, add:	14-hour cruise to Helsinki—and slow down
14 days, add:	Ærø, Odense, Roskilde, Frederiksborg (all in Denmark)
17 days, add:	Jutland (Denmark), Kalmar (Sweden)
21 days, add:	Tallinn (Estonia) and more time in capitals
24 days, add:	More Norwegian countryside

Itinerary Specifics

Design an itinerary that enables you to hit the festivals and museums on the right days. As you read through this book, note special days (such as festivals and days when sights are closed). Saturday morning feels like any bustling weekday morning, but at lunchtime, many shops close down through Sunday. Sundays have pros and cons, as they do for travelers in the United States (special events, limited hours, shops and banks closed, limited public transportation, no rush hours). Popular places are even more popular on weekends. Many sights are closed on Monday.

Plan ahead for banking, laundry, postal chores, and picnics. To maximize rootedness, minimize one-night stands. Mix intense and relaxed periods. Every trip (and every traveler) needs at least a few slack days. Pace yourself. Assume you will return.

RESOURCES

Scandinavian Tourist Office in the United States

This office is a wealth of information. Before your trip, get the free general information packet and request any specifics you want (such as regional and city maps and festival schedules).

For questions and brochures, call tel. 212/885-9700 (P.O. Box 4649, Grand Central Station, New York, NY 10163, fax 212/885-9710, www.goscandinavia.com, info@goscandinavia.com).

Rick Steves' Books and Public Television Shows

Rick Steves' Europe Through the Back Door 2005 gives you budget travel tips on minimizing jet lag, packing light, planning your itinerary, traveling by car or train, finding budget beds, avoiding rip-offs, using mobile phones, hurdling the language barrier, staying healthy, using your bidet, taking great photographs, and lots more. The book also includes chapters on 38 of my favorite "Back Doors," two of which are in Scandinavia.

Rick Steves' Country Guides, an annually updated series that covers Europe, offer you the latest on the top sights and destinations, with tips on how to make your trip efficient and fun.

My **City and Regional Guides,** freshly updated every year, focus on Europe's most compelling destinations. Along with specifics on sights, restaurants, hotels, and nightlife, you'll get self-guided, illustrated tours of the outstanding museums and most characteristic neighborhoods.

Rick Steves' Easy Access Europe, written for travelers with limited mobility, covers the Rhine River Valley, London, Paris, Bruges, and Amsterdam.

Rick Steves' Europe 101: History and Art for the Traveler (with Gene Openshaw) gives you the story of Europe's people, history, and art. Written for smart people who were sleeping in their history and art classes before they knew they were going to Europe, *101* really helps Europe's sights come alive.

Rick Steves' Guidebooks

Rick Steves' Europe Through the Back Door
Rick Steves' Best European City Walks & Museums
Rick Steves' Easy Access Europe

Country Guides
Rick Steves' Best of Europe
Rick Steves' Best of Eastern Europe
Rick Steves' France
Rick Steves' Germany & Austria
Rick Steves' Great Britain
Rick Steves' Ireland
Rick Steves' Italy
Rick Steves' Portugal
Rick Steves' Scandinavia
Rick Steves' Spain
Rick Steves' Switzerland

City and Regional Guides
Rick Steves' Amsterdam, Bruges & Brussels
Rick Steves' Florence & Tuscany
Rick Steves' London
Rick Steves' Paris
Rick Steves' Prague & the Czech Republic*
Rick Steves' Provence & the French Riviera
Rick Steves' Rome
Rick Steves' Venice

*New in 2005

(Avalon Travel Publishing)

Rick Steves' Best European City Walks & Museums (with Gene Openshaw) gives you self-guided tours of the major museums and historic neighborhoods in London, Paris, Amsterdam, Rome, Florence, Venice, and Madrid.

My public television series, *Rick Steves' Europe,* keeps churning out shows. Out of 95 episodes (the new series plus *Travels in Europe with Rick Steves*), three shows cover Copenhagen, Stockholm, and Oslo.

Rick Steves' Postcards from Europe, my autobiographical book, packs more than 25 years of travel anecdotes and insights into the ultimate 2,000-mile European adventure.

Other Guidebooks

You may want some supplemental information, especially if you'll be traveling beyond my recommended destinations. When you consider the improvements they'll make in your $3,000 vacation, $25 or

$35 for extra maps and books is money well spent. Especially for several people traveling by car, the weight and expense are negligible.

Lonely Planet's *Scandinavian Europe* is thorough, well-researched, and packed with good maps and hotel recommendations for low- to moderate-budget travelers, but it's not updated annually. The hip *Rough Guide: Scandinavia* is thick with encyclopedic background material, but is also not updated annually. Because of the relatively small market, there just aren't many guidebooks out on Scandinavia. Of all my European-destination guidebooks, this one fills the biggest void.

For Estonia, consider the *Bradt Guide to Estonia* (published by Globe Pequot Press).

Maps

The black-and-white maps in this book, drawn by Dave Hoerlein, are concise and simple. Dave, who is well traveled in Scandinavia, has designed the maps to help you locate recommended places and get to the tourist offices, where you can pick up a more in-depth map (usually free) of the city or region. Better maps are sold at newsstands—take a look before you buy to be sure the map has the level of detail you want.

Train travelers can use a simple rail map (such as the one that comes with your train pass). But drivers shouldn't skimp on maps—get one good overall road map for Scandinavia (either the Michelin *Scandinavia* or the Kummerly & Frey *Southern Scandinavia* 1:1,000,000 edition). The Collins Road Atlas is also good. The only detailed map worth considering is the *Southern Norway-North* (Sør Norge-nord, 1:325,000) by Cappelens Kart ($15 in Scandinavian bookstores).

PRACTICALITIES

Red Tape: Traveling throughout this region requires only a passport—no shots and no visas. Border crossings between Norway, Sweden, Denmark, and Finland are a wave-through. Getting into and out of Estonia, even though it's in the European Union, takes a little longer. When you change countries, you change money, phone cards, and postage stamps.

Time: Norway, Sweden, and Denmark share the same time zone as continental Europe, but Finland and Estonia are one hour ahead. (Continental European time is six/nine hours ahead of the East/West Coast of the United States.)

In Scandinavia—and in this book—you'll be using the 24-hour clock. After 12:00 noon, keep going—13:00, 14:00, and so on. For anything over 12, subtract 12 and add p.m. (14:00 is 2:00 p.m.).

Begin Your Trip at www.ricksteves.com

At ricksteves.com you'll find a wealth of **free information** on destinations covered in this book, including fresh European travel and tour news every month and helpful "Graffiti Wall" tips from thousands of fellow travelers.

While you're there, Rick Steves' **online Travel Store** is a great place to save money on travel bags and accessories specially designed by Rick Steves to help you travel smarter and lighter. These include Rick's popular carry-on bags (wheeled and rucksack versions), money belts, day bags, totes, toiletries kits, packing cubes, clotheslines, locks, clocks, sleep sacks, adapters, and a wide selection of guidebooks, planning maps, and *Rick Steves' Europe* DVDs.

Traveling through Europe by rail is a breeze, but choosing the right railpass for your trip (amidst hundreds of options) can drive you nutty. At ricksteves.com you'll find **Rick Steves' Annual Guide to European Railpasses**—your best way to convert chaos into pure travel energy. Buy your railpass from Rick, and you'll get a bunch of free extras to boot.

Travel agents will tell you about mainstream tours of Europe, but they won't tell you about **Rick Steves' tours**. Rick Steves' Europe Through the Back Door travel company offers more than two dozen itineraries and 250-plus departures reaching the best destinations in this book...and beyond. You'll enjoy the services of a great guide, a fun bunch of travel partners (with group sizes in the mid-20s), and plenty of room to spread out in a big, comfy bus. You'll find tours to fit every vacation size, from weeklong city getaways (Paris, London, Venice, Florence, Rome), to 12- to 18-day country tours, to three-week "Best of Europe" adventures. For details, visit www.ricksteves.com or call 425/771-8303 ext. 217.

Discounts: I have not listed special age-based discounts in this book. But in keeping with its liberal orientation, Scandinavia is Europe's most generous corner when it comes to youth, student, senior, and family discounts. If you are any of the above, always mention it. Students should travel with an ISIC (International Student Identity Card, normally available at university foreign-study offices in North America; www.isic.org). Spouses often pay half price when doing things as a couple. Seniors should ask about senior discounts. Children usually sleep and sightsee for half price or for free.

Watt's up? If you're bringing electrical gear, you'll need a two-prong adapter plug and a converter. Travel appliances often have convenient, built-in converters; look for a voltage switch marked 120V (U.S.) and 240V (Europe).

MONEY

Exchange Rates

I've priced things in local currencies throughout the book.

$1 equals about...
6 Danish kroner (1 krone equals about $.17)
6.5 Norwegian kroner (1 krone equals about $.15)
7 Swedish kronor (1 krona equals about $.14)
.85 euro in Finland (€1 equals about $1.20)
12 Estonian krooni (1 kroon equals about $.08)

In Scandinavia, kroner are decimalized: 100 øre = 1 krone. Kroner from one Scandinavian country are not accepted in the next (except at foreign-exchange services and banks, and then only bills).

Standard abbreviations are Danish krone, DKK; Swedish krona, SEK; and Norwegian krone, NOK. I'll keep it simple. For all three countries, I'll use the kroner abbreviation "kr." To roughly translate Danish and Norwegian prices into U.S. dollars, divide by 6 (e.g., 100 kr = about $16). In Sweden, divide prices by 7 (65 kr = about $9).

Finland's currency is the euro (€). To roughly convert prices in euros to dollars, add 20 percent (€20 = about $24).

Tallinn's kroon, officially abbreviated as EEK, also appears as "kr" in this book. To roughly convert prices from krooni into dollars, drop the last two digits and multiply by eight (500 kr = about $40; 1,255 kr = about $96). Anything under 100 kr is less than $8.

Banking

Bring a debit card (or ATM card) and a credit card, along with a couple hundred dollars in cash as a backup. Traveler's checks are a waste of your time and money.

The best and easiest way to get cash in euros is to use the omnipresent bank machines (always open, low fees, and quick processing). You'll need a PIN code—numbers only, no letters—to use with your Visa or MasterCard.

Before you go, verify with your bank that your card will work and alert them that you'll be making withdrawals in Europe; otherwise, the bank may not approve transactions if it perceives unusual spending patterns. Bring two cards in case one gets damaged.

Just like at home, credit or debit cards work easily at larger hotels, restaurants, and shops. Visa and MasterCard are more commonly accepted than American Express. Smart travelers function with plastic and cash. Smaller businesses prefer—and sometimes require—payment in hard kroner rather than plastic.

Banking in Scandinavia is straightforward, and exchange rates are nearly standard. Buy and sell rates are within about 2 percent of each other. If you plan to bring traveler's checks, get them in large denominations because bank fees are very stiff and can be per check rather than transaction. (In Norway, some banks charge 1 or 2 percent rather than per check.) American Express offices in each capital change AmEx checks (and sometimes other brands as well) for no extra fee. Even with their worse-than-banks' exchange rates, AmEx can save you money if you're changing less than $1,000. Post offices, which have long hours, decent rates, and smaller fees, can be a good place to change money.

Bring some $20 American bills along for those times when you need just a little more local cash (e.g., if you're just passing through or about to leave a country). In many cases, small cash exchanges are cheaper outside of banks, at places that offer worse rates but smaller (or no) fees, such as the handy FOREX window at the Copenhagen train station or exchange desks on international boats.

Keep your credit and debit cards and most of your money hidden away in a money belt (a cloth pouch worn around your waist and tucked under your clothes). Thieves target tourists. A money belt provides peace of mind and allows you to carry lots of cash safely. Don't be petty about getting money. Withdraw a week's worth of money, stuff it in your money belt, and travel!

Tipping

Tipping in Europe isn't as automatic and generous as it is in the United States—but for special service, tips are appreciated, if not expected. As in the United States, the proper amount depends on your resources, tipping philosophy, and the circumstance, but some general guidelines apply.

Restaurants: Tipping is an issue only at restaurants that have waiters and waitresses. If you order your food at a counter, don't tip.

At Scandinavian restaurants that have a wait staff, service is included, although it's common to round up the bill after a good meal (usually 5–10 percent; so, for a 140-kr meal, pay 150 kr). In Estonia, where the service charge isn't included in the bill, tip 10 percent.

Taxis: To tip the cabbie, round up. For instance, to pay a 85-kr fare, give 90 kr (about 5 percent). If the cabbie hauls your bags and zips you to the airport to help you catch your flight, you might want to toss in a little more. But if you feel like you're being driven in circles or otherwise ripped off, skip the tip.

Hotels: I don't tip at hotels, but if you do, give the porter a few kroner for carrying your luggage.

When in doubt, ask: If you're not sure whether (or how much) to tip for a service, ask your hotelier or the tourist information office; they'll fill you in on how it's done on their turf.

Damage Control for Lost or Stolen Cards

You can stop thieves from using your ATM, debit, or credit card by reporting the loss immediately to the proper company. Call these 24-hour U.S. numbers collect: Visa (tel. 410/581-9994), MasterCard (tel. 636/722-7111), and American Express (tel. 336/393-1111).

Providing the following information will help expedite the process: the name of the financial institution that issued you the card, full card number, the cardholder's name as printed on the card, billing address, home phone number, circumstances of the loss or theft, and identification verification including a Social Security number or birth date and your mother's maiden name. (Packing along a photocopy of the front and back of your cards helps you answer the harder questions.) If you are the secondary cardholder, you'll also need to provide the primary cardholder's identification verification details. You can generally receive a temporary card within two or three business days in Europe.

If you promptly report your card lost or stolen, you typically won't be responsible for any unauthorized transactions on your account, although many banks charge a liability fee of $50.

VAT Refunds for Shoppers

Wrapped into the purchase price of your Scandinavian souvenirs is a Value Added Tax (VAT) of 20–25 percent. You're entitled to get most of that tax back if you make a purchase of a certain amount ($50 in Denmark, $49 in Finland, $27 in Sweden, and $210 in Estonia) at a store that participates in the VAT refund scheme. (In Denmark, for instance, look for the Danish Tax-Free Shopping emblem.) VAT is called MVA in Norway and MOMS in Denmark, Finland, and Sweden. Note that you can't get refunds on meals, hotel stays, or transportation in Scandinavia, and you can't collect any VAT refunds at all from Estonia.

Personally, I've never felt that VAT refunds are worth the hassle, but if you do, here's the scoop.

If you're lucky, the merchant will subtract the tax when you make your purchase (this is more likely to occur if the store ships the goods to your home). Otherwise, you'll need to do all this:

- **Get the paperwork.** Have the merchant completely fill out the necessary refund document, called a "cheque." You'll have to present your passport at the store.
- **Get your stamp at the border.** If you've made purchases in Denmark, Finland, Sweden, and/or Estonia, get your cheque(s) stamped at your last stop in the European Union by the customs agent who deals with VAT refunds. If you've shopped hard in Norway (a non-EU country), get your cheque(s)

stamped at the border or at your point of departure from Norway.

It's best to keep your purchases in your carry-on for viewing, but if they're too large or dangerous (such as knives) to carry on, then track down the proper customs agent to inspect them before you check your bag. You're not supposed to use your purchased goods before you leave. If you show up at customs wearing your new clogs, officials might look the other way—or deny you a refund.

- **Collect your refund.** To collect your refund, you'll need to return your stamped documents to the retailer or its representative. Many merchants work with a service such as Global Refund or Premier Tax Free, which have offices at major airports, ports, or border crossings. These services, which extract a 4 percent fee, can refund your money immediately in your currency of choice or credit your card (within 2 billing cycles). If you have to deal directly with the retailer, mail the store your stamped documents and then wait. It could take months.

Customs Regulations

You can take home $800 in souvenirs per person duty-free. The next $1,000 is taxed at a flat 3 percent. After that, you pay the individual item's duty rate. You can also bring in duty-free a liter of alcohol (slightly more than a standard-size bottle of wine), a carton of cigarettes, and up to 100 cigars. As for food, anything in cans or sealed jars is acceptable. Skip dried meat, cheeses, and fresh fruits and veggies. To check customs rules and duty rates, visit www.customs.gov.

TRAVEL SMART

Your trip to Scandinavia is like a complex play—easier to follow and really appreciate on a second viewing. While no one does the same trip twice to gain that advantage, reading this book in its entirety before your trip accomplishes much the same thing.

Reread entire chapters as you travel, and visit local tourist information offices. Upon arrival in a new town, lay the groundwork for a smooth departure. Buy a phone card and use it for reservations and confirmations. Enjoy the friendliness of the local people. Ask questions. Most locals are eager to point you in their idea of the right direction. Wear your money belt, pack along a pocket-size notebook to organize your thoughts, and practice the virtue of simplicity. Those who expect to travel smart, do.

Tourist Information

The tourist information office is your best first stop in any new town or city. In this book, I'll refer to a tourist information office as a **TI**. Have a list of questions and a proposed sightseeing plan to confirm.

If you're arriving late, telephone ahead (and try to get a map for your next destination from a TI in the town you're leaving). Important: Each big city publishes a *This Week In...* guide (to Copenhagen, Stockholm, Oslo, Bergen, Helsinki, Århus, and Tallinn). These are free, found all over town, and packed with all the tedious details about each city (24-hour pharmacy, embassies, tram/bus fares, restaurants, sights with hours/admissions/phone numbers), plus a useful calendar of events and a map of the town center.

While the TIs offer room-finding services, they're a good deal only if you're in search of summer and weekend deals on business hotels. The TIs can help you with small pensions and private homes, but you'll save both yourself and your host money by going direct with the listings in this book.

TRANSPORTATION

Getting to Scandinavia

Copenhagen is usually the most direct and least expensive Scandinavian capital to fly into from the United States (though Stockholm and Helsinki offer similarly easy connections on Icelandair from the East Coast of the United States). Copenhagen is also Europe's gateway to Scandinavia from points south. There are often cheaper flights from the United States into Frankfurt and Amsterdam than into Copenhagen, but it's a long, rather dull, one-day drive (with a 2-hour, $75-per-car-and-passenger ferry crossing at Puttgarten, Germany). By train, the trip is an easy overnight ride from Amsterdam, Paris, or Frankfurt. The trip ($150–200) is covered if you have the comprehensive Eurailpass or a railpass covering the particular countries.

In Scandinavia: By Car or Train?

While a car gives you the ultimate in mobility and freedom, enables you to search for hotels more easily, and carries your bags for you, the train zips you effortlessly and scenically from city to city, usually dropping you in the center and near the tourist office. Cars are great in the countryside but an expensive headache in big cities. Three or four people travel cheaper by car. With a few exceptions, trains cover my recommended destinations wonderfully. Pick up train schedules from stations as you go. To study ahead on the Web, check http://bahn.hafas.de/bin/query.exe/en (Germany's excellent Europe-wide timetable). The local train companies also have their own sites with fare and timetable information; see http://dsb.dk (Denmark), www.nsb.no (Norway), and www.sj.se (Sweden).

Trains

One of the great Nordic bargains, the Scanrail pass is your best railpass deal for a trip limited to Scandinavia. Those sold in the United

Railpasses

Prices listed are for 2004. My free *Rick Steves' Guide to European Railpasses* has the latest prices and details (and easy online ordering) at: www.ricksteves.com/rail.

SCANRAIL PASS

	2nd Cl. Adult	2nd Cl. Senior	2nd Cl. Youth
5 days in 2 months	$291	$258	$203
10 days in 2 months	390	348	273
21 consecutive days	453	400	316

Trolls 4-11 half adult price, under 4 free. Senior = 60+. Youth = under 26. Covers Denmark, Norway, Sweden, and Finland.

NORWAY RAILPASS

	2nd Cl. Adult	2nd Cl. Sr./Youth
3 days in a month	$209	$151
Extra rail days (max. 5)	35	25

Kids 4-15 half price, under 4 free. Senior = 60+. Youth = under 26. Not valid on Airport Express.

FINNRAIL PASS

	1st Class	2nd Class
3 days in a month	$214	$143
5 days in a month	286	191
10 days in a month	387	259

Kids 2-15 half price when accompanied by parent, under 2 free.

Scandinavia:
Point-to-point 1-way
2nd class rail fares in $US.
1st class costs 50% more.
Add up fares for your itinerary
to see whether a railpass
will save you money.

EURAIL SELECTPASSES

This pass covers travel in three, four, or five adjacent countries. Visit www.ricksteves.com/rail for additional country choices.

		1st Class Individual	1st Class Saver	2nd Class Youth
Three Countries	5 days in 2 months	$356	$304	$249
	6 days in 2 months	394	336	276
	8 days in 2 months	470	400	329
	10 days in 2 months	542	460	379
Four Countries	5 days in 2 months	$398	$340	$279
	6 days in 2 months	436	372	306
	8 days in 2 months	512	436	359
	10 days in 2 months	584	496	409
Five Countries	5 days in 2 months	$438	$374	$307
	6 days in 2 months	476	406	334
	8 days in 2 months	552	470	387
	10 days in 2 months	624	530	437
	15 days in 2 months	794	674	556

Saverpass prices are per person for two or more people traveling together. Kids 4-11 half price, under 4 free.

SCANRAIL & DRIVE PASS

5 days of rail travel + 2 days of Avis car rental in 2 months.

Car category	2nd Class	Extra car day
Economy	$339	$59
Compact	359	69
Intermediate	369	79

No extra rail days. Price per person for two traveling together. To order Scanrail & Drive passes, call Rail Europe at 800/438-7245. *This pass is not sold by Europe Through the Back Door.*

Scandinavia: Main Train Lines

TO BODØ   TO NARVIK

ÖSTERSUND

TRONDHEIM   STORLIEN

HELL

ÅNDALSNES

DOMBÅS

BALESTRAND

LILLEHAMMER   MORA

FLÅM

VOSS   MYRDAL

GOL   TO TURKU

GEILO   KONGS-VINGER

BERGEN   UPPSALA

OSLO   STOCKHOLM

NORWAY   DRØBAK   TO HELSINKI

LAXÅ

TO ENG.   STAVANGER   LAR-VIK

HIRTS-HALS   MJÖLBY

GÖTE-BORG   SWEDEN   GOTLAND

KRISTIANSAND   ALVESTA   VÄXJÖ   ÖLAND

HJØRRING   FRED.   KALMAR

ÅLBORG

DENMARK   KARLS-KRONA

NORTH   ÅRHUS   HEL-SINGØR

ESBJERG   VEJLE   COPE.   MALMÖ   BALTIC

ODENSE   YSTAD

TO HARWICH   FREDE-RICIA   ÆRØ   SEA

RØDBY   ROSKILDE

PUTTGARTEN   GEDSER

SEA   SASS.   TO POLAND

ROSTOCK

TO   LÜBECK   DCH
HAMBURG

TO BERLIN

KEY: — RAIL ╤╤ PRIVATE RAIL ---- BUS ⋯ SHIP
(DISCOUNT ✔ RAILPASS)

States are listed on page 16. More restrictive 5-days-out-of-15 or 21-consecutive-day variations are also available for a similar price at any major train station in Scandinavia (www.scanrail.com). Although Scanrail passes are available only for second-class seats, Scandinavian second class is like Southern European first class, and I find it plenty comfortable. Some trains, including those that cover part of the popular Norway in a Nutshell route (see page 155), do not offer first class.

Driving in Scandinavia: Distance and Time

If your trip extends south of Scandinavia, consider the flexible Eurail Selectpass, which allows you to choose three, four, or five adjoining countries connected by land or ferry (for instance, Germany–Sweden–Finland). A more expensive Eurailpass is a good value only for those spending more time throughout Europe. A three-week first-class Eurailpass costs $762 (or $648 apiece for a Eurail Saverpass if you travel with a companion).

Railpasses give you free or discounted use of many boats (such as Stockholm to Finland) and cover virtually all trains in the region (though you'll need 50-kr reservations for long rides and express trains, plus a 105-kr supplement for Norway's Myrdal-to-Flåm ride—part of the Norway in a Nutshell route).

A Scanrail 'n' Drive pass offers a flexible, economical way to mix rail and car rental, and is handy if you plan to explore Sweden's Glass Country or the Norwegian mountains and fjords.

Consider the efficiency of night travel. A bed in a compartment on a night train is a good value in Scandinavia. Beyond the cost of your first- or second-class ticket or pass, you'll pay about $25 for a bed in a triple, $40 for a bed in a double, or $100 for a single.

Car Rental

Car rental is usually cheapest when arranged (well in advance) in the United States through your travel agent, rather than in Scandinavia. You'll want a weekly rate with unlimited mileage. If you're traveling for more than three weeks, ask about leasing a car (which includes CDW insurance, described below). Each major rental agency has an office in the Copenhagen airport. Comparison-shop directly or through your travel agent.

For peace of mind, consider CDW insurance (Collision Damage Waiver, about 25 percent extra). In case of an accident, CDW insurance lowers your deductible (generally to about $1,200, rather than the standard value-of-the-car deductible). Some companies sell additional coverage to buy down the deductible when you pick up the car. Increasingly, it's a better deal to waive the car rental company's CDW insurance entirely and opt instead for the coverage that comes with many "gold" credit cards (often with a zero deductible). Ask your credit-card company how it works, and quiz them about deductibles and worst-case scenarios (for example, they may only cover damage up to the credit limit of your card). Another alternative is to buy CDW coverage from a third party, such as Travel Guard ($7/day, U.S. tel. 800-826-4919, www.travelguard.com).

Driving

Except for the dangers posed by the scenic distractions and moose crossings, Scandinavia is a great place to drive. Your American license is accepted. Gas is expensive—more than $4 per gallon (gas is cheaper in Denmark than in its northern neighbors)—but roads are good (though nerve-rackingly skinny in western Norway). Traffic is generally sparse, and drivers are sober and civil. Signs and road maps are excellent. Local road etiquette is similar to that in the United States. Use your headlights day and night; it's required in most of Scandinavia. Seat belts are mandatory. Bikes tend to whiz by close and quiet, so be on guard.

There are plenty of good facilities, gas stations, and scenic rest stops. Snow is a serious problem off-season in the mountains. Parking on the street is a headache only in major cities, where expensive garages are safe and plentiful. Denmark uses a parking windshield-clock disk (free at TIs, post offices, and newsstands; set it when you arrive and be back before your posted time limit is up). Even in the Nordic countries, thieves break into cars. Park carefully, use the trunk, and show no valuables. Never drink and drive. Even one drink can get a driver into serious trouble.

As you navigate, you'll find town signs followed by the letters N, S, Ø (Ö in Sweden), V, or C. These stand for north *(nord)*, south *(sud)*, east *(øst)*, west *(vest)*, and center *(centrum)*, respectively, and understanding them will save you lots of wrong exits. Due to recent changes, many maps have the wrong road numbers. It's safest to navigate by town names.

COMMUNICATING

The Language Barrier

In Scandinavia, English is all you need. These days every well-educated person seems to speak English. Still, knowing the key words is good style and helpful.

A few words you'll see and hear a lot: *takk* (thanks), *gammel* (old), *lille* (small), *stor* (big), *slot* (palace), *fart* (trip), *centrum* (center), *gate* (street), *øl* (beer), *forbudt* (not allowed), and *udsalg* or *salg* (sale).

One Region, Different Countries

Scandinavia is Western Europe's least populated, most literate, most prosperous, most demographically homogeneous, most highly taxed, most socialistic, and least churchgoing corner. While the state religion is Lutheranism, only a small percentage of Scandinavians actually attend church other than at Easter or Christmas.

Denmark, Norway, and Sweden are each constitutional monarchies with a royal family who knows how to stay out of the tabloids and work with the parliaments. Scandinavia is the home of cradle-to-grave security and, consequently, residents (and visitors) pay hefty taxes. Blessed with pristine natural surroundings, the Scandinavians are environmentalists (except for the Norwegians' stubborn appetite for whaling). The region is also a leader in progressive lifestyles. More than half the couples in Denmark are "married" only because they've lived together for so long and have children.

Denmark, packing five million fun-loving Danes into a flatland the size of Switzerland, is the most densely populated Scandinavian country. Sweden, the size of California, has 8.5 million people; and 4.2 million Norwegians stretch out in vast yet skinny Norway. Oslo is as far from the northern tip of Norway as it is from Rome.

Each country has its own language. Danish, Norwegian, and Swedish are so closely related that locals can laugh at each other's TV comedies. The languages are similar to English but with a few letters we don't have (Æ, Ø, Ö, Å, Ä). These letters barely affect pronunciation, but do affect alphabetizing. If you can't find, say, Århus in a map index, look after Z.

Telephones

Savvy travelers learn the phone system and use it daily to reserve or reconfirm rooms, get tourist information, reserve restaurants, confirm tour times, or phone home.

Phone Cards: Phone cards have mostly replaced coin-operated phones in Scandinavia. Instead of putting coins in pay phones, today's Europeans buy cards with prepaid time. There are two types of phone cards:

1. Insertable phone cards that you stick into the slot of a public pay phone. Each country's telephone company sells a basic phone card (usually in denominations of $5 and $10), good for use only in that country's phone booths. You can buy phone cards at the post office, newsstands, and tobacco shops. To make a call, simply take the phone off the hook, insert the prepaid card, wait for a dial tone, and dial away. The price of the call (local or international) is automatically deducted while you talk.

2. International phone cards, which are not inserted, can be used from virtually any phone, even from the one in your hotel room. Dial the toll-free number listed on the card, reaching an automated operator. When prompted, you dial in a code number, also written on the card. A voice tells you how much is left in your account. Then dial your number. The card is good for local, long-distance, or international calls.

Calls to the United States cost about $1 for 10 minutes. Cards, offered in denominations of $5 and $10, are sold at small newsstand kiosks and hole-in-the-wall long-distance phone shops. Because there are so many brand names, simply ask for an international telephone card and tell the vendor where you'll be making most calls ("to America"), and he'll select the brand with the best deal. Get small denominations in case the card is a dud.

Beware: Most merchants promise that the cards work throughout Scandinavia (because each card has local access numbers for each country), but often they don't work in neighboring countries, and you're stuck with extra minutes that you can't use. The Go Bananas card is more reliable than most—good in Denmark, Norway, Sweden, and Germany.

Dialing Direct: In Denmark, Estonia, and Norway, which don't use area codes, just dial local numbers direct from anywhere in the country. Sweden and Finland do have area codes. When making long-distance calls within Sweden or Finland, include the entire area code (which starts with a zero).

Calling internationally to a Scandinavian country, you'll need to:
- Dial the international access code (011 if calling from the U.S. or Canada, 00 from Europe).
- Dial the country code of the country you're calling. For a list of country codes, see the appendix.
- If the country you're calling uses area codes, dial the code, omitting the initial zero. If the country does not use area codes, skip this step.
- Dial the local number.

To call one of my recommended B&Bs in Copenhagen from anywhere in Denmark, just dial its local number directly (32 95 96 22). To call the Copenhagen B&B from the United States, dial 011 (U.S. international access code), 45 (Denmark's country code), then 32 95 96 22.

To call Stockholm's hostel-in-a-ship from anywhere in Sweden outside of Stockholm, dial 08 (Stockholm's area code), then the local number, 679-5015. To call the Stockholm hostel from the United States, dial 011 (U.S. international access code), 46 (Sweden's country code), 8 (Stockholm's area code without the initial zero), then

679-5015. To call my office from Sweden, dial 00 (Sweden's international access code), 1 (the United States' country code), then 425/771-8303. Remember that European time is six/nine hours ahead of the East/West Coast of the United States.

Hotel-room phones are a terrible rip-off if you're calling the United States. Never call home from your hotel room unless you're using a phone card.

Calling Cards from American Companies: Calling cards offered by AT&T, MCI, and Sprint used to be a good value until direct-dialing rates dropped and international calling cards appeared. Now it's much cheaper to dial direct using an international calling card (see above).

Mobile Phones: Many travelers buy cheap mobile phones in Europe to make both local and international calls. (Typical American mobile phones don't work in Europe, and those that do have horrendous per-minute costs.) For about $100 you can get a phone with $20 worth of calls that will work in the country where you purchased it. (You can buy more time at newsstands and mobile phone shops.) For about $120 you can get a phone that will work in most countries once you pick up the necessary chip per country (about $25 each). If you're interested, stop by any European shop that sells mobile phones; you'll see prominent store window displays. Depending on your trip and budget, ask for a phone that works only in that country or one that can be used throughout Europe. If you're on a budget, skip mobile phones and use phone cards instead.

E-mail and Mail

E-mail: E-mail use among Scandinavian hoteliers is quite common. Internet cafés and little hole-in-the-wall Internet-access shops (offering a few computers, no food, and cheap prices) are popular in most cities. Your hotelier can direct you to the nearest place.

Mail: While you can arrange for mail delivery to your hotel (allow 10 days for a letter to arrive), phoning and e-mailing are so easy that I've dispensed with mail stops altogether.

SLEEPING

For each destination, I recommend the best accommodations values, from $15 bunk beds to $200 doubles. An overall average of $80 per night in humble doubles is possible using this book's listings. I like small, central, clean, traditional, friendly places that aren't listed in other guidebooks. Most places listed meet five of these six virtues. For smart use of your time, I favor hotels and restaurants handy to your sightseeing activities and public transportation.

Room-finding services offered by tourist information offices, if you have no place in mind, can be worth the 50-kr fee (about $8).

Sleep Code

To help you sort easily through these listings, I've divided the rooms into three categories based on the price for a standard double room with bath:

$$$ **Higher Priced**
$$ **Moderately Priced**
$ **Lower Priced**

To give maximum information with a minimum of space, I use the following code to describe accommodations listed in this book. Prices are listed per room, not per person. When a range of prices is listed for a room, the price fluctuates with room size or season. You can assume a hotel takes credit cards unless you see "cash only" in the listing.

    S = Single room (or price for one person in a double).
    D = Double or Twin. Double beds are usually big enough for non-romantic couples.
    T = Triple (often a double bed with a single bed moved in).
    Q = Quad (an extra child's bed is usually cheaper).
    b = Private bathroom with toilet and shower or tub.
    s = Private shower or tub only (the toilet is down the hall).
    SE = Speaks English.
    NSE = Does not speak English. Used only when it's unlikely you'll encounter English-speaking staff.

You can assume credit cards are accepted unless otherwise noted. According to this code, a couple staying at a "Db-995 kr" hotel in Sweden would pay a total of 995 kr (about $140) for a double room with a private bathroom. The hotel accepts credit cards or hard kronor in payment.

Be very clear about what you want. (Say "cheap" and mention that you have sheets or a sleeping bag, whether you will take a twin or double, if a bathroom down the hall is acceptable, and so on.) They know the hotel quirks and private-room scene better than anybody. Official "rack rates" (the highest rates a hotel charges) are often misleading, since they omit cheaper oddball rooms and special clearance deals.

To sleep cheaply, bring your own sheet or sleeping bag and offer to provide it in low-priced establishments. This can save $10 per person per night, especially in rural areas. Families can get a price break; normally a child can sleep free or for very little in Mom and Dad's room.

To get the most sleep for your dollar, pull the dark shades (and even consider bringing your own night shades) to keep out the early morning sun.

Hotels

Hotels are expensive ($80–200 doubles), with some exceptions. Business-class hotels drop prices to attract tourists with summer rates (late June–early Aug) and weekend rates (Fri, Sat, and sometimes Sun). Some chains such as Rainbow Hotels in Norway offer 400-kr discounts (about $60) per night if you purchase a 90-kr Skanplus discount card from them (about $15). You need to ask about these—receptionists don't volunteer the information.

To sleep in a fancy hotel in a big city, it's cheapest to arrive without a reservation and let the local tourist office book you a room. When a classy, modern $200 place has a $100 summer special that includes two $10 buffet breakfasts, the dumpy $60 hotel room without breakfast becomes less exciting.

There are actually several tiers of rates, including tourist office referral, weekend, summer, summer weekend, and walk-in. Walk-ins at the end of a quiet day can often get a room even below the summer rate. Many modern hotels have "combi" rooms (singles with a sofa that makes the room into a perfectly good double), which are cheaper than a full double. Also, many places have low-grade older rooms, considered unacceptable for the general public and often used by workers on weekdays outside of summer; if you're on a budget, ask for cheaper rooms with no windows or no water. And if a hotel is not full, any day can bring out summer discounts.

Hostels

Scandinavian hostels, Europe's finest, are open to travelers of all ages. They offer classy facilities, members' kitchens, cheap hot meals (often breakfast buffets), plenty of doubles (for a few extra kroner), and great people experiences. Receptionists will hold a room if you promise to arrive by 18:00. Note that many hostels close in the off-season.

Buy a hostel membership card before you leave home ($28 a year, free if you're under 18 and $15 if you're over 54; sold at your local student travel office, any hostel office, Hostelling International—U.S. tel. 301/495-1240, or online at www.hiayh.org). Those without hostel cards are admitted for a $7-per-night guest membership fee. Bring bedsheets from home or plan on renting them for about $6 per stay.

You'll find lots of Volvos in hostel parking lots, as Scandinavians know that hostels provide the best (and usually only) $20 beds in town. Hosteling is ideal for families who fit into two sets of bunk beds (4-bed rooms, kitchens, washing machines, discount family memberships). Pick up each country's free hostel directory at any hostel or TI.

Making Reservations

You can do this entire trip easily without reservations during most of the year (except, for instance, in the capitals during conventions—early June is packed in Oslo and Stockholm). Still, given the high stakes, erratic accommodations values, and the quality of the gems I've found for this book, I'd recommend calling ahead for rooms. For maximum flexibility, call between 9:00 and 10:00 on the day you plan to arrive, when the hotelier knows who'll be checking out and just which rooms will be available. But if you know your itinerary in advance, consider making telephone reservations before leaving home.

A hotel receptionist will trust you and hold a room until 16:00 without a deposit, though some will ask for a credit-card number. All proprietors speak English. Honor (or cancel by phone) your reservations. Long distance is cheap and easy from public phone booths. Don't let these people down—I promised you'd call and cancel if for some reason you won't show up. Don't needlessly confirm rooms through the tourist office; they'll take a commission.

To reserve from home, call, e-mail, or fax the hotel. Phone and fax costs are reasonable, e-mail is a breeze, and simple English is fine. To fax, use the form in the appendix (online at www.ricksteves.com/reservation). In Europe, dates appear as day/month/year, so a two-night stay in August would be "2 nights, 16/8/05 to 18/8/05" (hotel jargon includes your day of departure). You'll often receive a response back from the hotel requesting one night's deposit. If you provide your credit-card number as the deposit, you can pay with your card or with cash when you arrive; if you don't show up, you'll be billed for one night. Reconfirm your reservations a day or two in advance for safety.

Private Rooms

Throughout Scandinavia, people rent out rooms in their homes to travelers for about $50 per double (or about $75 for a double with private bath). While some put out a *Værelse, Rom, Rum,* or *Hus Rum* sign, most operate solely through the local TI (which occasionally keeps these B&Bs a secret until all hotel rooms are taken). You'll get your own key to a clean, comfortable but usually simple private room (sometimes without a sink), with free access to the family shower and WC (unless the room has a private bath). Booking direct saves both you and your host the cut the TI takes. The TIs are very protective of their lists. If you enjoy a big-city private home that would like to be listed in this book, I'd love to hear from you.

Camping

Scandinavian campgrounds are practical, comfortable, and cheap (about $6–7 per person with camping card, available on the spot). The national tourist office has a fine brochure/map listing all their campgrounds. This is the middle-class Scandinavian family way to travel: safe, great social fun, and no reservation problems.

Huts

Most campgrounds provide huts *(hytter)* for wanna-be campers with no gear. Huts normally sleep four to six in bunk beds, come with blankets and a kitchenette, and charge one fee (about 300 kr or $50, plus extra if you need sheets). Since locals typically move in for a week or two, many campground huts are booked for summer long in advance. If you're driving late with no place to stay, find a campground and try to grab a hut.

EATING

Breakfast

Hotel breakfasts are a huge and filling buffet, generally included but occasionally a $10-or-so option. This includes fruit, cereal, and various milks *(skummet* is skim, *lett* is low-fat, *sød* or *hel* is whole, *kefir* is buttermilk). Grab a drinkable yogurt and go local by pouring it in the bowl and sprinkling your cereal over it. The great selection of breads and crackers comes with jam, butter *(smør),* margarine (same word), and cheese. The brown cheese with the texture of earwax and a slightly sweet taste is *geitost*—goat's cheese; your trip will go better when you develop a taste for it. And you'll get cold cuts, pickled herring, caviar paste (in a squeeze tube), and boiled eggs *(bløt* is soft-boiled, *kokt* is hard-boiled); use the plastic egg cups and small spoons provided to eat your soft-boiled egg Scandinavian-style.

For beverages, it's orange juice *(appelsin* is OJ—get used to getting OJ when you ask for AJ) and coffee or tea. Coffee addicts can buy a thermos and get it filled in most hotels and hostels for $3 or $4. While it is bad form to take freebies from the breakfast buffet to eat later, many hotels will provide you with wax paper and a plastic bag to pack yourself a lunch, legitimately, for $6–7. Ask for a *matpakke.*

If you skip your hotel's breakfast, you can visit a bakery to get a sandwich and cup of coffee. Bakeries have wonderful inexpensive pastries. The only cheap breakfast is the one you make yourself. Many simple accommodations provide kitchenettes or at least coffeepots with heated bases.

Lunch

Many restaurants offer cheap daily lunch specials *(dagens rett)* and buffets for office workers. Scandinavians, not big on lunch, often just grab a sandwich *(smørrebrød)* and a cup of coffee at their work desk.

Especially in Denmark, you'll find *smørrebrød* shops turning sandwiches into an art form. These open-faced delights taste as good as they look. My favorite is the one piled high with *rejer* (shrimp). The roast beef is good, too. Shops will wrap sandwiches up for a perfect picnic in a nearby park.

If you want to enjoy a combination of picnics and restaurant meals on your trip, you'll save money by eating in restaurants at lunch (when there's usually a special and food is generally cheaper) and picnicking for dinner.

Picnics

Scandinavia has colorful markets and economical supermarkets. Picnic-friendly mini-markets at gas and train stations are open late. Samples of picnic treats: *Wasa* cracker bread (Sport is my favorite; Ideal *flatbrød* is ideal for munchies), packaged meat and cheese, goat cheese (*geitost; ekte* means pure and stronger), drinkable yogurt, freshly cooked or smoked fish from markets, fresh fruit and vegetables, lingonberries, squeeze tubes of mustard and sandwich spreads (shrimp, caviar), rye bread, and boxes of juice

and milk. Grocery stores sell a cheap, light breakfast: a handy yogurt with cereal and a spoon. Most places offer cheap ready-made sandwiches. If you're bored with sandwiches, some groceries and most delis have hot chicken, salads by the portion, and picnic portables.

Dinner

The large meal of the Nordic day is an early dinner. Alternate between cheap, forgettable, but filling cafeteria or fast-food dinners ($10) and atmospheric, carefully chosen restaurants popular with locals ($20). One main course and two salads or soups fill up two travelers without emptying their pocketbooks. The cheap eateries close early. In Scandinavia, a normal, practical, fill-the-tank dinner is usually eaten around 18:00. Anyone eating out later is "dining," will linger longer, and can expect to pay much more. A $15 Scandinavian meal is not that much more than a $10 American meal, since tax and tip are included in the menu price. Waitresses and waiters are well paid, and tips are normally included, although it's polite to round up the bill. (But in Estonia, where the service charge isn't included in the bill, tip 10 percent.)

In most Scandinavian restaurants, you can ask for more potatoes, so a restaurant entrée is basically an all-you-can-eat deal. First servings are often small, so take advantage of seconds. Fast-food joints, pizzerias, Chinese food, and salad bars are inexpensive. Booze is pricey. A beer costs $6 in Oslo. Water is served free with an understanding smile at most restaurants.

Most Scandinavian nations have one inedible dish that is cherished with a perverse but patriotic sentimentality. These dishes, which often originated during a famine, now remind the young of their ancestors' suffering. Norway's penitential food, *lutefisk* (dried cod marinated for days in lye and water), is used for Christmas and jokes.

Smörgåsbord

At least once in your trip, seek out a Scandinavian feast, the *smörgåsbord* (known in Denmark and Norway as the *store koldt bord*). This all-you-can-eat buffet allows you to sample the culinary delights of the Nordic lands.

Resist the urge to pile everything on your plate at once, as many Americans do, "Royal Fork" style. Instead, watch the locals. Take your time and dine in stages. Dirty lots of dishes.

Your first course is fish. Start with *sild* (pickled herring) on a slice of dense rye bread called *rugbrød*. Then maybe *gravad laks* (smoked salmon) with caviar on the side. Wash it down with beer or an ice-cold shot of *akvavit* (liquor distilled from potatoes—like vodka—flavored with anise, fennel, caraway, or other herbs). *"Skål!"* (skole) means "Cheers!"

Then get a new plate and move on to the main course of fish, chicken, or another meat, often accompanied by potatoes. The seafood is usually wonderful.

Next comes the cheese and fruit course with *franskbrød* white bread. Try creamy Havarti, blue Castello (a soft, mild blue cheese), and, in Norwegian buffets, goat cheese. For dessert there are often cakes or cookies with coffee.

You'll find these buffets for lunch and dinner; lunch is usually cheaper. Some good places for a Nordic buffet: Bergen's Hotel Norge, Stockholm's Grand Hotel, and on the boats between Copenhagen and Oslo and between Stockholm and Helsinki or Tallinn. Note that many hotels offer a mini-version of the feast mentioned above.

Dessert

Scandinavians love sweets. A meal is not complete without a little treat and a cup of coffee at the end. Bakeries *(konditori)* fill their window cases with all varieties of cakes, tarts, cookies, and pastries. The most popular ingredients are marzipan, almonds, hazelnuts, chocolate, and fresh berries. Many cakes are covered with entire sheets of solid marzipan. To find the neighborhood bakery, just look for a golden pretzel hanging above the door or windows.

Scandinavian chocolate is some of the best in Europe. In Denmark, seek out Anthon Berg's dark chocolate and marzipan treats as well as Toms' chocolate-covered caramels (Toms Guld are the best). Sweden's biggest chocolate producer, Maribou, makes huge bars of solid milk chocolate, as well as some with dried fruits or nuts. *Daim* are milk chocolate–covered hard toffees, sold in a variety of sizes, from large bars to bite-size pieces, all in bright-red wrappers. The Freia company, Norway's chocolate goddess (named for the Norse goddess Freya), makes a wonderful assortment of delights, from *Et lite stykke Norge* ("A little piece of Norway"—bars of creamy milk chocolate wrapped in pale-yellow paper) and *Smil* (chocolate-covered soft caramels sold in rolls) to *Firkløver* (bars of milk chocolate with hazelnuts). For those who can't decide on one type, the company sells bags of assorted chocolates called *Twist* and red gift boxes of chocolates called *Kong Haakon*, named after Norway's first king.

While chocolate rules, licorice and gummy candies are also popular. Black licorice *(lakrits)* is at its best here, except for *salt lakrits*, (salty licorice) which is not for the timid. Black licorice flavors everything from ice cream to chewing gum to liquor (for a strong, sweet, black licorice-infused shot, try *små grå*, called *salmiakki* in Finland).

TRAVELING AS A TEMPORARY LOCAL

We travel all the way to Scandinavia to enjoy differences—to become temporary locals. One of the beauties of travel is the opportunity to see that there are logical, civil, and even better alternatives to "truths" we always considered God-given and self-evident. While the materialistic culture of the United States is sneaking into these countries, simplicity has yet to become subversive. Scandinavians are into "sustainable affluence." They have experimented aggressively in the area of social welfare—with mixed results. Travel in high-tax/high government–service Scandinavia can rattle capitalist Americans. The people seem so happy and the society seems so genteel. Fit in, don't look for things American on the other side of the Atlantic, and you're sure to enjoy some thought-provoking stimulation and a full dose of Scandinavian hospitality.

Send Me a Postcard, Drop Me a Line
If you enjoy a successful trip with the help of this book and would like to share your discoveries, please fill out the survey at www.ricksteves .com/feedback or e-mail me at rick@ricksteves.com. I personally read and value all feedback.

Judging from the happy postcards I receive from travelers, it's safe to assume you'll enjoy a great, affordable vacation—with the finesse of an independent, experienced traveler.

Thanks, and happy travels!

BACK DOOR TRAVEL PHILOSOPHY

from *Rick Steves' Europe Through the Back Door*

Travel is intensified living—maximum thrills per minute and one of the last great sources of legal adventure. Travel is freedom. It's recess, and we need it.

Experiencing the real Europe requires catching it by surprise, going casual..."through the Back Door."

Affording travel is a matter of priorities. (Make do with the old car.) You can travel—simply, safely, and comfortably—anywhere in Europe for $100 a day plus transportation costs. In many ways, spending more money only builds a thicker wall between you and what you came to see. Europe is a cultural carnival, and, time after time, you'll find that its best acts are free and the best seats are the cheap ones.

A tight budget forces you to travel close to the ground, meeting and communicating with the people, not relying on service with a purchased smile. Never sacrifice sleep, nutrition, safety, or cleanliness in the name of budget. Simply enjoy the local-style alternatives to expensive hotels and restaurants.

Extroverts have more fun. If your trip is low on magic moments, kick yourself and make things happen. If you don't enjoy a place, maybe you don't know enough about it. Seek the truth. Recognize tourist traps. Give a culture the benefit of your open mind. See things as different but not better or worse. Any culture has much to share.

Of course, travel, like the world, is a series of hills and valleys. Be fanatically positive and militantly optimistic. If something's not to your liking, change your liking. Travel is addictive. It can make you a happier American as well as a citizen of the world. Our Earth is home to six billion equally important people. It's humbling to travel and find that people don't envy Americans. They like us, but, with all due respect, they wouldn't trade passports.

Globe-trotting destroys ethnocentricity. It helps you understand and appreciate different cultures. Travel changes people. It broadens perspectives and teaches new ways to measure quality of life. Many travelers toss aside their hometown blinders. Their prized souvenirs are the strands of different cultures they decide to knit into their own character. The world is a cultural yarn shop. And Back Door travelers are weaving the ultimate tapestry.

Come on, join in!

DENMARK
(Danmark)

Denmark is the smallest of the Scandinavian countries, but at one point it was the largest. In the 16th century, Denmark ruled all of Norway and the three southern provinces of Sweden. Danes are proud of their mighty history and are the first to remind you that they were a lot bigger and a lot stronger in the good old days.

Before its heyday as a Scan-superpower, Denmark was, like Norway and Sweden, home to the Vikings. More than anything else, these warriors were known for their great shipbuilding, which enabled them to travel far. Denmark's Vikings traveled west to Great Britain and Ireland (and founded Dublin), bringing back many influences to Denmark, including Christianity.

Today Denmark is one of the most environmentally conscious European countries. They are front-runners in renewable energy sources, recycling, and organic farming. The countryside is dotted with modern windmills, or wind turbines. Wind power accounts for 18 percent of Denmark's energy today, with a goal of 50 percent by 2030. In 1971, Denmark became the first country to create a cabinet-level ministry dealing exclusively with the environment. Half of all waste is recycled, and 80 percent of new paper is made from used paper. Twenty percent of the Department of Agriculture's budget is dedicated to promoting organic farming. In grocery stores, organic products are shelved right alongside nonorganic ones—for the same price.

Like the other Scandinavian countries, Denmark is predominantly Lutheran, but only a small minority attends church regularly. Danes are more inclined to treat their home like a sanctuary and spend a great deal of time improving their gardens and houses—inside and out. The Danish word for cozy, *hyggelig* (HEW-glee), describes this penchant for cozying up one's personal space. It's something the Danes do best. If you have an opportunity

How Big, How Many, How Much

- Denmark is 16,600 square miles (almost twice the size of Massachusetts).
- Population is 5.4 million (about 325 per square mile).
- 6 Danish kroner = about $1

Denmark

to do so, adopt some Danes while you are in Denmark so you can enjoy their *hyggelig* surroundings.

Although the Danish language is notoriously difficult for foreigners to pronounce, luckily for us almost everyone speaks English as well. Danes have playful fun teasing tourists who attempt to say Danish words.

Sample Denmark's sweet treats. *Rød grød med fløde* is a delightful red fruit porridge topped with cream. The pastries that we call Danish in the United States are called *wienerbrød* in Denmark. Bakeries line their display cases with several varieties of *wienerbrød* and other delectable sweets.

COPENHAGEN
(København)

Copenhagen, Denmark's capital, is the gateway to Scandinavia. And now, with the bridge connecting Sweden and Denmark (creating the region's largest metropolitan area), Copenhagen is energized and ready to dethrone Stockholm as Scandinavia's powerhouse city. A busy day cruising the canals, wandering through the palace, and

taking an old-town walk will give you your historical bearings. Then, after another day strolling the Strøget (Europe's first and greatest pedestrian shopping mall), biking the canals, and sampling the Danish good life, you'll feel right at home. Copenhagen is Scandinavia's cheapest and most fun-loving capital. So live it up.

Planning Your Time
A first visit deserves a minimum of two days.

Day 1: Catch a 10:30 city walking tour (departs from TI May–Sept daily except Sun; see "Tours," below). After lunch at Riz-Raz, visit the Use It information center and catch the relaxing canal-boat tour out to *The Little Mermaid* and back. Enjoy the rest of the afternoon tracing Denmark's cultural roots in the National Museum (touring the Victorian Apartment if possible) and visiting the Ny Carlsberg Glyptotek art gallery (some wings closed in 2005) or the National Art Museum (Impressionists and Danish artists). Spend the evening strolling Strøget (follow my self-guided walk, described on page 44).

Day 2: At 10:00, go neoclassical at Thorvaldsen's Museum. At 11:00, take the 50-minute guided tour of Denmark's royal Christiansborg Palace. After a *smørrebrød* lunch in a park, spend the afternoon seeing the Rosenborg Castle/crown jewels and the Museum of Danish Resistance. Spend the evening at Tivoli Gardens.

Remember the efficiency of sleeping while traveling in and out of town. Consider taking an overnight train to Stockholm (via Malmö) or an overnight boat to Oslo. Kamikaze sightseers see Copenhagen as a Scandinavian bottleneck. They sleep in and out heading north and in and out heading south, with two days and no nights in Copenhagen. Considering the joy of Oslo and Stockholm, this isn't all that crazy if you have limited time. You can check your bag at the station.

ORIENTATION

Nearly all of your sightseeing is in Copenhagen's compact old town. By doing things by bike or on foot, you'll stumble into some charming bits of Copenhagen that many miss. I rent a bike for my entire visit (for the cost of about a single cab ride per day) and park it safely in my hotel courtyard. I get anywhere in the town center literally faster than by taxi. The city is an absolute delight by bike.

Study the map to understand the city: The medieval walls are now roads that define the center—Vestervoldgade (literally, "West Rampart Street"), Nørrevoldgade, and Østervoldgade. The fourth side is the harbor and the island of Slotsholmen, where København ("merchants' harbor") was born in 1167. The next of the city's islands is Amager, where you'll find the local "Little Amsterdam" district of Christianshavn. What was Copenhagen's moat is now a string of pleasant lakes and parks, including Tivoli Gardens. You can still make out some of the zigzag pattern of the moats in the city's greenbelt. In 1850, Copenhagen's 120,000 residents all lived within this defensive system. Building in the no-man's-land outside the walls was only allowed with the understanding that in the event of an attack, you'd burn your dwellings to clear the way for a good defense. Today, the buildings of historic importance lie within the *voldgade* ring.

In the 17th century, King Christian IV extended the fortifications to the north, doubling the size of the city, while adding a grid plan of streets and his Rosenborg Castle. This old "new town" has the Amalienborg Palace and *The Little Mermaid.*

For most visitors, the core of the town is the axis formed by the train station, Tivoli Gardens, Rådhuspladsen (City Hall Square), and the Strøget pedestrian street. Bubbling with street life and colorful pedestrian zones, this main drag is fun. But be sure to get off the Strøget.

You need to remember one character in Copenhagen's history: Christian IV. Ruling from 1588 to 1648, he was Denmark's Renaissance king and a royal party animal. The personal energy of this "Builder King" sparked a golden age when Copenhagen prospered and many of the city's grandest buildings were erected. Locals love to tell stories of everyone's favorite king, whose drinking was legendary.

Tourist Information

Copenhagen This Week is a free, handy, and misnamed monthly guide to the city, worth reading for its good maps, museum hours with telephone numbers, sightseeing tour ideas, shopping suggestions, and calendar of events, including free English tours and concerts (online at www.ctw.dk). This is *the* essential listing of everything in town, and it's always the most up-to-date information in print. While the "TIs" are really just an advertising agency (see below), you should be ready to roll with a map and *Copenhagen This Week*—both free and available at TIs and most hotels. The Danish Tourist Board's Web site also has a wealth of information on activities and events in Copenhagen (www.visitdenmark.com).

Wonderful Copenhagen, as the tourist office is called, is a for-profit company. This colors the advice and information it provides. Mindful of this, drop by to get a city map and *Copenhagen This Week,* browse the racks of brochures, and get your questions answered (July–Aug Mon–Sat 9:00–20:00, Sun 9:00–18:00, May–June Mon–Sat 9:00–18:00, closed Sun, Sept–April Mon–Fri 9:00–16:00, Sat 9:00–14:00, closed Sun, across from train station on Vesterbrogade 4A, tel. 70 22 24 42, www.visitcopenhagen.dk). They also book rooms for a 75-kr fee. The TI (unlike the excellent "Use It" service described below) only posts information from outfits that pay for the shelf space. You'll find this week's entertainment program for Tivoli on posts outside Tivoli's main entrance (around the corner from the TI).

Use It is a better information service (10-min walk from train station). Government-sponsored, it caters to Copenhagen's young but welcomes budget travelers of any age. It's a friendly, driven-to-help, energetic, no-nonsense source of budget-travel information, offering a free room-finding service, free Internet access, and free short-term luggage lockers. Their free annual *Playtime* publication has Back Door–style articles on Copenhagen and the Danish culture, special budget tips, and self-guided tours. Read it! They book private rooms (350-kr doubles, no booking fee). From the station, head down Strøget, and then turn right on Rådhustræde for three blocks to #13 (mid-June–mid-Sept daily 9:00–19:00, otherwise Mon–Wed 11:00–16:00, Thu 11:00–18:00, Fri 11:00–14:00, closed Sat–Sun, tel. 33 73 06 20, www.useit.dk).

The **Copenhagen Card,** which includes free entry to many of

Copenhagen Overview

the city's sights, can save you some money if you're sightseeing like crazy (199 kr for 24 hours, the 72-hour version for 399 kr also covers outlying sights and public transportation).

Arrival in Copenhagen

By Train: The main train station is called Hovedbanegården (HOETH-bahn-gorn). It's a temple of travel and a hive of travel-related activity, offering lockers (35 kr/day), a checkroom (*garderobe,* 40 kr/day per backpack, Mon–Sat 5:30–24:00, Sun 6:00–24:00), a post office (Mon–Fri 8:00–21:00, Sat 9:00–16:00, Sun 10:00–16:00), a grocery store (daily 8:00–24:00), 24-hour thievery, and the best bike-rental shop in town (see "Getting Around Copenhagen," page 39). The station has ATMs and long-hours FOREX exchange desks (daily 8:00–21:00, FOREX is the least expensive place in town to change money). Showers for 10 kr are available in the public rest rooms at the back of the station.

While you're in the station, reserve your overnight train seat or *couchette* out at the Rejse-bureau (Mon–Fri 10:00–17:00, closed Sat–Sun, tel. 33 54 55 10). Some international rides and IC (fast) trains require reservations (usually 23–51 kr). If you have a railpass, you must make your reservations at the *Billetsalg* office (Mon–Fri 9:00–18:00, Sat–Sun 10:00–17:00). The *Kviksalg* office sells tickets within Denmark (plus the regional train to Malmö, Sweden). This "quick sale" office will also help you with reservations for international trips if the *Billetsalg* office is closed, and you're departing by train within one hour or early the next day (daily 5:45–23:30).

To get to the recommended Christianshavn B&Bs from the train station, catch bus #2A or #48 (15 kr, 4/hr, in front of station on near side of Bernstorffsgade, with back to the station heading to right, get off at stop just after *Knippelsbro*—Knippels Bridge). Note the time the bus departs, and then stop by the TI (across the street) and pick up a free Copenhagen city map that shows bus routes.

By Plane: Kastrup, Copenhagen's international airport, is a traveler's dream, with a TI, baggage check, bank, post office, shopping mall, grocery store, and bakery. You can use dollars or euros at the airport—but you'll get change back in kroner (airport info tel. 32 47 47 47, SAS info tel. 70 10 20 00). Need to kill a night at the airport? The Transfer Hotel, under the transit hall, rents compact fetal rest cabins. Called *hvilekabiner*, they are especially handy for early flights, but you must have a ticket, and if you stay there, you're stuck in the transit area (Sb-415 kr, Db-620 kr for 8 hrs, prices vary for 2- to 16-hr periods, reception open daily 5:30–23:30, easy telephone reservations, sauna and showers available at a cost for non-guests, tel. 32 31 24 55, fax 32 31 31 09, transferhotel@cph.dk).

Getting Downtown from the Airport: Taxis are fast, civil, accept credit cards, and, at about 200 kr to the town center, are a reasonable deal for foursomes. The slick and easy Air Rail train links the airport with the train station, as well as the Nørreport stations (25 kr, 3/hr, 12 min). City bus #250S gets you downtown to the Rådhuspladsen (at the train station) in 30 minutes for 25 kr (6/hr, across the street and to the right as you exit airport).

If you're going from the airport to Christianshavn, just hop on bus #2A, which takes you right through the middle of Christianshavn (30 min). Or you could take the Air Rail shuttle to Nørreport, then change to the Metro for Christianshavn (same 25-kr ticket works for entire trip). In a few years, the Metro will connect the airport and Christianshavn directly in 10 minutes.

Helpful Hints

Emergencies: Dial 112 and specify fire, police, or ambulance. Emergency calls from public phones are free.

U.S. Embassy: It's at Dag Hammerskjölds Alle 24 (tel. 35 55 31 44).

Pharmacy: Steno Apotek is across from the train station (open 24 hrs daily, Vesterbrogade 6c, tel. 33 14 82 66).

Telephones: Use the telephone liberally. Everyone speaks English, and *Copenhagen This Week* and this book list phone numbers for everything you'll be doing. All telephone numbers in Denmark are eight digits, and there are no area codes. Calls anywhere in Denmark are cheap; calls to Norway and Sweden cost 6 kr per minute from a booth (half that from a private home). Get a phone card (sold at newsstands, starting at 30 kr). To make inexpensive international calls, buy a phone card (with a scratch-off personal identification number). The Go Bananas card is particularly reliable (sold at kiosks for 100 kr—giving you more than 100 minutes of talk time to the United States, same card good in Germany, Denmark, Sweden, and Norway).

Ferries: Book any ferries now that you plan to take later in Scandinavia. Visit a travel agent or call direct. For the Denmark–Norway ferry, call DFDS (Mon–Fri 8:30–18:00, Sat–Sun 9:00–17:00, tel. 33 42 30 00, www.dfdsseaways.com). For the cruise from Stockholm to Helsinki, call Silja Line (tel. 96 20 32 00, generally 400 kr one-way, 800 kr round-trip, www.silja.com) or visit the DSB terminus at the Central Station. With the new Øresund Bridge, you'll no longer need a ferry to drive to Sweden, but the toll (230 kr) is the same as the Helsingør-Helsingborg ferry, which still runs twice hourly.

Jazz Festival: The Copenhagen Jazz Festival—10 days starting the first Friday in July (July 1–10 in 2005)—puts the town in a rollicking slide-trombone mood. The Danes are Europe's jazz enthusiasts, and this music festival fills the town with happiness. The TI prints up an extensive listing of each year's festival events, or get the latest at www.jazzfestival.dk. There's also an autumn jazz festival the first week of November.

Getting Around Copenhagen

By Bus, S-tog, and Metro: It's easy to navigate Copenhagen with its fine buses, Metro, and S-tog, a suburban train system with stops in the city (Eurail valid on S-tog). A 17-kr two-zone ticket (pay as you board buses, buy from station ticket offices or vending machines for the Metro) gets you an hour's travel within the center. Consider the blue two-zone *klippekort* (105 kr for 10 1-hr rides and the 24-hour pass (100 kr, validate day pass in yellow machine on bus or at station, both sold at stations and the TI). Assume you'll be within the middle two zones. Buses go every five to eight minutes during daytime hours. Bus drivers are patient, have change, and speak English. City maps list bus and subway routes. Locals are friendly and helpful. The HUR Kundecenter (big black building) on Rådhuspladsen (City Hall Square) is very helpful and has a fine, free map showing all the bus routes (tel. 36 13 14 15).

Copenhagen's super-futuristic Metro line connects Christianshavn and Nørreport (2 stops on S-tog from main train station). Eventually the Metro will run from Copenhagen to the airport and on to Ørestad, the industrial and business center created after the Øresund Bridge was built between Denmark and Sweden (for the latest, see www.m.dk).

By Bus Tour: Open Top Tour buses do a hop-on, hop-off 60-minute circle connecting the city's top sights (for details, see "Tours," page 42).

By Taxi: Taxis are plentiful, easy to call or flag down, and pricey (24-kr drop charge, and then 10 kr per kilometer, credit cards accepted). For a short ride, four people spend about the same by taxi as by bus (for example, 50 kr from train station to recommended Christianshavn B&Bs). Calling 35 35 35 35 will get you a taxi within minutes...with the meter already way up there.

Free Bikes: From May through November, 2,000 clunky but practical little bikes are scattered around the old-town center (basically the terrain covered in the Copenhagen map in this chapter). Simply locate one of the 150 racks, unlock a bike by popping a 20-kr coin into

the handlebar, and pedal away. When you're done, plug your bike back into any other rack and your deposit coin will pop back out (if you can't find a rack, just abandon your bike and a homeless person will take it back and pocket your coin). These simple bikes come with theft-proof parts (unusable on regular bikes) and—they claim—computer tracer chips embedded in them so that bike patrols can retrieve strays. These are funded by advertisements painted on the wheels and by a progressive electorate.

Copenhagen's radical city bike program is a clever idea. But in practice, it doesn't work great for sightseers. It's hard to find bikes in working order, and when you get to the sight and park your bike, it'll be gone by the time you're ready to pedal on. (There's a 20-kr deposit coin as an incentive for any kid to pick up city bikes not plugged back into their special racks.) Use the free bikes for a one-way pedal here and there. But if you really want to bike efficiently, pay to rent one.

Good Bikes: For a comfortable bike that's yours for the duration and in great working order, rent one at the main train station's

Copenhagen

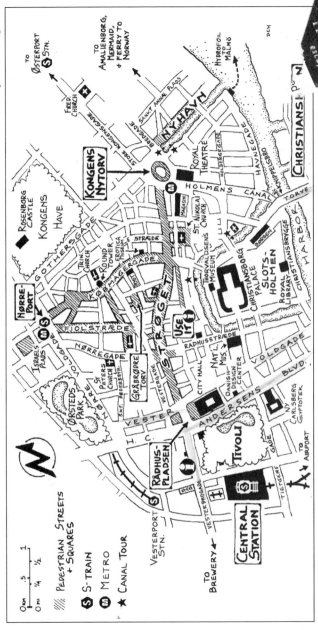

PRINCE
escape c

Okm .5 1
Omi ¼ ½

/// PEDESTRIAN STREETS
+ SQUARES

Ⓢ S-TRAIN

Ⓜ METRO

★ CANAL TOUR

TO ØSTERPORT Ⓢ STN.

FRED. CHURCH

TO AMALIENBORG, MERMAID, + FERRY TO NORWAY

NYHAVN

SAINT ANNE PLADS

STORE KONGENSGADE

BREDGADE

HYDROFOIL TO MALMÖ

CHRISTIANSH

N

KONGENS NYTORV

ROYAL THEATRE

HOLMENS CANAL

HAVNEGADE

KNIPPELSBRO

HOLMENS

TORVE

HARBOR

CHRISTIANSBRYGGE

ROSENBORG CASTLE

KONGENS HAVE

GOTHERSGADE

MAGASIN Ⓜ

ST. NIKOLAJ CHURCH

TRIN. CHURCH

ROUND TOWER

EROTICA MUSEUM

STRÆDE

THORVALDSENS MUSEUM

CHRISTIANSBORG PALACE

SLOTS-HOLMEN

ROYAL LIBRARY

NØRRE-PORT

Ⓜ

Ⓢ

ISRAELS PLADS

FIOLSTRÆDE

NØRREGADE

KØBMAGERGADE

STRØGET

USE IT!

RÅDHUSSTRÆDE

ØRSTEDS PARK

NØRRE VOLDGADE

ST. PETERS CHURCH

SKT. PEDERSTR.

GRÅBRØDRE TORV

VESTERGADE

NAT'L MUS.

VOLDGADE

VESTER VOLDGADE

I.C. ANDERSENS BLVD.

CITY HALL

DANISH DESIGN CENTER

NY CARLSBERG GLYPTOTEK

RÅDHUS-PLADSEN

Ⓘ

TIVOLI

TO AIRPORT

VESTERPORT STN. Ⓢ

VESTERBROGADE

TIETGENS GADE

Ⓢ

CENTRAL STATION

TO BREWERY ←

PCH

Cykelcenter (75 kr/24 hrs, cheaper for longer if paid in advance, Mon–Fri 8:00–17:30, Sat 9:00–13:00, July–Aug open Sun 9:00–13:00, otherwise closed Sun, no helmets, tel. 33 33 86 13). Cykelcenter also has a shop at the Østerport S-tog station (same prices, Mon–Fri 8:00–18:00, Sat 9:00–13:00, closed Sun, tel. 33 33 85 13). Cyclists see more, save time and money, and really feel like locals.

TOURS

▲▲▲Walking Tours—Once upon a time, American **Richard Karpen** visited Copenhagen and fell in love with the city (and one of its women). Now, dressed as Hans Christian Andersen, he leads daily 90-minute tours that wander in and out of buildings, courtyards, backstreets, and unusual parts of the old town. Along the way, he gives insightful and humorous background on the history and culture of Denmark, Copenhagen, and the Danes.

Richard offers three entertaining walks: "Castles and Kings," "Royal Copenhagen," and "Romantic Copenhagen." Each walk is a little more than a mile with breaks, and covers different parts of the historic center (75 kr apiece, kids under 12 free, departs from TI May–Sept Mon–Sat at 10:30). His tours, while all different, complement each other and are of equal introduction value.

Richard also does excellent tours of Rosenborg Castle (50 kr, doesn't include castle entry, Mon and Thu at 13:30, 90 min, led by dapper Renaissance "Sir Richard," meet outside castle ticket office). No reservations are needed for Richard's tours—just show up.

For details, pick up Richard's schedule in *Copenhagen This Week,* at the TI, or see www.copenhagenwalks.com.

Go with the Danes: These Danish guides give a fine basic two-hour introductory walk to Copenhagen (100 kr, Sat–Sun at 10:00, confirm schedule in *Copenhagen This Week,* tours start outside TI across from train station, simply show up, www.copenhagen-walkingtours.dk). This outfit also runs tours of Rosenborg Castle (60 min, Sun and Tue at 13:30 in July and Aug).

Copenhagen History Tours: Christian Donatzky, a charming young Dane with a master's degree in history, offers three walking tours. On Saturday at 10:00, the "Reformed Copenhagen" tour covers Copenhagen from 1400–1600—the era before, during, and after the Protestant Reformation. On Sunday at 10:00, the "Commercial Copenhagen" tour focuses on 1600–1800, when Copenhagen became an international business center. On Monday at 18:00 is the "Hans Christian Andersen's Copenhagen" tour (1800–2000), set in a time when Denmark turned democratic. The tours are thoughtfully designed, and those with a serious interest in Danish history find them time well spent (70 kr, 60–90 min each in small groups, depart from statue of Bishop Absalon on Højbro Plads between Strøget and Christiansborg Palace, tel. 28 49 44 35, www .copenhagenhistorytours.dk).

Local Guides: The Danish tour guide organization has a huge staff of well-trained guides ready to show you around (www.guides .dk). Or hire a guide from Go with the Danes (1,000 kr/2-hr tour, see above).

Bus Tours—A variety of guided bus tours depart from Rådhuspladsen in front of the Palace Hotel. The hop-on, hop-off **Open Top Tour** does the basic 60-minute circle of the city sights—Tivoli Gardens, the royal Christiansborg Palace, National Museum, *The Little Mermaid*, Rosenborg Castle, Nyhavn sailors' quarter, and more—with a taped narration (120 kr, 2/hr, 140 kr for access to all 3 tour lines, ticket good for 48 hrs, April–Oct daily 9:30–17:00; you can get off, see a sight, and catch a later bus; bus departs City Hall below the *Lur Blowers* statue—to the left of City Hall—or at many other stops throughout city, pay driver, tel. 32 54 06 06, run by Copenhagen Excursions—www.sightseeing.dk). The same company also runs jaunts into the countryside, with themes such as Vikings, castles, and Hamlet.

▲▲**Harbor Cruise and Canal Tours**—Two companies offer essentially the same live, three-language, 50-minute tours through the city canals. Both boats leave at least twice an hour from near Christians-

borg Palace, cruise around the palace and Christianshavn area, and then proceed into the wide-open harbor. It's a relaxing way to see *The Little Mermaid* and munch a lazy picnic during the slow-moving narration.

The low-overhead **Netto-Bådene** tour boats leave from Holmen's Bridge in front of the palace and from Nyhavn (25 kr, late-April–Sept daily 10:00–17:00, later in summer, sign at dock shows next departure, 2–5/hr, dress warmly—boats are open-top until Sept, tel. 32 54 41 02, www.havnerundfart.dk). Don't mix up the boats—this cheaper line advertises less. Its Nyhavn dock is midway down the canal (on the city side), while the expensive boat is at the head of the canal.

The pricey option, **DFDS Canal Tours,** does the same tour for 50 kr (departs from Gammel Strand, 200 yards away, and from Nyhavn, April–mid-Oct daily 10:00–17:00). They also offer unguided "water bus" hop-on, hop-off tours for 45 kr (mid-May– early Sept 10:15–16:45, tel. 33 93 42 60).

Go with Netto. There's no reason to pay double.

Copenhagen at a Glance

▲▲▲**Tivoli Gardens** Copenhagen's classic amusement park, with rides, music, food, and other fun. **Hours:** Mid-April–mid-Sept daily 11:00–23:00, later on Fri, Sat, and in summer, also open mid-Nov–Christmas daily 11:00–22:00.

▲▲▲**National Museum** History of Danish civilization with tourable 19th-century Victorian Apartment. **Hours:** Museum Tue–Sun 10:00–17:00, closed Mon; Victorian Apartment tours Sat and Sun (likely also Thu and Fri) at 12:00, 13:00, 14:00, and 15:00.

▲▲▲**Rosenborg Castle and Treasury** Renaissance castle of larger-than-life "warrior king" Christian IV. **Hours:** Daily June–Aug 10:00–17:00, May and Sept 10:00–16:00, Oct 11:00–15:00, Nov–April Tue–Sun 11:00–14:00, closed Mon.

▲▲▲**Christiania** Colorful counterculture squatters' colony where marijuana is sold and smoked openly. **Hours:** Always open.

▲▲**Christiansborg Palace** Royal reception rooms with dazzling tapestries. **Hours:** Visit only with tour, May–Sept daily at 11:00, 13:00, and 15:00; Oct–April Tue, Thu, Sat, and Sun at 15:00.

▲▲**Museum of Danish Resistance** Chronicle of Denmark's struggle against the Nazis. **Hours:** May–mid-Sept Tue–Sat

Bike Tours—City Safari offers three-hour guided bike tours of Copenhagen, a general city intro including Christiania (200 kr includes bike, in English and Danish as needed, tours available upon pre-booking either by mail or phone, show up 10 min in advance at Danish Center for Architecture, Gammel Dok Storehouse, Strandgade 27B, tel. 33 23 94 90, www.citysafari.dk, or ask at Use It, energetic Steen is a one-man show and speaks fine English).

Self-Guided Walk:
Strøget and Copenhagen's Heart and Soul

Start from **Rådhuspladsen (City Hall Square),** the bustling heart of Copenhagen, dominated by the tower of the City Hall. This was Copenhagen's fortified west end. For 700 years, Copenhagen was contained within its walls. In the mid-1800s, 140,000 people were packed inside. The overcrowding led to hygiene problems. (A cholera outbreak killed 5,000.) It was clear: The walls needed to come down...and they did.

In 1843, magazine publisher Georg Carstensen convinced the

10:00–16:00, Sun 10:00–17:00, off-season Tue–Sat 10:00–15:00, Sun 10:00–16:00, closed Mon.

▲**City Hall (Rådhus)** Copenhagen's landmark, packed with Danish history and topped with a tower. **Hours:** Mon–Fri 8:00–17:00, open Sat only for tours, closed Sun.

▲**Thorvaldsen's Museum** Works of the Danish neoclassical sculptor. **Hours:** Tue–Sun 10:00–17:00, closed Mon.

▲**Ny Carlsberg Glyptotek** Scandinavia's top art gallery, featuring Egyptians, Greeks, Etruscans, French, and Danes. **Hours:** Tue–Sun 10:00–16:00, closed Mon.

▲**National Art Museum** Good Danish and Impressionist collections. **Hours:** Tue–Sun 10:00–17:00, Wed until 20:00, closed Mon.

▲**Amalienborg Palace Museum** Quick and intimate look at Denmark's royal family. **Hours:** May–Oct daily 10:00–16:00, Nov–April Tue–Sun 11:00–16:00.

▲**Our Savior's Church** Spiral-spired church with bright Baroque interior. **Hours:** April–Aug Mon–Sat 11:00–16:30, Sun 12:00–16:30, closes off-season at 15:30.

king to let him build a pleasure garden outside the walls of crowded Copenhagen. The king quickly agreed, knowing that happy people care less about fighting for democracy. **Tivoli Gardens** became Europe's first great public amusement park. When the train lines came, the station was placed just beyond Tivoli. Those formidable

walls faded away, surviving only in echoes— a circular series of roads and remnants of moats, now people-friendly city lakes.

The **City Hall,** or Rådhus, is worth a visit (Mon–Fri 8:00–17:00, open Sat only for tours, closed Sun; described on page 53). Old **Hans Christian Andersen** sits to the right of City Hall, almost begging to be in another photo (as he used to in real life). Climb onto his well-worn knee. (While up there, you might take off your shirt for a racy photo, as many Danes enjoy doing.) In 2005, Copenhagen will be celebrating

H. C. A.'s 200th birthday (see www.hca2005.com for more details).

On a pedestal left of City Hall, note the *Lur Blowers* sculpture honoring the earliest warrior Danes. The *lur* is a horn that was used 3,500 years ago. The ancient originals (which still play) are displayed in the National Museum. (City tour buses leave from below these Vikings.)

The golden **weather girls** high up on the tower (marked *Philips* in blue) opposite the Strøget's entrance tell the weather: on a bike (fair) or with an umbrella. These two have been called the only women in Copenhagen you can trust. But for years, they've been stuck in the almost-sunny mode...with the bike just peeking out. Notice that the red temperature dots only go to 28 degrees Celsius (that's 82 Fahrenheit).

Here in the traffic hub of this huge city, you'll notice...not many cars. Denmark's 180 percent tax on car purchases makes the bus or bike a sweeter option.

The **SAS building** is Copenhagen's only skyscraper. Locals say it seems so tall because the clouds hang so low. When it was built in 1960, Copenhageners took one look and decided—that's enough of a skyline.

The American trio of Burger King, 7-Eleven, and KFC marks the start of the otherwise charming **Strøget.** Finished in 1962, Copenhagen's experimental, tremendously successful, and most-copied pedestrian shopping mall is a string of lively (and individually named) streets and lovely squares that bunny-hop through the old town from City Hall to the Nyhavn quarter, a 20-minute stroll away.

As you wander down this street, remember that the commercial focus of a historic street like Strøget drives up the land value, which generally trashes the charm and tears down the old buildings. Look above the modern window displays and street-level advertising to discover bits of 19th-century character that still survive. While Strøget has become hamburgerized, historic bits and attractive chunks of old Copenhagen are just off this commercial cancan.

Copenhagen was fortified around large mansions with expansive **courtyards.** As the population grew, the walls constricted the city's physical size. These courtyards were gradually filled with higgledy-piggledy secondary buildings. Today, throughout the old center you can step off a busy pedestrian mall and back in time into these characteristic half-timbered time-warps. Replace the parked car with a tired horse, replace the bikes with a line of outhouses, and you are in 19th-century Copenhagen. If you see an open door, you're welcome to discreetly wander in and look around. Don't miss the courtyards of Copenhagen.

After one block (at Kattesundet), make a side-trip three blocks left into Copenhagen's colorful **university district.** Formerly the old

Self-Guided Walk: Strøget and Copenhagen's Heart and Soul

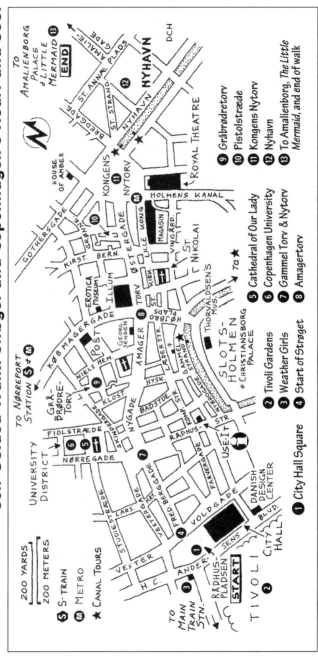

1 City Hall Square
2 Tivoli Gardens
3 Weather Girls
4 Start of Strøget
5 Cathedral of Our Lady
6 Copenhagen University
7 Gammel Torv & Nytorv
8 Amagertorv
9 Gråbrødretorv
10 Pistolstræde
11 Kongens Nytorv
12 Nyhavn
13 To Amalienborg, The Little Mermaid, and end of walk

brothel neighborhood, later the heart of Copenhagen's hippie community in the 1960s, today this "Latin Quarter" is Soho chic.

At Sankt Peders Stræde, turn right and walk to the end of the street. On your right is the big neoclassical **Cathedral of Our Lady.** Stand across the street from its facade. The Reformation Memorial celebrates the date Denmark broke from the Roman Catholic Church and became Lutheran (1536). Walk around and study the reliefs of great Danish reformers protesting from their pulpits. The relief facing the church shows King Christian III, who, after being influenced by Luther in his German travels (and realizing the advantages of being the head of his own state church), oversaw the town council meeting that decided on this break. Because of 1536, there's no Mary in the Cathedral of Our Lady.

The cathedral's **facade** is a Greek temple. (To the right in the distance, notice more neoclassicism—the law courts.) You can see why golden-age Copenhagen (early 1800s) fancied itself a Nordic Athens. Old Testament figures (King David and Moses) flank the cathedral's entryway. Above, John the Baptist stands where you'd expect to see Greek gods. He invites you in...to the New Testament.

Enter the cathedral—a world of neoclassical serenity (free, open daily 7:30–17:00). This pagan temple now houses Christianity. The nave is lined by the 12 apostles (all clad in Roman togas)—masterpieces by the great Danish sculptor Bertel Thorvaldsen. They lead to a statue of the risen Christ—standing where the statue of Caesar would have been. Rather than wearing an imperial toga, Jesus wears his burial shroud and says, "Come to me." The marvelous acoustics are demonstrated in free organ concerts each Saturday at noon. This is where Copenhagen gathers for extraordinary events. After September 11, 2001, the queen, her government, and the entire diplomatic core held a memorial service here.

Head back outside. If you face the facade and look to the left, you'll see **Copenhagen University**—home of 30,000 students. The king began the university in the 17th century to stop the Danish brain drain to Paris. Today tuition is free (but room, board, and beer are not). Locals say it's easy to get in...but (given the wonderful lifestyle) very hard to get out.

Step up the middle steps of the university's big building and enter a colorful lobby, starring Athena and Apollo. The frescoes celebrate high thinking, with themes such as the triumph of wisdom over barbarism. Notice how harmoniously the architecture, sculpture, and painting work together. Outside, busts honor great minds from the faculty, including (at the end) Niels Bohr—a professor who won the 1922 Nobel Prize for theoretical physics. He evaded the clutches of the Nazi science labs by fleeing to America in 1943, where he helped develop the atomic bomb.

Rejoin Strøget (down where you saw the law courts) at

Gammel Torv and **Nytorv** (Old Square and New Square). This was the old town center. In Gammel Torv, the Fountain of Charity (Caritas) is named for the figure of Charity on top. It has provided drinking water to locals since the early 1600s. Featuring a pregnant woman squirting water from her breasts next to a boy urinating, this was just too much for people of the Victorian age. They corked both figures and raised the statue to what they hoped would be out of view. The Asian-looking kiosk was one of the city's first community telephone centers from the days before phones were privately owned. Look at the reliefs ringing its top: an airplane with bird wings (c. 1900) and two women talking on the newfangled phone. (It was thought business would popularize the telephone, but actually it was women... Now, 100 years later, look at the mobile phones.)

While Gammel Torv was a place of happiness and merriment, Nytorv was a place of severity and judgment. Walk to the small raised area in front of the old, ancient Greek–style former City Hall. Do a 360. The entire square is neoclassical. Read the old Danish on the City Hall facade: "With Law Shall Man Land Build." Look down at the pavement and read the plaque: "Here stood the town's Kag (whipping post) until 1780."

Next, walk down **Amagertorv,** prime real estate for talented street entertainers and pickpockets (past the Gad Bookstore— excellent selection of English-language guidebooks and cookbooks), to the stately brick Holy Ghost church. The fine spire is typical of old Danish churches. Under the stepped gable was a medieval hospital run by monks. A block behind the church (walk down Valkendorfs-gade and through a passage under a rust-colored building) is the leafy and caffeine-stained **Gråbrødretorv** (Grey Friars' Square)—a popular place for an outdoor meal or drink in the summer—surrounded by fine old buildings. At the end of the square, the street Niels Hemmingsens Gade returns (past the Copenhagen Jazz House, a good place for live music nightly—see page 66) to Strøget. Continue down the pedestrian street, with its fine inlaid Italian granite stonework, to the next square with the stork fountain (actually a heron). The Victorian WCs here (steps down from fountain, 2 kr) are a delight.

Amagertorv—the next stretch of Strøget—is a highlight for shoppers. A line of Royal Copenhagen stores here sell porcelain (with demos), glassware, jewelry, and silverware. Illums Bolighus is known for modern design (Mon–Sat 10:00–18:00, Sun 12:00– 17:00). From here, you can see the imposing Parliament building, Christiansborg Palace, and an equestrian statue of Bishop Absalon, the city's founder (canal boat tours depart nearby). A block toward the canal, running parallel to Strøget, starts Strædet, which is a second Strøget featuring cafés, antique shops, and no fast food. North of Amagertorv, a broad pedestrian mall, Købmagergade, leads past the Museum of Erotica to Christian IV's Round Tower and the

Latin Quarter (university district). Café Norden overlooks the fountain—a smoky but good place for a coffee with a view. The second floor offers the best vantage point.

The final stretch of Strøget leads to **Pistolstræde** (leading off Strøget to the left from Østergade at #24), a cute lane of shops in restored 18th-century buildings. Wander back into the half-timbered section. The Kransekagehuset bakery (see "Eating," page 73) has a rack of tourist fliers including the very handy-for-shoppers *Local Life*, which highlights small specialty shops in the area.

Continuing along Strøget, you'll pass McDonald's (good view from top floor) and major department stores (Illum and Magasin—see "Shopping," page 65) to Kongens Nytorv.

Kongens Nytorv, the biggest square in town, is home to the Royal Theatre, French embassy, and venerable Hotel D'Angleterre. The statue in the middle of the square celebrates Christian V who, in the 1670s, enlarged Copenhagen by adding this "King's New Square" (Kongens Nytorv). The entire center is a happy skating rink for three months each winter.

On the right (just before the Metro station, at #19), Hviids Vinstue, the town's oldest wine cellar (from 1723), is a colorful if smoky spot for an open-face sandwich and a beer (3 sandwiches and a beer for 50 kr at lunchtime). Wander around inside, if only to see the old photos.

Just off Kongens Nytorv (30 yards from Hviids Vinstue) is the entrance to the futuristic Metro. Ride the escalators down and up to see the latest in Metro design (automated cars, no driver...sit in front to watch the tracks coming at you).

Head back up to ground level. Across the square is the trendy harbor of Nyhavn.

Nyhavn is a recently gentrified sailors' quarter. (Hong Kong is the last of the nasty bars from the rough old days.) With its trendy cafés, jazz clubs, and tattoo shops (pop into Tattoo Ole at #17—fun photos, very traditional), Nyhavn is a wonderful place to hang out. The canal is filled with glamorous old sailboats of all sizes. Any historic sloop is welcome to moor here in Copenhagen's ever-changing boat museum. Hans Christian Andersen lived and wrote his first stories here (in the red double-gabled building on the right at #20). Wander the quay, enjoying the frat-party parade of tattoos (hotter weather reveals more tattoos).

Celtic and Nordic mythological designs are in (as is bodybuilding, by the looks of things). The place thrives—with the cheap-beer drinkers dockside and the richer and older ones looking on from comfier cafés.

A note about all this public beer-drinking: There's no more beer consumption here than in the United States; it's just out in public. Many young Danes can't afford to drink in a bar. So they "picnic drink" their beers in squares and along canals, spending a quarter of the bar price for a bottle from a nearby kiosk (just past the bridge on the right).

Just past the first bridge, a line of people wait for the best ice cream around—packed into fresh-baked waffles (look through the window to see the waffle iron in action).

Continuing north along the harborside (from end of Nyhavn canal, turn left), you'll stroll a delightful waterfront promenade to the modern fountain of Amaliehaven Park (immediately across the harbor from the new opera house).

The orderly **Amalienborg Palace and Square** is a block inland, behind the fountain. Queen Margrethe II and her family live in the mansion to your immediate left as you enter the square from the harborside. Her son and heir to the throne, Crown Prince Frederik, recently moved into the mansion directly opposite his mother's. While the guards change with royal fanfare at noon only when the queen is in residence, they shower every morning. The small

Amalienborg Palace Museum offers an intimate look at royal living (see page 61). If in need of a very traditional cheap lunch, head inland two blocks just past the Marble Church, to Svend Larsen's Smørrebrød (fine little 8-kr open-face sandwiches to go, St. Kongensgade 83, Mon–Fri 8:00–14:00, closed Sat–Sun).

From the square, Amaliegade leads north to Kastellet (Citadel) Park and Denmark's fascinating WWII-era Museum of Danish Resistance (see "Near *The Little Mermaid*," page 61). A short stroll past the Gefion fountain (illustrating the myth of the goddess who was given one night to carve a chunk out of Sweden to make into Denmark's main island, Zealand—which you're on) and an Anglican church built of flint brings you to the overrated, overfondled, and overphotographed symbol of Copenhagen, *Den Lille Havfrue—The Little Mermaid.*

You can get back downtown on foot, by taxi, or on bus #1A, #15, or #19 from Store Kongensgade on the other side of Kastellet Park, or bus #29 from behind the Museum of Danish Resistance on Langelinie Street.

SIGHTS

Near the Train Station

▲▲▲**Tivoli Gardens**—The world's grand old amusement park—since 1843—is 20 acres, 110,000 lanterns, and countless ice cream cones of fun. You pay one admission price and find yourself lost in a

Hans Christian Andersen wonderland of rides, restaurants, games, marching bands, roulette wheels, and funny mirrors. Tivoli doesn't try to be Disney. It's wonderfully and happily Danish.

Cost, Hours, Location: The park is open every day—but only from about April 10 to September 20 (daily 11:00–23:00, later on Fri, Sat, and in summer, 65 kr gets you in, tel. 33 15 10 01, www.tivoli.dk). Rides range in price from 15 to 70 kr (195 kr for all-day pass). All children's amusements are in full swing by 12:00; the rest of the amusements open by 16:30. Tivoli is across from the train station. If you're catching an overnight train, this is *the* place to spend your last Copenhagen hours. Tivoli also opens for a Christmas Market (mid-Nov–Christmas daily 11:00–22:00—with ice skating on Tivoli Lake).

Entertainment in Tivoli: Upon arrival (through main entrance, on right in shop), pick up a map and events schedule. Take a moment to sit down and plan your entertainment for the evening. Events are spread between 15:00 and 23:00; the 19:30 concert in the concert hall can be free or may cost up to 500 kr, depending on the performer (box office tel. 33 15 10 12). If the Tivoli Symphony is playing, it's worth paying for. The ticket box office is outside, just to the left of the main entrance (daily 11:00–20:00, if you buy a concert ticket you get into Tivoli for free). You'll also find the daily events schedule on the posts outside the main entrance.

Free concerts, pantomime theater, ballet, acrobats, puppets, and other shows pop up all over the park, and a well-organized visitor can enjoy an exciting evening of entertainment without spending a single krone beyond the entry fee. The children's theater, Valmuen, plays excellent traditional fairy tales daily at 12:00, 13:00, and 14:00. Friday evenings feature a (usually free) rock or pop show at 22:00. On Saturday from late April through late September, fireworks light up the sky at 23:45. The park is particularly romantic at dusk, when the lights go on.

Eating at Tivoli: Inside the park, expect to pay amusement-park prices for amusement park–quality food. **Søcafeen,** by the lake, allows picnics if you buy a drink. The *pølse* (sausage) stands are cheap. **Færgekroen** is a good lakeside place for typical Danish food, beer, and an impromptu sing-along with a bunch of drunk Danes. The Croatian restaurant, **Hercegovina,** overlooks a leafy section of the amusement park and serves a 129-kr lunch buffet (mostly cold, 12:00–16:00) and a 169-kr dinner buffet (salads, veggies, and lots and lots of meat, daily 17:00–22:00, music nightly after 19:00). For a cake and coffee, consider the **Viften** café. **Georg,** to the left of the concert hall, has tasty 45-kr sandwiches and 150-kr dinners (which include a glass of wine).

▲**Rådhus (City Hall)**—This city landmark, between the train station/Tivoli/TI and Strøget pedestrian mall, offers private tours and trips up its 345-foot-tall tower. It's draped, inside and out, in Danish symbolism. The city's founder, Bishop Absalon, stands over the door. The polar bears climbing on the rooftop symbolize the giant Danish protectorate of Greenland.

Step inside. The lobby has racks of tourist information (city maps and *Copenhagen This Week*). The building was inspired by the City Hall in Siena, Italy (with the necessary addition of a glass

roof). Huge functions fill this grand hall (the iron grill in the center of the floor is an elevator for bringing up 1,200 chairs) while the busts of four illustrious local boys—the fairy-tale-writer Hans Christian Andersen, the sculptor Bertel Thorvaldsen, the physicist Niels Bohr, and the building's architect Martin Nyrop—look on. Underneath the floor are national archives dating back to 1275, popular with Danes researching their family roots. The City Hall is free and open to the public (Mon–Fri 8:00–17:00, open on Sat only for tours—see below, closed Sun).

You can wander throughout the building and into the peaceful garden out back. Guided English-language **tours** get you into more private, official rooms (30 kr, 45 min, year-round Mon–Fri at 15:00, Sat at 10:00 and 11:00).

Tourists romp (in groups with an escort) up the **tower**'s 300 steps for the best aerial view of Copenhagen (20 kr, June–Sept: Mon–Fri 10:00, 12:00, and 14:00, Sat 12:00; Oct–May: Mon–Sat 12:00, tel. 33 66 25 82).

▲▲**Christiansborg Palace**—A complex of government buildings stands on the ruins of Copenhagen's original 12th-century fortress: the Parliament, Supreme Court, prime minister's office, royal reception rooms, royal library, several museums, and the royal stables.

While the current palace dates only from 1928 and the royal family moved out 200 years ago, the building is the sixth to stand here in 800 years and is rich with tradition. The information-packed 50-minute English-language tours of the royal reception rooms are excellent. As you slip-slide on protect-the-floor slippers through 22 rooms, you'll gain a good feel for Danish history, royalty, and politics. (For instance, the family portrait of King Christian IX shows why he's called the "father-in-law of Europe"—with children eventually becoming or marrying royalty in Denmark, Russia, Greece, Britain, France, Germany, and Norway.) The highlight is the dazzling set of modern tapestries—Danish-designed but Gobelin-made in Paris. This gift, given to the queen on her 60th birthday in 2000, celebrates 1,000 years of Danish history with wild wall-hangings from the Viking age to our chaotic times (admission by tour only, 40 kr, May–Sept daily at 11:00, 13:00, and 15:00; Oct–April Tue, Thu, Sat, and Sun at 15:00; from equestrian statue in front, go through wooden door, past entrance to Christiansborg Castle ruins, into courtyard, and up stairs on right; tel. 33 92 64 92).

Christiansborg Castle Ruins—An exhibit in the scant remains of the first fortress built by Bishop Absalon, the 12th-century founder of Copenhagen, lies under the palace. There's precious little to see, but it's old and well described (20 kr, May–Sept daily 9:30–15:30; Oct–April Tue, Thu, Sat, and Sun 9:30–15:30, closed Mon, Wed, and Fri; good 1-kr guide). Early birds note that this sight opens 30 minutes before other nearby sights.

▲**Thorvaldsen's Museum**—This museum, which has some of the best swoon-worthy art you'll see anywhere, tells the story and shows the monumental work of the great Danish neoclassical sculptor Bertel Thorvaldsen (1770–1844). Considered Canova's equal among neoclassical sculptors, Thorvaldsen spent 40 years in Rome. He was lured home to Copenhagen with the promise to showcase his work in a fine museum—which opened in the revolutionary year of 1848 as Denmark's first public art gallery. The ground floor showcases his statues (pull open the little black "information" cases for descriptions). Upstairs, get into the mind of the artist by perusing his personal possessions and the private collection of paintings from which he drew inspiration (30 kr, free Wed, open Tue–Sun 10:00–17:00, closed Mon, well-described, located in neoclassical building with colorful walls next to Christiansborg Palace, tel. 33 32 15 32).

Royal Library—Copenhagen's "Black Diamond" library is a striking building made of shiny black granite, leaning over the harbor at the edge of the palace complex. Wander through the old and new sections, read a magazine, and enjoy a classy—and pricey—lunch (restaurant, café, library hours: Mon–Sat 10:00–19:00, closed Sun, tel. 33 47 43 63).

▲▲▲**National Museum**—Focus on the excellent and curiously enjoyable Danish collection, which traces this civilization from its ancient beginnings. Exhibits are laid out chronologically and described in English. Pick up the museum map. The audioguide (25 kr) describes the highlights but adds little to the printed descriptions you'll find inside. Start with "Denmark's Old Tide" at room #1 (right of entrance, through glass tunnel), and follow the numbers through the "prehistory" section circling the ground floor—oak coffins with still-clothed and -armed skeletons from 1300 B.C., ancient and still-playable *lur* horns, the 2,000-year-old Gundestrup Cauldron of art-textbook fame, lots of Viking stuff, and a bitchin' collection of well-translated rune stones. Then go upstairs, find room 101, and carry on to find fascinating material on the Reformation, an exhibit on everyday town life in the 16th and 17th centuries, and, in room 126, a unique "cylinder perspective" of the noble family (from 1656) and two peep shows. The next floor takes you into modern times, with historic toys and a slice-of-Danish-life 1600–2000 gallery where you'll see everything from rifles and old bras to early jukeboxes (50 kr, free Wed, Tue–Sun 10:00–17:00, closed Mon, mandatory bag check—10-kr coin deposit, cafeteria, enter at Ny Vestergade 10, tel. 33 13 44 11).

▲National Museum's Victorian Apartment—The museum inherited an incredible Victorian apartment just around the corner, a tour of which is included with your admission. The wealthy Christensen family managed to keep its plush living quarters a 19th-century time capsule until the granddaughters passed away in 1963. Since then, it's been part of the National Museum with all but two of its rooms looking like they did around 1890. Visit it if the tour schedule works for you (45-min tours leave from museum ticket desk Sat and Sun at 12:00, 13:00, 14:00, and 15:00; tours also likely at those times on Thu and Fri).

▲Ny Carlsberg Glyptotek—Scandinavia's top art gallery is an impressive example of what beer money can do. Because of ongoing renovation during 2005, some collections (Danish painting, French and Danish sculpture) will not be on view—but the admission price will be reduced to soften the blow. The museum has intoxicating Egyptian, Greek, and Etruscan collections; a fine sample of early 19th-century Danish golden-age painting (may not be viewable); and a heady, if small, exhibit of 19th-century French paintings (in the new "French Wing," including Géricault, Delacroix, Manet, Impressionists, and Gauguin before and after Tahiti). Linger with marble gods under the palm leaves and glass dome of the very soothing winter garden. Designers, figuring Danes would be more interested in a lush garden than in classical art, used this wonderful space as leafy bait to cleverly introduce locals to a few Greek and Roman statues. (It works for tourists, too.) One of the original Rodin *Thinker*s (wondering how to scale the Tivoli fence?) is in the museum's backyard (20 kr, free Wed and Sun, Tue–Sun 10:00–16:00, closed Mon, 2-kr English brochure/guide, classy cafeteria under palms, behind Tivoli at Dantes Plads 7, tel. 33 41 81 41, www.glyptoteket.dk).

Danish Design Center—This center, its building a masterpiece in itself, shows off the best in Danish design as well as top examples from around the world, including architecture, fashion, and graphic arts. A visit to this low-key display case for sleek Scandinavian design offers an interesting glimpse into the culture. The basement showcases the Industrial Design prizewinners from 1965 through 1999. Here's a sample English description: "He taught the materials to do things not even they realized they were able to do" (40 kr, Mon–Fri 10:00–17:00, Wed until 21:00, Sat–Sun 11:00–16:00, across from Tivoli at H. C. Andersen Boulevard 27, tel. 33 69 33 69, www.ddc.dk). The boutique next to the ticket counter features three themes: travel light (chic travel accessories and gadgets), modern Danish classics, and books and posters. The café on the main level, under the atrium, serves light lunches (60–100 kr).

Hovedbanegården—Copenhagen's great train station is a fascinating mesh of Scandinavian culture and transportation efficiency. Even if you're not a train traveler, check it out (see "Arrival in Copenhagen," page 37). Notice how the classical music effectively keeps the junkies away from the back door.

Rosenborg Castle and Nearby

▲▲▲**Rosenborg Castle and Treasury**—This finely furnished Dutch Renaissance–style castle was built by Christian IV in the early 1600s as a summer castle. Open to the public since 1838, it houses the Danish crown jewels and 500 years of royal knickknacks, including some great Christian IV memorabilia, such as the shrapnel (removed from his eye and forehead after a naval battle) that he had made into earrings for his girlfriend. Because nothing is explained in English, a tour—or the following self-guided tour—is essential.

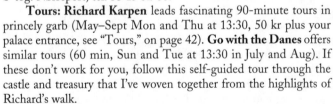

Cost, Hours, Location: 60 kr, daily June–Aug 10:00–17:00, May and Sept 10:00–16:00, Oct 11:00–15:00, Nov–April Tue–Sun 11:00–14:00, closed Mon. S-tog: Nørreport, tel. 33 15 32 86.

Tours: Richard Karpen leads fascinating 90-minute tours in princely garb (May–Sept Mon and Thu at 13:30, 50 kr plus your palace entrance, see "Tours," on page 42). **Go with the Danes** offers similar tours (60 min, Sun and Tue at 13:30 in July and Aug). If these don't work for you, follow this self-guided tour through the castle and treasury that I've woven together from the highlights of Richard's walk.

Self-Guided Tour: You'll tour the first floor room by room, then climb to the third floor for the big throne room. After a quick sweep of the middle floor, finish in the basement for the jewels. Begin the tour on the ground floor, in the Audience Room.

Ground floor: Here in the **Audience Room,** all eyes were on Christian IV. Today, your eyes should be on him, too. Take a close look at his bust by the fireplace. Check this guy out—earring and fashionable braid, a hard drinker, hard lover, energetic statesman, and warrior king. Christian IV was dynamism in the flesh, wearing a toga: a true Renaissance guy. During his reign, the size of Copenhagen doubled. Rosenborg was his favorite residence, and where he chose to die. You're surrounded by Dutch paintings (the Dutch had a huge influence on 17th-century Denmark). Note the smaller statue of the 19-year-old king, showing him jousting jauntily on his coronation day. The astronomical clock—with musical works and moving figures—did everything you can imagine.

The **study** (nearest where you entered) was small (and easy to heat). Kings did a lot of corresponding. We know a lot about Christian because 3,000 of his handwritten letters survive. The painting shows eight-year-old Christian—after his father died, but still too young to rule. A portrait of his mother hangs above the boy, and opposite is a portrait of Christian in his prime.

In the **bedroom,** paintings show the king as an old man...and as a dead man. In the case are the clothes he wore when wounded in battle. Riddled with shrapnel, he lost an eye. No problem for the warrior king with a knack for heroic publicity stunts: He had the shrapnel bits taken out of his eye and forehead made into earrings. (They hang in the case above the blood-stained cloth.) Christian lived to be 70 and fathered 26 children (with two wives and one mistress).

The next room displays **wax casts** of royal figures. This was the way famous and important people were portrayed back then. The **chair** is a forerunner of the whoopee cushion. When you sat on it, metal cuffs pinned your arms down, allowing the prankster to pour water down the back of the chair (see hole)—making you "wet your pants." When you stood up, the chair made embarrassing tooting sounds.

The next room has a particularly impressive inlaid **marble floor.** Imagine the king meeting emissaries here in the center, with the emblems of Norway (right), Denmark (center), and Sweden (left) behind him.

The end room was a **dining room.** Study the box made of amber (petrified tree resin, 30–50 million years old). The tiny figures show a healthy interest in sex. (You might want to shield children from the more graphic art in the case next to the door you just passed.) By the window (opposite where you entered), a hole in the wall let the music performed by the band in the basement waft in. (Who wants the actual musicians in the dining room?) The audio hole was also used to call servants.

The **long hall** leading to the staircase exhibits an intriguing painting of Frederick III being installed as the absolute monarch. Study it closely for slice-of-life details. Next, a sprawling family tree makes it perfectly clear that Christian IV comes from good stock. Note the tree is labeled in German—the second language of the realm.

The queen had a hand-pulled elevator, but you'll need to hike up two flights of stairs to the top-floor throne room.

Throne room (top floor): The **Long Hall**—considered one of the best-preserved Baroque rooms in Europe—was great for banquets. The decor trumpets the great accomplishments of Denmark's great kings.

The four corners of the ceiling feature the four continents known at the time. (America was still considered pretty untamed—notice the decapitated head with the arrow sticking out of it.) In the center, of course, is the proud seal of the Danish Royal Family. The tapestries are from the late 1600s, designed for this room. Effective propaganda, they show the Danes defeating their Swedish rivals on land and at sea. The king's throne was made of "unicorn horn" (actually narwhal tusk from Greenland)—believed to bring protection from evil and poison. It was about the most precious material in its day. The queen's throne is of hammered silver—the 150-pound lions are 300 years old.

The small room to the left holds a delightful **royal porcelain** display with Chinese, French, German, and Danish examples of the "white gold." For five centuries, Europeans couldn't figure out how the Chinese made this stuff. The difficulty in just getting it back to Europe in one piece made it precious. The Danish pieces, called "Flora Danica" (on the left as you enter) are from a huge royal set showing off the herbs and vegetables of the realm.

On your way back down, the **middle floor** is worth a look: Circling counterclockwise, you'll see more fine clocks, fancy furniture, and royal portraits. In the first room, notice the double portrait of the king and his sister. The queen enjoyed her royal lathe (with candleholders for lighting and pedals to spin it hidden away below). The small mirror room (on the side) was where the king played Hugh Hefner—using mirrors on the floor to see what was under those hoop skirts. In hidden cupboards, he had a fold-out bed and a handy escape staircase.

Back outside, find the stairs leading down to the...

Royal Danish Treasury (castle basement): The palace was a royal residence for a century and has been the royal vault right up until today. As you enter, peek into the royal **wine cellar,** with thousand-liter barrels, to right of ticket checker. Then continue into the treasury.

The diamond- and pearl-studded **saddles** were Christian IV's—the first for his coronation, the second for his son's wedding. When his kingdom was nearly bankrupt, Christian had these constructed lavishly—complete with solid-gold spurs—to impress visiting dignitaries and bolster Denmark's credit rating.

Next case: **tankards.** Danes were always big drinkers, and to drink in the top style, a king had narwhal steins (#4030 and #4031). Note the fancy Greenland Inuit (Eskimo) on the lid. The case is filled with exquisitely carved ivory.

Next case: What's with the mooning snuffbox (#4063)? Also, check out the amorous whistle (#4064).

Case in corner: The 18th century was the age of **brooches.** Many of these are made of freshwater pearls. Find the fancy combination toothpick and ear spoon (#1140). A queen was caught having an affair after 22 years of royal marriage. Her king gave her a special present: a golden ring—showing the hand of his promiscuous queen shaking hands with a penis (#4146).

Step downstairs, away from all this silliness. Passing through the serious vault door, you come face to face with a big, jeweled **sword.** The tall, two-handed, 16th-century coronation sword was drawn by the new king, who cut crosses in the air in four directions, symbolically promising to defend the realm from all attacks. The cases surrounding the sword contain everyday items used by the king (all solid gold, of course). What looks like a trophy case of gold records is actually a collection of dinner plates with amber centers (#5032).

Go down the steps. In the center case is Christian IV's **coronation crown** (from 1596, 7 pounds of gold and precious stones, #1524), which some consider to be the finest Renaissance crown in Europe. Its 12 gables radiate symbolism. Find the symbols of justice (sword and scales), fortitude (a woman on a lion with a sword), and charity (a woman nursing—meaning the king will love God and his people as a mother loves her child). The pelican, which famously pecks its own flesh to feed its children, symbolizes God sacrificing his son, just as the king would make great sacrifices for his people. Climb the footstool to look inside—it's as exquisite as the outside. The shields of various Danish provinces remind the king that he's surrounded by his realms.

Circling the cases along the wall (right to left), notice: the fine enameled lady's goblet with traits of a good woman spelled out in Latin (#5128); above that, an exquisite prayer book (with handwritten favorite prayers, #5134); the big solid-gold baptismal basin (#5262) hanging above tiny boxes that contained the royal children's umbilical chords (handy for protection later in life, #5272); and royal writing sets with wax, seals, pens, and ink (#5320).

Go down a few more steps into the lowest level of the treasury and last room. The two **crowns** in the center cases are more modern (from 1670), lighter, and more practical—just gold and diamonds without all the symbolism. The king's is only four pounds, and the queen's is a mere two.

The cases along the walls show off the **crown jewels.** These were made in 1840 of diamonds, emeralds, rubies, and pearls from earlier royal jewelry. The saber (#5540) shows emblems of the 19 provinces of the realm. The sumptuous pendant features a 19-carat diamond cut (like its neighbors) in the 58-facet "brilliant" style for maximum reflection. Imagine these on the dance floor. The painting shows the coronation of Christian VIII at Frederiksborg Chapel in 1840. The crown jewels are still worn by the queen on special occasions several times a year.

▲**Rosenborg Gardens**—The Rosenborg Castle is surrounded by the royal pleasure gardens and, on sunny days, a minefield of sunbathing

Danish beauties and picnickers. While "ethnic Danes" grab the shade, the rest of the Danes worship the sun. When the royal family is in residence, there's a daily changing-of-the-guard mini-parade from the Royal Guard's barracks adjoining Rosenborg Castle (at 11:30) to Amalienborg Castle (at 12:00). The Queen's Rose Garden (across the moat from the palace) is a royal place for a picnic (cheap open-face sandwiches to go at Sos's Smørrebrød, nearby at the corner of Borgergade and Dronningens Tværgade, Mon–Fri 8:00–14:00, closed Sat–Sun). The fine statue of Hans Christian (H. C., pronounced *hoe see*) Andersen in the park, actually erected in his lifetime (and approved by him), is meant to symbolize how his stories had a message even for adults.

▲**National Art Museum (Statens Museum for Kunst)**—The museum fills an impressive building with Danish and European paintings from the 14th century through today. Of most interest is the Danish golden age of paintings and those from the late 19th and early 20th centuries. Its Impressionist collection is impressive (with works by Manet, Monet, Renoir, Cézanne, Gauguin, and van Gogh). It's complemented with works by Danish artists, who, inspired by the Impressionists, introduced that breezy movement to Scandinavia. Make a point to meet the "Skagen" artists. They gathered in the fishing village of Skagen on the northern tip of Denmark, surrounded by the sea and strong light, and painted heroic folk fishermen themes in the late 1800s (50 kr, extra for special exhibitions, Tue–Sun 10:00–17:00, Wed until 20:00, closed Mon, Sølvgade 48, tel. 33 74 84 94).

Near Strøget

Museum of Erotica—This museum's focus is the love life of *Homo sapiens.* Better than the Amsterdam equivalent, it offers a chance to visit a porn shop and call it a museum. It took some digging, but they've put together a history of sex from Pompeii to the present day. Visitors get a peep into the world of 19th-century Copenhagen prostitutes and a chance to read up on the sex lives of Mussolini, Queen Elizabeth, Charlie Chaplin, and Casanova. After reviewing a lifetime of Playboy centerfolds and an entire room filled with Marilyn Monroe, visitors sit down for the arguably artistic experience of watching the "electric *tabernakel*," a dozen silently slamming screens of porn (worth the 79-kr entry fee only if fascinated by sex, they'll try to charge you 99 kr with optional graphic booklet, daily May–Sept 10:00–23:00, Oct–April 11:00–20:00, a block north of Strøget at Købmagergade 24, tel. 33 12 03 11). Copenhagen's dreary little red light district along Istedgade behind the train station has withered away to almost nothing. If you came to Copenhagen to sightsee sex...it's in the museum.

Round Tower—Built in 1642 by Christian IV, the tower connects a church, library, and observatory (the oldest functioning observatory in Europe) with a ramp that spirals up to a fine view of Copenhagen (20 kr, June–Aug Mon–Sat 10:00–20:00, Sun 12:00–20:00, Sept–May Mon–Sat 10:00–17:00, Sun 12:00–17:00, nothing to see inside but the ramp and the view, just off Strøget on Købmagergade).

Near *The Little Mermaid*

▲▲**Museum of Danish Resistance (Frihedsmuseet)**—The compelling story of Denmark's heroic Nazi-resistance struggle (1940–1945) is well explained in English, from Himmler's eyepatch to fascinating tricks of creative sabotage (40 kr, free on Wed, open May–mid-Sept Tue–Sat 10:00–16:00, Sun 10:00–17:00, off-season Tue–Sat 10:00–15:00, Sun 10:00–16:00, closed Mon; guided tours at 14:00 Tue, Thu, and Sun in the summer; on Churchillparken between Amalienborg Palace and *The Little Mermaid,* bus #26 from Langelinie or bus #1, #6, #19, or #29 from farther away, tel. 33 13 77 14).

▲**Amalienborg Palace Museum**—While Queen Margrethe II and her family live quite privately in one of the four mansions that make up the palace complex, another mansion has been open to the public since 1994. It displays the private studies of four kings of the House of Glucksborg, who ruled 1863–1972. Your visit is short—six or eight rooms on one floor. But it affords an intimate and unique peek into Denmark's royal family (45 kr, May–Oct daily 10:00–16:00, Nov–April Tue–Sun 11:00–16:00, enter on side of palace square farthest from the harbor, tel. 33 12 08 08).

Amalienborg Palace Changing of the Guard—This noontime event is boring in the summer when the queen is not in residence— the guards just change places. For more information about the palace and Amalienborg Square, see page 51.

Christianshavn

▲**Our Savior's Church (Vor Frelsers Kirke)**—The church's bright Baroque interior (1696), with its pipe organ supported by the royal elephants, is worth a look (free, helpful English flier, April–Aug Mon–Sat 11:00–16:30, Sun 12:00–16:30, off-season closes 1 hr earlier, bus #2A, #8, #19, or Metro: Christianshavn, Sankt Annægade 29, tel. 32 57 27 98). You can climb the unique spiral spire for great views of the city and of the Christiania commune below (20 kr, 400 steps, 311 feet high, closed in bad weather and Nov–March).

▲▲▲**Christiania**—In 1971, the original 700 Christianians established squatters' rights in an abandoned military barracks just a 10-minute walk from the Danish parliament building. A generation later, this "free city" still stands—an ultra-human mishmash of idealists, hippies, potheads, nonmaterialists, and happy children

(250 kids, 250 dogs, and 600 adults). There are even a handful of Willie Nelson–type seniors among the 180 remaining here from the original takeover. And an amazing thing has happened: The place has become the third-most-visited sight among tourists in Copenhagen. Move over, *Little Mermaid*.

Pusher Street is Christiania's main drag. Get beyond this touristy side of Christiania, and you'll find a fascinating, ramshackle world of moats and earthen ramparts, alter-native housing, cozy tea houses, carpenter shops, hippie villas, children's playgrounds, peaceful lanes, and people who believe that "to be normal is to be in a straightjacket." Be careful to distinguish between real Christianians and Christiania's motley guests—druggies (mostly from other coun-tries) who hang out here in the summer for the freedom. Part of the original charter guaranteed that the community would stay open to the public.

The Community: Christiania is broken into 14 administrative neighborhoods on a former military base. The land is still owned by Denmark's Ministry of Defense. Locals build their homes but don't own the land. There's no buying or selling of property. When some-one moves out, the community decides who will be invited in to replace that person. A third of the adult population works on the outside, a third works on the inside, and a third doesn't work much at all. There are nine rules: no cars, no hard drugs, no guns, no explosives, and so on. The Christiania flag is red and yellow because when the original hippies took over, they found a lot of red and yellow paint on site. The three yellow dots in the flag are from the three "i"s in Christiania.

The community pays the city about $1 million a year for utili-ties and has about $1 million a year more to run its local affairs. A few "luxury hippies" have oil heat, but most use wood or gas. The ground here was poisoned by its days as a military base, so nothing is grown in Christiania. The community has one mailing address (for 25 kr/month, you can receive mail here). A phone chain provides a system of communal security (they have had bad experiences calling the police). Each September 26, the day those first squatters took over the barracks here in 1971, Christiania has a big birthday bash.

Tourists are entirely welcome here, because they've become a major part of the economy. Visitors react in very different ways to the place. Some see dogs, dirt, and dazed people. Others see a haven of peace, freedom, and no taboos. Locals will remind judgmental Americans (whose country incarcerates more than a quarter of the world's prison inmates) that a society must make the choice: Allow for alternative lifestyles...or build more prisons.

Christiania

1. Carl Madsens Place
2. Nemoland
3. Green Hall
4. Månefiskeren Café
5. Morgenstedet Vegetarian Restaurant
6. Spiseloppen Restaurant
7. Old Entrance

Even since its inception, Christiania has been a political hot potato. No one in the Danish establishment wanted it. And no one had the nerve to mash it. In the last decade, Christiania has connected better with the rest of society—paying its utilities and taxes, and so on. But since taking over in 2001, Denmark's conservative government (with pressure from the United States) has vowed to "normalize" Christiania, and in recent years police have regularly conducted raids on pot sellers. In January 2004, to minimize governmental hassles, residents tore down the hash stands along Pusher Street. (Although the shops may be gone, the merchants remain.) And there's talk about developing posh apartments to replace existing residences—perhaps as early as 2006, according to one government plan.

Many predict that Christianians will withstand the government's challenge, as they have in years past. The community, which also calls itself Freetown, fended off a similar attempt in 1976 with the help of fervent supporters from around Europe. *Bevar Christiania*—"Save Christiania"—banners fly everywhere, and locals are confident that their free way of life will survive. As history has shown, the challenge may just make that hippie haven a bit stronger.

Orientation Tour: Passing under the gate, take Pusher Street directly into the community. The first square—a kind of market square (souvenirs and marijuana-related stuff)—is named Carl Madsens Place, honoring the lawyer who took the squatters' case to the Danish supreme court in 1976 and won. Beyond that is Nemoland (a food circus, on the right). A huge warehouse called the Green Hall (Den Gronne Hal) is a recycling center

(where people get most of their building material) that does double duty at night as a concert hall and as a place where children work on crafts. On the left, a lane leads to the Månefiskeren café, and beyond that, to the Morgenstedet vegetarian restaurant. Going straight on Pusher Street takes you to the ramparts that overlook the lake. A walk or bike ride through Christiania is a great way to see how this community lives. (When you leave, look up—the sign above the gate says, "You are entering the EU.")

Smoking Marijuana: Beefy marijuana plants stand on proud pedestals at the market square. The open-air food circus (or the canal-view perch above it, on the earthen ramparts) creates just the right ambience for losing track of time.

While hard drugs are out and government crackdowns continue, marijuana is still sold and smoked happily (cheap, in joints or loose, bars have bongs). Local dealers are friendly, talkative, and helpful to Americans. They claim you're safe within Christiania. You can buy and smoke marijuana legally anytime of year, but don't take it out of the neighborhood or you'll risk arrest. Because of the possibility of losing its favored trade status with America, Denmark is required by Uncle Sam to make an occasional bust of someone leaving the "free city" with pot.

About hard drugs: For the first few years, junkies were tolerated. But that led to violence and polluted the mellow ambience residents envisioned. In 1979, the junkies were expelled— an epic confrontation in the community's folk history now—and since then, the symbol of a fist breaking a

syringe is as prevalent as the leafy marijuana icon. Hard drugs are emphatically forbidden in Christiania.

Eating in Christiania: The people of Christiania appreciate good food and count on tourism as a big part of their economy. Consequently, there are plenty of decent eateries. Most of the restaurants are closed on Monday (the community's weekly holiday). **Pusher Street** has a few grungy but tasty falafel stands. **Nemoland** is a fun food circus with Thai food, fast hippie food, and great tented outdoor seating. Its stay-a-while atmosphere comes with backgammon, foosball, bakery goods, and fine views from the ramparts. **Morgenstedet** is a good, cheap vegetarian café (60-kr meals, Tue–Sun 12:00–21:00, closed Mon, left after Pusher Street).

Månefiskeren (Moonfisher Bar) looks like a Brueghel painting—from 2004—with billiards, chess, light meals, and drinks. **Spiseloppen** is *the* classy, good-enough-for-Republicans restaurant in the community (closed Mon, described in "Eating," page 73).

Hours and Tours: Christiania is open all the time (main entrance is down Prinsessegade behind Vor Frelsers' spiral church spire in Christianshavn). You're welcome to snap photos, but ask residents before you photograph them. Guided tours leave from the front entrance of Christiania at 15:00 (just show up, 30 kr, 90 min, daily late June–Aug, Sat–Sun rest of year, in English and Danish, tel. 32 57 96 70). For a private tour, contact Nina Pontoppidan. Nina and her husband have been part of the community since its early days, and she charges 180 kr for a 90-minute tour (tel. 32 57 69 51, pontoppidan@mail.mira.dk).

Greater Copenhagen

Carlsberg Brewery—Denmark's beloved source of legal intoxicants, Carlsberg welcomes you to its Visitors Center for a self-guided tour and a half-liter of beer (free, Tue–Sun 10:00–16:00, closed Mon, bus #18, enter at Gamle Carlsbergvej 11 around corner from brewery entrance, tel. 33 27 13 14).

Open-Air Folk Museum (Frilandsmuseet)—This park is filled with traditional Danish architecture and folk culture (50 kr, free Wed, open April–Sept Tue–Sun 10:00–17:00, closed Mon and off-season, outside of town in the suburb of Lyngby, S-tog: Sorgenfri and 10-min walk to Kongevejen 100, tel. 33 13 44 11).

Bakken—Danes gather at Copenhagen's other great amusement park, Bakken (free, April–Aug daily 12:00–24:00, S-tog: Klampenborg then walk 10 min through the woods, tel. 39 63 73 00, www.bakken.dk—in Danish only).

Dragør—If you don't have time to get to the idyllic island of Ærø (see Central Denmark chapter), consider a trip a few minutes out of Copenhagen to the fishing village of Dragør (bus #250S or #5A from station 5 stops at Sundbyvesterplads, change to #350A).

SHOPPING *STRØGET STREET*

Shops are generally open Monday through Friday from 10:00 to 19:00 and Saturday from 9:00 to 16:00. While the big department stores dominate the scene, many locals favor the characteristic, small artisan shops and boutiques that are listed in the *Local Life* flier. You can't get this flier at the TI, but keep your eyes peeled for it (for example, at the bus info center on Rådhuspladsen and at the bakery on Pistol Street).

For a street's worth of shops selling **"Scantiques,"** wander down Ravnsborggade from Nørrebrogade.

Copenhagen's colorful **flea markets** are small but feisty and surprisingly cheap (Sat May–Nov 8:00–14:00 at Israels Plads, Fri and Sat May–Sept 8:00–17:00 along Gammel Strand and on Kongens Nytorv). For other street markets, ask at the TI.

The city's top **department stores** (Illum at Østergade 52, tel. 33 14 40 02; and Magasin at Kongens Nytorv 13, tel. 33 11 44 33) offer a good, if expensive, look at today's Denmark. Both are on Strøget and have fine cafeterias on their top floors. The department stores and the Politiken Bookstore on Rådhuspladsen have a good selection of maps and English travel guides.

Shoppers who like jewelry look for amber, known as "gold of the North." Globs of this petrified sap wash up on the shores of all the Baltic countries. **House of Amber** has a shop and a tiny two-room museum with about 50 examples of prehistoric insects trapped in the amber (remember *Jurassic Park*?) under magnifying glasses (25 kr, daily 10:00–18:00, 50 yards off Nyhavn at Kongens Nytorv 2).

If you buy anything substantial (more than 300 kr, about $50) from a shop displaying the **Danish Tax-Free Shopping** emblem, you can get a refund of the Value Added Tax, roughly 25 percent of the purchase price (VAT is MOMS in Danish). If you have your purchase mailed, the tax can be deducted from your bill. For details, call 32 52 55 66, and see "VAT Refunds for Shoppers" on page 13.

NIGHTLIFE

For the latest on the city's hopping jazz scene, inquire at the TI, study your *Copenhagen This Week* booklet, or pick up the "alternative" *Playtime* magazine at Use It. To locate the following places, see the map on pgae 76. The **Copenhagen Jazz House** is a good bet for live jazz (around 90 kr, Tue–Thu and Sun at 20:30, Fri–Sat at 21:30, closed Mon, Niels Hemmingsensgade 10, tel. 33 15 26 00 for the schedule in Danish, www.jazzhouse.dk). For blues, try the **Mojo Blues Bar** (50 kr Fri–Sat, otherwise no cover, nightly 20:00–5:00, music starts at 22:00, Løngangsstræde 21c, tel. 33 11 64 53). Christiania always seems to have something musical going on after dark. **Tivoli** has evening entertainment daily from mid–April through mid–September until 23:00 (see page 51).

If you'd rather dance, join Denmark's salsa wave at **Sabor Latino Salsa Club.** Located one block south of Rådhuspladsen, it offers free salsa lessons in English. Salsa dancing is surprisingly easy to learn in this friendly environment, and you'll get a chance to know the fun-loving Danes (free on Thu, 50 kr Fri–Sat, Thu–Sun 21:00–3:00, free lesson 22:00–23:00, closed Mon–Wed, no reservation required, wear comfortable shoes, Vestervoldgade 85, tel. 26 16 46 96).

SLEEPING

I've listed a few big business-class hotels, the best budget hotels in the center, cheap rooms in private homes in great neighborhoods an easy bus ride from the station, and a few backpacker dorm options.

Big Copenhagen hotels have an exasperating pricing policy. Their high rack rates are actually charged only about 20 or 30 days a year (unless you book in advance and don't know better). Hotels are swamped at certain times and need to keep their gouging options open. Therefore, you need to check their Web site for deals or be bold enough to simply show up and let the TI (for a 75-kr fee) find you a room on their push list. The TI swears that, except for maybe 10 days a year, they can land you a deeply discounted room in a three- or four-star business-class hotel in the center. That means a 1,400-kr American-style comfort double for about 800 kr, including a big buffet breakfast.

Hotels in Central Copenhagen

Prices include breakfast unless noted otherwise. All are big, modern places with elevators and non-smoking rooms upon request, and all accept credit cards. Beware, many hotels have rip-off phone rates even for local calls. The Mayfair, Webers, Sophie Amalie, and Ibis hotels are big and soulless. The rest are smaller, cheaper, and more characteristic.

$$$ **Ibsens Hotel** is an elegant 118-room hotel in a charming neighborhood away from the main train station commotion and a short walk from the old center (Sb-935–1035 kr, Db-1,150–1350 kr, discounted rooms available May–June and Aug–Sept—ask about these and other discounts when booking or check their Web site for the latest offers, Vendersgade 23, S-tog: Nørreport, tel. 33 13 19 13, fax 33 13 19 16, www.ibsenshotel.dk, hotel@ibsenshotel.dk).

$$$ **Hotel Mayfair** is a comfortable but sterile place on a quiet street three blocks behind the station (Sb-1,295 kr, Db-1,395 kr rack rate but Db often go for 800 or 900 kr, a half a block away from busy Vesterbrogade at Helgolandsgade 3, tel. 33 31 48 01, fax 33 23 96 86, www.choicehotels.dk, info.mayfair@comfort.choicehotels.dk).

$$$ **Webers Scandic Hotel** faces busy Vesterbrogade (some noisy rooms), but has a peaceful garden courtyard and a modern, inviting interior (high-season rack rates: small Sb-1,145 kr, Sb-1,395 kr, Db-1,545 kr, but ask about summer/weekend rates June–Aug and Fri–Sun all year—you can save 20–30 percent, 10 percent discount when you show this book, both discounts depend on availability, sauna, exercise room, particularly expensive phone rates, Vesterbrogade 11B, tel. 33 31 14 32, fax 33 31 14 41, www.scandic -hotels.com, webers@scandic-hotels.com).

Sleep Code

(6 kr = about $1, country code: 45)
S = Single, **D** = Double/Twin, **T** = Triple, **Q** = Quad,
b = bathroom, **s** = shower. Breakfast is generally included at hotels
but not at private rooms or hostels. Unless otherwise noted, credit
cards are accepted. Everybody speaks English.

To help you sort easily through these listings, I've divided
the rooms into three categories, based on the price for a standard
double room with bath during high season:

$$$ **Higher Priced**—Most rooms 1,000 kr or more.
$$ **Moderately Priced**—Most rooms between 450–1,000 kr.
$ **Lower Priced**—Most rooms 450 kr or less.

$$$ Sophie Amalie Hotel is a classy and modern Danish-style
hotel a block from the big cruise-ship harbor and a block from trendy
Nyhavn (134 rooms, Sb-875/1,075/1,275 kr, Db-1,075/1,175/1,275
kr, prices vary with size of room from pretty tight to very spacious,
breakfast-115 kr, Sankt Annæ Plads 21, tel. 33 13 34 00, fax 33 11 77
07, www.remmen.dk, booking.hsa@remmen.dk).

$$$ Hotel Guldsmeden, a boutique hotel with comfortable,
well-appointed rooms, feels more like a B&B than a 64-room hotel.
It's situated in the trendy Vesterbro district, between Frederiksborg
park and the central train station. Although located on busy
Vesterbrogade, most rooms are clustered around a quiet courtyard
(Sb-995 kr, Db-1,295 kr, 20 percent discount with this book through
2005, includes breakfast, Internet access, Vesterbrogade 66, tel. 33
22 15 00, fax 33 22 15 55, www.hotelguldsmeden.dk, reception
@hotelguldsmeden.dk).

$$ Ibis Copenhagen, a big chain, has several hotels with
cookie-cutter rooms at reasonable prices in the center (mid-
June–Oct: Sb-599 kr, Db-799 kr, Nov–April: Sb-599 kr, Db-659
kr, breakfast-60 kr, elevator). Two identical hotels a block behind
the station are **Ibis Triton Hotel** (Helgolandsgade 7, tel. 33 31 32
66, triton@accorhotel.dk) and **Ibis Star Hotel** (Colbjornsensgade
13, tel. 33 22 11 00, star@accorhotel.dk).

$$ Hotel Nebo, a secure-feeling refuge with a friendly welcome
and comfy, spacious rooms, is half a block from the station on the
edge of Copenhagen's red light district (S-460 kr, Sb-760 kr, D-690
kr, older Db-860 kr, these prices promised with this book through
2005, cheaper Oct–April, extra bed-150 kr, Istedgade 6, tel. 33 21
12 17, fax 33 23 47 74, www.nebo.dk, nebo@email.dk).

$$ Hotel Bethel Somandshjem is a calm and stately former sea-
men's hotel facing the boisterous Nyhavn canal and offering 30 fine

Copenhagen Hotels

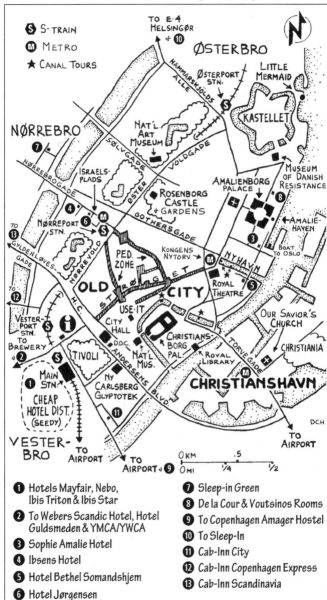

S S-TRAIN
M METRO
★ CANAL TOURS

TO E·4
HELSINGØR
10

ØSTERBRO

ØSTERPORT
STN.

LITTLE
MERMAID

KASTELLET

NØRREBRO

7

NAT'L
ART
MUSEUM

SØLVGADE

VOLDGADE

MUSEUM
OF DANISH
RESISTANCE

NØRREBROGADE

ISRAELS-
PLADS

ØSTER

ROSENBORG
CASTLE
& GARDENS

AMALIENBORG
PALACE

8

4

NØRREPORT
STN.

6

M

S

GOTHERSGADE

AMALIE-
HAVEN

3

BOAT
TO OSLO

TO
13

GYLDENLØVES
GADE

NØRREVOLD

PED.
ZONE

KONGENS
NYTORV

M

NYHAVN

TO
12

H.C.

OLD

STRØGET

CITY

ROYAL
THEATRE

5

OUR SAVIOR'S
CHURCH

VESTER-
PORT
STN.

S

i

CITY
HALL

USE IT

★

CHRISTIANIA

TO
BREWERY

2

S

TIVOLI

D.D.C.

ANDERSENS BLVD.

NAT'L
MUS.

CHRISTIANS-
BORG
PAL.

ROYAL
LIBRARY

TORVE GADE

MAIN
STN.

1

CHEAP
HOTEL DIST.
(SEEDY)

NY
CARLSBERG
GLYPTOTEK

11

M

CHRISTIANSHAVN

DCH

VESTER-
BRO

TO
AIRPORT

TO
AIRPORT

TO
AIRPORT
9

0 KM   .5

0 MI   1/4   1/2

1 Hotels Mayfair, Nebo,
Ibis Triton & Ibis Star

2 To Webers Scandic Hotel, Hotel
Guldsmeden & YMCA/YWCA

3 Sophie Amalie Hotel

4 Ibsens Hotel

5 Hotel Bethel Somandshjem

6 Hotel Jørgensen

7 Sleep-in Green

8 De la Cour & Voutsinos Rooms

9 To Copenhagen Amager Hostel

10 To Sleep-In

11 Cab-Inn City

12 Cab-Inn Copenhagen Express

13 Cab-Inn Scandinavia

rooms at the most reasonable rack rates in town. It's an old-fashioned place—no e-mail, but it's easy to reserve a room with a phone call and a promise to show up. A third of their rooms are non-smoking and newly renovated, but the older rooms are a bit more spacious (Sb-595 kr, Db-745 kr, harborview Db-795 kr, big Db on corner-895 kr, extra bed-150 kr, includes breakfast, bus #650S from station or Metro to Kongens Nytorv, facing bridge over the canal at Nyhavn 22, tel. 33 13 03 70, fax 33 15 85 70).

$$ **Hotel Jørgensen** is a friendly little 30-room hotel beautifully located just off Nørreport with some cheap, depressing rooms and some good-value, nicer rooms. While the lounge is classy and welcoming, the halls are a narrow, tangled maze (basic S-475 kr, Sb-575 kr, very basic D-575 kr, more elegant Db-700 kr, includes breakfast, Romersgade 11, tel. 33 13 81 86, fax 33 15 51 05, www .hoteljoergensen.dk, hoteljoergensen@mail.dk). They also rent 135-kr dorm beds to those under 35 (6–14 beds in rooms, sheets-30 kr, includes breakfast).

A Danish Motel-6

$$ **Cab-Inn** is a radical innovation: identical, mostly collapsible, tiny but comfy, cruise ship–type staterooms, all bright, molded, and shiny with TV, coffeepot, shower, and toilet. Each room has a single bed that expands into a twin with one or two fold-down bunks on the walls. The staff will hardly give you the time of day, but it's tough to argue with this efficiency (Sb-510 kr, Db-630 kr, Tb-750 kr, Qb-870 kr, breakfast-50 kr, easy parking-60 kr, www.cabinn.dk). There are two virtually identical Cab-Inns in the same neighborhood (a 15-min walk northwest of the station): **Cab-Inn Copenhagen Express** (86 rooms, Danasvej 32–34, tel. 33 21 04 00, fax 33 21 74 09, express@cabinn.com) and **Cab-Inn Scandinavia** (201 rooms, "Commodore" rooms have a real double bed for 100 kr extra, Vodroffsvej 55, tel. 35 36 11 11, fax 35 36 11 14, scandinavia @cabinn.com). A third location recently opened just south of Tivoli: **Cab-Inn City** (350 rooms, Mitchellsgade 14, tel. 33 46 16 16, fax 33 46 17 17, city@cabinn.com).

Rooms in Private Homes

Lots of travelers seem shy about rooms in private homes. Don't be. I almost always sleep in a private home. And, at 450 kr or so per double, they're a great value. The experience is as private or as social as you want it to be, offering great "at home in Denmark" opportunities in good neighborhoods (in Christianshavn and near Amalienborg Palace) for a third of the price of hotels. You'll get a key and come and go as you like. Always call ahead—they book in advance. All speak English and afford a fine peek into Danish domestic life. Rooms generally have no sink. While they usually don't include breakfast, you'll have access to the kitchen. If their rooms are booked up, they can often find you a place with a neighbor. You can trust the quality of their referrals. If you still can't snare a place, remember that the TI or Use It would love to send you to one from their stable of locals renting out rooms. For more listings, visit www.bbdk.dk.

Private Rooms in Christianshavn

This area is a never-a-dull-moment hodgepodge of the chic, artistic, hippie, and hobo, with historic fixed-up warehouses in the shadow of government ministries. Colorful with shops, cafés, and canals, Christianshavn is an easy 10-minute walk to the center and has good bus connections to the airport and downtown. The bus stop is just outside the 7-Eleven on Torvegade. Take bus #2A or #48 to City Hall or the main train station and #2A to the airport. The Metro connects Christianshavn and Nørreport (2 stops on S-tog from main train station).

$ **Annette and Rudy Hollender** enjoy sharing their 300-year-old home with my readers. Even with a long and skinny staircase, sinkless rooms, and two rooms sharing one toilet/shower, it's a comfortable and cheery place to call home (S-350 kr, D-450 kr, T-625 kr, cash only, closed Nov–April, half a block off Torvegade at Wildersgade 19, Metro: Christianshavntorv, tel. 32 95 96 22, hollender@city.dk).

$ **Chicken's Private Pension** rents basic rooms in a funky old house, with steep stairs and rustic furniture. It's right on Christianshavn's main drag (S-350 kr, D-450 kr, T-625 kr, Q-800 kr, extra bed-125 kr, kitchen available for breakfast on your own, cash only, Torvegade 36, Metro: Christianshavntorv, tel. 32 95 32 73, mobile 20 41 32 73, www.chickens.dk, morten@chickens.dk, Morton Frederiksen).

South of Christianshavn: $$ **Gitte Kongstad** rents two apartments, each taking up an entire spacious floor in her 100-year-old house. You'll have a kitchen, little garden, Internet connection, and your own bike as you settle comfortably far from the big-city intensity (Sb-400 kr, Db-475 kr, extra bed-150 kr, cash only, family-friendly, bus #2A from airport, bus #12 or #13 from station, and just 75 yards from Metro stop: Lergravsparken, Badensgade 2, tel. & fax 32 97 71 97, mobile 21 65 75 22, g.kongstad@post.tele.dk). You'll feel at home here, and the bike ride into town (or to the beach) is a snap.

Lower-Priced Private Rooms a Block from Amalienborg Palace

Amaliegade is a stately cobbled street in a quiet neighborhood (a 10-min walk north of Nyhavn and Strøget). You can look out your window and see the palace guard changing. Catch bus #1A or #15 from the station to Fredericiagade.

Christianshavn

1 Hollender House

2 Chicken's Private Pension

3 To Gitte Kongstad Rooms

4 Færge Cafeen

5 Ravelin Restaurant

6 Bastionen & Løven Restaurant

7 Lagkagehuset Bakery

8 Spicy Kitchen Indian

9 Spiseloppen Restaurant

$ The following people are artistic and professional folks who each rent out two rooms in their utilitarian, modern, and very Danish flats: **Puk and Holger De la Cour** (S-375 kr, D-425 kr with do-it-yourself breakfast, extra bed-150 kr, cash only, kitchen/lounge available, Amaliegade 34, 4th floor, tel. 33 12 04 68, mobile 23 72 96 45, holgerdelacour@private.dk) and **Line** (pronounced LEE-nuh) **Voutsinos** (2 double rooms, 1 with queen bed, 1 with 2 large single beds, D-425 kr, includes breakfast, extra bed-150 kr, cash only, family deals, May–Sept only, Amaliegade 34, 3rd floor, tel. & fax 33 14 71 42, line.voutsinos@privat.dk).

Hostels

Copenhagen energetically accommodates the young vagabond on a shoestring. The Use It office (see page 36) is your best source of information. Each of these places charges about 100 kr per person for a bed and breakfast. Some don't allow sleeping bags, and if you don't have your own hostel bedsheet, you'll usually have to rent one for about 30 kr. IYHF hostels normally sell non-cardholders a guest pass for 25 kr.

$ The modern **Copenhagen Amager Hostel** (IYHF) is huge (528 beds), with 300-kr doubles, 390-kr triples, 460-kr quads, and five-bed dorms at 95 kr per bed (membership required, sheets-35 kr, no curfew, excellent facilities, breakfast-45 kr, dinner-65 kr, Internet access, self-serve laundry). It's on the edge of town, but the Metro gets you within a 10-minute walk (Metro: Balla Center). By bus, it's 30 minutes from the center (#250S with change to #100S, direction: Svanmøllen S, Vejlands Allé 200, tel. 32 52 29 08, fax 32 52 27 08, www.danhostel.dk).

$ The following two big, grungy, central crash pads are open in July and August only: **Danish YMCA/YWCA** (dorm bed-90 kr, 4- to 10-bed rooms, breakfast-25 kr, sheets-15 kr, Valdemarsgade 15, 10-min walk from train station or bus #6, tel. 33 31 15 74) and **Sleep-In** (dorm bed-110 kr, sheets-30 kr, 4- or 6-bed cubicles in a huge 286-bed room, no curfew, breakfast-20 kr, lockers, always has room and free condoms, Blegdamsvej 132, bus #1, #6, or #14 to Triangle stop and look for sign, tel. 35 26 50 59, www.sleep-in.dk, copenhagen@sleep-in.dk).

$ **Sleep-in Green,** the "ecological hostel," is very young, cool, and open mid-April through October (100-kr bunks, organic breakfast-30 kr, in a quiet spot a 15-min walk from center or catch bus 5A from station to Ravnsborggade, off Nørrebrogade at Ravnsborggade 18, tel. 35 37 77 77, www.sleep-in-green.dk).

EATING

Cheap Meals

For a quick lunch, try a *smørrebrød,* a *pølse,* or a picnic. Finish it off with a pastry.

Smørrebrød

Denmark's 300-year-old tradition of open-face sandwiches survives. Find a *smørrebrød* take-out shop and choose two or three that look good (about 10 kr each). You'll get them wrapped and ready for a park bench. Add a cold drink, and you have a fine, quick, and very Danish lunch. Tradition calls for three sandwich courses: herring first, then meat, and then cheese. Downtown, you'll find these handy local alternatives to Yankee fast-food chains:

Near Kongens Nytorv: Try Tria Cafe (Mon–Fri 8:00–14:00, closed Sat–Sun, Gothersgade 12).

Near the Round Tower: Café Halvvejen is good for sit-down *smørrebrød* (lunch only, on Krystalgade).

Near Gammeltorv/Nytorv: Sorgenfri offers a local experience in a dark, woody spot just off Strøget (Mon–Sat 11:00–21:00,

Sun 12:00–21:00, Brolæggerstræde 8, tel. 33 11 58 80). Or consider Domhusets Smørrebrød (Mon–Fri 7:00–14:30, closed Sat–Sun, Kattesundet 18, tel. 33 15 98 98).

Near Amalienborg Palace: Head inland two blocks just past the Marble Church to Svend Larsen's Smørrebrød (8-kr sandwiches to go, Mon–Fri 8:00–14:00, closed Sat–Sun, St. Kongensgade 83).

Near Rosenborg Palace: Sos's Smørrebrød delights local office workers (Mon–Fri 8:00–14:00, closed Sat–Sun, at corner of Borgergade and Dronningens Tværgade). The nearby Rosenborg Gardens are perfect for your picnic.

The Pølse

The famous Danish hot dog, sold in *pølsevogn* (sausage wagons) throughout the city, is another typically Danish institution that has resisted the onslaught of our global, Styrofoam-packaged, fast-food culture. Study the photo menu for variations. These are fast, cheap, tasty, and—like their American cousins—almost worthless nutritionally. Even so, what the locals call the "dead man's finger" is the dog Danish kids love to bite.

There's more to getting a *pølse* than simply ordering a hot dog. Employ these handy phrases: *rød* (red, the basic weenie), *medister* (spicy, better quality), *knæk* (short, stubby, tastier than *rød*), *ristet* (fried), *brød* (a bun, usually smaller than the sausage), *svøb* ("swaddled" in bacon), *Fransk* (French style, buried in a long skinny hole in the bun with sauce), and *flottenheimer* (a fat one with onions and sauce). *Sennep* is mustard and *ristet løg* are crispy, fried onions. Wash everything down with a *sodavand* (soda pop).

By hanging around a *pølsevogn,* you can study this institution. Denmark's "cold feet cafés" are a form of social care: People who have difficulty finding jobs are licensed to run these wiener-mobiles. As they gain seniority, they are promoted to work at more central locations. Danes like to gather here for munchies and *pølsesnak*—the local slang for empty chatter (literally, "sausage talk").

Picnics

Throughout Copenhagen, small delis *(viktualiehandler)* sell fresh bread, tasty pastries, juice, milk, cheese, and yogurt (drinkable, in tall liter boxes). Two of the largest supermarket chains are **Irma** (in arcade on Vesterbrogade next to Tivoli) and **Super Brugsen. Netto** is a cut-rate outfit with the cheapest prices. The little grocery store in the main train station is expensive but handy (daily 8:00–24:00).

Pastry

Find your way to the famous Danish pastries by looking for the golden pretzel sign hanging over the door or windows—it's the Dane's age-old symbol for a bakery. Danish pastries, called *wienerbrød*

(Vienna bread) in Denmark, are named for the Viennese bakers who brought the art of pastry-making to Denmark, where the Danes say they perfected it. Try these bakeries: **Nansens** (on corner of Nansensgade and Ahlefeldtsgade, near Ibsens Hotel), **Kransekagehuset** (on Pilestræde—Pistol Street, just off Strøget, near Kongens Nytorv; for their cheaper takeout, go around the corner to Ny Ostergade 9), and **Lagekagehuset** (on Torvegade in Christianshavn). For a genteel bit of high-class 1870s Copenhagen, pay a lot for a coffee and a fresh danish at **Conditori La Glace,** just off Strøget at Skoubogade 3.

Dining with the Danes

For a unique experience and a great opportunity to meet locals in their homes, consider dining with a Danish family. You get a homey two-course meal with lots of conversation. Some effort is made to match your age and interests (but not occupations). Book in advance, by phone or online. **Dine with the Danes** costs 350 kr per person (reserve at least a day in advance, tel. 26 85 39 61, www.dinewiththedanes.dk). **Meet the Danes** charges 395 kr per person (tel. 33 46 46 46, www.meetthedanes.dk).

Restaurants

In the Center

Det Lille Apotek ("The Little Pharmacy") is a reasonable, candlelit place. It's been popular with locals for 200 years, and now it's also quite touristy (sandwich lunches, traditional dinners for 120–170 kr nightly from 17:30; just off Strøget, between Frue Church and Round Tower at St. Kannikestræde 15; tel. 33 12 56 06). Their specialty is "Stone Beef," a big slab of tender, raw steak plopped down in front of you on a scalding-hot lava stone. Flip it over a few times and it's cooked within minutes.

Riz-Raz Vegetarian Buffet has two locations in Copenhagen: around the corner from the canal boat rides at Kompagnistræde 20 (tel. 33 15 05 75) and across from Det Lille Apotek at Store Kannikestræde 19 (tel. 33 32 33 45). At both places, you'll find a healthy all-you-can-eat Mediterranean/vegetarian buffet lunch for 59 kr (daily 11:30–16:00) and an even bigger dinner buffet for 69 kr (16:00–24:00). The dinner has to be the best deal in town. And they're happy to serve free water with your meal.

Café Norden, smoky and very Danish with fine pastries, overlooks Amagertorv by the swan fountain. They have good light meals and salads and great people-watching from window seats on the second floor (order at the bar upstairs).

Kobenhavner Cafeen, cosy yet classy, dishes up traditional food at a reasonable price. Their lunch specials are served until 17:00, when the more expensive dinner menu kicks in (daily until

Copenhagen Restaurants

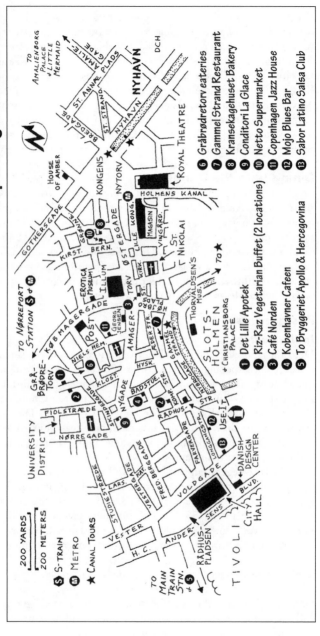

1 Det Lille Apotek
2 Riz-Raz Vegetarian Buffet (2 locations)
3 Café Norden
4 Kobenhavner Cafeen
5 To Bryggeriet Apollo & Hercegovina
6 Gråbrødretorv eateries
7 Gammel Strand Restaurant
8 Kransekagehuset Bakery
9 Conditori La Glace
10 Netto Supermarket
11 Copenhagen Jazz House
12 Mojo Blues Bar
13 Sabor Latino Salsa Club

22:00, 2 blocks off Nytorn at Badstuestraede 10, tel. 33 32 80 81).

Bryggeriet Apollo, just outside the main entrance to Tivoli, offers pub atmosphere Danish-style. Beer is brewed on the premises while the kitchen cranks out generous portions of meat-and-potatoes dishes for reasonable prices (140–200-kr dinners, Mon–Sat 11:30–22:00, Sun 15:00–24:00, Vesterbrogade 3, tel. 33 12 33 13). Order a one-liter mug of beer and they take a surprising security deposit.

Hercegovina, a Croatian restaurant with folksy seating over-looking a leafy section of Tivoli, serves a 129-kr lunch buffet (mostly cold, 12:00–16:00) and a 169-kr dinner buffet (salads, veggies, and lots and lots of meat, including a lamb on a spit, daily 17:00–22:00, music nightly after 19:00). While this is technically in Tivoli, diners can get in from the outside by going through the restaurant's office (facing the train station, next to the TI). You can eat here without a Tivoli ticket, but you will not be allowed into the park.

Gråbrødretorv is perhaps the most popular square in the old center for a meal. It's a food court—especially in good weather. Choose from Greek, Mexican, Danish, or a meal in the old street-car #14.

Department stores serving cheery, reasonable meals in their cafeterias include **Illum** (head to the elegant glass-domed top floor, Østergade 52) and **Magasin** (Kongens Nytorv 13), which also has a great grocery and deli in the basement.

Gammel Strand, which serves "Danish-inspired French cuisine," is ideal for a dressy splurge in the old center (lunch-80–200 kr, entrees-200 kr, 3-course menu-300–450 kr, Mon–Sat 12:00–15:00 & 17:30–22:00, closed Sun, reservations wise, across from Canal Tours Copenhagen tour boats at Gammel Strand 42, tel. 33 91 21 21). Outdoor tables enjoy a canal and strolling people scene. Indoor tables are white-tablecloth elegant.

In Christianshavn

This neighborhood is so cool, it's worth combining an evening wander with dinner even if you're not staying here. It's a 10-minute walk across the bridge from the old center (or a 3-min ride on the Metro). For restaurants locations, see map on page 72.

Færge Cafeen is a fun-loving pub with a local following. They serve inexpensive traditional Danish specialties indoors or along the canal (daily specials about 70 kr, daily 12:00–16:00 & 17:00–21:00, Strandgade 50, tel. 32 54 46 24).

Ravelin Restaurant, on a tiny island on the big road 100 yards south of Christianshavn, serves good, traditional Danish food at reasonable prices to happy local crowds. Dine indoors or on the lovely lakeside terrace (*smørrebrød* lunches-40–100 kr, dinners-100–200 kr, daily mid-April–mid-Sept, Torvegade 79, tel. 32 96 20 45).

Bastionen & Løven, at the little windmill (Lille Mølle), serves gourmet Danish: nouveau cuisine from a small but fresh menu, on a Renoir terrace or in its Rembrandt interior (lunches for 60–95 kr, dinners for 145–190 kr, 3-course menu for 310 kr, 135-kr weekend brunch, daily 10:00–24:00, brunch Sat–Sun 10:00–14:00, Voldgade 50, walk to end of Torvegade and follow ramparts up to restaurant, at south end of Christianshavn, tel. 32 95 09 40 for reservations indoors). The inside feels like a colonial mansion—but smoky.

Lagkagehuset, with a big selection of pastries, sandwiches, and excellent fresh-baked bread, is a great place for breakfast (take-out coffee and pastries for 15 kr, Torvegade 45). **Spicy Kitchen** serves cheap and good Indian food (Torvegade 56).

Spiseloppen ("The Flea Eats") is a wonderfully classy place in Christiania. It serves great 140-kr vegetarian meals and 160–220-kr meaty ones by candlelight. It's gourmet anarchy—a good fit for Christiania, the free city/squatter town (restaurant open Tue–Sun 17:00–22:00, closed Mon, live music Fri and Sat, reservations often necessary on weekends; 3 blocks behind spiral spire of Vor Frelser's church, on top floor of old brick warehouse, turn right just inside Christiania's gate, enter the wildly empty warehouse, and climb the graffiti-riddled stairs; tel. 32 57 95 58). Beware, the people at the next table are likely to light up a joint while waiting for their ribs. Other, less-expensive Christiania eateries are listed above (see page 64).

Near Nørreport

These places—near the recommended Ibsens and Jørgensens hotels—are all close enough to survey before making a choice.

Kost Bar serves good-sized portions of pub fare indoors or outdoors (60-kr salads, 50–75 kr for lunch, 75–120 kr for dinner, daily 11:00–24:00, later on weekends, Vendersgade 16, tel. 33 33 00 35).

Café Klimt, which draws a young, hip, but sometimes heavy-smoking crowd, offers omelettes, sandwiches, and modern world cuisine (50–100 kr, daily 10:00–24:00, later Fri–Sat, Frederik-borggade 29, tel. 33 11 76 70).

Café Marius, with a jazzy elegance, dressy indoor tables, and casual sidewalk seating, is popular for its homemade pasta, hearty burgers, and big salads. Marius is from Chicago, so don't expect traditional Danish here (85–135-kr plates, brunch served daily with American-style pancakes, daily 12:00–23:00, Nørre Farimagsgade 55, tel. 33 11 83 83).

TRANSPORTATION CONNECTIONS

From Copenhagen by train to: Hillerød/Frederiksborg (6/hr, 40 min), **Roskilde** (1–3/hr, 30 min), **Odense** (2/hr, 1.75 hrs), **Helsingør** (3/hr, 50 min), **Malmö** (3/hr, 35 min), **Ærøskøbing** (5/day, 2.5 hrs to

Svendborg with a transfer in Odense, then 75-min ferry crossing to Ærøskøbing), **Stockholm** (11/day, 5 hrs on X2000 high-speed train, night service via Malmö 23:10–6:10; take regional train to Malmö first, but if you get off at Malmö Syd, you'll miss your connection—wait for Malmö C, for Central), **Växjö** (5/day, 3 hrs), **Kalmar** (5/day, 4 hrs), **Oslo** (2/day departing 8:20 and 13:36, 8–9 hrs, you must change in Göteborg, Sweden; no night train), **Berlin** (4/day, 9 hrs, via Hamburg), **Amsterdam** (2/day, 11 hrs), and **Frankfurt/Rhine** (4/day, 8 hrs). Convenient overnight trains from Copenhagen run to Stockholm, Amsterdam, and Frankfurt, some with one connection. National train info tel. 70 13 14 15. International train info tel. 70 13 14 16. Cheaper bus trips are listed at Use It (see page 36).

Overnight Cruises to Oslo

Luxurious DFDS cruise ships leave nightly from Copenhagen for Oslo, and from Oslo for Copenhagen. The 16-hour sailings leave at 17:00 and arrive at 9:00 the next day. So you can spend eight hours in Norway's capital and then return to Copenhagen, or take this cruise from Oslo and do Copenhagen as a day trip. Or just go one-way in either direction.

One-way costs about $163–214 per person in a standard double cabin; round-trip is simply double that unless you take a "mini-cruise," returning the same day you arrive (costs $186–281). The big dinner is $33 and the breakfast is $14. Fares vary with season, day (Friday is more expensive), and cabin.

DFDS operates two ships on this route—the M.S. *Pearl of Scandinavia* and the M.S. *Crown of Scandinavia*. Both offer all the cruise-ship luxuries: big buffets for breakfast and dinner (at an additional cost), a kids' playroom, pool (indoor on the *Crown,* indoor and outdoor on the *Pearl*), sauna, nightclub, and tax-free shopping (Danish office tel. 33 42 30 00, www.dfdsseaways.com, U.S. tel. 800/533-3755, www.seaeurope.com).

Near Copenhagen:
Roskilde, Frederiksborg Castle, Louisiana, Kronborg Castle, and the Øresund Region

Copenhagen's the star, but there are several worthwhile sights nearby, and the public transportation system makes side-tripping a joy. Visit Roskilde's great Viking ships and royal cathedral. Tour Frederiksborg, Denmark's most spectacular castle, and slide along the cutting edge at Louisiana—a superb art museum with a coastal setting as striking as its art. At Helsingør, do the dungeons of Kronborg Castle before heading on to Sweden.

Planning Your Time

Roskilde's Viking ships and the Frederiksborg Castle are the area's essential sights. Each take a half day; they're both easy 30- to 40-minute commutes from Copenhagen (followed by a 15-min walk). You'll find fewer tour-bus crowds in the afternoon. While you're in Roskilde, you can also pay your respects to the tombs of the Danish royalty.

If you're choosing between castles, Frederiksborg is the beautiful showpiece, and Kronborg—darker and danker—is more typical of the way most castles really were.

By car, you can see these sights on your way into or out of Copenhagen. By train, do day trips from Copenhagen—then sleep to and from Copenhagen while traveling to Oslo (overnight cruise) or Stockholm (night train). Consider getting a Copenhagen Card (see "Orientation," page 35), which covers your transportation and admission to all major sights.

Roskilde

Denmark's roots, both Viking and royal, are on display in Roskilde, a pleasant town 18 miles west of Copenhagen. Eight hundred years ago, Roskilde was the seat of Denmark's royalty—its center of power. Today the town that introduced Christianity to Denmark in A.D. 980 is most famous for hosting northern Europe's biggest annual rock/jazz/folk festival (July 1–July 10 in 2005). Wednesday and Saturday are flower/flea/produce market days (8:00–14:00). Its **TI** is helpful (Mon–Fri 9:00–17:00, Sat 10:00–13:00, open 1 hour later late June–Aug, closed Sun, 3 blocks from cathedral, follow signs to *Turistbureau*, tel. 46 31 65 65). Roskilde is an easy side-trip from Copenhagen by train (1–3/hr, 30 min).

▲▲**Roskilde Cathedral**—Roskilde's imposing 12th-century, twin-spired cathedral houses the tombs of 38 Danish kings and queens. It's a stately, modern-looking old church with great marblework, paintings (notice the impressive 3-D painting with Christian IV looking like a pirate, in the room behind the small pipe organ), wood carvings in and around the altar, a great 16th-century Baroque organ, and a silly little glockenspiel that plays high above the entrance at the top of every hour (15 kr, good 25-kr guidebook, April–Sept Mon–Fri 9:00–16:45, Sat 9:00–12:00, and Sun 13:00–16:45, Oct–March Tue–Sat 10:00–15:45, Sun 12:30–15:45, closed Mon, occasionally closes during the day for baptisms and weddings, private tours available for 450 kr, tel. 46 31 65 65). From the cathedral, it's a pleasant walk through a park down to the harbor and Viking ships.

▲▲▲**Viking Ship Museum (Vikingeskibshallen)**—Roskilde is strategically located on a shallow inlet. (*Vik* means "shallow inlet.")

Near Copenhagen

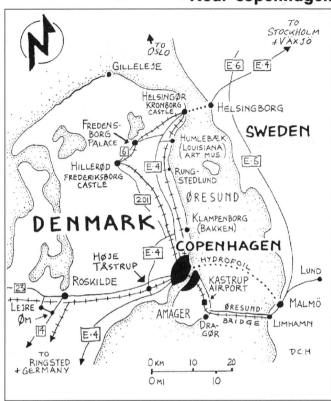

Vikings are people who lived along them. Roskilde's award-winning museum displays five different Viking ships—one boat is like the one Leif Eriksson took to America 1,000 years ago; another is like those depicted in the Bayeux Tapestry in Normandy, France. The descriptions are excellent—and in English. It's the kind of museum where you want to read everything. As you enter, buy the 15-kr guidebook and request the 22-minute English-language movie introduction. These ships were deliberately sunk 1,000 years ago to block a nearby harbor and were only recently excavated, preserved, and pieced together. The ships aren't as intact or as ornate as those in Oslo, but this museum does a better job of explaining shipbuilding (60-kr entry, less off-season, daily 10:00–17:00, from station catch bus #607 toward Boserup, 2/hr, 7-min ride, tel. 46 30 02 00, www.vikingeskibsmuseet.dk).

The museum's archaeological workshop lets visitors observe (10:00–15:00) the completed reproduction of a 100-foot-long, eight-man long boat built using ancient techniques. They plan to practice sailing it for two years, relearning the techniques. And, in 2007, they'll reconquer Ireland.

Frederiksborg Castle

The castle, rated ▲▲, is located in the cute town of Hillerød. The town's traffic-free center is worth a wander (just outside the gates of the mighty Frederiksborg Castle, past the TI). Hillerød's TI can book rooms in private homes for about 200 kr per person (Mon–Fri 10:00–17:00, Sat 10:00–13:00, closed Sun, Slangerupgade 2, tel. 48 24 26 26, www.hillerodturist.dk, turistbureau@hillkomm.dk).

To reach the castle from Copenhagen, take the S-tog to Hillerød (6/hr, 45 min) and enjoy a pleasant 20-minute walk or catch bus #701 or #702 (free with S-tog ticket or Copenhagen Card) from the train station (tel. 48 26 04 39).

Frederiksborg Castle, the grandest castle in Scandinavia, is often called the Danish Versailles. Frederiksborg (built 1602–1620) is the castle of Denmark's King Christian IV. Much of it was reconstructed after an 1859 fire, with the normal Victorian over-the-top flair, by the brewer J. C. Jacobsen and his Carlsberg Foundation.

A museum since 1878, it takes you on a chronological walk through the story of Denmark from 1500 until today (the third floor covers modern times). Many rooms have a handy English-language information sheet. The countless musty paintings are a fascinating scrapbook of Danish history.

Cost and Hours: 60 kr, daily April–Oct 10:00–17:00, Nov–March 11:00–15:00 (tel. 48 26 04 39). Drivers will find easy parking.

Approach: You can almost hear the clopping of royal hooves as you walk over the moat through the first island (which housed the stables and small businesses needed to support a royal residence). Then, down a windy (easy to defend) lane to the second island (home to the government when the king was here—domestic and foreign ministries), and then over the last moat to the main palace—where the king lived.

Main Courtyard: Survey the castle exterior from the Fountain of Neptune in the main courtyard. Christian IV imported Dutch architects to create this Christian IV style, which you'll see all over Copenhagen. The brickwork and sandstone are products of the local clay and sandy soil. The building, with its horizontal lines, triangles, and squares, is generally Renaissance style. But notice how this is interrupted by a few token Gothic elements on the church's facade. Some say this homey touch was to let the villagers know the king was "one of them."

Royal Chapel: Christian IV wanted the grandest royal chapel in Europe. For 200 years the coronation place of Danish kings, it's still used for royal weddings (and extremely popular for commoner weddings—book long in advance). The chapel is nearly all original, dating back to 1620. As you walk around the upper level, notice the graffiti scratched on the windows by the diamond rings of royal kids visiting for the summer back in the 1600s. Most of the coats of arms show off noble lineage (Eisenhower's, past the organ, is an exception). The organ is from 1620 with the original hand-powered bellows. (If you like music, listen for hymns on the old carillon at the top of each hour.) Leaving the chapel, you step into the king's oratory, with evocative romantic paintings (restored after a fire) from the mid-19th century.

Audience Room: Here, where formal meetings with the king took place, a grand painting shows Christian V as a Roman emperor firmly in command (with his 2 sons prominent for extra political stability). Christian's military victories line the walls and the four great continents—Europe, America, Asia, and Africa—circle the false cupola.

Dutch Reformation: In Room 26, note the effort noble families put into legitimizing themselves with family trees and family seals. Over the door to the next room is the image of a monk invited by the king to preach the new thinking of the Reformation. In the case is the first Bible translated into Danish (access to the word of God was a big part of the Reformation, from 1550).

Time for Lunch: You can picnic in the castle's moat park or enjoy the elegant Spisestedet Leonora at the moat's edge (35–70-kr *smørrebrød*, 65-kr salads, hot dishes from 120 kr, daily 10:00–17:00, slow service, tel. 48 26 75 16).

Louisiana

This is Scandinavia's most-raved-about modern-art museum. Located in the town of Humlebæk, beautifully situated on the coast 18 miles north of Copenhagen, Louisiana is a holistic place that masterfully mixes its art, architecture, and landscape. Wander from famous Chagalls and Picassos to more obscure art. Poets spend days here nourishing their creative souls with new angles, ideas, and perspectives. Frequent special exhibitions allow visitors an extra treat (visit www.louisiana.dk for the latest). The views over the Øresund, one of the busiest passages in the nautical world, are nearly as inspiring as the art. The cafeteria (indoor/outdoor) is reasonable and welcomes picnickers who buy a drink (74-kr museum admission, discount with Copenhagen Card, included in a special 120-kr round-trip tour ticket from Copenhagen—ask at Copenhagen's TI or any train station, daily 10:00–17:00, Wed until 22:00, tel. 49 19 07 91).

Take the train from Copenhagen toward Helsingør, get off at Humlebæk (3/hr, 40 min), and follow the signs to Louisiana along a busy road about 15 minutes. Or walk 10 minutes through the woods—exit the station and immediately go left onto Hejreskor Allé, a residential street, and then along a path through the woods. If you're coming from Frederiksborg Castle, catch the Lille Nord train at Hillerød station toward Helsingør. Change trains at Snekkersten or Helsingør, and go south to reach Humlebæk.

Kronborg Castle

Kronborg Castle is located in Helsingør, a small, pleasant little Danish town that's often confused with its Swedish sister, Helsingborg, just two miles across the channel. Helsingør has a TI (tel. 49 21 13 33), a medieval center, Kronborg Castle, and lots of Swedes who come over for the lower-priced alcohol.

Helsingør has a fine beachfront hostel, **$ Vandrerhjem Villa Moltke** (dorm bed-110 kr, S-250 kr, Sb-400 kr, D-300 kr, Db-400 kr, T-350 kr, Tb-400 kr, larger rooms available, nonmembers 30-kr extra per night, breakfast-45 kr, 1 mile north of castle, Nedre Strandvej 24, tel. 49 21 16 40, fax 49 21 13 99, www.helsingorhostel .dk). People who prefer small towns and small prices can day-trip to Copenhagen by train (5/hr, 50 min) with this hostel as their base.

Kronborg Castle (also called Elsinore) is a ▲▲ sight famous for its questionable (but profitable) ties to Shakespeare. Most of the "Hamlet" castle you'll see today, darling of every big bus tour and travelogue, was built long after the historical Hamlet died (more than a thousand years ago), and Shakespeare never saw the place. But this Renaissance castle existed when a troupe of English actors performed here in Shakespeare's time (Shakespeare may have known them). To see or not to see? It's most impressive from the outside.

If you're heading to Sweden, Kalmar Castle (see the South Sweden chapter) is a better medieval castle. But you're here, and if you like castles, see Kronborg. Duck into the creepy casements under the castle where the servants and guards lived.

The royal apartments include English explanations (75 kr, daily May–Sept 10:30–17:00, April and Oct Tue–Sun 11:00–16:00, Nov–March Tue–Sun 11:00–15:00, closed Mon, tel. 49 21 30 78 for recorded info or 49 21 80 88). Free 45-minute English tours are given daily at 14:00. In the basement, notice the statue of Holger Danske, a mythical Viking hero revered by Danish children. The story goes that if the nation is ever in danger, this Danish superman will awaken and restore peace and security to the land.

The free grounds between the walls and sea are great for picnics, with a pleasant view of the strait between Denmark and Sweden.

Øresund Region

When the Øresund (UH-ra-soond) Bridge, which connects Denmark and Sweden, opened in July 2000, it created Europe's most dynamic new metropolitan area. Overnight, the link forged an economic power with the 12th-largest gross domestic product in Europe. The Øresund region has surpassed Stockholm as the largest metro area in Scandinavia. Now 3.5 million Danes and Swedes—a highly trained and highly technical workforce—are within a quick commute of each other.

The bridge opens up new questions of borders. Historically, southern Sweden (the area across from Copenhagen, called Skåne) had Danish blood. It was Danish for 1,000 years before Sweden took it in 1658. Notice how Copenhagen is the capital on the fringe of its realm—at one time it was in the center.

The 10-mile-long link, which has a motorway for cars (255-kr toll) and a two-track train line, ties together the main islands of Denmark with Europe and Sweden. The $4 billion project consists of a 2.5-mile-long tunnel, an artificial island called Peberholm, and a five-mile-long bridge. With speedy connecting trains, Malmö in Sweden is now an easy half-day side-trip from Copenhagen (70 kr each way, 3/hr, 35 min). The train drops you at the station right in the center of Malmö, with all the important sights within a short walk. The *Malmö This Week* publication (free from Copenhagen TI) has everything you need for a well-organized visit.

TRANSPORTATION CONNECTIONS

Route Tips for Drivers

Copenhagen to Hillerød (45 min) **to Helsingør** (30 min) **to Kalmar** (6 hrs): Just follow the town-name signs. Leave Copenhagen, following signs for E-4 and Helsingør. The freeway is great. Hillerød signs lead to the Frederiksborg Castle, not to be confused with the nearby Fredensborg *slot* (palace) in the pleasant town of Hillerød. Follow signs to Hillerød C (for "center") then *slot* (for "castle"). While the E-4 freeway is the fastest, the Strandvejen coastal road (152) is pleasant, passing some of Denmark's finest mansions (including that of Danish writer Karen Blixen, a.k.a. Isak Dinesen of *Out of Africa* fame, in Rungstedlund, which is now a museum: 40 kr, May–Sept Tue–Sun 10:00–17:00, closed Mon, off-season shorter hours and closed Mon–Tue, tel. 45 57 10 57).

The 10-mile Øresund Bridge linking Denmark with Sweden (toll-255 kr) now lets drivers and train travelers skip nonstop from one country to the next.

Despite the bridge, some travelers will still take the ferry to Sweden (follow the signs to Helsingborg, Sweden—freeway leads to dock). Boats leave every 30 minutes. Buy your ticket as you roll on board (230 kr one-way for car, driver, and up to 5 passengers; round-trip gives you the return at less than half price). Reservations are free and smart (tel. 33 15 15 15, or book online at www.scandlines.dk). If you arrive before your time, you can probably drive onto any ferry. The 20-minute Helsingør–Helsingborg ferry ride gives you just enough time to enjoy the view of the Kronborg "Hamlet" castle, be impressed by the narrowness of this very strategic channel, and change money. The ferry exchange desk's rate is decent.

In Helsingborg, follow signs for E-4 and Stockholm. The road is good, traffic is light, and towns are all clearly signposted. At Ljungby, road 25 takes you to Växjö and Kalmar. Entering Växjö, skip the first Växjö exit and follow the freeway into Centrum, where it ends. It takes about four hours to drive from Copenhagen to Kalmar.

CENTRAL DENMARK

Ærø and Odense

The sleepy isle of Ærø is the cuddle after the climax. It's the perfect time-passed world in which to wind down, enjoy the seagulls, and take a day off. Get Ærø-dynamic and pedal a rented bike into the essence of Denmark. Stop for lunch in a traditional *kro* (country inn). Settle into a cobbled world of sailors, who, after the invention of steam-driven boat propellers, decided that building ships in bottles was more their style.

Between Ærø and Copenhagen, drop by bustling Odense, home of Hans Christian Andersen and a fine open-air folk museum.

Planning Your Time

Odense is a transportation hub, the center of the island of Funen. Geared up to celebrate Hans Christian Andersen's 200th anniversary in 2005, it's an easy stop, worth a few hours on the way to or from Ærø. More out of the way, Ærø is worth the journey. Once there, you will want two nights and a day to properly enjoy it.

Ærø

This small (22 by 6 miles) island on the south edge of Denmark is as salty and sleepy as can be. A typical tombstone reads: "Here lies

Christian Hansen at anchor with his wife. He'll not weigh until he stands before God." It's the kind of island where baskets of strawberries sit in front of houses—for sale on the honor system.

Ærø statistics: 7,000 residents, 500,000 visitors annually, 80,000 boaters annually, 350 deer, seven priests, no

Central Denmark

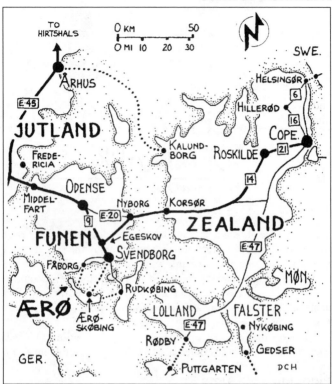

crosswalks, and three police officers. The three big industries are farming, shipping, and tourism—in that order. Twenty percent of the Danish fleet still resides on Ærø. But jobs are scarce, the population is slowly dropping, and family farms are consolidating into larger units. Ærø's going "green," and soon it's likely all local energy will be wind and solar, and all the produce will be organically grown.

Since Ærø is only nine miles across the water from Germany, you'll see plenty of Germans who return regularly to this peaceful retreat.

Ærøskøbing

Ærøskøbing is Ærø's town in a bottle. The government, recognizing the value of this amazingly preserved little town, prohibits modern building anywhere in the center. It's the only town in Denmark protected in this way. Drop into the 1680s, when Ærøskøbing was the wealthy home port of a hundred windjammers. The many Danes and Germans who come here for the tranquility—washing up the cobbled main drag in waves with the landing of each boat—call it the fairy-tale town. The Danish word for "cozy" *(hyggelig)* describes Ærøskøbing well.

Ærøskøbing is simply a pleasant place to wander. Stubby little porthole-type houses, with their birth dates displayed in proud decorative rebar, lean on each other like drunk, sleeping sailors. Wander under flickering old-time lamps. Snoop around town. It's OK. Peek into living rooms (if people want privacy, they shut their drapes). Notice the many "snooping mirrors" on the houses. Antique locals are following your every move. The harbor now caters to holiday yachts, and on midnight low tides you can almost hear the crabs playing cards.

The town economy, once rich with the windjammer trade, hit the rocks in modern times. Kids 15 to 18 years old go to a boarding school in Svendborg; many don't return. It's an interesting discussion: Should the island folk pickle their culture in tourism or forget about the cuteness and get modern?

ORIENTATION

Ærøskøbing is tiny. Everything's just a few cobbles from the ferry landing.

Tourist Information: The TI faces the ferry landing (Mon–Fri 10:00–16:00, Sat 9:30–12:30, closed Sun and off-season, tel. 62 52 13 00, fax 62 52 14 36). They have Internet access, give out brochures about the various sights and activities in the area, and can help you find a room if the listings below are booked (25-kr fee).

Helpful Hints

ATMs: The town has two cash machines (at the top of Vestergade and on Torvet Square).

Internet Access: Try the TI or the library on Torvet.

Rainy-Day Activities: The cute little 30-seat theater near Torvet Square plays movies in their original languages nightly (new titles begin every Mon). The best antiques shopping is at Vestergade 60 (its rejects fill the nearby alley and courtyard, both open June–Sept only). Or hit the bowling alley (hot dogs and cheese sandwiches, arcade games, usually open late).

Ferries: Drivers should call well in advance—especially in summer—to reserve a spot on the ferry (free and easy, just give name and license-plate number, Mon–Fri 8:00–16:00, Sat–Sun 9:00–15:00, tel. 62 58 17 17 or 62 52 40 00, fax 62 52 20 88, booking also possible online at www.aeroe-ferry.dk, info@aeroe-ferry.dk). If you haven't booked ahead, try parking your car overnight in the "ticketless" lane; up to four spots are opened up on a first-come first-served basis in the morning if not needed for ambulance service.

Bike Rental: Rent a bike from the Energi Station at the top of town on Pilebækken (45 kr for 3-speeds, 20 kr for worthwhile "*cykel* map," Mon–Fri 9:00–17:00, Sat 9:00–13:00, closed Sun except in July open 10:00–13:00; go through green door at Søndergade end of Torvet Square, past garden to next road; Pilebækken 7, tel. 62 52 11 10). The hostel and the campground also rent bikes (longer hours, see "Sleeping," page 95, for contact information). On Ærø there are no deposits and few locks.

Laundry: A self-service launderette is on Gyden between Vestergade and Brogade (daily 7:30–21:00). Instructions are posted in English, soap is available, and they'll make change. Beware: Doors lock automatically at 21:00, whether you're in with your laundry or not.

Self-Guided Walk: Ærøskøbing's Old Town

Ideally, take this ▲▲▲ stroll with the sun low, the shadows long, and the colors rich. From the harbor and TI, walk up the main street a block and go left on **Smedegade** (the poorest street in town, with the most architectural charm). Have a close look at the "street spies" on the houses—clever mirrors letting old women inside keep an eye on what's going on outside. The ship-in-a-bottle **Bottle Peter Museum** is on the right. Notice the gutters—some protect only the doorway. Appreciate the finely carved old doors. Number 37, from the 18th century, is Ærøskøbing's cutest house. Its tiny dormer is from some old ship's poop deck.

Smedegade ends at the Folkehojskole (folks' high school). Inspired by the Danish philosopher, Nikolaj Gruntvig—who wanted people to be able to say "I am good at being me"—it offers people of any age the benefit of government-subsidized cultural education (music, art, theater, and so on).

Jog left and stroll along the peaceful harborside **Molestien Lane,** lined with gardens, a quiet beach, and a row of small-is-beautiful houses—beginning with humble and progressing to captain's class. Each garden is cleverly and lovingly designed. Nicknamed "Virgin's Lane," this was where kids could court within view of their parents.

The dreamy-looking **island** immediately across the way is a natural preserve and a resting spot for birds making their long journey from the north to the Mediterranean. In the winter, when the water freezes, locals slip and slide over for a visit.

From the end of the lane, a trail leads farther along the water to

Ærøskøbing

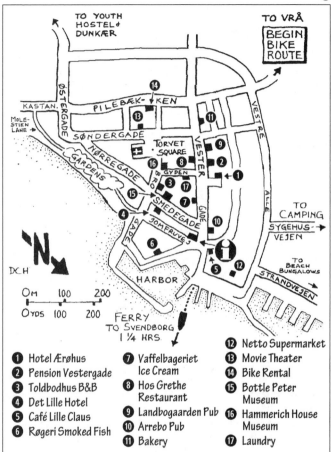

TO YOUTH
HOSTEL &
DUNKÆR

TO VRÅ

BEGIN
BIKE
ROUTE

ØSTERGADE

KASTAN.

PILEBÆK-KEN

MOLE-
STIEN
LANE

SØNDERGADE

NØRREGADE

GARDENS

TORVET
SQUARE

VESTER

GYDEN

SMEDEGADE

GADE

JOMFRUVEJ

TO
CAMPING

SYGEHUS-
VEJEN

TO
BEACH
BUNGALOWS

STRANDVEJEN

DCH

N

0m 100 200

0yds 100 200

HARBOR

FERRY
TO SVENDBORG
1 ¼ HRS.

❶ Hotel Ærøhus
❷ Pension Vestergade
❸ Toldbodhus B&B
❹ Det Lille Hotel
❺ Café Lille Claus
❻ Røgeri Smoked Fish

❼ Vaffelbageriet
Ice Cream
❽ Hos Grethe
Restaurant
❾ Landbogaarden Pub
❿ Arrebo Pub
⓫ Bakery

⓬ Netto Supermarket
⓭ Movie Theater
⓮ Bike Rental
⓯ Bottle Peter
Museum
⓰ Hammerich House
Museum
⓱ Laundry

a place the town provides for fishermen to pull out their boats and
tidy up their nets.

Molestien Lane leads around to the right (past the modern fire-
house) to **Østergade**, Ærøskøbing's east gate. In the days of German
control, all island trade was legal only within the town. All who
passed this point would pay various duties and taxes at a tollbooth
that once stood here.

Look through windows to see the sea. Peek into living rooms.
Catch snatches of Danish life. Ponder the beauty of a society with
such a keen sense of civic responsibility that fishing permits commit
you "to catch only what you need."

At the first square, stay left on Sondergade. Wrought-iron
anchors were added to hold together bulging houses. Ærøskøbing's

oldest houses—the only ones that survived a fire from a Swedish war—are #36 and #32. Notice the dates and the hatches upstairs where masts and sails were stored for the winter. The red on #32's door is the original paint job—ox blood, which, when combined with the tannin in the wood, really lasts. It never rots.

The **courtyard** behind #18 was a parking lot in pre-car days. Farmers, in town for their shopping chores, would leave their horses here. Even today, the wide-open fields are just beyond.

Wander down to Torvet, Ærøskøbing's **main square.** Notice the two pumps. Until 1951, townspeople came here for their water. The linden tree is the town symbol. The rocks around it celebrate the reunion of a big chunk of southern Denmark, which was ruled by Germany from 1864 to 1920. See the town seal featuring a linden tree, over the door of the old city hall (now the library). On the wall read the Danish: "With law shall man a country build."

SIGHTS AND ACTIVITIES

▲**Bottle Peter Museum**—This fascinating house has 750 different bottled ships. Old Peter Jacobsen, who made his first bottle at 16 and his last at 85, bragged that he drank the contents of each bottle, except those containing milk. He died in 1960 (and is most likely buried in a glass bottle), leaving a lifetime of tedious little creations for visitors to squint and marvel at (25 kr, daily mid-June–Aug 10:00–17:00, April–mid-June and Sept–mid-Oct 10:00–16:00, mid-Oct–March 13:00–15:00, at Smedegade 22, guided tours and demonstrations available in July—call for details, tel. 62 52 29 51).

▲**Hammerich House**—These 12 funky rooms in three houses are filled with 200- to 300-year-old junk (20 kr, daily mid-June–mid-Sept Mon–Fri 12:00–16:00, closed off-season, just east of Torvet Square, on Brogade). The third sight in town, the Ærø Museum, is across the street but is not as interesting as Hammerich House.

▲▲**Beach Bungalow Sunset Stroll**—At sunset, stroll to Ærøskøbing's sand beach. Facing the ferry dock, go left, following the harbor. Upon leaving the town you'll pass a children's playground and see a row of tiny, Monopoly-like huts past the wavy wheat field. This is Vestre Strandvejen, facing the sunset. And these tiny huts are beach escapes. Each is different, but all are stained with merry memories of locals enjoying themselves Danish-style. It's a fine walk out to the end of Urehoved, as this spit of land is called.

Ærø Island Bike Ride

0 KM 1   3
0 MI 1   2

100 KM

DENMARK

ÆRØ   COPE

TO
SVENDBORG

CAMPING

TO
SØBY

BORGNÆS

VRÅ

ÆRØSKØBING

BREG-
NINGE

VINDE-
BALLE

←YOUTH
HOSTEL

VODRUP
KLINT

TING-
STEDET

LILLE
RISE

TO
RUD-
KØBING

MARSTAL

TRANDERUP

STORE
RISE

DUNKÆR

GRAASTEN
B+B

DCH

BALTIC   SEA

Ærø Island Bike Ride (or Car Tour)

While serious biking maps take you on more complicated routes, this 18-mile trip shows you the best of this windmill-covered island's charms. The highest point on the island is only 180 feet above sea level, but the wind can be strong and the hills seem long. This ride is good exercise. Rent a bike from the Energi Station at the top of town on Pilebækken (see "Helpful Hints," page 89).

Leave Ærøskøbing to the west on the road to Vrå (Vråvejen, signed Bike Route 90). You'll see the first of many **U-shaped farms,** typical of Denmark. The three sides block the wind and store cows, hay, and people. *Gaard* (farm) shows up on many local surnames. At Osemarksvej, bike along the coast in the protection of the dike built in 1856 to make the once-salty swampland to your left farmable. Today, the soil is good for hay and little else. At the T-junction, go right toward Borgnæs. Keep to the right (passing two Vindeballe turnoffs), following signs to Bregninge. After a secluded beach, head inland (to O. Bregninge). Pass the island's only water mill, and climb uphill over the island's 2,700-inch-high summit to Bregninge. The tallest point on Ærø is called Synnes Hoej ("seems high"). Turn right and roll through Denmark's "second-longest village" to the church.

The interior of the 12th-century **Bregninge church** is still painted as a Gothic church would have been. Tradition says if the painter (his self-portrait is behind the pulpit, right of front pew) wasn't happy with his pay, he'd paint a fool's head in the church. Note the hole for a bell-ringing rope (left above first pew).

The **altarpiece**—gold leaf on carved oak—is from 1528, six years before the Reformation came to Denmark. The cranium carved into the bottom indicates it's a genuine masterpiece by Claus Berg (from Lübeck, Germany). This crucifixion scene is such a commotion it seems to cause Christ's robe to billow up. Strangely, the three wise men, each a Danish king, made it to this crucifixion. Notice the escaping souls of the two thieves—the one who converted on the cross being carried happily to Heaven, and the other, with its grim-winged escort, heading straight to Hell. Since this is a Catholic altarpiece, a roll call of saints lines the wings. During the restoration, the identity of the two women on the lower right was unknown, so the lettering—even in Latin—is clearly gibberish. (Public WC in churchyard.)

Roll back through Bregninge past many more U-shaped *gaards*. About a mile down the main road, in Vindeballe, take the Vodrup Klint turnoff to the right. (The Vindeballe Kro is a traditional inn serving decent food and cold draft beer.)

A road leads downhill (with a jog to the right) to a rugged bluff called **Vodrup Klint.** If I were a pagan, I'd worship here—the sea, the wind, and the chilling view. Notice how the land steps in sloppy slabs down to the sea. When saturated with water, the slabs of clay that make up the land here get slick and entire chunks can slide.

Hike down to the foamy beach (where you can pick up some flint, chalk, and wild thyme). While the wind at the top could drag a kite-flier, the beach below can be ideal for sunbathing. Since Ærø is warmer and drier than the rest of Denmark, this island is home to plants and animals found nowhere else in the country.

Backtrack 200 yards and follow the sign to Tranderup. You'll pass a lovely pond famous for its bell frogs, happy little duck houses, and the Sami-style tepee (a nature camp). Still following signs for Tranderup, stay parallel to the big road through town. You'll pass a lovely farm and a potato stand. At the main road, turn right. At the Ærøskøbing turnoff, just before the tiny little white house, turn left to the big stone (commemorating the return of the island to Denmark from Germany in 1750) and a grand **island panorama.** Seattleites might find Claus Clausen's rock interesting (in the picnic area, next to WC). It's a memorial to an extremely obscure pioneer from the state of Washington.

Return to the big road, pass the little white house, pass through Olde, and head toward Store Rise (REE-zuh), the next church spire in the distance. (Think of medieval travelers using spires as navigational aids.) Thirty yards after the Stokkeby turnoff, follow the rough, tree-lined path on the right to the Langdysse Tingstedet, just behind the church spire. This is a 6,000-year-old **early-Neolithic burial place.** Though Ærø had more than 200 of these prehistoric tombs, only 13 survive. *Ting* means assembly spot. Imagine a thousand years ago: Viking chiefs representing the island's various communities gathering here around their ancestors' tombs. For 6,000 years, this has been a holy spot. (A possible reason: Two underground streams cross here.) The stones were considered fertility stones. For centuries, locals in need of virility ground up bits and took the powder home (the hollows in the rock near the information post are mine).

Bundle up your powder and carry on down the lane to the **Store Rise church.** Inside you'll find little ships hanging in the nave, a fine 12th-century altarpiece, and Martin Luther keeping his Protestant hand on the rudder in the stern. The list in the church allows today's pastor to trace his pastoral lineage back to Doctor Luther himself. The churchyard is circular—echoing the shape of the Viking holy spot, which stood here long before the church. Can you find anyone buried in the graveyard whose name doesn't end in "sen"?

Continue down the main road (direction: Dunkær) with the three, 330-foot-high modern **windmills** on your right. These windmills are communally owned and—since they are a nonpolluting source of energy—state-subsidized. The Dunkær Kro is a handy place for an open-face-sandwich lunch (daily 12:00–14:00, tel. 62 52 15 54).

From Dunkær, take the small road, signed Lille Rise, past the topless windmill. Except for the Lille Rise, it's all downhill from here, as you coast past great sea views and the hostel back home to Ærøskøbing.

Still rolling? Bike past the campground along the **Urehoved beach** (*strand* in Danish) for a look at the coziest little beach houses you'll never see back in the "big is beautiful" United States. This is Europe, where the concept of sustainability is neither new nor subversive.

SLEEPING

In Ærøskøbing

$$$ **Hotel Ærøhus** is big and sprawling with 33 rooms. Although it is less personal and cozy than some of the other listings here, it's the closest thing to a grand hotel in this capital of quaint (Sb-770–860 kr, Db-1,090–1,190 kr, higher prices for rooms with more comforts and/or terrace, on Vestergade, 2 blocks up from ferry, tel. 62 52 10 03,

Sleep Code

(6 kr = about $1, country code: 45)
S = Single, **D** = Double/Twin, **T** = Triple, **Q** = Quad,
b = bathroom, **s** = shower. You can assume credit cards are
accepted and breakfast is included unless otherwise noted.

To help you sort easily through these listings, I've divided
the rooms into three categories, based on the price for a standard
double room with bath during high season:

    $$$ **Higher Priced**—Most rooms 800 kr or more.
    $$ **Moderately Priced**—Most rooms between 400–800 kr.
    $ **Lower Priced**—Most rooms 400 kr or less.

fax 62 52 21 23, www.aeroehus-hotel.dk, mail@aeroehus.dk). They
also rent holiday apartments with kitchenettes at the nearby Hotel
Ærø Marina; these can be a good value for families.

$$ Pension Vestergade is your best home away from home in
Ærøskøbing. It's lovingly run by Susanna Greve and her daughters,
Henrietta and Celia, who speak the Queen's English. Susanna is a
wealth of knowledge about the town's history and takes good care
of her guests. Built in 1784 for a sea captain's daughter, this eight-
room place—with each room named for its particular color
scheme—is on the main street in the town center. Reserve well in
advance (S-450 kr, D-680 kr, 2 nights minimum, cuddly hot-water
bottles, no smoking, Vestergade 44, tel. & fax 62 52 22 98, www
.pension-vestergade44.dk). Picnic in the back garden.

$$ Toldbodhus B&B, once a toll house, now rents four
delightful rooms to travelers. Three rooms share two bathrooms in
the main house, and a small garden house has a double room with a
detached bathroom (includes bathrobes). Karin and John Steenberg
named each room after cities they've lived in—Amsterdam,
København (Copenhagen), London, and Hong Kong (D-630 kr,
near harbor on corner of Smedegade at Brogade 8, tel. 62 52 18 11,
fax 62 52 18 02, www.toldbodhus.com, toldbodhus@mail.dk).

$$ Det Lille Hotel, a former 19th-century captain's home with
six tidy rooms, is warm, modern, and shipshape (S-580 kr, D-620
kr, extra bed-245 kr, Smedegade 33, 5970 Ærøskøbing, tel. & fax
62 52 23 00, www.det-lille-hotel.dk—in Danish only).

Just Outside of Town

Drivers may opt for this countryside B&B, a 10-minute drive or bus
ride from Ærøskøbing: **$$ Graasten B&B** is a non-smoking, family-
friendly cattle farm 300 yards from the sea run by a British/
Danish couple, Julie and Aksel Hansen (S-350 kr, D-450 kr,

extra bed-225 kr, under age 7-200 kr, cash only, fridge and cof-feemaker, laundry-30 kr, bike rental service arranged for guests, Østermarksvej 20, short bus ride on #990—direction Marstal, or drive from Ærøskøbing toward Marstal, tel. 62 52 24 25, fax 62 52 13 49, www.graastenfarmb-b.com, greyfarm@adr.dk).

$ Ærøskøbing Youth Hostel comes equipped with a fine living room, members' kitchen, and family rooms with two or four beds. When you add in all the extras, it's not much less than the hotels (dorm bed-105 kr, S-165, D-270 kr, T-315 kr, breakfast-45 kr, sheets-40 kr, required hostel membership card-30 kr, Smedevejen 15, 500 yards out of town, tel. 62 52 10 44, fax 62 52 16 44). The place is packed in July and closed October through March.

The three-star **$ campground,** on a fine beach, offers a lodge with a fireplace, campsites (60 kr per person), and cottages (110–250 kr, May–Sept, a short walk from "downtown"—facing the water, follow waterfront to the left, tel. 62 52 18 54).

EATING

Ærøskøbing has a handful of eateries and each summer a few other burger-joint-type places seem to pop up for a couple of months. Starting at the ferry dock (with your back to the harbor), you'll find a *pølse* stand to the right and a kiosk selling candy, ice cream, and telephone cards to your left.

Café Lille Claus, an inexpensive Danish-style diner, has good, reasonably priced entrées for 50–150 kr. Order at the bar (May–Sept daily 12:00–22:00, closed off-season, on Vestergade).

Ærøskøbing Røgeri, facing the harbor, is great for a light meal of smoked fish served with potato salad and bread for about 60 kr. They have picnic tables outside, or take it to go. Find a pleasant picnic site at the beach or at the park located on the street behind the fish house (daily May–Sept 10:00–18:00, later in July, Havnen 15, tel. 62 52 40 07). A smoked fish dinner and a couple of cold Carlsbergs are a welcome reward after a long bike ride.

Det Lille Hotel serves dinners in an inviting dining room or garden (from 150 kr, daily 18:00–21:00, Smedegade 33, tel. 62 52 23 00).

Hotel Ærøhus (also listed under "Sleeping," above) offers a traditional Danish menu in addition to a summertime grill menu, with seating indoors or on the patio (open daily, on Vestergade, tel. 62 52 10 03).

Heading up Vestergade, past the pink and popular **Vaffelbageriet** (ice cream–filled homemade waffle cones—try the Ærø special), you'll find a few summer cafés cooking up burgers or light meals. Across the street from Pension Vestergade is the classy **Hos Grethe Restaurant** (130–180-kr entrées). Further up is **Landbogaarden,** a pub offering basic meat-and-potatoes and fish dinners for around 100 kr.

For cheaper fare, the **bakery** serves homemade bread, cheese, yogurt, and tasty pastries (Mon and Wed–Fri 7:00–17:00, Sat–Sun 7:00–14:00, closed Tue, top of Vestergade).

Ærøskøbing's two bars are at the top and bottom of Vestergade: **Arrebo Pub** (near the ferry landing, young crowd) and **Landbogaarden** (top of Vestergade, older crowd).

Supermarket: Try Netto for picnic fixings plus wine and beer (Mon–Fri 9:00–19:00, Sat 8:00–19:00, closed Sun, across street from ferry dock).

TRANSPORTATION CONNECTIONS

Ærøskøbing is accessible by ferry from **Svendborg.** It's a relaxing 75-minute crossing (295 kr round-trip per car and driver, 135 kr round-trip per person, you can leave the island via any of the three different Ærø ferry crossings, you'll save a little money with round-trip tickets).

Svendborg–Ærø ferry: Departures from Svendborg occur Monday through Saturday at 7:30, 10:30, 13:30, 16:30, 19:30, and 22:30—but no 7:30 departure on Saturday. Departures from Ærøskøbing are daily at 6:00, 8:55, 11:55, 14:55, 17:55, 20:55—no 6:00 departure on weekend mornings. While walk-ons always get on, cars need reservations (tel. 62 52 40 00 or reserve online at www .aeroe-ferry.dk, info@aeroe-ferry.dk). A ferry/bus combo-ticket gives you the whole island with stopovers (178 kr round-trip, must return within 24 hrs, bus runs throughout island, same contact info as above). If you won't use your car in Ærø, park it in Svendborg (big, safe lot 2 blocks in from ferry landing). On Ærø, parking is free.

Trains connecting with Svendborg–Ærø ferry: Train arrivals and departures are coordinated with the ferry schedule. If you're arriving by train in Svendborg (to continue by ferry to Ærø), a ferry will leave five minutes after your train arrives. From Svendborg's train station it's a short walk to the ferry dock. Head downhill to the harbor and look right for the Ærø sign. When you depart Ærø by ferry and dock at Svendborg, a train will leave for Copenhagen (via Odense) within 15 minutes of your arrival. The Copenhagen–Svendborg trip takes about 2.5 hours (with a 30-min wait for a connection in Odense).

Odense

Founded in A.D. 988 and named after Odin (the Nordic Zeus), Odense is the birthplace of storyteller Hans Christian Andersen. He once said, "Perhaps Odense will one day become famous because of me." Today Odense (OH-then-za) is one of Denmark's most visited towns. As Denmark's third-largest city, with 183,000 people, it is big and industrial. But its old center retains some of the fairy-tale charm it had in the days of H. C. A.

Tourist Information: The TI is in the Town Hall (Rådhuset) right downtown (Mon–Fri 9:30–18:00, Sat–Sun 10:00–15:00, off-season Mon–Fri 9:30–16:30, Sat 10:00–13:00, closed Sun, tel. 66 12 75 20, fax 66 12 75 86). From the train station, cross through the Kongens Have (King's Garden) park and head south (away from train station) down Jernabanegade. When you come to Vestergade, take a left and follow this fine pedestrian street 100 yards to the TI (about a 10-minute walk total). The TI can help you book a room for a 35-kr booking fee. For a quick visit to Odense, all you need is the free map/guide from the Hans Christian Andersen Hus (Note: The Danes call him "Hoe See" for "H. C." Andersen).

SIGHTS

▲▲**Hans Christian Andersen Hus**—This museum is packed with mementos from the writer's life and hordes of children and tourists. To commemorate the 200-year anniversary of the author's birth (on April 2, 1805), the museum completed renovations of the home where Andersen was born. Exhibits in the modern section of the museum include a display on the era in which Andersen lived (1805–1875), a library of Andersen's books from around the world (his tales were translated into nearly 150 languages), and headsets and benches throughout for you to listen to a selection of fairy tales. It's fun if you like the man and his tales (50-kr entry, 20 kr for kids, daily mid-June–Aug 9:00–19:00, off-season Tue–Sun 10:00–16:00, closed Mon, Bangs Boder 29, tel. 66 14 88 14, ext. 4601). Since the museum includes good descriptions in English, the guidebook is unnecessary (but pick up the free map/city guide next to entrance turnstiles).

The garden fairy-tale parade—with pleasing vignettes—thrills kids daily in July in the museum garden at 11:00, 13:00, and 15:00 (in English Wed and Thu at 15:00). The museum gift shop is full of mobiles, papercut models, and English versions of Andersen's fairy tales. An attached café offers seating indoors and out with sandwiches, soups, and salads (50–100 kr).

▲**Møntergården Urban History Museum**—The humble little museum, very close to the Hans Christian Andersen Hus, offers Odense history and early town photos (free, Tue–Sun 10:00–16:00, closed Mon, Overgade 48, tel. 65 51 46 01).

▲**Funen Art Museum**—This small pleasant museum collects Danish art from 1750 to the present, paying particular attention to artists of the island of Funen, or *Fyn* in Danish (40 kr, Tue–Sun 10:00–16:00, closed Mon, Jernbanegade 13, tel. 66 14 88 14).

▲**Den Fynske Landsby Open-Air Museum**—The sleepy gathering of 26 old buildings preserves the 18th-century culture of this region. There are no explanations in the buildings, because the many school groups who visit play guessing games. Pick up the 15-kr guidebook (60-kr admission, Mon–Sat mid-June–mid-Aug 9:30–19:00, April– mid-June and mid-Aug–mid-Oct 10:00–17:00, Sun 11:00–15:00, closed Mon and mid-Oct–March, tel. 65 51 46 01). From mid-July to early August, there are H. C. Andersen musicals (in Danish) in the theater daily at 16:00. The 70-kr ticket for the musical includes admission 90 minutes early (not before 14:30) to see the museum.

SLEEPING

(6 kr = about $1, country code: 45)
$$$ Radisson H. C. A. Hotel is big, comfortable, impersonal, and a block from the Hans Christian Andersen museum (Sb-1,225 kr, Db-1,425 kr, special summer deal mid-June–Aug: Sb or Db-850 kr with breakfast, Claus Bergs Gade 7, tel. 66 14 78 00, fax 66 14 78 90, radissonsas@odense.dk).

$$ Hotel Domir, located on a quiet side street just a few minutes from the train station, offers 35 tidy, simple, little rooms amidst its tiny halls. Many of the rooms are clustered around a courtyard (Sb-495 kr, Db-545–645 kr, Tb-745 kr, higher prices for slightly larger rooms, includes breakfast, extra charge if you pay by credit card, Hans Tausensgade 19, tel. 66 12 14 27, fax 66 12 14 13, www .domir.dk).

$$ Ydes Hotel, down the street and run by the same reception as Hotel Domir, offers 25 slightly larger rooms with similar comforts (Sb-390 kr, Db-495–595 kr, Tb-700 kr, includes breakfast, extra charge if you pay with credit card, Hans Tausensgade 11, tel. 66 12 11 31, www.ydes.dk).

$ Jytte (U-ter) Gamdrup rents two well-appointed rooms in her 17th-century home a few doors down from the Hans Christian Andersen Hus. This is probably your best Odense home, located on a fairy-tale street (D-350 kr, breakfast-35 kr, Ramsherred 17, 5000 Odense C, tel. & fax 66 13 89 36, mobile 21 45 49 72, www .jyttes-bb.dk).

EATING

If you are in town for a just short stopover to visit the H. C. Andersen Hus, consider the café at the museum for lunch (see details under "Sights" above). Otherwise, Odense's main pedestrian shopping streets, Vestergade and Kongensgade, offer the best atmosphere and most options for lunch and dinner.

Vintapperstræde is an alleyway full of restaurants just off Vestergade, one street before Kongensgade if you're walking from the TI. Choose from Danish, Mexican, Italian, and more. Study the menus posted outside each restaurant to decide, then grab a table inside or join the locals at an outdoor table.

Eydes Pub and Restaurant is a woodsy old pub serving mostly grilled meat, chicken, potatoes, and other kinds of pub grub. They also offer a global beer menu—but you're better off sticking with the local Albani brand brew. Pick a table, note the number and place your order at the bar. Servings are huge, but thankfully they offer small-portion alternatives at dinner (lunches and small portions for 60–100 kr, large portions for 85–180 kr, daily 12:00–22:00, bar open much later, Kongensgade 31A, tel. 66 19 19 50).

TRANSPORTATION CONNECTIONS

From Odense by train to: Copenhagen (3/hr, 90 min), **Århus** (2/hr, 90 min), **Svendborg** (hrly, 1 hr, to Ærø ferry), **Roskilde** (2/hr, 75 min).

Route Tips for Drivers
Århus or Billund to Ærø: Figure about two hours to drive from Billund (or 2.5 hours from Århus) to Svendborg. The freeway takes you over a suspension bridge to the island of Fyn; from Odense, take the highway south to Svendborg.

Leave your car in Svendborg (at the convenient long-term parking lot 2 blocks from the ferry dock) and sail for Ærø. It's an easy 75-minute crossing; note there are only five or six boats a day (see "Transportation Connections" for Ærøskøbing, page 98). Cars need reservations but not walk-on passengers. A ferry/bus combo-ticket gives you the whole island with stopovers.

Ærø to Copenhagen via Odense: From Svendborg, drive north following signs to Fåborg, past Egeskov Castle, and on to Odense. For the open-air folk museum (Den Fynske Landsby), leave Route 9 just south of town at Højby, turning left toward Dalum and the Odense campground (on Odensevej). Look for Den Fynske Landsby signs (near the train tracks, south edge of town). If you're going directly to Hans Christian Andersen Hus, follow the signs.

Continuing toward Copenhagen, you'll take the world's second-longest suspension bridge (250-kr toll, 12.5 miles long, opened to traffic in 1998, free exhibition center on bridge in Halsskov, daily 10:00–20:00, until 17:00 off-season, take exit 43 off E-20). Follow signs marked København (Copenhagen). At Ringsted, signs take you to Roskilde. Aim toward the twin church spires and follow signs for Vikingskibene (Viking ships).

Copenhagen is 30 minutes from Roskilde. If you're heading to the airport, stay on the freeway to the end, following signs to København C, then to Dragør/Kastrup Airport.

JUTLAND
Legoland and Århus

Jutland, the part of Denmark that juts up from Germany, is a land of sand dunes, Lego toys, moated manor houses, and fortified old towns. Make a pilgrimage to the most famous land in all of Jutland: the pint-sized kids' paradise, Legoland. In Århus, the lively capital of Jutland, wander the pedestrian street of this busy port, tour its boggy prehistory, and visit centuries-old Danish town life in its open-air folk museum.

Planning Your Time

Jutland, or Jylland in Danish, is worth a day (more if you have kids) on a three-week trip through Scandinavia. If you arrive in Århus by early afternoon (after catching the 9:00 boat from Kristiansand, Norway, and driving two hours), spend the rest of the afternoon at Den Gamle By (the Old Town open-air museum) and the next morning in downtown Århus. Stop by the ARoS art museum and have lunch at a canalside café before moving on. If you have kids, visit Legoland on the way to or from Århus. Speedy travelers can make Århus an afternoon stop and drive to Legoland that evening (which is free if you enter late).

Legoland

Legoland is Scandinavia's top kids' sight. If you have a child (or think you might be one), it's a fun stop. This huge park is a happy combination of rides, restaurants, trees, smiles, and 33 million Lego bricks creatively arranged into such wonders as Mount Rushmore, the Parthenon, "Mad" King Ludwig's castle, and the Statue of Liberty. It's a Lego world here, as everything is cleverly related to this popular toy. Surprisingly, the restaurants don't serve Legolamb.

Jutland

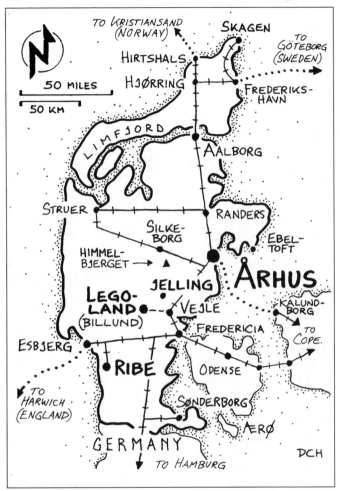

The indoor museum features the company history, high-tech Lego creations, a great doll collection, and a toy museum full of mechanical wonders from the early 1900s, many ready to jump into action with the push of a button. There's a Lego playroom for hands-on fun—and a campground across the street if your kids refuse to move on.

Cost and Hours: 180 kr entry, 160 kr for kids ages 3–13, 160 kr for kids over 60 (gets you on all the rides), April–Oct daily 10:00–20:00, until 21:00 in summer, one hour less on weekdays in Sept, closed Nov–March (tel. 75 33 13 33, see "Legoland Billund" at www.lego.com/legoland). Legoland doesn't charge in the evening (free after 19:30 in July and late Aug, otherwise after 17:30). Activities close an hour before the park, but it's basically the same place after dinner as during the day—with fewer tour groups.

SIGHTS

Near Legoland

Jelling—If you've always wanted to see the hometown of the ancient Danish kings Gorm the Old and Harald Bluetooth, this is your chance. The village of Jelling (12 miles from Legoland, just off highway near Vejle) has a church with Denmark's oldest frescoes and two ancient runic stones in its courtyard—often called "Denmark's birth certificate."

▲Ribe—A Viking port 1,000 years ago, Ribe is the oldest, and possibly loveliest, town in Denmark. It's an entertaining mix of cobbled lanes and leaning medieval houses, with a fine church (12 kr, modern paintings under Romanesque arches). The **TI** can find beds in B&Bs for a 35-kr booking fee (Torvet 3, tel. 75 42 15 00). Take the free Night Watchman tour (daily May–mid-Sept at 22:00, extra tour at 20:00 June–Aug). The **Weis' Stue,** a smoky, low-ceilinged, atmospheric inn, rents primitive rooms and serves good meals (S-395 kr, D-595 kr, includes breakfast, across from the church, tel. 75 42 07 00).

SLEEPING

Legoland or Nearby, in Billund

$$$ **Legoland Hotel** adjoins Legoland (Sb-1,265 kr, Db-1,755 kr, special family deals: 2,455 kr for room big enough for 2 adults and 2 kids, room prices include 2-day admission to park, prices slightly lower Sept–May or for 2 or more nights, tel. 75 33 12 44, fax 75 35 38 10, www.lego.com/hotel).

Sleep Code

(6 kr = about $1, country code: 45)
S = Single, **D** = Double/Twin, **T** = Triple, **Q** = Quad, **b** = bathroom, **s** = shower. You can assume credit cards are accepted unless otherwise noted.

To help you sort easily through these listings, I've divided the rooms into three categories based on the price for a standard double room with bath during high season:

$$$ **Higher Priced**—Most rooms 1,000 kr or more.
$$ **Moderately Priced**—Most rooms between 450–1,000 kr.
$ **Lower Priced**—Most rooms 450 kr or less.

$$ Hotel Svanen is close by in Billund (Sb-850–950 kr, Db-950–1,050 kr, extra bed-175 kr, Nordmarksvej 8, tel. 75 33 28 33, fax 75 35 35 15, www.hotelsvanen.dk, info@hotelsvanen.dk).

$$ Legoland Village is a family youth hostel offering inexpensive rooms that sleep one to five people (Ds-500–930 kr, sheets and towels-40 kr, includes breakfast, Ellehammers Alle 2, tel. 75 33 27 77, fax 75 33 28 77, www.legolandvillage.dk, info@legolandvillage.dk).

$ Private rooms are the key to a budget visit here. **Erik and Mary Sort** have four doubles and a great setup in a forest just outside of town. Their guests enjoy a huge living room, a kitchen, lots of Lego toys, and a kid-friendly yard (170 kr per person, breakfast-35 kr, cash only, leave Billund on Grindsted Road, turn right on Stilbjergvej, go a half mile to Stilbjergvej 4, tel. 75 33 23 27).

TRANSPORTATION CONNECTIONS

Legoland is easiest to visit by car, but doable by public transportation (at Vejle, the nearest train station to Billund, transfer to the #28 bus to travel the remaining 25 miles to Billund). For details on transportation, see www.lego.com/legoland.

To Billund from: Copenhagen (hrly trains, 2.25 hr to Vejle, then take bus #28 to Billund, allow 3.5 hrs total), **Odense** (2/hr, 50 min to Vejle, transfer to bus #28, figure on 2 hrs total), **Århus** (2/hr, 45 min to Vejle, switch to bus #28, allow 2 hrs total).

Århus

Århus (OAR-hoos), Denmark's second-largest city, has a population of 300,000 and calls itself the "World's Smallest Big City." Århus is Jutland's capital and cultural hub. Its Viking founders, ever conscious of aesthetics, chose a lovely wooded setting where the river hits the sea. Today, Århus bustles with a lively port, an important university, and an adorable "Latin Quarter" filled with people living very, very well. The town has a great pedestrian street that lasts at least two ice cream cones from the cathedral to the train station (Søndergade/Clements Torv). Århus is well worth a stop.

Tourist Information: The TI is 200 yards from the station at the town hall (May–mid-June Mon–Fri 9:30–17:00, Sat 10:00–13:00, closed Sun; mid-June–early-Sept Mon–Fri 9:30–18:00, Sat 9:30–17:00, Sun 10:00–13:00; early Sept–April Mon–Fri 9:30–14:30, Sat 10:00–13:00, closed Sun; tel. 89 40 67 00, fax 86 12 95 90). Consider the **Århus Passet,** which covers all sights, a 2.5-hour introductory bus tour, and public transportation (100 kr/day, 125 kr/2 days).

Århus

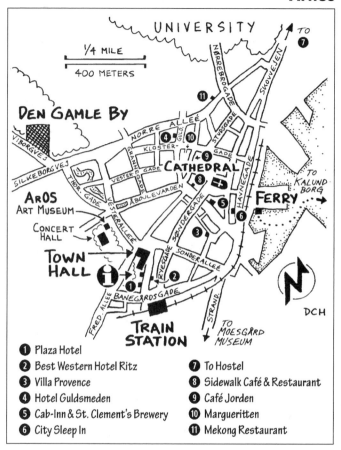

1 Plaza Hotel
2 Best Western Hotel Ritz
3 Villa Provence
4 Hotel Guldsmeden
5 Cab-Inn & St. Clement's Brewery
6 City Sleep In
7 To Hostel
8 Sidewalk Café & Restaurant
9 Café Jorden
10 Margueritten
11 Mekong Restaurant

Getting Around Århus: City buses (19-kr tickets) easily connect the downtown and train station with the Den Gamle By open-air folk museum and the Forhistorisk Museum Moesgård prehistory museum.

TOURS

▲▲**City Bus Tour**—The TI's great 2.5-hour bus tour winds all over the city. You'll tour the cathedral, have 40 minutes to blitz Den Gamle By, drive through the university (30,000 students, Denmark's first outside Copenhagen), and see Denmark's biggest container port (60 kr, tours daily mid-June–early Sept at 10:00, departs from TI, includes 24 hrs unlimited bus travel in city).

SIGHTS

▲▲▲**ARoS**—The new Århus Art Museum, which opened in April 2004, is a must-see sight, if only for the building's architecture. Square and unassuming from the outside, the bright white interior—with its spiral staircase winding up the museum's three floors—is surprising. The building has two sections, one for the exhibits and one for administration. The halves are divided by a passageway, which has free entry if you just want to peek at the building itself. You'll also see the squatting sculpture of *Boy* (by Australian artist Ron Mueck), realistic yet 15 feet high.

The permanent collection features paintings from the Danish Golden Age (1800–1850) to modern art, including many multimedia installations and works by Danish artist Per Kirkeby. Be sure to visit the basement, where (amid the black walls) artists from around the world exhibit their works of light and sound in each of the nine rooms *(De 9 Rum)*.

Pick up a museum floor plan at the ticket counter. Don't miss the rooftop terrace and its super view of the city (60 kr, Tue–Sun 10:00–17:00, until 22:00 on Wed, closed Mon, lunch café on ground floor, exclusive restaurant on top floor, ARoS Allé 2, tel. 87 30 66 00, www.aros.dk).

▲**Århus Cathedral**—Denmark's biggest church, more than 330 feet long and tall, began as Romanesque in 1201 and finished as Flamboyant Gothic in the 15th century (free, Mon–Sat 9:30–16:00, off-season 10:00–15:00). The altarpiece, dating from 1479, features the 12 Apostles surrounding John the Baptist and St. Clement, the patron saint of Århus and sailors (his symbol is the anchor). On top, Jesus is crowning Mary in heaven. This is a polyptych (a many-paneled altarpiece). The model in the apse behind demonstrates how it flips to different scenes through the church year. The fresco on the aisle (right of altar) shows a three-part universe: heaven, earth (at Mass), and—under the thick black line—hell (with the tortuous bagpipe band). The kid on the gallows illustrated medieval disciplinary sermons for children. Notice the angels trying desperately to save the damned. Just a little more money to the Church... and...I...think we can...pull...grandpa...OUT.

▲**Latin Quarter**—The small, trendy, pedestrian-friendly streets just beyond the cathedral will make you fall in love with Århus.

▲▲▲**Den Gamle By**—The Old Town open-air folk museum puts Århus on the touristic map. Seventy half-timbered houses and crafts shops come with old furnishings. Highlights include Torvet (the main square), the Mayor's House (from 1597), and the toy museum (Legetoj). Unlike other Scandinavian open-air museums that focus on rural folk life, Den Gamle By re-creates old Danish town life (75 kr, daily June–Aug 9:00–18:00, April–May and Sept–Oct

10:00–17:00, shorter hours off-season, the 10-kr mini-guide adds little to the brief English building descriptions and maps throughout the park; from train station catch bus #3, #14, #55, or #25, or walk 15 min to Viborgvej 2; tel. 86 12 31 88). For lunch, consider eating at the cheery indoor/outdoor Simonsens Have tea garden. After hours, the buildings of the open-air museum are locked but the peaceful park is open. A fine botanical garden is next door.

▲**Forhistorisk Museum Moesgård**—This prehistory museum at Moesgård, just south of Århus, is famous for its incredibly well-preserved Grauballe Man. This 2,000-year-old "bog man" looks like a fellow half his age. You'll see his skin, nails, hair, and even the slit in his throat he got at the sacrificial banquet. The museum has fine Stone Age exhibits (45 kr, April–Sept daily 10:00–17:00, Oct–March Tue–Sun 10:00–16:00, closed Mon, museum cafeteria sells picnics to go; take bus #6, 20 min, 2/hr, from Århus train station to last stop, Moesgård Allé 20; tel. 89 42 11 00).

Behind the museum, an **open-air museum** with a few model Viking buildings, including a 12th-century stave church (included in Forhistorisk Museum admission, same hours, good 15-kr guide booklet), stretches two miles down to a fine beach from which, in the summer, bus #19 takes you back downtown.

Other Attractions—There's lots more to see in Århus, such as the small Viking museum (free, Mon–Wed and Fri 10:00–16:00, Thu until 17:30, closed Sat–Sun, in a bank basement across from cathedral) and the "Tivoli" amusement park offering great fun for the family (55 kr, daily 12:00–22:00, less off-season; bus #1, #4, #6, #8, or #18 to edge of town; tel. 86 14 73 00).

SLEEPING

(6 kr = about $1, country code: 45)

All accommodations come with a breakfast buffet and are centrally located near the train station and TI. The TI can set you up in a 300-kr double (with shared bath) in a private home for a 30-kr fee. They also have summer deals on ritzy hotels (Db-about 750 kr).

$$$ **Plaza Hotel** rents 162 well-furnished, business-class rooms 100 yards from the station. The lower range of prices listed apply to summer, from late June through early August (Sb-670–875/995–1,405 kr, Db-875–980/1,510–1,615 kr, bedroom suite-2,160 kr, extra bed-200 kr, kids under 14 free, includes breakfast, sauna/gym/hot tub, smoke-free rooms, Banegardspladsen 14, tel. 87 32 01 00, fax 87 32 01 99, www.scandic-hotels.com,plaza.aarhus@scandic-hotels.com).

$$$ **Best Western Hotel Ritz,** across the street from the Plaza Hotel, has similar-quality rooms but less enthusiasm for its clients

(Sb-895–1,050 kr, Db-1,095–1,455 kr; Db on Fri, Sat, Sun, or July–Aug-795 kr; extra bed-300 kr, extra bed for child under 14-150 kr, tel. 86 13 44 44, fax 86 13 45 87, www.hotelritz.dk, hotel.ritz@image.dk).

$$$ **Villa Provence,** named for the owners' favorite vacation destination, is a *petit* taste of France in the center of Århus. Its 39 rooms, impeccably and uniquely decorated, surround a quiet courtyard. Prices vary depending on the size and elegance of the room, and the most expensive have large bathtubs and a sitting area (Sb-895–1,470 kr, Db-995–1,590 kr, includes breakfast, suites available, 10-min walk from station, near Åboulevarden at Fredens Torv 12, tel. 86 18 24 00, fax 86 18 24 03, www.villaprovence.dk, hotel@villaprovence.dk).

$$ **Hotel Guldsmeden** is a small, welcoming, and sparkling-clean hotel with 20 rooms, fluffy comforters, and a young, disarmingly friendly staff. A steep staircase takes you to the best rooms, while the cheaper rooms (without private facilities) are in a ground-floor annex behind the stay-awhile garden (S-495 kr, Sb-795 kr, D-745 kr, Db-995 kr, extra bed-200 kr, 10 percent off with this book in 2005, suites available, penthouse apartment available for longer stays, includes breakfast, 15-min walk or 70-kr taxi from the station, in Århus' quiet Latin Quarter at Guldsmedgade 40, tel. 86 13 45 50, fax 86 13 76 76, www.hotelguldsmeden.dk, hotel_guldsmeden@mail.tele.dk).

$$ **Cab-Inn,** overlooking the atmospheric Åboulevarden canal, has small but comfortable rooms with a single bed that expands into a twin and one or two fold-down bunks on the walls. The service, like the rooms, is no-nonsense (Sb-435 kr, Db-630 kr, Tb-750 kr, Qb-870 kr, breakfast-50 kr, easy parking-60 kr, rooms overlook canal or quieter courtyard, Kannikegade 14, tel. 86 75 70 00, fax 86 75 71 00, cabinn@cabinn.dk).

$ The creative **City Sleep In,** open 24 hours a day year-round, has a kitchen, fun living and games room, laundry service, lockers, and bikes for rent. It's on a busy road facing the harbor a 10-minute hike from the station (dorm beds-110 kr, D-340 kr, Db-380 kr, sheets-45 kr, breakfast-45 kr, Havnegade 20, tel. 86 19 20 55, fax 86 19 18 11, www.citysleep-in.dk, sleep-in@citysleep-in.dk).

$ The **hostel,** with 108-kr beds and plenty of two- and four-bed rooms, is near the water two miles out of town (sheets-45 kr, breakfast-46 kr, bus #1 to the end, follow signs, Marienlundsvej 10, tel. 86 16 72 98, fax 86 10 55 60, www.hostel-aarhus.dk, info @aarhus-danhostel.dk).

EATING

The **Åboulevarden** canal (2 blocks south of cathedral in old center) is lined with trendy eateries, such as the **Sidewalk Café and Restaurant,** a fine place for a canalside drink or meal. Big salads, pasta dishes, burgers, and tipsy, toppling sandwiches run 60–100 kr (daily 9:00–24:00, later Fri–Sat, indoor seating available, Åboulevarden 56, tel. 86 18 18 66).

The Latin Quarter, north of the cathedral, is a *hyggelig* neighborhood of small lanes and charming little cafés. A good bet here for lunch or a light dinner is cozy **Café Jorden** (daily 10:00–24:00, Badstuegade 3, tel. 86 19 72 22). They serve a fun and fruity "brunch" (80 kr, daily 10:00–15:00, carnivorous or vegetarian) indoors or on the quiet but people-filled square.

St. Clement's Brewery is the only pub in town that has a built-in brewery. Choose from a hearty menu and eat amid shiny copper vats. Lunch and light meals are 60–100 kr; hearty dinners are 120–200 kr (Mon–Sat 11:30–24:00, closed Sun, Bryggeriet Sct. Clemens, Kannikegade 10-12, tel. 86 13 80 00).

Margueritten, tucked into a small alley between Badestuegade and Guldsmedgade, has both a casual, candlelit indoor setting and a cozy courtyard. Choose from a variety of meat and fish dishes, stylishly presented and served with lots of vegetables and delectable sauces (lunches 70–80 kr, dinners 160–240 kr, Mon–Sat 11:30–21:30, Fri–Sat until 22:30, Sun 17:00–21:30, Guldsmedgade 20, tel. 86 19 60 33).

For cheap and good Vietnamese or Thai food, try the homey little **Mekong Restaurant** (Tue–Sat 17:00–22:30, Sun 17:00–21:30, closed Mon, Nørregade 10, tel. 86 18 49 55).

TRANSPORTATION CONNECTIONS

From Århus by train to: Hirtshals (1/hr, 2.5 hrs), **Odense** (1–2/hr, 2 hrs), **Copenhagen** (1–2/hr, 3 hrs), **Hamburg** (5/day, 5.5 hrs).

Ferries: Ferries sail between Hirtshals, Denmark, and Kristiansand, Norway (for details, see South Norway's Setesdal Valley chapter).

Route Tips for Drivers
From the ferry dock at Hirtshals to Århus to Billund: From the dock in Hirtshals, drive south (signs to Hjørring, Ålborg). It's about 2.5 hours to Århus. (To skip Århus, skirt the center and follow E-45 south.) To get to downtown Århus, follow signs to the center, then Domkirke. Park in the pay lot across from the cathedral. Signs all over town direct you to Den Gamle By open-air folk museum. From Århus, it's 60 miles to Billund/Legoland (go south on Skanderborg Road; follow signs to Vejle, Kolding). For Legoland, take the Vejle S (after Vejle N) exit for Billund.

NORWAY
(Norge)

Norway is stacked with superlatives—it's the most mountainous, most scenic, most prosperous, and least populated of all the Scandinavian countries. Ice ages have carved out and shaped the steep mountains and deep fjords the country is famous for.

Norway is a land of rich harvests—timber, oil, and fish. In fact, its wealth of resources is a major reason why Norwegians have voted *"nei"* to membership in the European Union. They don't want to be forced to share fishing rights with EU countries.

The country's relatively recent independence (in 1905, from Sweden) makes Norwegians notably patriotic and proud of their traditions and history.

Norway's Viking past (8th–11th centuries) can still be seen today in the 29 remaining stave churches throughout the country and Viking artifacts found in Oslo's Viking Ship Museum.

Beginning in the 14th century, Norway was under Danish rule for more than 400 years, before the Danes took the wrong side in the Napoleonic Wars. The Treaty of Kiel forced Denmark to cede Norway to Sweden in 1814. Sweden's rule of Norway lasted until 1905, when Norway voted to dissolve the union.

Like many European countries, Norway temporarily lost its independence during World War II. April 1940 marked the start of five years of Nazi occupation, during which a strong resistance movement developed and hindered some of the Nazi war efforts.

Each year on May 17, Norwegians celebrate their new constitution with fervor and plenty of flag-waving. Men and women wear folk costumes *(bunads),* each specific to a region of Norway. Parades are held throughout the country. The parade in Oslo marches past the Royal Palace, where the royal family waves to the populace from their balcony. While Norway is ruled by a parliament and prime minister, the royal family is still highly revered

How Big, How Many, How Much

- Norway is 148,900 square miles (slightly larger than New Mexico).
- Population is 4.5 million (about 30 per square mile).
- 6.5 kroner = about $1

Norway

and respected, but plays only a ceremonial role in government.

Four holidays in May disrupt transportation schedules: Ascension Day (May 5 in 2005) and Whitsunday (May 15), followed by Whitmonday (May 16) and Constitution Day (May 17, mentioned above).

High taxes contribute to Norway's high standard of living. Norwegians receive cradle-to-grave social care: university education, health care, nearly year-long maternity leave, and an annual six weeks of vacation. Norwegians feel there is no better place than home and have voted Norway the most livable country in the world (UN Human Development Index, 2002).

Despite being looked down upon as less sophisticated by their Scandinavian neighbors, Norwegians are proud of their rich folk traditions—from handmade sweaters and folk costumes to the small farms that produce sweet goat cheese, called *geitost*. Less than 7 percent of the country's land is arable, resulting in numerous small farms. The government recognizes the value of farming, especially in the remote reaches of the country, and provides rich subsidies to keep this tradition alive. These subsidies would not be allowed if Norway joined the European Union—yet another reason the country is an EU holdout.

While the majority of the population under 70 years of age speaks English, a few words in Norwegian will serve you well. If you visit a Norwegian home, be sure to leave your shoes at the door; indoors is usually meant for stocking feet only. At the end of a meal, it's polite to say "Thanks for the food"—"*Takk for maten*" (tahk for MAH-ten). Norwegians rarely feel their guests have eaten enough food, so be prepared to say *"Nei, takk"* (nigh tahk; "No, thanks"). You can always try *"Jeg er met"* (yigh ahr met; "I am full"), but be careful not to say *"Jeg er full"*—"I am drunk."

OSLO

While Oslo is the smallest and least earthshaking of the Nordic capitals, this brisk little city offers more sightseeing thrills than you might expect. Sights of the Viking spirit—past and present—tell an exciting story. Prowl through the remains of ancient Viking ships and marvel at more peaceful but equally gutsy modern boats (the *Kon-Tiki, Ra,* and *Fram*). Dive into the traditional folk culture at the Norwegian open-air folk museum and get stirred up by the country's heroic spirit at the Norwegian Resistance Museum.

For a look at modern Oslo, browse through the yuppie-style harbor shopping complex, tour the striking City Hall, take a peek at sculptor Gustav Vigeland's people pillars, and climb the towering Holmenkollen ski jump.

Situated at the head of a 60-mile-long fjord, surrounded by forests, and populated by more than 500,000 people, Oslo is Norway's cultural hub and an all-you-can-see *smörgåsbord* of historic sights, trees, art, and Nordic fun.

Planning Your Time

Oslo offers an exciting two-day slate of sightseeing thrills. Ideally, spend two days and leave on the night boat to Copenhagen, or on the scenic train to Bergen the third morning. Spend the two days like this:

Day 1: Take my self-guided walk and say "hello" to Oslo (see page 119). Tour the Akershus Fortress (see Christiania City Model film if it's showing) and the Norwegian Resistance Museum. Catch the City Hall tour. Spend the afternoon at Vigeland Park and at the Holmenkollen ski jump and museum. For dinner, consider hiking to the classy Frognerseteren Hovedrestaurant near the ski jump, or taking a picnic or fast-food meal on the harbor mini-cruise.

Day 2: Ferry across the harbor to Bygdøy and tour the *Fram, Kon-Tiki,* and Viking Ship museums. Spend the afternoon at the Norwegian Folk Museum. Back downtown, browse the National Gallery and stroll the harborfront Akerbrygge mall/restaurant complex.

ORIENTATION

Oslo is easy to manage. Its sights cluster around the main boulevard, Karl Johans Gate (with the Royal Palace at one end and the train station at the other), and in the Bygdøy district, a 10-minute ferry ride across the harbor.

Tourist Information

Oslo has two TIs: across from the City Hall and in the train station.

The **Oslo Information Center** faces the City Hall at Fridtjof Nansens Plass 5 (June–Aug Mon–Sat 9:00–17:00, closed Sun; April–May and Sept Mon–Sat 9:00–17:00, closed Sun; Oct–March Mon–Fri 10:00–16:00, closed Sat–Sun; tel. 24 14 77 00, www.visitoslo .com, info@visitoslo.com). The TI at the **train station,** though simpler, has much longer hours and handles your needs just as well (daily in summer 8:00–23:00, shorter hours off-season). A late-night visit avoids the lines.

At either TI, pick up the Oslo map, the annual *Oslo Guide* (with plenty of details on sightseeing, shopping, and eating), the *What's On in Oslo* monthly (for the most accurate listing of museum hours and special events), *Streetwise* magazine (hip, fun to read, and full of offbeat ideas—see below), and (if you're traveling on) the *Bergen Guide* and information for the rest of Norway. It's all free. Consider buying the Oslo Pass (described below) unless you get the Oslo Package, which includes your hotel accommodation and an Oslo Pass (see "Sleeping," page 145).

Use It, a hardworking information center, is geared for youths and students but is happy to offer anyone of any age its solid, money-saving, experience-enhancing advice (July–Aug Mon–Fri 9:00–18:00, closed Sat–Sun; Sept–June Mon–Fri 11:00–17:00, Thu until 18:00, closed Sat–Sun; Møllergata 3, tel. 22 41 51 32, fax 22 42 63 71, www.unginfo.oslo.no). They can find you the cheapest beds in town (no booking fee), and offer free Internet access (30-min limit, may have to wait for a computer). Their free *Streetwise* magazine—packed with articles on Norwegian culture, ideas on eating and sleeping cheap, good nightspots, the best beaches, and so on—is a must for young travelers and worthwhile for anyone curious to probe the Oslo scene.

The **Oslo Pass** covers the city's public transit and boats, entry to all sights, and parking, plus lots of discounts—described in a useful handbook (195 kr/24 hrs, 285 kr/48 hrs, 375 kr/72 hrs; family of four-395 kr/24 hrs, or kids ages 4–15 save almost 40 percent on individual passes). Do the arithmetic carefully before buying; add up the individual costs of the sights you want to see to find out if an Oslo Pass will save you money (sample charges: 24-hr transit pass-55 kr, ski jump-60 kr, City Hall-40 kr, 3 boat museums at Bygdøy-110 kr, National Gallery-free). Students with an ISIC card may be better off without the Oslo Pass. The TI's special Oslo Package hotel deal (see "Sleeping," page 145) includes this card with your discounted hotel room.

Arrival in Oslo

By Train: Oslo Sentralstasjon (or "Oslo S" for short)—the central train station—is slick and helpful. You'll find a late-hours TI (daily in summer 8:00–23:00, less off-season; the brochure rack has the free, important *Oslo Guide* booklet), a room-finding service, an Internet café, and a long-hours exchange desk. The station is plugged into a lively modern shopping mall called Byporten (Mon–Sat 10:00–21:00, Sun 10:00–18:00) and a Bit sandwich shop with seating for a cheap meal (see "Eating," page 151).

For tickets and train info, go to the station's ticket office (Mon–Fri 6:30–20:00, Sat 7:00–19:00, Sun 7:30–20:00) or to the helpful train office at the National Theater railway and T-bane station, which can have shorter lines (Mon–Fri 7:00–21:00, Sat–Sun 10:00–21:00, Ruseløkkveien, southwest of National Theater). At either office, you can buy domestic, international, and Norway in a Nutshell tickets (for the most scenic way to connect Oslo and Bergen by train, boat, and bus, see the Norway in a Nutshell chapter). Pick up leaflets on the Flåm and Bergen Railway.

By Plane: Oslo Airport (Lufthavn) is about 30 miles north of Oslo. Call tel. 81 55 02 50 for a great automated departure-confirming system for all flights (www.osl.no). For SAS, dial tel. 81 52 04 00.

The speedy **Flytoget** train zips travelers between the airport and the central train station (or farther, to the National Theater station) in 20–25 minutes (150 kr, 8/hr, runs 5:34–24:34 from airport, 4:45–24:05 from station, less on weekends, not covered by railpass, buy and validate ticket before boarding, keep it to exit, www.flytoget.no). **InterCity trains** cost half as much and take only a little longer, but do not run as frequently (75 kr, hrly, 30 min, covered by railpass). To reach the Flytoget and InterCity train counters at the airport, exit right after you leave customs and walk all the way to the corner; you'll see two separate ticket counters (one for Flytoget, NSB for the cheaper InterCity trains) and separate TV screens showing the timetables for Flytoget and the "lokal-intercity-fjerntog" trains.

Flybus airport buses make several downtown stops, including the central train station (100 kr one-way, 4/hr, 40 min).

A **taxi** (525 kr) to or from the airport—given the much faster shuttle train—wastes time and money.

Helpful Hints

Pickpocket Alert: They're a problem in Oslo, particularly in crowds on the street and in subways and buses. To call the police, dial 112.

U.S. Embassy: It's at Drammensveien 18 (tel. 22 44 85 50).

Pharmacy: Jernbanetorgets Apotek is open 24/7 (across from train station on Jernbanetorget, tel. 22 41 24 82).

Internet Access: **@rtic Internet Café** in the station's main hall above track 13 is good (daily 8:00–24:00, sells international phone cards). **Studenten Café,** on the corner of Karl Johans Gate and Universitets Gata, offers Internet access in the basement (Sun–Mon 12:00–22:00, Tue–Sat 12:00–20:00, tel. 22 42 56 80).

Post Office: The central P.O. is near the train station at Dronningens Gate 15 (tel. 23 14 78 20).

Currency Exchange: American Express is near the City Hall (Mon–Fri 9:00–17:00, Sat 10:00–15:00, closed Sun, Fridtjof Nansens Plass 6, tel. 22 98 37 35).

Laundry: Selva Laundromat is on the corner of Wesselsgate and Ullevålsveien at Ullevålsveien 15, a half mile north of the train station (daily 8:00–21:00, walk or catch bus #37 from station, tel. 41 64 08 33).

Getting Around Oslo

By Public Transit: Commit yourself to taking advantage of Oslo's excellent transit system. It's made up of buses, trams, ferries, and a subway (*Tunnelbane,* or T-bane for short). The wonderful and free *Visitor's Map Oslo* (available at TIs and major T-bane stations) makes sightseeing by public transit easy. The system runs like clockwork, with schedules clearly posted and followed. **Trafikanten,** the public-transit information center under the glass tower, faces the train station (Mon–Fri 7:00–20:00, Sat–Sun 8:00–18:00, info tel. 177 or 81 50 01 76, www.trafikanten.no).

Individual **tickets** work on buses, trams, ferries, and T-bane for one hour (20 kr if bought at a Narvesen kiosk, or 30 kr if bought on board). Other options include the **Flexicard** (150 kr for 8 rides, shareable), the 24-hour **Dagskort Tourist Ticket** (55 kr, pays for itself in 3 rides), and the **Oslo Pass** (free run of entire system—see page 117).

By Taxi: Taxis come with an expensive minimum fare of 80 kr. To get a taxi, wave one down, find a taxi stand, or have one called (tel. 02323).

By Bike: Oslo is a good biking town, especially if you'd like to get out into the woods or ride a tram uphill out of town and coast back. (You need to buy a half-price child's ticket for your bike.) Vestbanen Sykkelutleie rents bikes on the harbor at Akerbrygge Plass 1 (150 kr/3 hrs, 210 kr/6 hrs, 265 kr/24 hrs, daily 10:00–20:00, may close earlier off-season, tel. 22 83 52 08).

TOURS

Boat Tours—Several tour boats leave regularly from pier 3 in front of the City Hall. **Båtservice** has a relaxing and scenic 50-minute mini-cruise—with a boring three-language commentary—that departs on the hour and costs 105 kr (discount with Oslo Pass, daily July–late Aug 10:00–19:00, late Aug–June 10:00–16:00, tel. 23 35 68 90, www.boatsightseeing.com). They won't scream if you bring something to Munch. They also offer two-hour fjord tours (190 kr, 3–4/day late May–Sept) and a Summer Evening on the Fjord dinner cruise (315 kr, includes shrimp buffet, daily late June–Aug 19:00–22:00; all tours depart from pier 3 in front of City Hall).

The cheapest way to enjoy the scenic Oslofjord is to simply ride the ferries that regularly connect the nearby islands with downtown (free with Oslo Pass or transit pass).

Bus Tours—**Båtservice,** which runs the harbor cruises (above), offers bus tours of Oslo, with stops at the ski jump, Bygdøy museums, and Vigeland Sculpture Park on the longer tours (300 kr/3 hrs, 310 kr/4 hrs, 455 kr/7.5 hrs, each tour 1/day June–Aug, departs from ticket office on pier 3, tel. 23 35 68 90, www.boatsightseeing.com). **HMK** also does daily city bus tours (195 kr/2 hrs, 265 kr/3 hrs, departs from TI across from City Hall, tel. 23 15 73 00, www.hmk.no).

While there is a hop-on, hop-off bus service for Oslo, the city doesn't really work well with this kind of tour bus. Again, commit yourself to public transit to save lots of time.

Local Guide—To hire a private guide, call the guides' association at tel. 22 42 70 20.

Self-Guided Walk: Hello Oslo

This stroll, worth ▲▲, covers the heart of Oslo—the zone most tourists find themselves walking—from the train station, up the main drag, and past City Hall to the harborfront. It takes a brisk 15 minutes if done nonstop.

Train Station: Start at the main entrance of Oslo's central train station (Sentralstasjon)—still marked *Østbanehallen,* or "East Train Station," from when Oslo had two stations. The statue of the tiger commemorates the 1,000th birthday of the town nicknamed Tigerstad (Tiger Town). With your back to the entrance, look for the glass Trafikanten tower that marks the **public transit office;** from here, trams zip to City Hall (with main TI, harbor, and boat to

Immigration in Norway

Oslo has a big and growing immigrant community. These new "ethnic Norwegians" have provided a labor force for jobs that wealthy Norwegians would rather not do. And immigrants have literally added spice to the local cuisine. But, especially near the train station, you see some of the downside of a country that is disinclined to be a melting pot. There have been scuffles between gangs and immigrant groups. Locals complain that the Norwegian government gives refuge to various ethnic groups who are historic enemies, and then houses them side-by-side. Another source of friction among blonde locals is the tough love Norwegians get from their government compared to the easy ride needy immigrants get: "They even get pocket money in jail!" While Norway is a leader among rich nations in per-capita giving to the developing world, the issue of "ethnic Norwegians" is an awkward one for locals to discuss. While many aren't eager to have their country become the next melting pot, they're careful not to object too strenuously, wary of being labeled racist.

Bygdøy), and the underground T-bane goes to the Vigeland Sculpture Park and Holmenkollen ski jump.

The green building behind the Trafikanten tower is a shopping mall called **Byporten** (literally "City Gate"), built to greet those arriving from the airport on the shuttle train. Oslo's 37-floor **skyscraper**—the Radisson/SAS Hotel—looms behind that. Its 34th-floor pub welcomes the public with air-conditioned views and pricey drinks (daily 16:00–24:00). The tower was built with reflective glass, so it almost disappears from a distance. The area behind the Radisson—the lively and colorful "Little Pakistan," where most of Oslo's immigrant population settled—has become a vibrant nightspot offering a fun contrast to the predictable homogeneity of Norwegian cuisine and culture (see "Immigration in Norway," above).

Oslo allows hard-drug addicts and prostitutes to mix and mingle in a **little park** just south of the station. Troubled young people come here from small towns in the countryside for anonymity and community. The two cameras near the top of the Trafikanten tower monitor drug deals.

Norway's grand boulevard—**Karl Johans Gate**—leads directly from the train station to the Royal Palace. The street is named for the French prince Jean Baptiste Bernadotte, who was given a Swedish name, established the current Swedish dynasty, and ruled as a popular king (1818–1844) during the period after Sweden took Norway from Denmark.

Walk three blocks up Karl Johans Gate. This stretch is referred to as **"Desolation Row"** by locals—it has no soul. (Shoppers can

Self-Guided Walk: Hello Oslo

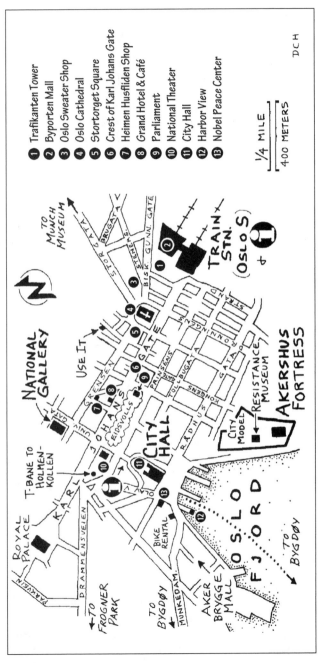

1 Trafikanten Tower
2 Byporten Mall
3 Oslo Sweater Shop
4 Oslo Cathedral
5 Stortorget Square
6 Crest of Karl Johans Gate
7 Heimen Husfliden Shop
8 Grand Hotel & Café
9 Parliament
10 National Theater
11 City Hall
12 Harbor View
13 Nobel Peace Center

¼ MILE
400 METERS

DCH

detour to the Oslo Sweater Shop, a block to the right down Skippergata—see "Shopping," page 144.) Hook around the curved old brick structure and to the cathedral.

Oslo Cathedral (Domkirke): This Lutheran church is where Norway celebrates and mourns its royal marriages and deaths. The most recent royal wedding was of Crown Prince Haakon Magnus and commoner Mette-Marit Tjessem Høiby—a single unwed mom—in August 2001. Her father is a pensioner, poor enough to be a cheap source of gossip for the tabloids. Locals enjoy all the latest...and he has new teeth and a free mobile phone paid for by Oslo's tabloid.

The cathedral's cornerstone (right of entrance), a thousand-year-old carving from Oslo's first and long-gone cathedral, shows how the forces of good and evil tug at each of us. Step inside beneath the red, blue, and gold seal of Oslo and under an equally colorful ceiling (free, daily 10:00–16:00, services in Norwegian on Sun at 11:00). The box above on the right is for the royal family.

Back outside, notice the tiny square windows midway up the copper cupola—once the lookout quarters of the fire watchman. Walk behind the church. The **courtyard** is lined by a circular row of stalls from an old market. The rusty meat hooks now decorate the lamps of a peaceful café. The atmospheric **Café Bacchus,** at the far left end of the arcade, serves outside and in a classy café downstairs (light 100-kr meals, salads, good cakes, coffee, daily 11:00–23:00, tel. 22 33 34 30).

Stortorget: The big square that faces the cathedral was once a cattle market. Now it's a flower market (Mon–Fri). The statue is of Christian IV, the Danish king who ruled Norway around 1600. In 1624, he moved higgledy-piggledy old Oslo from here to the shelter of the fortress, built a fortified new town in a fine Renaissance grid plan, and named it (immodestly) Christiania. Oslo took back its old name only in 1925. Christian was serious about Norway. During his 60-year reign, he visited it 30 times (more than all other royal visits over 300 years of Danish rule combined).

Return to Karl Johans Gate and continue up the boulevard past street musicians, cafés, shops, and hordes of people. Kongens Gate leads left past that first grid-plan town to the fortress. Hike to the crest of the hill and pause to enjoy some of the street musicians along the way. Jim Pizza—the one-man band from Hawaii—summers here.

The Crest of Karl Johans Gate: Look back at the train station. A thousand years ago, the original (pre-1624) Oslo was located near the wooded hill behind the station. Now look ahead to the Royal Palace in the distance—built in the 1830s "with nature and God behind it and the people at its feet." If the flag flies atop the palace, the king is home. Karl Johans Gate is a parade ground from here to the palace—the axis of modern Oslo. Each May 17th, Norway's Independence Day, this street turns into a sea of marching bands and costumed flag-wavers while the royal family watches from the palace balcony. King Harald V and Queen Sonja moved back into the palace in 2001, after extensive (and costly) renovations. To quell the controversy caused by this expense, the public is now allowed in each summer.

The "T" sign marks a stop of the *Tunnelbane* (or T-bane, Oslo's subway). Let W. B. Samson's bakery tempt you with its pastries. And next to that, David Andersen's jewelry store displays traditional silver art. Just inside on the right is a display of fine Bunad jewelry—worn on big family occasions and church holidays. (From here, the street called Akersgata kicks off a worthwhile stroll—a 30-min sidetrip, described in "Walk up the Akers River to Grünerløkka" on page 142—past the national cemetery and through a park-like river gorge to the trendy Grünerløkka quarter.)

Hike two blocks down Karl Johans Gate, past the big brick parliament building (left). On the right, a statue of the painter Christian Krohg marks a square nicknamed "the toilet lid"—since it covers the public WC. A block down Arbeidergata is a **Heimen Husfliden** shop for Norsk souvenirs (see "Shopping," page 144); just beyond it is the cheap, cheery Kaffistova cafeteria (see "Eating," page 151). Farther down Karl Johans Gate, just past the Freia shop (Norway's oldest and best chocolate), the venerable **Grand Hotel** (Oslo's celebrity hotel—Nobel Peace Prize winners sleep here) overlooks the boulevard. Ask the waiter at the Grand Café if you can pop inside for a little sightseeing (he'll generally say, "Ya, sure").

Grand Café: This historic café was long the meeting place of Oslo's intellectual and creative elite. Just inside the door by the window is the little round table the playwright Henrik Ibsen virtually called home. Notice the photos and knickknacks on the wall. At the back of the café, a mural shows Norway's literary and artistic clientele—from a century ago—enjoying this fine hangout. On the far left, find Ibsen, coming in as he did every day at 13:00. Edvard Munch is on the right, leaning against the window, looking pretty drugged. Names are below the mural.

Cross the street to the little park facing Norway's Danish-designed...

Parliament Building: Stortinget, Norway's parliament, meets here. Built in 1866, the building seems to counter the Royal Palace at the other end of Karl Johans Gate. If the flag's flying, parliament's in session. Today the king is a figurehead, and Norway is run by a parliament and prime minister. Guided tours of Stortinget are offered for those interested in Norwegian government (free, July–mid-Aug daily at 10:00 and 13:00, arrive 10 min early to get a spot, enter on Karl Johans Gate side).

Continue walking toward the palace through the park, past the fountain, to the...

Oslo at a Glance

▲▲▲**Vigeland Sculptures and Museum** Sprawling park with works by Norway's greatest sculptor. **Hours:** Garden—always open; Museum—June–Aug Tue–Sun 11:00–17:00, closed Mon; Sept–May Tue–Sun 12:00–16:00, closed Mon.

▲▲**City Hall** Oslo's artsy 20th-century government building, lined with huge, vibrant, municipal-themed murals, best visited with a tour. **Hours:** Daily May–Aug 9:00–17:00, until 16:00 off-season, tours Mon–Fri at 10:00, 12:00, and 14:00.

▲▲**National Gallery** Norway's cultural and natural essence, captured on canvas. **Hours:** Mon and Wed–Fri 10:00–18:00, Thu until 20:00, Sat 10:00–16:00, Sun 11:00–16:00, closed Tue.

▲▲**Norwegian Folk Museum** Norway condensed into 150 historic buildings in a large open-air park. **Hours:** Daily mid-May–mid-Sept 10:00–18:00, off-season 11:00–15:00.

▲▲**Viking Ship Museum** An impressive trio of 9th-century Viking ships, with exhibits on their builders. **Hours:** Daily May–Sept 9:00–18:00, Oct–April 11:00–16:00.

▲▲**Fram Museum** Captivating exhibit on the Arctic exploration ship. **Hours:** Mid-June–Aug daily 9:00–18:45, shorter hours off-season.

▲▲**Kon-Tiki Museum** Adventures of primitive *Kon-Tiki* and *Ra II* ships built by Thor Heyerdahl. **Hours:** Daily June–Aug 9:30–17:45, Sept–May 10:30–17:00 or 16:00.

Statue of Wergeland: The poet Henrik Wergeland helped inspire the movement for Norwegian autonomy. In the winter, the pool here is frozen and covered with children happily ice-skating. Across the street behind Wergeland stands the **National Theater** and statues of Norway's favorite playwrights: Ibsen and Bjørnstjerne Bjørnson. A block to the right is the National Gallery, with Norway's best collection of paintings (free entry; see self-guided tour on page 128).

Follow Roald Amundsens Gate left to the towering brick...

City Hall (Rådhuset): Built in the 1930s with contributions from Norway's leading artists, the City Hall is worth touring (see "Sights," below). For the best exterior art, circle the courtyard clockwise, studying the colorful woodcuts in the arcade. Each shows a scene from Norwegian mythology, well-explained in English: Thor

▲▲**Holmenkollen Ski Jump and Ski Museum** Dizzying vista and schuss through skiing history. **Hours:** Daily June–Aug 9:00–20:00, Sept and May 10:00–17:00, Oct–April 10:00–16:00.

▲▲**Norwegian Resistance Museum** Gripping look at Norway's tumultuous WWII experience. **Hours:** Mid-June–Aug Mon–Sat 10:00–17:00, Tue and Thu until 18:00, Sun 11:00–17:00; spring and fall Mon–Sat 10:00–16:00, Sun 11:00–16:00; winter Mon–Fri 10:00–15:00, Sat–Sun 11:00–16:00.

▲**Akershus Fortress Complex** Historic military base and fortified old center, offering tours, a couple museums (including Norwegian Resistance Museum listed above), and Christiania City Model with a film showing the early history of the city. **Hours:** 45-minute tours offered mid-June–mid-Aug Mon–Fri at 10:00, 12:00, 14:00, and 16:00; Sat–Sun at 12:00, 14:00, and 16:00; no tours off-season. Film runs continuously June–Aug Sat–Sun 12:00–17:00, closed Mon–Fri and Sept–May.

▲**Edvard Munch Museum** Works of Norway's famous modern art painter. **Hours:** June–Aug daily 10:00–18:00; Sept–May Tue–Fri 10:00–16:00, Sat–Sun 11:00–17:00, closed Mon.

▲**Norwegian Maritime Museum** A cruise through Norway's rich seafaring heritage. **Hours:** Daily mid-May–Aug 10:00–18:00, off-season 10:30–16:00.

with his billy-goat chariot, Ask and Embla (a kind of Norse Adam and Eve), Odin on his eight-legged horse guided by ravens, the swan maidens shedding their swan disguises, and so on. Circle around City Hall on the right to the front. The statues (especially the 6 laborers who seem to guard the facade) celebrate the nobility of the working class. The 1930s were a period of labor rule in Norway—and the art wanted to imply a classless society, showing everyone working together.

A few years ago, you would have dodged several lanes of busy traffic to get to the harborfront. But Oslo has made its town center pedestrian-friendly by levying a traffic-discouraging 20-kr toll for every car entering town. At the water's edge, find the shiny metal plaque (just left of center) listing the contents of a time capsule planted in the harbor for 1,000 years. You can see the little lighthouse in the harbor ahead. Go to the end of the stubby pier (on the right). This is the ceremonial "enter the city" point for momentous occasions, such as that exciting day in 1905 when Norway gained its independence from Sweden, and its Danish prince sailed in from Copenhagen to become the first modern king of Norway.

Harborfront Spin Tour: Oslofjord is a playground, with 40 city-owned parklike islands. Stand at the harbor and give it a sweeping counterclockwise look. Big, white cruise ships—a large part of the local tourist economy—dock just under the Akershus Fortress on the left. The historic *Christian Radich* tall ship calls this harbor home. Just past the fort's impressive 13th-century ramparts, a statue of FDR grabs the shade. Enjoy the grand view of City Hall. The

yellow building farther to the left was the old West Train Station. A new museum honoring Nobel Peace Prize winners is slated to open here in June of 2005. The next pier is the launch-pad for harbor boat tours and the shuttle boat to the Bygdøy museums. A fisherman is often moored here, selling shrimp from the back of his boat (70 kr/liter, daily from 8:00).

Shrimp doesn't get fresher: He catches them, and while making the four-hour sail back into Oslo, cooks them up. At the other end of the harbor, warehouses have been transformed into Akerbrygge—Oslo's hottest restaurant/shopping/nightclub zone (see "Eating," page 151).

From here, you can tour City Hall (see below), hike up to Akershus Fortress (see page 132, below), take a harbor cruise (see "Tours," above), or catch a boat across the harbor to the museums at Bygdøy (from pier 3; see "Oslo's Bygdøy Neighborhood," page 137).

SIGHTS AND ACTIVITIES

Central Oslo

▲▲**City Hall (Rådhuset)**—City halls, rather than churches, are the dominant buildings in this your-government-loves-you northern corner of Europe. The main hall of Oslo's City Hall actually feels like a temple to good government (the altar-like mural celebrates "work, play, and civic administration"). The Nobel Peace Prize is awarded here each December (though the general Nobel Prize ceremony occurs in Stockholm's City Hall).

In 1931, Oslo tore down a slum and began constructing its richly decorated City Hall. It was finished—after a WWII delay—in 1950 to celebrate the city's 900th birthday. Norway's leading artists all contributed to the building, an avant-garde thrill in its day. The interior's 20,000 square feet of bold and colorful "Romantic Social Realism" murals show town folk, country folk, and people from all classes and walks of life working harmoniously for a better society. The huge paintings take you on a voyage through the collective psyche of Norway, from its simple rural beginnings through the scar tissue of the Nazi occupation and beyond. But they're meaningful only with the excellent, 50-minute guided tours (40 kr, included tours Mon–Fri at 10:00, 12:00, and 14:00; City Hall open daily May–Aug 9:00–17:00, until 16:00 off-season; enter on Karl Johans Gate side, tel. 23 46 16 00).

Fans of the explorer Nansen might enjoy a coffee or beer across the street at Fridtjof, a bar filled with memorabilia of Nansen's Arctic explorations (daily until late, Nansens Plass 7, near American Express).

▲▲Browsing—Oslo's pulse is best felt strolling. Three good areas are along and near the central Karl Johans Gate (from train station to palace); in the trendy harborside Akerbrygge mall—a glass-and-chrome collection of sharp cafés and polished produce stalls (really lively at night, trams #10 and #12 from train station); and along Bogstadveien. While most tourists never get out of the harbor/Karl Johans Gate district, the real, down-to-earth Oslo is better seen elsewhere. Bogstadveien is a thriving shopping street with no-nonsense modern commerce, lots of locals, and no tourists (T-bane to Majorstuen and follow this street back toward the palace and tourist zone). The up-and-coming Grünerløkka district is described on page 142.

National Gallery (Nasjonalgalleriet)

While there are many schools of painting and sculpture displayed in Norway's National Gallery—a ▲▲ sight—focus on what's uniquely Norwegian. Why? Because Norway rocks. Check out Leif Ericson discovering America at the top of the stairs in the entry hall. If he

were here today, he'd be saying, "This way to the first floor—because that's where all the great Norwegian paintings are." Paintings come and go in this museum, but the rooms generally maintain their themes. A thoughtful visit here gives those heading into the mountains and fjord country a chance to pack along a little of Norway's cultural soul. Tuck these images carefully away with your goat cheese—they'll sweeten your explorations.

The gallery also has several Picassos, a noteworthy Impressionist collection, some Vigeland statues, and a raving roomful of Munch's work, including one of his famous *Scream* paintings. His artwork here makes a trip to the Edvard Munch Museum unnecessary for most (see page 141).

Cost, Hours, Location: Free, Mon and Wed–Fri 10:00–18:00, Thu until 20:00, Sat 10:00–16:00, Sun 11:00–16:00, closed Tue, Universitets Gata 13, tel. 22 20 04 04, www.museumsnett.no /nasjonalgalleriet.

Self-Guided Tour: This easy-to-handle museum gives an effortless tour back in time and through Norway's most beautiful valleys, mountains, and villages—with the help of its Romantic painters (especially Dahl). Here are some of the highlights.

Room 17—*Stalheim* (Johan Christian Dahl): This painting epitomizes the Norwegian closeness to nature. It shows the climactic view 21st-century travelers enjoy on their Norway in a Nutshell excursion (see page 155)—the mountains at the head of the Sognefjord as seen from the famous, romantic Stalheim Hotel. Painted in 1842, it's classic Romantic style. Nature rules—the background is as detailed as the foreground, and you are sucked in.

Dahl (his portrait hangs just to the left) is considered the father of Norwegian Romanticism. Romantics like Dahl (and Turner, Beethoven, and Lord Byron) all put emotion over rationality. They reveled in the power of nature—death and pessimism ripple through their work. The rainbow says it all: This is God's work. Nature is big. God is great. Man is small...and he's gonna die. The birch tree—standing boldly front and center—is a standard symbol for the (politically downtrodden) Norwegian people: hardy, cut down, but defiantly sprouting new branches. The tiny folks are in traditional dress. In the mid-19th century, Norwegians were awakening to their national identity. Throughout Europe, nationalism and Romanticism went hand-in-hand.

Find four typical Norse farms. They remind us that these are hardworking, independent, small landowners. There was no feudalism in medieval Norway. People were poor...but they owned their own land. You can almost taste the *geitost*.

Look around this biggest room in the gallery. Dahl's paintings and those by his Norwegian contemporaries, showing heavy clouds and wrecked ships, repeat these same themes—drama over rationalism, nature pounding humanity. Characters are melancholy. Norwegians, so close to nature, are fascinated by those plush magic hours of dawn and twilight. The dusk makes us wonder: What will the future bring?

In *Waterfall* (*Labrofossen*, Thomas Fearnley), man cannot control nature or his destiny. Lumber mills are churning upstream. But the eagle says, "While you can cut these logs, they'll always be mine."

Room 29: In many ways, German culture has dominated Norway's. In the mid-19th century, a group of Norwegian painters went to Düsseldorf to study. They traded the emotions of

National Gallery

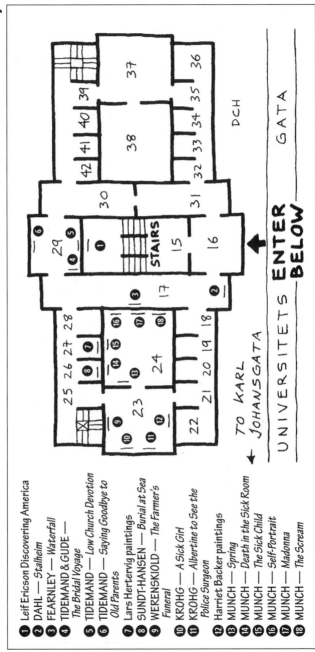

① Leif Ericson Discovering America
② DAHL — *Stalheim*
③ FEARNLEY — *Waterfall*
④ TIDEMAND & GUDE — *The Bridal Voyage*
⑤ TIDEMAND — *Low Church Devotion*
⑥ TIDEMAND — *Saying Goodbye to Old Parents*
⑦ Lars Hertervig paintings
⑧ SUNDT-HANSEN — *Burial at Sea*
⑨ WERENSKIOLD — *The Farmer's Funeral*
⑩ KROHG — *A Sick Girl*
⑪ KROHG — *Albertine to See the Police Surgeon*
⑫ Harriet Backer paintings
⑬ MUNCH — *Spring*
⑭ MUNCH — *Death in the Sick Room*
⑮ MUNCH — *The Sick Child*
⑯ MUNCH — *Self-Portrait*
⑰ MUNCH — *Madonna*
⑱ MUNCH — *The Scream*

Romanticism for more slice-of-life detail. This was Realism.

The Bridal Voyage **(Tidemand and Gude, 1848):** This famous painting shows the ultimate Norwegian scene—a wedding party with everyone decked out in traditional garb leaving the stave church and floating down the quintessential fjord (Hardanger). It's a studio work (not real) and a collaboration: Hans Gude painted the landscape, and Adolph Tidemand painted the people. Study their wedding finery. This work trumpets the greatness of the landscape and the Norwegian culture.

Low Church Devotion **(Tidemand, 1848):** This scene shows a dissenting Lutheran church group (of which there were many in the 19th century) worshipping in a smokehouse. The light of God powers through the chimney, illuminating salt-of-the-earth people with strong faiths. Only aristocrats such as Tidemand had the luxury to devote their lives to painting. They observed folk life without dirtying their fingers in it.

Saying Goodbye to Old Parents **(Tidemand):** This somber scene, painted in 1855, was not uncommon. Millions of Scandinavians emigrated to America. Imagine the sadness of a younger generation saying goodbye forever to grandma and grandpa. The mom—gripping her staff, reluctantly releasing her mother's hand—is determined to make a better life for the baby on her back. Tidemand painted this as a still life with loving attention to detail, focusing on every cobble, the reflection on the pewter, and the texture of the cloth.

Room 27: This small room is filled with small paintings (by Gude and Tidemand) that are not studio paintings but easel paintings done on-site—quick takes on Norwegian life.

Lars Hertervig (1830–1902) was depressed, and his torment empowered his canvases. Under demonic clouds, crushed by the density of nature, he was abandoned, alone in a mystical world. Treatment for mental illness at that time would have not provided artists' materials to help him vent his inner feelings through his creativity. He had to paint with whatever he could get his hands on. Now in vogue, his anguished paintings and drawings—dashed on scraps of paper and cloth—fetch big prices in auctions.

Room 26: Paintings in this room show how artists such as Gude and Tidemand worked to promote Norway's national awakening in the late 19th century. Norway drafted a constitution with guarantees of free speech and self-determination, leading to a bloodless dissolution of the union with Sweden in 1905. But prosperity was threatening traditional ways. These paintings were the artists' attempt to preserve the endangered culture.

Burial at Sea: Carl Fr. Sundt-Hansen (1841–1907) was an early photo-realist. He finished only a few paintings and is therefore not well known. But study the faces of his *Burial at Sea* (1890) and you'll wish there were more of his works.

Room 23: In the 1880s, Europe's artistic community (and that included a few Norwegians) turned to Paris. Impressionism took the art world by storm. French artists abandoned reality, using the physical object only as a rack upon which to hang light and color—their true subject matter. Inhibited Norwegians couldn't go quite that far. While their Naturalism (parallel to Impressionism) came with a new appreciation of light, their subjects remained real things.

The Farmer's Funeral (**Erik Werenskiold, 1885**): Werenskiold had the rough brushwork of Monet, but his scene is firmly rooted in Realism. Before, artists invited you in by putting a figure in the foreground (as in Dahl's *Stalheim*). But now the viewer is a participant, part of a moment captured by the painter.

A Sick Girl (**Christian Krohg, 1880**): This extremely realistic painting shows a child dying of tuberculosis—as so many did in Norway in the 19th century. The girl looks directly at you. You can almost feel the cloth, with its many shades of white. Krohg (1852–1925) is known as Edvard Munch's inspiration. But to Norwegians, he is famous in his own right for his artistry and giant personality.

Albertine to See the Police Surgeon (**Krohg, c. 1885–1887**): Krohg had a sharp interest in social injustice. In this painting, Albertine—a sweet girl from the countryside—has fallen into the world of prostitution in the big city. She's the new kid on the red light block in the 1880s, as Oslo's prostitutes are pulled into the police clinic for their regular checkup. Note her traditional dress and the disdain she gets from the more experienced girls.

Harriet Backer: Several paintings in this room are by Harriet Backer, a female Norwegian painter—rare in that age. Backer was from an aristocratic family and therefore had the means to travel to Paris and hobnob with the Impressionists. Her paintings, while not as airy as Monet's, still have strong Impressionist influences.

Room 24: View the paintings in clockwise order. **Edvard Munch** (1863–1944) is Norway's most famous and influential painter. His life was rich, complex, and sad. His father was a doctor who had a nervous breakdown. His mother and sister both died of tuberculosis. He knew suffering.

Spring (**1889**): This shows a girl with TB and her heartbroken mom. Munch is radical in his abandonment of detail for bigger brush strokes. At last, a Norwegian painter is free from Realism. Munch is called the first Expressionist. His subject: angst.

Death in the Sick Room (**c. 1895**): Munch's sister died and his extended family has gathered—the sister (unseen in the chair), the aunt who cared for the household, and Edvard himself (likely the shadowy guy in the left corner).

The Sick Child (**1896**): The girl's face melts into the pillow. She's halfway between life and death. Everything else is peripheral.

You can see how Munch scraped and repainted the face until he got it right.

Self-Portrait (1895): Munch was considered a very good-looking man. Here his hand hovers, and the cigarette only adds to the mist—demons, threats, and troubles—filling his world. His eyes are spooked. Munch had an alcohol problem, typical of Norwegian painters. He did drugs in Berlin.

Madonna **(1894–1895):** Munch had an awkward relationship with women (he never married). In his paintings, they are a threat. Munch's women are Medusas with wild locks and cascading vampire hair.

Survey the room: Moonbeams at sea were phallic. Man plus woman equals need chained to exasperation. The hair becomes blood, which becomes sperm. After a nervous breakdown (around 1910), Munch emerged less troubled—but a less powerful painter. His late works were as a colorist—big, bright, less tormented...and less noticed.

The Scream: Munch's most famous work shows a man screaming, capturing the fright many feel as the human "race" does just that. He made many copies (this one from 1893) of the scene—*the* textbook example of Expressionism. On one, he graffitied: "This painting is the work of a madman." He explained that this "shows today's society, reverberating within me...making me want to scream." The people on the bridge seem to be going—leaving the artist locked up in himself, unable to stifle his scream.

Akershus Fortress Complex

This parklike complex of sights scattered over Oslo's fortified old center—worth ▲ overall—is still a military base. But as you dodge patrol guards and vans filled with soldiers, you'll see the castle, a prison, war memorials, the Norwegian Resistance Museum, the Armed Forces Museum, and cannon-strewn ramparts affording fine harbor views and picnic perches. There's an unimpressive changing of the guard daily at 13:30 (at the parade ground, deep in the castle complex). The park is open daily 6:00–21:00.

Fortress Information Center: Located immediately inside the gate, the information center has an interesting exhibit tracing the story of Oslo's fortifications from medieval times through the struggles (environmental) of today. Stop here to pick up a castle overview booklet, quickly browse through the museum, and consider catching a tour (see below; museum entry free, mid-June–mid-Aug Mon–Fri 9:00–17:00, Sat–Sun 11:00–17:00, shorter hours off-season, tel. 23 09 39 17).

▲**Fortress Tours**—The free 45-minute, English-language walking tours of the grounds help you make sense of the most historic piece of real estate in Oslo (mid-June–mid-Aug Mon–Fri at 10:00, 12:00, 14:00, and 16:00; Sat–Sun at 12:00, 14:00, and 16:00; no tours off-season, depart from Fortress Information Center).

Christiania City Model (Bymodell)—In a half-timbered hay barn, a 25-minute presentation shows the history of Christiania (as Oslo was called from 1624–1840). After the city suffered repeated destruction, King Christian IV directed that old Oslo be moved closer to the fortress, rebuilt on a Renaissance grid plan (that survives today), and renamed Christiania (after himself). While heavy on the history for some, it's well done (free, presentations run continuously, June–Aug Sat–Sun 12:00–17:00, closed Mon–Fri and Sept–May, outside entrance of the castle, tel. 23 28 41 70).

Akershus Castle—Though one of Oslo's oldest buildings, this castle overlooking the harbor is mediocre by European standards. The big, empty rooms recall Norway's medieval poverty. Standing in the courtyard, steps on the left lead to a one-way circuit of rooms open to the public. After hiking through these rooms, head for the chapel (at the far end of the courtyard). Behind the chapel altar, steps lead down to some royal tombs and deeper into the dungeon (40 kr, sparse English descriptions throughout, May–mid-Sept Mon–Sat 10:00–16:00, Sun 12:30–16:00, closed mid-Sept–April). The castle is interesting only with the tour (free 50-min English tours summer only; Mon–Sat at 11:00, 13:00, and 15:00; Sun at 13:00 and 15:00; tel. 22 41 25 21). There are terrific harbor views from the rampart just outside.

▲▲Norwegian Resistance Museum (Norges Hjemmefront- museum)—This fascinating museum tells the story of Norway's WWII experience: appeasement, Nazi invasion, resistance, liberation, and, finally, the return of the king. (It's a one-way, chronological, can't-get-lost route—enter through 1940 door.) The museum is particularly poignant since many patriots featured were executed by the Germans right outside the front door. With wonderful English descriptions, this is the best look in Europe at how national spirit endured total German occupation (30 kr; mid-June–Aug Mon–Sat 10:00–17:00, Tue and Thu until 18:00, Sun 11:00–17:00; spring and fall Mon–Sat 10:00–16:00, Sun 11:00–16:00; winter Mon–Fri 10:00–15:00, Sat–Sun 11:00–16:00; next to castle, overlooking harbor, tel. 23 09 31 38).

Armed Forces Museum—Across the fortress parade ground, a too-spacious museum traces Norwegian military history from Viking days to post–World War II. The early stuff is sketchy, but the WWII story is compelling (free, June–Aug Mon–Fri 10:00–17:00, Sat–Sun 11:00–17:00, shorter hours off-season, tel. 23 09 35 82).

Frogner Park

▲▲▲Vigeland Sculptures and the Vigeland Museum—This 75-acre park contains a lifetime of work by Norway's greatest sculptor, Gustav Vigeland (1869–1943). In 1921, he made a deal with the city. In return for a great studio and state support, he'd spend his creative life beautifying Oslo with this sculpture garden. From 1924 to 1943 he worked on-site, sculpting 192 bronze and granite statues—600 figures, each nude and unique. Vigeland even designed the landscaping. Today the park is loved and respected (no police, no fences, and no graffiti) by the people of Oslo. The garden is always open and free (bus #20, bus #45, tram #12, and tram #15 all stop immediately in front of the main entry, or T-bane: Majorstuen and a 5-min walk). The Frogner-

badet swimming pool is also at Frogner Park (see page 142).

Vigeland's park is more than great art. It's a city at play. Appreciate its urban Norwegian ambience. The park is huge but this visit is a snap. Here's a quick, four-stop, straight-line, gate-to-monolith tour:

1. Enter the Park from Kirkeveien: For an illustrated guide and fine souvenir, pick up the 57-kr book in the Visitors Center (Besøkssenter) on your right as you enter. The modern cafeteria has sandwiches (indoor/outdoor seating, daily 9:00–20:30, less Sun and off-season), plus books, gifts, and WCs. Look at the statue of Gustav Vigeland (hammer and chisel in hand, drenched in pigeon poop) and consider his messed-up life as you enjoy his art. He lived with his many models. His marriages failed. His children entangled his artistic agenda. He didn't age gracefully. He didn't name his statues and refused to explain their meanings. While those who know his life story can read it clearly in the granite and bronze, I'd forget Gustav's troubles and see his art as observations on the bittersweet cycle of life in general—from a man who must have had a passion for living.

2. Bridge: The 100-yard-long bridge is bounded by four granite columns—three show a man fighting a lizard, the fourth shows a woman submitting to the lizard's embrace. Hmmm. But enough lizard love; the 58 bronze statues along the bridge deal with relationships between people. In the middle, on the right, find the circular statue of a man and woman going round and round—perhaps the eternal attraction and love between the sexes. But directly opposite,

another circle feels like a prison—and man fights to get out. From the man escaping, look down at the children's playground—eight bronze infants circling a head-down fetus.

On your left, see the famous *Sinnataggen*, the hot-headed little boy. It's said Vigeland gave him chocolate and then took it away to get this reaction. The statues capture the joys of life (and, on a sunny day, so do the Norwegians filling the park around you).

Greater Oslo

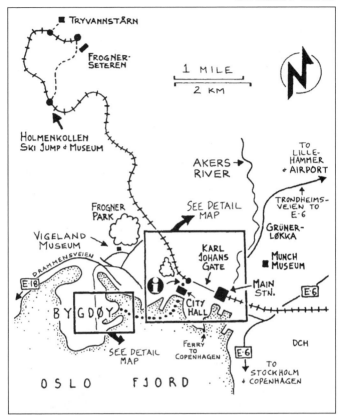

3. Fountain: Continue through a rose garden to the earliest sculpture unit in the park. Six giants hold a fountain, symbolically toiling with the burden of life, as water—a.k.a. fertility—cascades steadily around them. Twenty tree-of-life groups surround the fountain, each echoing the shape of the fountain in miniature. Four clumps of trees (on each corner) show humanity's relationship to nature and the seasons of life: childhood, young love, adulthood, and winter.

Take a quick swing through life, starting on the right with youth. In the branches you'll see a swarm of children (Vigeland called them "geniuses"): a boy sits in a tree, boys actively climb while most girls stand by quietly, and a girl glides through the branches wide-eyed and ready for life...and love. Circle clockwise to the next stage: love scenes. In the third corner, life becomes more complicated: a sad woman in an animal-like tree, a lonely child, a couple plummeting downward (perhaps falling out of love), and finally an

angry man driving away babies. The fourth corner completes the cycle, as death melts into the branches of the tree of life and new geniuses bloom.

The 60 bronze reliefs circling the basin develop the theme further, showing man mixing with nature and geniuses giving the carousel of life yet another spin.

The sidewalk surrounding the basin is a maze—life's long and winding road with twists, dead ends, frustrations, and ultimately a way out. If you have about an hour to spare, enter the labyrinth (on the side nearest the park's entrance gate) and follow the white granite path. Two miles later (on the monolith side) you finally get out. (Tracing this path occupies older kids, affording parents a peaceful break in the park.) Or you can go straight to the monolith.

4. Monolith: The centerpiece of the park—a teeming monolith of life surrounded by 36 granite groups—continues Vigeland's cycle-of-life motif. The figures are hunched and clearly earthbound, as Vigeland explores a lifetime of human relationships. At the center, 121 figures carved out of a single block of stone rocket skyward. Three stone carvers worked daily for 14 years cutting Vigeland's full-sized plaster model into the final 180-ton, 50-foot-tall erection.

Circle the plaza, once to trace the stages of life in the 36 statue groups and a second time to enjoy how Norwegian kids relate to the art. The statues—both young and old—seem to speak to children.

Vigeland lived barely long enough to see his monolith raised. Covered with bodies, it seems inert at the base and picks up speed as it ascends. Some people seem to naturally rise. Others struggle not to fall. Some help others. Although the granite groups around the monolith are easy to understand, Vigeland left the meaning of the monolith itself open. Like life, it can be interpreted many different ways.

From this summit of the park, look a hundred yards farther, where four children and three adults are intertwined and spinning in the Wheel of Life. Now, look back at the entrance. If the main gate is at 12 o'clock, the studio where Vigeland lived and worked—now the Vigeland Museum—is at 2 o'clock. His ashes sit in the top of the tower in clear view of the monolith. If you liked the park, visit the museum—it's a delightful five-minute walk—for an intimate look at the art and how it was made.

▲▲**Vigeland Museum**—Filled with original plaster casts and well-described exhibits on his work, this palatial city-provided studio was Vigeland's workplace. The high, south-facing windows provided just the right light.

Vigeland, who had a deeply religious upbringing, was also inspired by visits to Rodin's studio in Paris in 1893. Vigeland said, "The road between feeling and execution should be as short as possible." Here, immersed in his work, Vigeland supervised his craftsmen like a father, from 1924 until his death in 1943 (45 kr; June–Aug Tue–Sun 11:00–17:00, closed Mon; Sept–May Tue–Sun 12:00–16:00, closed Mon; bus #20 or #45 or tram #12 or #15 to Frogner Plass, Nobelsgate 32, tel. 22 54 25 30).

Oslo City Museum (Oslo Bymuseum)—This hard-to-be-thrilled-about little museum tells the story of Oslo (40 kr, Tue 12:00–19:00, Wed–Sun 12:00–16:00, closed Mon, shorter hours off-season, borrow English description sheet, located in Frogner Park at Frogner Manor Farm across street from Vigeland Museum, tel. 23 28 41 70).

Oslo's Bygdøy Neighborhood

This exciting cluster of sights—worth ▲▲▲—on a parklike peninsula just across the harbor from downtown provides a busy and rewarding half day (at a minimum) of sightseeing. Here, within a short walk, are five important sights:

- Norwegian Folk Museum, an open-air park with traditional log buildings from all corners of the country.
- Viking Ship Museum, showing off the best-preserved Viking long-boats in existence.
- *Fram* Museum, showcasing the modern Viking spirit with the ship of arctic-exploration fame.
- *Kon-Tiki* Museum, starring the *Kon-Tiki* and the *Ra II*, in which Norwegian explorer Thor Heyerdahl proved that early civilizations—with their existing technologies—could have crossed the oceans.

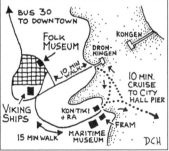

- Norwegian Maritime Museum, which is mediocre but has a wonderfully scenic movie of Norway.

Getting There: Sailing from downtown to Bygdøy is half the fun and gets you in a seafaring mood. Ride the Bygdøy ferry—marked "Public Ferry Bygdøy Museums"—from pier 3 in front of City Hall (20 kr, free with transit pass or Oslo Pass, May–Sept daily 8:00–21:00, usually 3/hr, doesn't run Oct–April). Nearby, much more expensive tour boats depart. You want the public ferry. For a less memorable

approach, you can take bus #30 (from train station or National Theater).

Getting Around Bygdøy: The Norwegian Folk and Viking Ship museums are a 10-minute walk from the ferry's first stop (Dronningen). The other museums (*Fram, Kon-Tiki,* Maritime) are at the second ferry stop (Bygdøynes). All Bygdøy sights are within a pleasant (when sunny) 15-minute walk of each other. The walk gives you a picturesque taste of small-town Norway. A goofy and overpriced tourist train shuttles tired tourists from sight to sight (2/hr, 9:30–18:00, 25 kr per segment or 50 kr for all day). A red city bus (#30) connects the sights four times hourly. If you take the bus within an hour of having taken the public ferry, your ticket is still good on the bus. Stops are immediately in front of the *Kon-Tiki* Museum, the Viking Ship Museum, and the Norwegian Folk Museum. In a strange and greedy twist of logic, the bus doesn't run on some peak-season days so that more people will pay to ride the ferry. But, generally, you can zip around on bus #30.

Eating at Bygdøy: Lunch options near the *Kon-Tiki* are a sandwich bar (relaxing picnic spots along the grassy shoreline), a cafeteria (with tables overlooking the harbor), or a stuffy indoor restaurant above the Maritime Museum (fancy 165-kr lunch buffet daily). Between the *Kon-Tiki* and the Viking Ship Museum, there's a **Spar** grocery store with a picnic-friendly deli section (closed Sun, on Fredericksbergveien, a 5-min walk off the main road, Langviksveien). The Norwegian Folk Museum has a decent cafeteria inside and a fun little farmers' market stall across the street from the entrance. **Restaurant Lanternen,** next to the Dronningen dock, serves *smørrebrød,* salads, and more (100–150 kr, daily 11:00–23:00, shorter hours on Sun, dressy interior or relaxing dockside tables, tel. 22 43 78 38).

▲▲**Norwegian Folk Museum (Norsk Folkemuseum)**—Brought from all corners of Norway, 150 buildings have been reassembled on these 35 acres. While Stockholm's Skansen was the first to open to the public (see page 237), this museum is a bit older, started in 1882 as the king's private collection (and the inspiration for Skansen).

Think of the visit in three parts: the park with old buildings; the old city; and the folk-art museum. In peak season, the park is lively with craftspeople doing their traditional things (pick up the daily schedule of activities as you pay) and costumed guides all around. (They're paid to happily answer your questions—so ask lots.) Don't miss the evocative old stave church. The old town comes complete with apartments from various generations offering an intimate look at lifestyles here in 1905, in 1930, and even an immigrant Pakistani family from the 1970s. The museum beautifully presents woody, colorfully painted folk art (ground floor), exquisite-in-a-peasant-kind-of-way folk costumes (upstairs), and the best Sami culture exhibit I've seen in Scandinavia (across the courtyard in the green building). Its final display—showing a Sami guy in traditional reindeer-hunter garb with a briefcase and an SAS plane ticket—reads: "For better or worse, Samiland is a society in transition." Everything in the museum is generously explained in English.

The place is lively only June through mid-August, when buildings are open and staffed. (Otherwise the indoor museum is fine, but the park is just a walk past lots of locked-up log cabins.) If you don't take a tour, glean information from the 10-kr guidebook and the informative attendants (90 kr, daily mid-May–mid-Sept 10:00–18:00, off-season 11:00–15:00, free lockers, Museumsveien 10). Bus #30 stops immediately in front.

Norwegian Evening performances are held at the museum at 17:30 on Tuesday, Wednesday, Friday, and Saturday from late June or early July through mid- to late August (200 kr, 125 kr with Oslo Pass, in English; includes museum tour, stories, music, folk-dancing, and even *lefse*). To get schedules for the folk evening, guided walking tours, and crafts demonstrations, call 22 12 37 00 or visit www .norskfolke.museum.no.

▲▲**Viking Ship Museum (Vikingskiphuset)**—Three great 9th-century Viking ships are surrounded by artifacts from their days of rape, pillage, and "ya-sure-you-betcha" plunder. There are no

museum tours, but everything is well described in English, and it's hard not to hear the English-speaking big-bus-tour guides. Climb to the viewpoints for a good look into the boats. There was a time when much of a frightened Europe closed every prayer with, "And deliver us from the Vikings, Amen." Gazing up at the prow of one of these sleek, time-stained vessels, you can almost hear the screams and smell the armpits of those redheads on the rampage. The ships tend to steal the show, but don't miss the wing with artifacts, including a dark room with impressive Viking weaving and textiles, or the temporary exhibit on Viking culture up the stairs above the ticket desk (40 kr, daily May–Sept 9:00–18:00, Oct–April 11:00–16:00, tel. 22 13 52 80, www.khm.uio.no).

▲▲*Fram* **Museum (Frammuseet)**—This great ship took modern-day Vikings Amundsen and Nansen deep into the Arctic and Antarctic, farther north and south than any ship before. For three years, the *Fram* was part of an Arctic ice drift. The exhibit is engrossing. Read the ground-floor displays, then explore the boat (30 kr, mid-June–Aug daily 9:00–18:45, shorter hours off-season, tel. 23 28 29 50, www.fram.museum.no).

▲▲**Kon-Tiki Museum (Kon-Tiki Museet)**—Next to the *Fram* is a museum housing the *Kon-Tiki* and the *Ra II*, the boats built by Thor Heyerdahl (1914–2002). Heyerdahl sailed the *Kon-Tiki* for 4,000 miles and the *Ra II* for 3,000 miles to prove that early South Americans could have sailed to Polynesia and Africans could have populated Barbados. Both boats are well displayed and described in English. Various 10-minute *Adventures of Thor Heyerdahl* movie clips play constantly in a small theater at the end of the exhibit (40 kr, daily June–Aug 9:30–17:45, Sept–May 10:30–17:00 or 16:00, tel. 23 08 67 67, www.kon-tiki.no).

▲**Norwegian Maritime Museum (Norsk Sjøfartsmuseum)**—If you like the sea, this museum is a salt lick, providing a look at Norway's maritime heritage (40 kr, daily mid-May–Aug 10:00–18:00, off-season 10:30–16:00, tel. 24 11 41 50, www.norsk-sjofartsmuseum.no). Don't miss the movie. *The Coast: A Way of Life*, included with your admission, is a breathtaking widescreen film swooping you scenically over Norway's dramatic sea and fishing townscapes from here all the way to North Cape, in a comfy theater (20 min, shown at the top of the hour and often at the bottom—schedule at door, follow signs to Supervideografen).

The polar sloop *Gjøa* is dry-docked next to the ferry dock. This is the boat Amundsen and a crew of six used from 1903 to 1906 to "discover" the Northwest Passage.

Outer Oslo
▲▲**Holmenkollen Ski Jump and Ski Museum**—Overlooking Oslo is a tremendous ski jump with a unique museum of skiing. The T-bane gets you out of the city, through the hills and forests and mansions that surround Oslo, and to the jump (take any westbound train—that's *tog mot vest*—to Majorstuen, then #1 to Holmenkollen, and hike up the road 10 min). After touring the history of skiing in the museum, ride the elevator and climb the 100-step stairway to the top of the jump for the best possible view of Oslo—and a chance to look down the long and frightening ramp that has sent so many tumbling into the agony of defeat.

The **ski museum**—a must for skiers—traces the evolution of the sport from 4,000-year-old rock paintings to crude 1,500-year-old skis to the slick and quickly evolving skis of modern times, including a fun exhibit showing the royal family on skis (60-kr ticket includes museum and jump, both open daily June–Aug 9:00–20:00, Sept and May 10:00–17:00, Oct–April 10:00–16:00, tel. 22 92 32 64, www.holmenkollen.com).

To cap your Holmenkollen experience, step into the **simulator** and fly down the Olympic slopes of Lillehammer in a virtual downhill ski race. My legs were exhausted after the five-minute terror. This simulator, parked in front of the ski museum, costs 45 kr, or

35 kr with an Oslo Pass. (Japanese tourists, who wig out over this one, are usually given a free ride after paying for 4.)

For an easy, downhill jaunt through the Norwegian forest, with a woodsy coffee or meal break in the middle, stay on the T-bane past Holmenkollen to the end of the line (Frognerseteren) and walk 10 minutes downhill to the **Frognerseteren Hovedrestaurant** (described on page 153—fine traditional place with sod roof, reindeer meat on the griddle, and a city view). Then continue on the same lane another 20 minutes downhill to the ski jump, and then to Holmenkollen T-bane stop.

▲**Edvard Munch Museum (Munch Museet)**—The only Norwegian painter to have had a serious impact on European art, Munch (pronounced "monk") is a surprise to many who visit this fine museum. Note that it may be closed until the summer of 2005 while new security measures are put in place in response to the bold in-broad-daylight theft of two Munch paintings—including his famous *Scream*—in 2004. The emotional, disturbing, and powerfully Expressionist work of this strange and perplexing man is arranged chronologically. You'll see paintings, drawings, lithographs, and photographs. You won't see *The Scream*, but you can see another version of this famous painting in the National Gallery downtown, alongside more Munch works; the free Gallery can be a good alternative if you find the Munch Museum, on the outskirts of the city, too expensive or time-consuming to reach (65 kr, June–Aug daily 10:00–18:00; Sept–May Tue–Fri 10:00–16:00, Sat–Sun 11:00–17:00, closed Mon; T-bane to Tøyen or bus #20, Tøyengata 53, tel. 23 49 35 00, www.munch.museum.no).

Forests, Lakes, and Beaches—Oslo is surrounded by a vast forest dotted with idyllic little lakes, huts, joggers, bikers, and sun worshipers. Mountain-biking possibilities are endless (as you'll discover if you go exploring without a good map). Consider taking your bike on the T-bane (for the cost of a child's ticket) to the end of line #1 (Frognerseteren, 30 min from National Theater) to gain the most altitude possible. Then follow the gravelly roads (mostly downhill but with some climbing) past several dreamy lakes to Sognsvann at the end of T-bane line #3. Farther east, from Maridalsvannet, a bike path follows the Aker River all the way back into town.

For plenty of trees and none of the exercise, ride the T-bane #3 to its last stop, Sognsvann (with a beach towel rather than a bike) and join in the lakeside scene. A pleasant trail leads around the lake.

Other popular beaches, located on islands in the harbor (such as Bygdøy Huk—direct boat from pier 3 in front of City Hall), are described in Use It's *Streetwise* magazine.

Tusenfryd—This giant amusement complex just out of town offers a world of family fun. It's sort of a combination Norwegian Disneyland/Viking Knott's Berry Farm, with more than 50 rides, plenty of entertainment, and restaurants (215 kr, daily June–late Aug

10:30–19:00, closed in winter, tel. 64 97 64 97, www.tusenfryd.no). A bus shuttles fun-seekers to the park from behind Oslo's train station (30 kr, 2/hr, 20-min ride).

Wet Fun—Oslo offers a variety of water play. In Frogner Park, the **Frognerbadet** has a sauna, outdoor pools, a water slide, high dives, a cafeteria, and lots of young families (65 kr, students half-price, free with Oslo Pass, late May–mid-Aug Mon–Fri 7:00–19:30, Sat–Sun 10:00–18:00, last entry 1 hr before closing, closed mid-Aug–late May, Middelthunsgate 28, tel. 23 27 54 50).

Tøyenbadet is a modern indoor/outdoor pool complex with a 330-foot-long water slide (60 kr, free with Oslo Pass, daily until 19:00, 10-min walk from Edvard Munch Museum, Helgengate 90, tel. 23 30 44 70). Oslo's free botanical gardens are nearby.

From Akers River to the Grünerløkka District

Connect the dots by following the self-guided walk below.

Akers River—This river, while only about five miles long, powered Oslo's early industry: flour mills in the 1300s, sawmills in the 1500s, and Norway's industrial revolution in the 1800s. A walk along the river not only spans Oslo's history, but also shows the contrast the city offers. The bottom of the river (where this walk doesn't go)— bordered by the high-rise Oslo Plaza Hotel and the "Little Pakistan" neighborhood of Grønland—has its share of drunks and drugs, reflecting a new urban reality in Oslo. Farther up, the river valley becomes a park as it winds past decent-sized waterfalls and red-brick factories. The source of the river (and Oslo's drinking water) is the pristine Lake Maridal, situated at the edge of the Nordmarka wilderness. The idyllic recreation scenes along Lake Maridal are a world apart from the rougher reality downstream.

▲**Grünerløkka**—The Grünerløkka district, the largest planned urban area in Oslo, was built in the latter half of the 1800s to house the legions of workers employed at factories powered by the Akers River. The first buildings were modeled on those built in Berlin. Visiting Berliners observe that there's now more of turn-of-the-century Berlin here than in present-day Berlin. While slummy in the 1980s, today it's trendy. Locals sometimes refer to it as "Oslo's Greenwich Village." Although that's way over the mark, it is a bustling area with lots of cafés, fine places for a fun meal, and few tourists.

Grünerløkka can be reached from the center of town by a short ride on tram #11, #12, or #13, or take the short but interesting walk described below.

▲**Walk up the Akers River to Grünerløkka**—While every tourist explores the harborfront and main drag of Oslo, few venture into a neighborhood evoking the Industrial Revolution, once housing poor workers and now attracting hip professionals. A 30-minute hike up the Akers River finishing in the stylish

Grünerløkka district shines a truly different light on Oslo. Navigate with the TI's free city map.

Leave Karl Johans Gate at the top of the hill, heading up Akersgata, which becomes Ullevålsveien. You'll walk past **Oslo's Fleet Street** (lined with major newspaper companies), past big government buildings on the right (red-brick Supreme Court building and the Department of Finance—an example of *Jugendstil,* or Art Nouveau, architecture), the Trefoldighets Church, and St. Olav's Church before reaching the cemetery.

Walking through the **Vår Frelsers Cemetery,** work your way left, then right, and out onto Akersveien. En route, you may want to check some of the tombstones of the illuminati and literati buried in the honorary Æreslund section. They include Munch, Ibsen, Bjørnson, and many of the painters seen in the National Gallery (all marked on a map posted at the entrance). Exiting on the far side of the cemetery, walk up Akersveien to the church.

The Romanesque **Gamle Aker Church** from the 1100s is the oldest building in Oslo and is worth a look inside (free, 12:00–14:00). The church, which fell into ruins and has been impressively rebuilt, is pretty bare except for a pulpit and baptismal font from the 1700s. From the church, head downhill on **Telthusbakken Road** toward the huge, gray former grain silos (now student housing). The cute lane is lined with old, wooden houses. The people who constructed these homes were too poor to meet the no-wood fire-safety building codes within the city limits, so they built in what used to be suburbs. At the bottom of Telthusbakken, cross the busy Maridalsveien and walk through the park to the Akers River. (The lively Grünerløkka district is straight across the river from here, but if you have 20 minutes and a little energy, detour upstream first and hook back down.) Don't cross yet.

Walk upstream through the **river gorge park,** crossing the Åmot footbridge and some impressive **falls.** Keep hiking uphill. At the big waterfall, cross over again, hiking up the stairs to the bridge with the statue of the women laborers. They're pondering the textile factory where they and 700 like them toiled long and hard. Cross over to the Ringnes Brewery and follow Thorvald Meyers Gate downhill into the heart of Grünerløkka. The square called Olaf Ryes Plass is a happening place to grab a meal or drink. Trams take you from here back to the center.

Near Oslo: Drøbak

This delightful fjord town is just an hour from Oslo by bus (60 kr one-way, 2/hr, bus #541 from Klingenberggate between City Hall and Royal Palace) or ferry (62 kr one-way, sporadic departures, check at pier 1 or ask at Oslo TI). Consider taking the boat trip down, exploring the town, having dinner, and taking the bus back.

For holiday cheer year-round, stop into **Tregaarden's Julehuset** Christmas shop, right off Drøbak's main square (generally Mon–Fri 10:00–17:00, Sat 10:00–15:00, variable hours on Sun, closed Jan–Feb, tel. 64 93 41 78, www.julehus.no). Then wander out past the church and cemetery on the north side of town to a pleasant park. Looking out into the fjord, you can see the old **Oscarsborg Fortress,** where Norwegian troops fired their cannons to sink Hitler's battleship, *Blücher.* The attack bought enough time for Norway's king and parliament to set up a government-in-exile in London during the Nazi occupation of Norway (1940–1945). Nearby, a monument is dedicated to the commander of the fortress, and the *Blücher*'s anchor rests aground. If you want to spend the night, the **TI** can recommend accommodations (June–Aug Mon–Fri 8:00–18:00, Sat–Sun 10:00–16:00; Sept–May Mon–Fri 8:00–16:00, closed Sat–Sun; tel. 64 93 50 87). **Restaurant Skipperstuen,** right on the harbor, has ghost stories to tell and huge dinner entrées to sell (from 200 kr), with outdoor seating overlooking the fjord (Mon–Sat 11:00–21:00, closed Sun, tel. 64 93 07 03).

SHOPPING

Shops are generally open 10:00–17:00. Many stay open until 20:00 on Thursday and close early on Saturday and all day Sunday. Shopping centers are open Monday–Friday 10:00–20:00, Saturday 10:00–18:00, and are closed Sunday.

For a superb selection of sweaters and other Norwegian crafts (at high prices), shop at **Heimen Husfliden** (Mon–Fri 10:00–17:00, Thu until 18:00, Sat 10:00–15:00, closed Sun, Rosenkrantz Gate 8, tel. 22 41 40 50). The **Oslo Sweater Shop** seems to have the best prices for sweaters (Mon–Sat 8:00–22:00, Sun 8:00–17:00, off Skippergate at Biskop Gunnerusgata 3, tel. 22 42 42 25). Oslo's **Byporten mall,** adjoining the central train station, has 70 shops (Mon–Sat 10:00–21:00, Sun 10:00–18:00). The street named **Bogstadveien,** running from behind the Royal Palace to Frogner Park, is lined with chic, high-quality shops.

NIGHTLIFE

For early-evening entertainment, consider the Norwegian Evening performances in the Bygdøy neighborhood (see page 139). Norwegians used to tell people who asked about nightlife in Oslo that Copenhagen was only an hour away by plane. Now Oslo has sprouted an ever-changing nightlife of its own. Ask the TI for the latest on hot spots, cafés, discos, and jazz clubs.

Sleep Code

(6.5 kr = about $1, country code: 47)
S = Single, **D** = Double/Twin, **T** = Triple, **Q** = Quad,
b = bathroom, **s** = shower. You can assume credit cards are
accepted and breakfast is included unless otherwise noted.

To help you sort easily through these listings, I've divided
the rooms into three categories, based on the price for a standard
double room with bath:

    $$$ **Higher Priced**—Most rooms 1,000 kr or more.
     $$ **Moderately Priced**—Most rooms between 450–1,000 kr.
      $ **Lower Priced**—Most rooms 450 kr or less.

SLEEPING

In Oslo, the season and type of hotel dictate the best deals. From
July through mid-August, and weekends (Fri–Sat) year-round, fancy
business-class hotels provide the best value because they discount
their double rooms to about 700–800 kr (includes breakfast). Like
those in its sister Scandinavian capitals, Oslo's hotels are designed
for business travelers; they're expensive during the tourists' off-
season (autumn through spring), full in May and June for conventions, and empty otherwise.

During business days (Mon–Thu) outside of summer, business
hotels are going for their inflated "rack rates," and budget travelers opt
for Oslo's dumpy-for-Scandinavia (but still nice by European standards) cheapie options: doubles for about 700 kr in central, "cheap"
hotels, or 350 kr in private homes on the outskirts of the city. For experience and economy—but not convenience—go for a private home. For
convenience and modern comfort, I like the Rainbow Hotels.

Only the TI can sort through all of the confusing hotel specials
and get you the best deal possible on fancy hotel rooms on the push
list. Although these rooms are still expensive—even at half-price
(about 700–800 kr)—you get a huge breakfast and a lot of extra
comfort for little more than the cost of a cheap hotel. If it's late in
the day, ask the TI about any half-price last-minute deals.

The most predictable special is the TI's **Oslo Package,** which
offers business-class rooms for 460–760 kr per person (based on
double occupancy); prices vary depending on the hotel you choose.
The Oslo Package is offered between mid-June and late August,
weekends year-round (Fri, Sat, and Sun, plus Thu if staying at least
2 nights), and, at certain hotels, daily year-round. It's a good deal
for couples and ideal for families with children under 16. Two kids
under 16 sleep free, breakfast is included, and up to four family

members get Oslo Passes, covering admission to sights and all public transportation (see page 117). The cards are valid for four days, even if you only stay one night at the hotel (allowing you to squeeze 2 days of sightseeing out of a 1-night stay—possible if, on your second evening, you take the overnight Oslo–Copenhagen boat or take an overnight train from Oslo to Bergen to do the Norway in a Nutshell route in reverse). Buy the Oslo Package through your travel agent at home, ScanAm World Tours in the United States (U.S. tel. 800/545-2204), or—easiest—upon arrival in Oslo at the TI. For details on the Oslo Package, see www.visitoslo.com.

Near the Train Station and Karl Johans Gate

These places are within a 15-minute walk of the station. While shades of an earlier shady time survive, the hotels feel secure and comfortable. The Paleet parking garage is handy (1 block south of train station) but not cheap—150 kr per 24 hours.

Rainbow Hotels

This fast-growing chain of business-class hotels (in Oslo, Bergen— see page 194—and throughout Norway) knows which comforts are worth paying for. They offer little character but provide maximum comfort per krone in big, modern, conveniently located buildings. There are umbrellas, televisions, telephones, and full modern bathrooms in each room. Each place has elevators, cheery staff and lobby, tight but well-designed rooms, non-smoking floors, and a big buffet breakfast included. And most Rainbow Hotels have the wonderful habit of leaving the juice and milk bar in the breakfast room open all day. There are usually three kinds of rooms available: singles (plenty of these for businesspeople), "combi" twins (slightly smaller rooms with twin beds or "combi" beds—a twin and a sofa bed, not available at all hotels), and full double rooms. Their two-tiered price system is pricier on Mon–Thu outside of summer, and cheaper on weekends all year plus every day during the summer (late June–mid-Aug). "Weekend" means Fridays and Saturdays (and Sun if you stayed at least Sat, too). In late June and early August, single rooms cost the same price as a double. The weekend and summer rates are possible only with the purchase of a 90-kr **Skanplus Hotel Pass** (which gives you more than 400 kr savings per night; easy to purchase with reservation or buy at hotels, www.rainbow-hotels.no). For each hotel, I've listed two sets of prices: the full price, followed by the discounted (summer and weekend) Skanplus rate.

$$$ **Rainbow Hotel Stefan,** two blocks off Karl Johans Gate, in a classy and central location, is a cut above its sisters in comfort, charm, and price (Sb-1,100/660 kr, Db-1,400/840 kr, some tram noise, Rosenkrantz Gate 1, tel. 23 31 55 00, fax 23 31 55 55, stefan @rainbow-hotels.no).

Oslo Hotels and Restaurants

1. Rainbow Hotel Spectrum
2. Rainbow Hotel Astoria
3. Rainbow Hotel Terminus
4. Rainbow Hotel Stefan
5. City Hotel
6. Centrum Hotel
7. Perminalen Hotel
8. Cochs Pensjonat
9. To Ellingsen's Pensjonat
10. To Anker Hostel
11. Vandrehjem Hostel
12. Hotell Bondeheimen & Kaffistova Cafeteria
13. Norrøna Cafeteria
14. Bit Takeaway
15. Brasserie 45 Restaurant
16. Christian Kvart Restaurant
17. Vegeta Vertshus Restaurant
18. Akerbrygge Restaurants

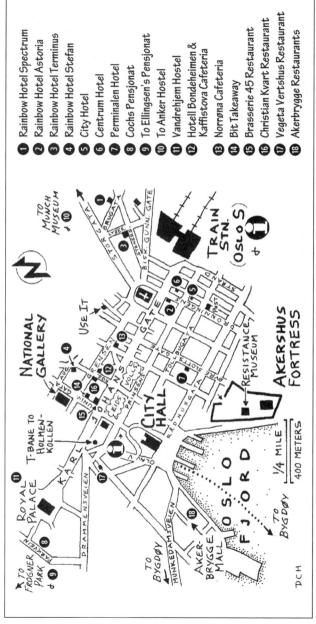

$$$ **Rainbow Hotel Spectrum** is not quite as central, but like the Stefan (above), is a tad more elegant than the others (Sb-995/630 kr, "combi" twin Db-1,145/790 kr, full Db-1,245/790 kr; 4 blocks from station, leave station out north entrance toward bus terminal, go across footbridge toward tall glass SAS Radisson Hotel, keep left around the front of the hotel, go through a parking lot next to a mostly concrete park, hotel is across Lilletorget street at Brugata 7; tel. 23 36 27 00, fax 23 36 27 50, spectrum@rainbow-hotels.no). A quarter of its rooms are plagued by disco noise on weekends.

$$$ **Rainbow Hotel Terminus** is similar and closer to the station (Sb-925/630 kr, Db-1,175/790 kr, Stenersgate 10, tel. 22 05 60 00, fax 22 17 08 98, terminus@rainbow-hotels.no).

$$ **Rainbow Hotel Astoria** has the least charm of my recommended Rainbow Hotels, but it's well located and perfectly serviceable (Sb-585/495 kr, Db-735/630 kr, 3 blocks in front of station, 50 yards off Karl Johans Gate, Dronningens Gate 21, tel. 24 14 55 50, fax 22 42 57 65, astoria@rainbow-hotels.no).

Other Hotels near the Train Station

$$$ **Best Western Hotell Bondeheimen** ("Farmer's Home") is a historic hotel run by the farmers' youth league, *Bondeungdomslaget*. It once housed the children of rural farmers attending school in Oslo. Today it has all the comforts of a modern hotel in its nearly 130 rooms (Sb-1,145–1,445 kr, or 785–1,085 kr Fri–Sun; Db-1,345–1,645 kr, or 1,045–1,345 kr Fri–Sun; non-smoking rooms, elevator, Rosenkrantz Gate 8, tel. 23 21 41 00, fax 23 21 41 01, www.bondeheimen .com, booking@bondeheimen.com). This nearly 100-year old building is also home to the simple Kaffistova restaurant (see "Eating," page 151) and the Heimen Husfliden shop (see "Shopping," page 144).

$$ **City Hotel** has clean, basic, and well-worn but homey rooms, a wonderful lounge, and a central location. The hotel originated 100 years ago as a cheap place for Norwegians to sleep while they waited to sail to their new homes in America. It now serves the opposite purpose. With prices the same throughout the year, this place is the best value on off-season weekdays (Mon–Thu), when other hotels are at their most expensive (S-450 kr, Sb-550 kr, D-650 kr, Db-750 kr, extra bed-180 kr, kids-100 kr, 10 percent discount by showing this book in 2005, non-smoking rooms, Skippergaten 19, enter from Prinsens Gate, tel. 22 41 36 10, fax 22 42 24 29, www.cityhotel.no, booking@cityhotel.no).

$$ **Centrum Hotel** is a simple, inexpensive option with basic, bright rooms in a great location (Sb-500 kr, Db-750 kr, 50-kr breakfast packet available, non-smoking rooms, Skippergaten 21, a half block off Karl Johans Gate, tel. 22 33 32 80, fax 22 33 32 90, www.centrumhotel.no, booking@centrumhotel.no). Apartments are also available, complete with small kitchen, TV, and living

space (2-room apartment-1,200 kr, 3-room apartment-1,500 kr).

$$ Perminalen Hotel, a hotel for military personnel on leave, is spartan, perfectly central, inexpensive, and welcomes civvies. Spliced invisibly into a giant office block on a quiet street, it feels like a dorm for adults, with vinyl floors, sleek woody furniture, a cheap mess hall, and a no-nonsense reception desk (beds in shared unisex quads-280 kr each, S-495 kr, bunk bed D-650 kr, includes sheets and breakfast, individual lockable closet, entirely non-smoking, elevator, Øvre Slotts Gate 2, tel. 23 09 30 81, fax 23 09 35 59, www.perminalen .com, post@perminalen.com).

The West End

$$ Cochs Pensjonat has 88 plain rooms (including 20 remodeled doubles), some with kitchenettes. It's right behind the Royal Palace (S-390 kr, Sb-490–530 kr, D-540 kr, Db-640–700 kr, extra bed-155 kr, no breakfast, elevator, non-smoking rooms, T-bane to National Theater and walk through park or ride tram #11 to Parkveien 25, tel. 23 33 24 00, fax 23 33 24 10, www.cochspensjonat.no, booking @cochs.no).

$$ Ellingsen's Pensjonat has clean, bright rooms with fluffy down comforters. It's located in a residential neighborhood four blocks behind the Royal Palace. Call well in advance for doubles (S-310 kr, Sb-430 kr, D-500 kr, Db-570 kr, extra bed-130 kr, no breakfast, cash only, non-smoking, tram #19 from train station, near Uranienborg church at Holtegata 25, tel. 22 60 03 59, fax 22 60 99 21, ep@tiscali.no).

Private Homes

The TI at the train station can find you a 350-kr double for a 25-kr fee (minimum 2-night stay, likely a tram ride out of the center). Here are several private homes to consider.

$ Arve Naess, young at heart, enthusiastically welcomes travelers in his warren of well-worn but clean budget rooms. It's like staying at your grandparents', but in the happening Grünerløkka neighborhood (see page 142) across the street from a park. His rooms are on the top three floors of a four-story building (S-175 kr, D-350 kr, 35 kr extra for 1-night stays, cash only, WC and small kitchen down the hall, no elevator, tram #12 from station to Olaf Ryes Plass stop on Thorvald Meyers Gate, then a block down Sofienberggata to Toftesgate 45, tel. 98 83 68 36).

$ Ragnar and Frode rent a dozen homey guestrooms in several 19th-century wooden houses that give you cozy old Norway with a garden (S-225 kr, D-340 kr, T-470 kr, WCs and kitchenettes down hall, 2-room apartments that sleep up to 5 people-600 kr, tram #10 or bus #31 or #32 from train station to Carl Berners Plass stop, walk up Trondheimsveien, turn right to Hasleveien 8, tel. 22 35 23 08, mobile 90 01 36 61, www.hasleveien.com, welcome@c2i.net).

$ The **Caspari Family** rents four comfortable rooms in their home (D-350 kr, cash only, no breakfast but kitchen access). Loosely run, it's set in a lush green yard in a peaceful suburb behind Frogner Park, a quick T-bane ride away (T-bane: Kålsås or Østerås, get off at Borgen and walk 100 yards more on the right-hand side of the tracks, Heggelbakken 1, tel. 22 14 57 70).

Hostels

$ **Anker Hostel,** a huge student dorm open to travelers of any age, offers 250 of Oslo's best cheap doubles. Though it feels like a bomb shelter, each of its rooms is spacious, simple, and clean. There are kitchens, free parking, and elevators (bed in 6-bed room-150 kr, bed in quad-175 kr, Sb-430 kr, Db-440 kr, sheets-45 kr, towel-15 kr, breakfast-60 kr at adjacent Best Western hotel; tram #10, #12, or #13, or bus #30, #31 or #32 from the station; Storgata 55, tel. 22 99 72 00, fax 22 99 72 20).

$ **Haraldsheim Youth Hostel (IYHF),** a huge, modern hostel open all year, comes with a grand view, laundry, self-service kitchen, 270 beds (4 per room)...and a long commute. Beds in the fancy quads with private showers and toilets are 195 kr per person, including buffet breakfast (bed in simple quad-175 kr, includes breakfast, non-members pay 25 kr extra, sheets-50 kr, 2.5 miles out of town, catch tram #10 or #17 from Oslo train station to Sinsenkrysset— then 5-min uphill hike, Haraldsheimveien 4, tel. 22 22 29 65, fax 22 22 10 25, www.haraldsheim.oslo.no, post@haraldsheim.oslo.no). Eurailers can train to the hostel with their railpass (2/hr, to Grefsen and walk for 10 min).

$ **Oslo Vandrehjem (IYHF)** is beautifully located near the Royal Palace, with a big lounge, laundry, Internet and kitchen access, and cheap beds—but only from June through mid-August (dorm bed in quad-190 kr, Sb-300 kr, D-400 kr, T-550 kr, non-members pay 25 kr extra, sheets-50 kr, towel-20 kr, a block north of the palace park at Staffelsgate 4 but enter on Linstowsgate, tel. 22 98 62 00, fax 22 98 61 01, oslo.imi.hostel@vandrehjem.no).

Sleeping on the Train

Norway's trains offer reasonable beds for budget travelers on the go (175 kr per person in a triple, 320 kr in a double, 640 kr in a single, more with private bathroom). Eurailers who sleep well to the rhythm of the rails have a couple of scenic overnight trips from which to choose (it's light until midnight for much of the early summer at Oslo's latitude). If you have a train pass, use the station's service center (across from the ticket windows) and avoid the long lines. The eight-hour trip between Bergen and Oslo leaves at about 23:00 in each direction (not Sat night). Eurail hobos sleep cheap—if not well—for the cost of a train reservation (sleep on a train ride out, cross platform, and sleep back), for example, Oslo–Vinstra (direction: Trondheim) 23:05–2:56, Vinstra–Oslo 3:15–7:10. While there are no longer overnight trains connecting Oslo with Stockholm or Copenhagen, the overnight cruise from Copenhagen to Oslo is a clever way to avoid a night in a hotel and travel while you sleep—saving a day in your itinerary (see "Overnight Cruise to Copenhagen," page 154).

EATING

Eating Cheap

How do the Norwegians afford their high-priced restaurants? They don't eat out much. This is one city in which you might just settle for simple or ethnic meals—you'll save a lot and miss little. Many menus list small plates and large plates. Since portions tend to be large, choosing a small plate or splitting a large one makes some otherwise pricey options reasonable. For a description of Oslo's classic (and expensive) restaurants, see the TI's *Oslo Guide* booklet.

Splurge for a hotel that includes breakfast or pay for it if it's optional. At 75 kr, a Norwegian breakfast fit for a Viking is a good deal. Picnic for lunch or dinner. Basements of big department stores have huge, first-class supermarkets with lots of picnic dinners—quality alternatives to sandwiches. The little yogurt tubs with cereal come with collapsible spoons. Wasa crackers and meat or shrimp or cheese spread in a tube is cheap and packs well. The train station has a late-hours grocery.

You'll save 12 percent by getting take-away food from a restaurant rather than eating inside. (The VAT on take-away food is 12 percent, for restaurant food 24 percent.) Fast-food places ask if you want to take away or not before they ring up your order on the cash register. Even McDonald's has a two-tiered price list.

Oslo is awash with little budget eateries (modern, ethnic, fast food, pizza, department-store cafeterias). **Baker Hansen** is a cheery bakery chain serving good light meals. There are 7-Elevens everywhere, and they've changed the local hot-dog culture.

Good Bets near Karl Johans Gate and the National Gallery

Kaffistova is where my thrifty Norwegian grandparents always took me. It's changed little in 30 years. This alcohol-free cafeteria serves simple, hearty, and typically Norwegian (read: bland) meals for a great price. For about 100 kr, you get your choice of an entrée (meatballs and other Norse classics) with salad, cooked vegetables, and "flat bread" (Mon–Fri 9:30–21:00, Sat–Sun 10:30–19:00, Rosenkrantz Gate 8, tel. 23 21 42 10).

Norrøna Cafeteria is a similar traditional budget-saver a block away (150-kr lunch buffet, 100-kr salad bar, 80-kr soup buffet, 100-kr meals, Mon–Fri 11:00–16:00, closed Sat–Sun, central at Grensen 19, near recommended Hotel Stefan, tel. 23 31 80 00).

Bit, a block from the National Gallery, is a favorite among locals for its fresh-made take-away calzones and sandwiches. With a drink, you've got a 70-kr meal to munch in the nearest park, next to the National Theater (Mon–Fri 8:00–19:00, Sat 10:00–17:00, closed Sun, Universitets Gata 20). Another branch is in the train station's Byporten mall (with seating).

Brasserie 45, overlooking Karl Johans Gate from its second-floor perch, is a modern place offering fine and affordable continental cuisine with energetic service. While larger entrées go for about 150 kr, their "light plates" (80–120 kr) were plenty for me (Mon–Sat 12:00–24:00, Sun 14:30–22:30, always a veggie option, on corner of Karl Johans Gate and Universitets Gata, tel. 22 41 34 00).

Christian Kvart, named for that mighty Danish king, is a hopping place serving Cajun meals ("light" meals for 120 kr, full entrées for 200 kr). The interior is dark, woody, and nautical with chandeliers, but on balmy nights their beach-party Bakgarden courtyard is the place to be (daily 12:00–24:00, corner of Christian Gate and Rosenkrantz Gate, tel. 23 13 95 00).

Vegeta Vertshus, while a bit tired, has kept Oslo vegetarians fat, happy, and low on the food chain for 60 years. It serves a huge selection of hearty vegetarian food that would satisfy even a hungry Viking. Fill your plate once (small plate-90 kr, large plate-100 kr) or eternally for 145 kr. How's your balance? (Daily 12:00–21:00, non-smoking, no meat, 30 yards off the top of Stortingsgata between palace and City Hall, Munkedamsveien 3B, tel. 22 83 42 32.)

Harborside in Akerbrygge

The **Akerbrygge** harborfront mall isn't cheap, but it has some inviting cafés, classy delis, and restaurants with outdoor harborview tables. Before choosing a place, I'd walk the entire lane, considering both the regular places (some with 2nd-floor view seating) and the various floating options. Nearly all are open for lunch and dinner. If you're on a budget, get a take-out meal from the fast-food stands and grab a bench along the boardwalk.

Druen, the first restaurant on the strip, is best for people-watching. I like the balcony seats upstairs—under outside heaters and with a harbor view. They serve international dishes—spicy Asian, French, and seafood—in small plates for 140 kr and big meals for 200–250 kr (daily, Stranden 1, Akerbrygge, tel. 23 11 54 60).

Two restaurants are actually on the water with a view of the harbor rather than the river of strolling people. **Lekter'n,** which has the best harbor view and offers live music nightly, serves hamburgers, pizza, and shrimp buckets. Budget eaters can split a 150-kr pizza (all outdoors, Stranden 3, tel. 22 83 76 46). **Herbern Marina,** farther out—just across from the naked ladies—is *the* place for shrimp. Couples, in the midst of lots of pleasure boats, enjoy the fun, laid-back dockside ambience and fill up by splitting a 190-kr liter bucket of shrimp with bread. Request a free peeling lesson; rinse in the finger bowl (Stranden 30, tel. 22 83 19 90).

Lofoten Fiskerestaurant serves perhaps Oslo's best fish amid a classy yacht-club atmosphere at the end of the strip. While it has harbor views, it's beyond the people-watching action (lunch-150–200 kr, dinner-250–300 kr, open daily, reservations smart, Stranden 75, tel. 22 83 08 08).

Roasted Rudolph under a Thatched Roof High on the Mountain

Frognerseteren Hovedrestaurant, nestled high above Oslo (and 1,400 feet above sea level), is a classy, sod-roofed old restaurant. Its terrace, offering a commanding view of the city, is a popular stop for the famous apple cake and coffee. The café is casual and less expensive, with indoor and outdoor seating (sandwiches-70 kr, hot dishes-100 kr, daily 10:30–22:30, reservations unnecessary). The elegant view restaurant is pricier (230–300-kr plates, 500-kr 3-course meals, reindeer specials, daily 12:00–22:00, reserve for evening dining, tel. 22 92 40 40).

You can combine a trip into the forested hills surrounding the city with lunch or dinner and get a chance to see the famous ski jump up close. Ride T-bane line #1 to the last stop (Frognerseteren), walk about 10 minutes down a traffic-free dirt lane, stop for your meal, and walk another 20 minutes (1.25 miles) downhill on the same lane to the ski jump (and the Holmenkollen T-bane station).

TRANSPORTATION CONNECTIONS

For train information, call 81 50 08 88 and press 4 for English. For international trains, dial 81 56 81 00. Even if you have a railpass, reservations are required for long rides (e.g., a reservation to Stockholm in first class costs 140 kr, second class for 60 kr). First class often comes with a hot meal, fruit bowl, and unlimited juice and coffee.

From Oslo by train to Bergen: Oslo and Bergen are linked by a spectacularly scenic train ride (6/day, 7 hrs). Many travelers take it as part of the **Norway in a Nutshell** route, which combines train, ferry, and bus travel in an unforgettably beautiful trip. For information on times and prices, see the next chapter.

By train to: Stockholm (3/day, departures at 6:30, 11:30, and 17:30, 5 hrs on the slick Linx train—reservation required, no night-train option), **Copenhagen** (2/day, 7.25 hrs, reservation required, no night-train option), **Lillehammer** (9/day, 2.5 hrs), **Kristiansand** (5/day, 4–5 hrs).

Overnight Cruise to Copenhagen

Consider the cruise that leaves daily from Oslo (departs at 17:00, arrives in Copenhagen at 9:00 the following morning; departs Copenhagen at 17:00 and returns to Oslo at 9:15 the next morning, giving you about 8 hours in Denmark's capital; 16 hours sailing each way). The boat leaves Oslo from the far (non-City Hall) side of the Akershus Fortress peninsula (get there via bus #60 from in front of train station). From Oslo, you'll sail through the Oslofjord—not as dramatic as Norway's western fjords, but impressive if you're not going to Bergen. On board are three gourmet restaurants, a sauna, hot tub, and swimming pool. This is fun and convenient, but more expensive and not as nice as the Stockholm–Helsinki cruise (see page 271).

You can take this cruise one-way or do a round-trip from either city. To make a reservation, call DFDS Seaways' Norwegian office at tel. 22 41 90 90 (Mon–Fri 8:00–17:00, www.dfdsseaways.com), or, in the United States, tel. 800/533-3755 (www.seaeurope.com). For specifics and sample prices, see "Overnight Cruises to Oslo" on page 79.

NORWAY
in a NUTSHELL
A Scenic Journey

While Oslo and Bergen are the big draws for tourists, Norway is essentially a place of natural beauty. There's a certain mystique about the "land of the midnight sun," but you'll get the most scenic travel thrills per mile, minute, and dollar by going west rather than north.

Norway's greatest claims to scenic fame are her deep, lush fjords. A series of well-organized and spectacular bus, train, and ferry connections, appropriately called Norway in a Nutshell, lays Norway's beautiful fjord country spread-eagled on a scenic platter. You can do it as a day trip from Oslo or from Bergen, or en route between Oslo and Bergen.

You'll see the seductive Sognefjord, with tiny but tough ferries, towering canyons, and isolated farms and villages marinated in the mist of countless waterfalls. You're an eager Lilliputian to the Gulliver of Norwegian nature.

Today the region enjoys mild weather for its latitude, thanks to the warm Gulf Stream. But three million years ago, the Ice Age made this land as inhabitable as the center of Greenland. Like the hairline on Dick Clark, the ice slowly receded. As the last glaciers of the Ice Age cut their way to the sea, they gouged out long grooves—today's fjords. Since the ice was thicker inland and only a relatively thin lip at the coast, the gouging was deeper inland. The average fjord is 4,000 feet deep far inland and only about 600 feet deep where it reaches the open sea.

The entire west coast is slashed by stunning fjords, but the Sognefjord, Norway's longest (120 miles) and deepest (1 mile), is

Norway in a Nutshell

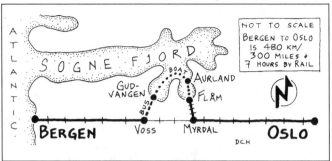

tops. Anything but the Sognefjord is, at best, foreplay. This is it—the ultimate natural thrill Norway has to offer.

Aurland, a good home base for your exploration, is on Aurlandsfjord, a remote, scenic, and accessible arm of the Sognefjord. The local weather is actually decent, with about 24 inches of rain per year, compared to 80 inches annually in nearby Bergen. (For more fjords in your life, consider extending your trip northwest of Aurland to the town of Balestrand for fewer crowds, more hikes, and lots of day-trip possibilities; see next chapter.)

Planning Your Time

Even the blitz tourist needs a day for the Norway in a Nutshell trip. This is easily done as a long day trip from Oslo or Bergen. (All connections are designed for tourists, explained in English, convenient, and easy—see below.) Ideally, break the trip with an overnight in Aurland, Flåm, or Balestrand (see next chapter) and carry on into Bergen, to enjoy a day there before sleeping on the night train (past all the scenery you saw westbound) back to Oslo.

Those with a car and only one day should leave the car in Oslo and take the train. With more time, drivers can improve on the Nutshell by taking a northern route: from Oslo, drive through Gudbrandsdal Valley, go over the Jotunheimen Mountains, then along Lustrafjord and/or Balestrand to Bergen. These sights are covered in the next two chapters.

ORIENTATION

The most exciting single-day trip you could make from Oslo or Bergen is this circular train/boat/bus/train jaunt through fjord country. It's famous, everybody does it...and if you're looking for the scenic grandeur of Norway, so should you.

Tourist offices and train stations have souvenir-worthy brochures with photos, descriptions, and exact times. The all-day trip starts by train every morning from Oslo and Bergen.

The Route: Leaving from Oslo, you'll ride the Oslo–Bergen train to Myrdal (MEER-doll), take the scenic train from Myrdal to Flåm, hop on the fjord cruise from Flåm to Gudvangen, and then take the bus from Gudvangen to Voss. (It's easier than it sounds—just follow the crowds.) At Voss, jump on the Oslo–Bergen train and head west for Bergen or east for Oslo. The Nutshell trip is possible all year. Some say it's most beautiful in winter (but not possible then as a day trip from Oslo).

Reservations: If you're traveling during peak season (July-mid-Aug), it's wise to make reservations several weeks in advance for the Oslo–Bergen train segment of your trip (for specifics, see Oslo–Bergen train listing under "Sights," page 158).

Sample Norway in a Nutshell Schedules

Nutshell connections are made even if trains, boats, or buses are running late. Off-season, limited train, bus, and boat schedules can cause frustrations. Note that trains leave throughout the day between Oslo and Bergen. The following schedules are the optimum times (based on 2004 schedules) for one-way and round-trips made within a day's time; if you'll be overnighting on the fjord in Flåm or Aurland, you can easily start your trip later in the day. Confirm all times and connections.

Oslo–Bergen: Train departs Oslo-8:11, arrives Myrdal-12:53; cogwheel train departs Myrdal-13:02, arrives Flåm-13:55; boat departs from Flåm-15:00, arrives Gudvangen-17:00; bus from Gudvangen-17:30 (or upon arrival), arrives Voss-18:50; train from Voss-19:20, arrives Bergen-20:35.

Day Trip from Oslo: Train departs Oslo-6:11, arrives Myrdal-11:07; cogwheel train departs Myrdal-12:11, arrives Flåm-13:05; boat departs from Flåm-13:25, arrives Gudvangen-15:25; bus from Gudvangen-15:30, arrives Voss-16:50; train from Voss-17:11, arrives Oslo-22:30.

A similar day trip can be done from Bergen to Oslo, or as a day trip from Bergen. There is also a fast-boat option for the Flåm–Bergen trip (see below).

Cost of Norway in a Nutshell

If you have a Scanrail, Eurailpass, or Eurail Selectpass, you can get discounts on the journey (but not on the package deals mentioned below).

Without a Railpass: Allow about 1,085 kr for a one-way trip from Oslo to Bergen and about 910 kr for a round-trip from Bergen. Buying and reserving the Nutshell journey on your own isn't difficult. For solo travelers, the package deals from Fjord Tours (described below) save you time, but not any money. Couples and families should buy and reserve the trip on their own (get train tickets, including Myrdal–Flåm segment, at the train station in Oslo or Bergen) and purchase your fjord-cruise ticket on the boat or from the TI in Flåm. You can buy the tickets for the Gudvangen bus on board from the driver.

With a Railpass: With a railpass, allow about 420 kr (50 kr for seat reservation on Oslo–Bergen train; 105 kr for Myrdal–Flåm train supplement; 185 kr for fjord cruise—discounts for students or couples; 80 kr for Gudvangen–Voss bus). Some fast trains, such as the 10:43 Oslo–Bergen departure, come with a meal in first class, raising the seat reservation to a whopping 300 kr with a first-class railpass.

Packages: Fjord Tours sells the Nutshell package (among other package trips, www.fjordtours.no) at all Norwegian State Railways stations, including Oslo and Bergen, or through their Customer Service line in Norway (tel. 81 56 82 22). The approximate costs of the Nutshell package are as follows: one-way from Bergen or Oslo-1,065 kr; round-trip from Oslo via Voss-1,505 kr mid-June–mid-Sept; round-trip from Oslo via Bergen-1,735 kr, departs year-round; round-trip from Bergen-750 kr.

SIGHTS

▲▲**The Oslo–Bergen Train**—This is simply the most spectacular train ride in northern Europe. The scenery crescendos as you climb over Norway's mountainous spine. After a mild three hours of deep woods and lakes, you're into the barren, windswept heaths and glaciers. The line was started in 1894 to link Stockholm and Bergen. But Norway won its independence from Sweden in 1905, so the line served to link the two main cities in the new country.

Note that the Nutshell route includes only part of this train ride (as a day trip from Oslo, for instance, you take the Oslo–Myrdal and Voss–Oslo segments).

The entire railway, an amazing engineering feat completed in 1909, is 300 miles long; peaks at 4,266 feet—which at this Alaskan latitude is far above the tree line; goes under 18 miles of snow sheds; trundles over 300 bridges; and passes through 200 tunnels in just under seven hours.

Reservations: This train can get booked up in peak season (July–mid-Aug), so it's smart to reserve a seat several weeks ahead if you're traveling during this time and your itinerary is set (dial 81 50 08 88, press 4 for English, and book with a credit card; if you have a railpass and want to book only a seat reservation, you can use a credit card to pay the 50-kr fee when you call, or go to www.nsb .no/internet/en/booking/agents for a list of U.S. agents).

Nutshell Route from Oslo to Myrdal: Leaving Oslo, you pass through a six-mile-long tunnel and stop in Drammen, Norway's fifth-largest town. The scenery stays mild and woodsy up Hallingdal Valley until you reach Geilo, a popular ski resort. Then you enter a land of big views and tough little cabins. Finse, at about 4,000 feet, is the highest stop on the line. From here, you enter the longest high-mountain stretch of railway in Europe. Much of the line is protected by snow tunnels. The scenery gets more dramatic as you approach Myrdal. Just before Myrdal, look to the right and down into Flåm Valley (Flåmsdalen), where the branch line winds its way down to the fjord. Nutshell travelers get off at Myrdal.

▲▲**Myrdal–Flåm Train**—The little 12-mile spur line leaves the Oslo–Bergen line at Myrdal (2,800 feet), which is nothing but a scenic high-altitude train junction with a decent cafeteria. From

Myrdal, the train winds down to Flåm (sea level) in 55 thrilling minutes (150-kr ticket or 105-kr supplement for Eurail and Scanrail passholders, departures nearly hourly). It's party time on board, and the engineer even stops the train for photos at the best waterfall (according to a Norwegian legend, a temptress lives behind

these falls and tries to lure men to the rocks with her singing). This line has 20 tunnels (more than 3 miles' worth) and is so steep that the train has five separate braking systems (stations have a cool souvenir pamphlet with lots of info on the trip; also see www.flaamsbana.no).

▲**Flåm**—On the Norway in a Nutshell route, this scenic, touristy "town" at the head of the Aurlandsfjord is little more than a transit junction with a train station, ferry landing, baggage check (20 kr, daily 8:00–19:45, next to train tracks, on your right as you depart the train, ring bell if nobody's there), grocery store (open Mon–Fri

9:00–18:00, Sat 9:00–15:00, closed Sun), post office, public WC, Internet access, souvenir shops (over-priced reindeer pelts—cheaper in Bergen), cluster of hotels and hostels, and a handy TI. At the **TI,** you can purchase your boat tickets and

load up on handy brochures (daily June–Aug 8:30–15:30 & 16:00–20:00, May and Sept 8:45–17:00, closed Oct–April, tel. 57 63 21 06). Answers to most of your questions can be found on the walls and at the counter here. Bus schedules, boat and train timetables, maps, and more are photocopied and available for your convenience (and the staff's). For accommodations in Flåm, see "Sleeping" (page 162)—or, better yet, stay in nearby Aurland (described below; see "Sleeping," page 162). For a longer stay, consider Balestrand (connected by express boat from Flåm, see next chapter). Nightlife in Flåm is sparse.

▲▲▲**Flåm–Gudvangen Fjord Cruise**—At Flåm, if you're doing the Nutshell route nonstop, follow the crowds and hop on the sightseeing boat. Boats leave Flåm daily at 9:00, 11:00, 13:25, and 15:00 (fewer off-season), dock briefly at the town of Aurland, then continue to Gudvangen (185 kr one-way, 95 kr for students with ISIC cards, 230 kr round-trip, no railpass discounts; couples ask for a family discount that lets 1 person go for half-price). With minimal English narration, the boat takes you close to the goats, sheep, waterfalls, and awesome cliffs.

You'll cruise up the lovely Aurlandsfjord and hang a left at the stunning Nærøyfjord. The trip is breathtaking in any weather. For two glorious hours, camera-clicking tourists scurry around the drool-stained deck like nervous roosters, scratching fitfully for a photo that will catch the magic. Waterfalls turn the black cliffs into bridal veils, and you can nearly reach out and touch the Nærøyfjord's cliffs. It's the world's narrowest fjord: six miles long and as little as 820 feet wide. On a sunny day, the ride is one of those fine times—like when you're high on the tip of an Alp—when a warm camaraderie spontaneously combusts between the strangers who came together for the experience.

Most people stay on the boat, but you can request to be dropped off in Undredal (see below) or Styvi (which has a farm museum, 20 kr). There's an idyllic 2.5-mile shoreline along the 17th-century postal road from Styvi to Bleikindli (ask if the boat stops at Bleikindli, but you'll likely have to walk back to Styvi for a ferry pickup to Gudvangen—if you're at the pier, the boat is supposed to stop).

Gudvangen–Voss Bus—Gudvangen is little more than a boat dock and giant tourist kiosk. Norway Nutshellers get off the boat at Gudvangen and take the bus up the Nærøydalen (Narrow Valley) to Voss. Try to catch a bus taking the extra-scenic route via Stalheim. At the end of Nærøydalen, the bus climbs a corkscrew series of switchbacks before stopping at the Stalheim Hotel for a last grand view back into fjord country (80 kr, pay on board, about a 1-hr ride, buses meet each ferry, but confirm this if you want to take the last boat of the day—at about 18:00).

Voss—A plain town in a lovely lake-and-mountain setting, Voss has a **TI** (June–mid-Aug Mon–Fri 8:00–19:00, Sat 9:00–19:00, Sun 14:00–19:00; off-season Mon–Fri 9:00–15:30, closed Sat–Sun; tel. 56 52 08 00), an interesting folk museum (45 kr, daily June–Aug 10:00-17:00, closes earlier off-season), a 13th-century church, and a few other historic sights, but it's basically a home base for summer or winter sports. **Nordic Ventures** offers kayak trips on the Sognefjord (495 kr/half-day, 890 kr/day, 1,395 kr/2-day excursion, includes meals, depart from their office—100 yards from Voss train station, tel. 56 51 00 17, mobile 95 20 80 36, www.nordicventures.com).

The Nutshell bus from Gudvangen drops you at the Voss train

station, which is on the Oslo–Bergen train line. Drivers should zip right through. You can spend the night (consider the luxurious **Voss Youth Hostel,** tel. 56 51 20 17), though I wouldn't.

▲▲**Sognefjord Scenic Express Boat**—Boats speed between Flåm and Bergen through the Sognefjord, making stops along the way, including Balestrand (see next chapter). In peak season (May–Sept), boats depart Bergen daily at 8:00, stop in Balestrand at 11:50, and arrive in Flåm at 13:25; depart Flåm at 15:30, stop in Balestrand at 16:55, and arrive in Bergen at 20:40 (Bergen to Flåm: 530 kr one-way, 685 kr round-trip, 890 kr round-trip if you return by train, round-trip fares not available if you travel late Fri or on Sun, discounted with ISIC card, all stop in Aurland, tel. 55 90 70 70). Ask if they'll pull up close to one of the scenic waterfalls.

More Fjord Sights

▲▲**Flåm Valley Bike Ride or Hike**—For the best single-day activity from Flåm, take the train to Myrdal, then hike or mountain bike the gravel road back down to Flåm (2 hrs, great mountain scenery but no fjord views). The Flåm TI rents bikes (30 kr/hr, 175 kr/day for mountain bikes; it costs 50 kr to take a bike to Myrdal on the train). You could just hike the best two hours from Myrdal to Berekvam, where you can catch the train into the valley.

▲▲**Aurland**—A few miles north of Flåm, Aurland is more of a town and less of a tourist depot. Nothing exciting, but it's a good, easygoing fjordside home base (see "Sleeping," next page). The harborside public library is a pleasant refuge, and the 800-year-old church is worth a peek.

The local *geitost* (goat's cheese) is sweet and delicious. Aurland has as many goats as people (1,900). The person who runs the **TI** speaks English (mid-June–Aug Mon–Fri 9:00–19:00, Sat–Sun 10:00–17:00, shorter hours and closed Sat–Sun off-season, tel. 57 63 33 13, fax 57 63 11 48, www.alr.no). The TI stocks the English-language *Bergen Guide.*

If you want to stay overnight in Aurland, note that every train (except for the late-night one) arriving in Flåm connects with a bus or boat to Aurland. Eleven buses and at least four ferries link the towns daily (bus-25 kr, 10 min; boat-60 kr, 20 min). The Flåm–Gudvangen boat stops at Aurland en route, so it's theoretically easy to continue the Nutshell route from Aurland without backtracking to Flåm. However, in July and August, when the boat from Flåm can be packed (and unable to take on more passengers in Aurland), it can make sense to double back to Flåm by bus (only 10 min) to ensure a spot on the boat.

▲**Undredal**—This almost impossibly remote community of 52 families was accessible only by boat until 1985, when the road from Flåm was opened. Undredal has Norway's smallest still-used church (built in the 12th century, pews for 40). The 15-minute drive from Flåm is mostly through a new tunnel. There's not much in the town, which is famous for its goat cheese and its church, but I'll never forget the picnic I had on the ferry wharf. For an overnight, **Undredal Overnatting** rents four modern, woody, comfortable rooms on a back street with little character (250 kr per person, includes breakfast, tel. 57 63 30 80).

You'll sail past Undredal on the Flåm–Gudvangen boat; you can request a stop here. To get the ferry to pick you up in Undredal, turn on the blinking light (though some express boats will not stop).

SLEEPING

Flåm

Note that the season is boom or bust here. It can be dead in June and packed in July and August.

$$ Heimly Pensjonat is doing its best to go big-time in a small-time town. It's clean, efficient, and the best small hotel in town (23 rooms, S-575 kr, Sb-680 kr, D-700 kr, Db-895 kr, extra bed-195 kr, includes breakfast, cheaper mid-Sept–May, attached restaurant; bike, boat, and car rental; try to reserve a room with a view, tel. 57 63 23 00, fax 57 63 23 40, www.heimly.no, post@heimly.no). Sit on the porch with new friends and watch the clouds roll down the fjord. Located along the harbor a quarter-mile from the station, they will pick up and drop off at the station/dock for 10 kr round-trip.

$ Flåm Youth Hostel and Camping Bungalows, recently voted Scandinavia's most beautiful campground, has the cheapest beds in the area. On the river just behind the Flåm train station, the place—run by the Håland family—offers dorm beds in four-bed hostel rooms (120 kr per bed with kitchenette). They also have some doubles from 330 to 380 kr, and four-bed cabins ranging from 450 kr to a deluxe cabin for 700 kr (50 kr for sheets, 25 kr extra if not a hostel member, tel. 57 63 21 21, fax 57 63 23 80, camping@flaam -camping.no) The folks at the check-in cabin can recommend local kayak and hiking tours, as well as some good hikes nearby.

Aurland

$$$ Aurland Fjordhotell is big (30 rooms), modern, and centrally located, with balconies and amenities such as a sauna and steam bath (Sb-630–735 kr, Db-850–1,080 kr, includes breakfast, attached restaurant, tel. 57 63 35 05, fax 57 63 36 22, www.aurland-fjordhotel .com, post@aurland-fjordhotel.com).

$$ The Aabelheim Pension/Vangen Motel complex, dominat-ing the old center of Aurland, is run from one reception desk (tel. 57 63 35 80, fax 57 63 35 95, vangsgas@online.no, Astrid). **Vangen Motel,** nestled between Aabelheim and the fjord, is a simple old

Sleep Code

(6.5 kr = about $1, country code: 47)
S = Single, **D** = Double/Twin, **T** = Triple, **Q** = Quad,
b = bathroom, **s** = sleeping. All of these places accept credit cards.
   To help you sort easily through these listings, I've divided
the rooms into three categories, based on the price for a standard
double room with bath:

   $$$ Higher Priced—Most rooms 1,000 kr or more.
   $$ Moderately Priced—Most rooms 500–1,000 kr.
   $ Lower Priced—Most rooms 500 kr or less.

hotel offering basic rooms, a large self-serve kitchen, and a dining
and living area (S-375 kr, Ds-550 kr, Db-750 kr, breakfast-70 kr,
open all year). The motel has four-bed cabins right on the water for
450 kr (sheets-50 kr). **Aabelheim Pension** is far and away Aurland's
best cozy-like-a-farmhouse place. "Cozy" is *koselig,* a good Norwegian
word (S-375 kr, D-550 kr, Db-750 kr; 2- to 6-person cabins including kitchen, bathroom, and 2 bedrooms-800–1,200 kr; sheets-60 kr,
extra bed-50 kr, 75-kr breakfasts are served in a wonderfully traditional dining room, open April–Oct, fine old-time living room).
   $$ At the **Skahjem Gård** farmhouse, Aurland's former deputy
mayor, Nils Tore, rents out family apartments (500–600 kr with pri-
vate bathroom and kitchenette, 400 kr without, 50 kr extra per
person for sheets and towels, 2.2 miles up the Oslo road, tel. 57 63
33 29, nskahjem@online.no). It's a 20-minute walk from town, but
Nils will pick up and drop off travelers at the ferry. This is best for
families who are driving.
   $ Lunde Camping offers 14 cabins overlooking the river one
mile out of Aurland (at the Aurland exit off the big road). Each cabin
has four beds in two bunks, a kitchenette, and a river view (350–400
kr, deluxe cabins for up to 4 people-500–700 kr, 50 kr extra per person
for sheets or towels, open April–Oct, generally full June 20–Aug 20,
tel. 57 63 34 12, fax 57 63 31 65, jelun@online.no, Jens Lunde).

EATING

Aurland
The Vangen Motel runs the **Duehuset Pub** (70–180-kr dinners,
daily 15:00–23:00). For cheap eats on dockside benches, gather a
picnic at the **grocery store** (Mon–Fri 9:00–20:00, Sat 9:00–18:00,
closed Sun, next to Vangen Motel).

MORE on the
SOGNEFJORD
Balestrand and Lustrafjord

Norway's world of fjords is decorated with medieval stave churches, fishing boats, and brightly painted shiplap villages. If you want to linger in fjord country, this chapter is for you.

Snuggle into the village of Balestrand on the Sognefjord, a handy jumping-off spot for adventures great and small that offers a variety of walking and biking options and a fun local arts scene. Farther east is Lustrafjord, a branch of the Sognefjord, offering drivers a scenic string of towns, churches, waterfalls, ferry rides, and rugged passes.

Planning Your Time

A day and a night in Balestrand is doable, but to take advantage of the various day-trip options, consider staying two days and a night (leaving by boat in the late afternoon of the second day).

Located on the express-boat route between Bergen and Flåm, Balestrand is easy to visit using public transportation. To add the town to the popular Norway in a Nutshell route (see previous chapter), you can take the express boat from Flåm to Balestrand, then return by express boat (transferring at Midtfjord—literally from boat to boat, in the middle of the fjord—to the Kaupanger–Gudvangen ferry) to continue the Nutshell route down the Nærøyfjord to Gudvangen.

The Lustrafjord, better by car, is a logical extension of the driver's route from Oslo to Bergen through the Gudbrandsdal Valley, Jotunheimen Mountains, then Lustrafjord (with a possible stop in

Balestrand). This trip can be done just as easily and scenically in reverse (rent a car in Bergen, drive to Oslo, drop off car).

Balestrand

This pleasant fjordside village (pop. 1,850) is away from the Norway in a Nutshell crowd. From here you can side-trip to nearby Fjærland (a.k.a. "Mundal") and the awesome Jostedal glacier. Consider this worthwhile detour to the typical fjord visit—so you can dig deeper into the Sogne-fjord, just like the glaciers did during the last Ice Age.

ORIENTATION

Most travelers arrive in Balestrand on the express boat from Bergen or Flåm. The tidy harbor area has a TI, two small grocery stores (Co-op and Spar), a couple of galleries, an art museum, and a small aquarium devoted to sea life found in the fjord. The historic wooden Kvikne's Hotel and its modern addition dominate Balestrand's waterfront. Balestrand is tiny. From the harbor to the Balestrand Hotel is a five-minute stroll. You can walk from the aquarium to Kvikne's Hotel in less than that.

The town has outdoor activities for everyone, from easy to strenuous mountain hikes and mostly flat bike rides. Note that Balestrand virtually shuts down from September through May. While rooms and dinner are available at Kvikne's Hotel during this period, the rest of the activities, sights, hotels, and restaurants listed below are likely closed.

Tourist Information

At the TI, located upstairs in the modern building next to the dock, pick up the free, helpful *Balestrand Guide*. The TI has numerous brochures about the Sognefjord area and detailed information on the more challenging hikes. It offers Internet access, rents bikes (35 kr/hr, 85 kr/half-day, 150 kr/day), sells day-trip excursions to the glacier, and more (late-June–Aug Mon–Fri 7:30–19:00, Sat–Sun 8:00–17:30, shorter hours in spring and fall, closed mid-Sept–April, tel. 57 69 12 55).

SIGHTS

In Balestrand

Town Walking Tour—Following the *Balestrand Guide* (free at the TI or your hotel), take the self-guided walking tour of town (20 min to an hour one-way, depending on your pace and how many stops you make along the way). You'll stroll along a lightly traveled paved road punctuated with benches (some with great fjord views)—perfect for a break or picnic. Most sights are signposted in English.

You'll stroll the "old road"—once the main road from the harbor—along the fjord's edge, passing numerous "villas" from the late 1800s. These were built in the popular Swiss style of the period by locals attempting to introduce a dose of Romanticism

into Norwegian architecture. Look for the dragons' heads, copied from Viking-age stave churches, decorating the gables. Along the walk, you'll see two burial mounds from the Viking age, marked by a ponderous statue of a Viking king. Check out the wooden shelters for the postboxes; some give the elevation (*m.o.h.* stands for "meters over *havn*"—the sea—not too high, are they?). If you'd prefer a guided walk, contact Bjørg Bjøberg (see "Galleries," below).

St. Olaf's Church—This distinctive stave church was built in 1897 by the wife of Knut Kvikne (of the Kvikne's Hotel family; see "Sleeping," below). This devout Englishwoman wanted a church in Balestrand where English services were held...and indeed they still are, by British clergy in summer (free, open daily, services in English every Sun).

Aquarium—The tiny aquarium gives you a good look at sea life in the Sognefjord. There are no English-language descriptions in the exhibit—but you can borrow a fine English brochure at the front desk (60 kr, mid-June–mid-Aug daily 9:00–22:00, closed off-season). Be sure to check out the tanks filled with live fish on the dock outside. You can fill your tank with seafood or land food at Café Fløfisken, the aquarium's cheery restaurant (see "Eating," below).

Galleries—Of the galleries on the harbor, Bjørg Bjøberg's is best. A local watercolorist and historian, she sells cards, prints, and calendars, as well as a 70-kr colorful brochure of the town walking tour (described above), illustrated with her watercolors and words (free, daily 11:00–17:00 & 20:00–21:00, tel. 91 56 28 42). Ask Bjørg about her walking tours of Balestrand.

Near Balestrand: Glacier Excursions

FJORD WIDTH
EXAGGERATED FOR CLARITY

HELLESYLT

GEIRANGER
FJORD

GEIRANGER

STRYN

15

TO LOM

GLACIER

BØVERDAL

OLDEN

NIGARDSBREEN
GLACIER

JOSTEDAL

SOGNEFJELL

TURTAGRO

FORTUN

FEIGUM FOSS

GAUPNE

FJÆR-LAND

SOLVORN

URNES

SOGNDAL

USTRA FJORD

BALE-STRAND

KAU-PANGER

MANNHELLER

FODNES

LÆRDALS-ØYRI

SOGN·EFJORD

ERDAL   BORGUND

GUD-VANGEN

AURLAND

FLÅM

TO VOSS
& BERGEN

"NUT SHELL"
ROUTE

TO MYRDAL
& OSLO

30 MILES

50 KM

DCH

Biking—The roads here are relatively flat, and you can cycle around town or farther by circling the Esefjord. Bike rentals are available from the TI and, for guests, at some hotels.

Near Balestrand

Glacier Excursions—You can see a glacier and the Norwegian Glacier Museum on a half-day or full-day excursion sold by the TI or on board the boat. This is the full-day version:

Depart Balestrand by boat and take a 90-minute fjord cruise along Fjærland's fjord. You'll see the Jostedal glacier in the distance, perched atop the mountains. Once you reach the town of Fjærland (a.k.a. "Mundal"), a bus meets the boat and takes you to the informative Glacier Museum, where you'll have free time.

At the **Norwegian Glacier Museum** (Norsk Bremuseum), you'll learn how glaciers were formed, experiment with your own hunk of glacier, and weigh evidence of the woolly mammoth's existence in Norway (75 kr, daily June–Aug 9:00–19:00, April–May and Sept–Oct 10:00–16:00, Nov–March on request, tel. 57 69 32 88, www.bre.museum.no).

After the museum, take a bus ride to a nearby arm of the glacier for a closer look.

Full-day excursions depart Balestrand at 8:15, allow almost two hours at the museum, visit two glaciers, and return to Balestrand at 16:55 (385 kr). Half-day excursions depart Balestrand at 12:00, allow one hour at the museum, visit only one glacier, and return at 16:55 (370 kr). Both excursions finish in time to allow you to catch the last express boat from Balestrand to Bergen.

SLEEPING

$$$ **Kvikne's Hotel,** a big, old, wooden hotel with a modern annex, is the place for a splurge. It's the classy grande dame of Balestrand,

dominating the town and packed with tour groups (Sb-745–960 kr, Db-1,030–1,460 kr, 200 kr more for rooms in the historic wooden hotel section, lower rates off-season, includes breakfast, demisuites and family rooms available; deals for stays of 3 or more nights, including half-pension with *store koldt bord* buffet dinner; tel. 57 69 42 00, fax 57 69 42 01, www.kviknes.no).

$$ **Balestrand Hotel,** well run by hardworking Unni-Marie Kvikne and her California-born husband Eric Palmer and their family, is your best fjordside home. This cozy, welcoming place has 30 well-appointed, comfortable, quiet rooms; a large, modern common area with lots of English paperbacks; balconies (in some rooms) and outdoor benches for soaking in the scenery; and Internet and laundry service available for extra. When reserving, let them know your arrival time, and they'll pick you up at the ferry (Sb-615 kr, Db-890 kr, 50–100 kr less without a view or balcony, includes breakfast, 5-min uphill walk from dock—or free pick-up, tel. 57 69 11 38, www.balestrand.com).

Sleep Code

(6.5 kr = about $1, country code: 47)
S = Single, **D** = Double/Twin, **T** = Triple, **Q** = Quad,
b = bathroom, **s** = shower. All of these places accept credit cards.

To help you sort easily through these listings, I've divided the rooms into three categories, based on the price for a standard double room with bath:

$$$ **Higher Priced**—Most rooms 1,000 kr or more.
$$ **Moderately Priced**—Most rooms between 500–1,000 kr.
$ **Lower Priced**—Most rooms 500 kr or less.

$ Kringsja School, a camp school for sixth-graders, rents beds to budget travelers mid-June to mid-Aug (bed in 4-bed dorm-190 kr, D-280 kr, includes breakfast, sheets/towels-40 kr, cash only, tel. 57 69 13 03).

EATING

Gekkens is an informal summer restaurant serving grilled meat, fish, and vegetarian dishes, along with burgers, fish and chips, and other fried fare (most meals 70–150 kr, May–Sept daily 12:00–22:00, closed Oct–April, at the harbor, next to TI, tel. 97 51 29 26).

Bistro Balholm, in the lobby of Kvikne's Hotel, is essentially a pub, but has a pleasant atmosphere and reasonable prices (lunch—sandwiches, soup, salads, and hot dishes from around 90 kr; dinner—pasta, meat, or fish dishes 180–250 kr; daily 12:00–22:00, closed off-season).

Kvikne's Hotel offers a splendid, spendy *store koldt bord* buffet dinner. Take your time. Get a new plate with each course and save room for dessert. Consider taking a preview tour before you dive in so you can budget your stomach space (375 kr per person,  May–Sept daily 17:00–22:00, closed Oct–April). After dinner, head into the grand lounges to pick up your (included) cup of coffee or tea, which you'll sip sitting on classy old-fashioned furniture and basking in fjord views.

Café Fløfisken, the informal café at the aquarium, serves sandwiches for lunch (50–80 kr) and seafood and landfood dinners (100–150 kr) at indoor or outdoor tables (mid-June–mid-Aug daily 9:00–22:00, kitchen closes 1 hour earlier, closed off-season).

Café Galleri, adjacent to Bjørg Bjøberg's art gallery at the harbor, serves sandwiches, cakes, and beverages throughout the day, and sometimes grilled meats and fish in the evening after 16:00 (indoor and outdoor seating, daily 10:00–21:00).

The Co-op and Spar **supermarkets** at the harbor have basic grocery supplies, including bread, meats, cheeses, and drinks—perfect for a picnic lunch. Co-op is bigger and has more selection (both open Mon–Fri 9:00–18:00, Sat 9:00–15:00, closed Sun). The local **bakery** sells bread, pastries, and open-face sandwiches (between Co-op and Spar, Mon–Fri 10:00–17:00, Sat 9:00–14:00, closed Sun).

TRANSPORTATION CONNECTIONS

Balestrand is connected to the rest of Norway via the **Fylkesbaatane express boat** (buy tickets on boat or at TI, discounts for students, seniors, and couples, tel. 55 90 70 70, www.fylkesbaatane.no)

From Bergen to Balestrand takes four hours (385 kr, departs Bergen May–Sept daily at 8:00, also Mon–Fri at 16:30, Sat at 14:15, some Sun at 16:30—but not mid-June–late Aug; Oct–April Sun–Fri at 16:30, Sat at 14:15). In summer, the 8:00 boat continues to **Flåm.**

From Flåm to Balestrand takes about 1.5 hours (185 kr, departs Flåm May–Sept daily at 15:30, stops at Aurland, arrives in Balestrand at 16:55; second boat sometimes runs Mon–Fri at 6:00, arrives Balestrand 7:55; no express Flåm–Balestrand boats Oct–April).

From Balestrand to Bergen takes about four hours (385 kr, departs Balestrand May–Sept daily at 16:55, sometimes also Mon–Sat at 7:55, some Sun at 11:20—but not mid-June–late Aug; Oct–April Mon–Sat at 7:55, Sun at 16:55).

From **Oslo,** you can take an early train to Flåm (no later than the 8:11 train, as part of the Norway in a Nutshell route—see previous chapter), then catch the 15:30 express boat to Balestrand. After your visit, you can continue on the express boat to Bergen, or return to the Nutshell route by taking the express boat to Midtfjord, and transferring to the next boat to Gudvangen.

For more on connecting Flåm and Bergen with this express boat (via Balestrand), see "Sognefjord Scenic Express Boat," page 161 of previous chapter.

Lustrafjord

This arm of the famous Sognefjord is rugged country. Only 2 percent of this land is fit to build or farm on. Lustrafjord is ringed with tiny villages where farmers sell cherries and giant raspberries. Drivers can pick and choose among the sights below.

SIGHTS

The towns and sights are listed from north to south.

Skjolden—This village, at the north tip of Lustrafjord, has a good **TI** (tel. 57 68 67 50) with advice on fjord ferries and glacier hikes, and a cozy youth hostel on the river (100 kr per bed, D-250 kr, non-members pay 50 kr extra, open mid-May–mid-Sept, tel. 57 68 66 15).

Nes and Waterfall View—From the little town of Nes on the west bank of the Lustrafjord, look across the fjord at the impressive Feigumfoss waterfall. Drops and dribbles come from miles around for this 650-foot tumble. **Viki Fjord Camping,** located directly across from Feigumfoss Waterfall, has great fjordside huts (tel. 57 68 64 20).

Dale—This village on the west bank boasts a 13th-century stone Gothic church with 14th-century frescoes; it's unique and worth a peek.

▲▲**Urnes' Stave Church**—The town of Urnes, perched on the east bank of Lustrafjord, has Norway's oldest stave church (1150), the most important artistic and historic sight in the region (40 kr, daily early June–Aug 10:30–17:30, call for an English tour, steep but pleasant 20-min walk from town, tel. 57 68 39 45).

Ferries running between Solvorn and Urnes depart Solvorn at the top of most hours and Urnes at the bottom of most hours (40-kr round-trip passenger fare, 15-min ride).

Solvorn—On the west bank of the Lustrafjord, 10 miles east of Sogndal, Solvorn is a sleepy little Victorian town. Its tiny fjerry crosses the fjord regularly to Urnes and its famous little stave church (see above).

Sleeping in Solvorn: $$$ Walaker Hotel, a former inn and coach station, has been run by the Walaker family since 1690 (that's a lot of pressure on the ninth generation). In the main house, tradition drips like butter through the halls and living rooms. A warm family feeling pervades the building and there are only patriotic hymns on the piano. Most of the rooms are simple but good, and four rooms are fancy, done in 18th-century style. The Walaker, set right on the Lustrafjord (in the perfect garden to relax and recover from stress), is open May through September. Oda and Hermod Walaker and their son, Ole Henrik, are a wealth of information, and they serve fine food (Sb-750–980 kr, Db-1,280–1,800 kr, higher prices are for rooms with a fjord view; includes breakfast, 3-course dinners-375 kr; tel. 57 68 20 80, fax 57 68 20 81, www.walaker.com, hotel@walaker.com). The cheery Linahagen Café, next door, has Internet access and a fun window full of live fish.

Sogndal—About 10 minutes (by car) from the Mannheller–Fodnes ferry, Sogndal is the only sizable town in this region. It's big enough to have a busy shopping street and a helpful **TI** (tel. 57 67 30 83).

   Sleeping in Sogndal: $$ Loftenes Pensjonat houses travelers June through August, and mostly students—but a few travelers—during the school year (S-400 kr, Sb-450 kr, D-650 kr, Db-700 kr, includes breakfast, cash only, near the water, tel. & fax 57 67 15 77).

   $ Sogndal has a fine **youth hostel** (beds in 3- and 4-bed rooms-100 kr, S-175 kr, D-250–400 kr, more for non-members, sheets extra, breakfast-50 kr, cash only, members' kitchen—bring your own pots, open mid-June–mid-Aug, closed 10:00–17:00, at fork in the road as you enter town, tel. 57 62 75 75).

SCENIC DRIVES FROM LUSTRAFJORD

Note that car ferries cost roughly $5 per hour for walk-ons and $15 per hour for a car, driver, and passenger. Reservations are generally not necessary (and sometimes not possible), but in summer—especially on Friday and Sunday—I'd get one to be safe (free and easy, tel. 55 90 70 60).

▲▲**From Sogndal to Aurland**—This drive to Aurland (via Mannheller, Fodnes, Lærdal, and Hornadalen—see map on page 173) takes you over an incredible mountain pass, offers classic aerial fjord views, and winds into the pleasant fjordside town of Aurland (accommodations listed in previous chapter).

   Near Sogndal, catch the Mannheller–Fodnes ferry (2/hr at :00 and :30 past the hour, 15 min, no reservations possible) and drive through the tunnel to Lærdal. Though the 15-mile-long tunnel (world's longest—paid for by North Sea oil) from Lærdal under Hornadalen to Aurland, the scenic route over the pass is worth the messy pants.

   From the ferry, take the first road to the right (to Erdal). Leave E-68 at Erdal (just west of Lærdal) for the breathtaking 60-minute, 30-mile drive to Aurland over 4,000-foot-high Hornadalen. This road, open only in summer, passes remote mountain huts and terrifying mountain views before its 12-hairpin zigzag descent into the Aurlandsfjord.

   Stop at the first fjord viewpoint (look for the *Utsiktspunkt* sign) as you begin your descent; it's the best. (Climb the rock just 30 feet above the road and it's better yet.)

▲**From Kaupanger to Bergen**—Car ferries take tourists between Kaupanger (on the southern end of Lustrafjord) and Gudvangen (on the Norway in a Nutshell route) through an arm and elbow of the Sognefjord, including the staggering Nærøyfjord. While this ferry ride is great and saves substantial time, this shortcut over the full

Fjords North of Nutshell Route

Aurland/Flåm–Gudvangen cruise does cost you some of the scenery. Boats leave Kaupanger daily at 9:20, 12:05, 16:05, and 18:50 for the two-hour trip (175 kr per adult passenger, car and driver-420 kr, reserve 1 day in advance, tel. 55 90 70 60). While Kaupanger is little more than a ferry landing set on the scenic Sognefjord, the small stave-type church at the edge of town merits a look.

From Gudvangen, it's a 90-mile drive to Bergen. Get off the ferry in Gudvangen and drive up the Nærøydalen (Narrow Valley) past a river bubbling excitedly about the plunge it just took. You'll see the two giant falls just before the road marked *Stalheimskleiva*. Follow the sign (exiting left) to the little Stalheimskleiva road. This incredible road doggedly worms its way up into the ozone. My car overheated in a few minutes. Take it easy. (The main road gets you there more easily—through a tunnel and 0.8 miles back up a smaller road.) As you wind up, you can view the falls from several turnouts. At the top, stop for a break at the touristy Stalheim Hotel. Though this hotel dates from 1885, there's been an inn here since about 1700, when the royal mailmen would change horses here. The hotel is geared for tour groups (genuine trolls sew the pewter buttons on the sweaters), but the priceless view from the backyard is free.

The road continues into a mellower beauty, past lakes and farms, toward Voss. Tvindefossen, a waterfall with a handy camp-ground/WC/kiosk picnic area right under it, is worth a stop. Unless you judge waterfalls by megatonnage, the 500-foot-long fall has nuclear charms. The grassy meadow and flat rocks at its base were made especially for your picnic lunch.

The highway takes you through Voss and into Bergen. From Monday through Friday (6:00–22:00), drivers pay a 15-kr toll to enter Bergen. (If you plan to visit Edvard Grieg's home and the nearby Fantoft stave church, now is the ideal time, since you'll be driving right by. Both are overrated but almost obligatory, a headache from downtown, and open until 17:30.)

GUDBRANDSDAL VALLEY and JOTUNHEIMEN MOUNTAINS

Norway in a Nutshell is a great day trip, but with more time and a car, consider meandering from Oslo to Bergen along a powerfully scenic arc up the Gudbrandsdal Valley and over the Jotunheimen Mountains, then along the Lustrafjord (see previous chapter).

After an introductory stop in Lillehammer, with its fine folk museum, you might spend the night in a log-and-sod farmstead-turned-hotel, tucked in a quiet valley under Norway's highest peaks. Next, Norway's highest pass takes you on an exhilarating roller-coaster ride through the heart of the myth-inspiring Jotunheimen ("Giants' Home"), bristling with Norway's biggest mountains. The road then hairpins down into fjord country (see previous chapter).

Planning Your Time

While you could spend five or six days in this area on a three-week Scandinavian rampage, this slice of the region is worth three days. By car, I'd spend them like this:

Day 1: Leave Oslo early, and spend midday at the Maihaugen Open-Air Folk Museum for a tour and picnic. Drive up Gudbrandsdal Valley, stopping at the Lom church. Stay overnight in Jotunheimen.

Day 2: Drive out of the mountains, along Lustrafjord (see previous chapter), over Hornadalen Pass, and into Aurlandsfjord. Sleep in Aurland.

Day 3: Cruise the Aurland and Nærøy fjords (round-trip or have the poor driver meet the rest at Gudvangen) before carrying on to Bergen.

Days two and three can be collapsed into one day if rushed. (For specifics on Aurland accommodations and the fjord cruise, see the Norway in a Nutshell chapter.)

Gudbrandsdal Valley and
Jotunheimen Mountains

① Spiterstulen Lodge
② Juvasshytta Lodge
③ Leirvassbu Lodge
④ Røisheim Hotel
⑤ Elvesæter Hotel
⑥ Youth Hostel
⑦ Strind Gård

Gudbrandsdal Valley

The Gudbrandsdal Valley is the tradition-steeped country of Peer Gynt, the Norwegian Huck Finn. This romantic valley of timeworn hills, log cabins, and velvet farms has connected northern and southern Norway since ancient times. Throughout this region, the government subsidizes small farms to keep the countryside populated and healthy. (These subsidies would not be permitted if Norway were a member of the European Union.)

Lillehammer

Lillehammer, a pleasant winter and summer resort town of 25,000, was the smallest town ever to host the Winter Olympics (1994).

Lillehammer has a happy, old, woody pedestrian zone and several interesting museums, including the Maihaugen Open-Air Folk Museum. The TI is right in the colorful pedestrian shopping zone (mid-June–mid-Aug Mon–Sat 9:00–19:00, less on Sundays and off-season, tel. 61 28 98 00). For accommodations, see "Sleeping," below.

SIGHTS

In Lillehammer

Norwegian Olympics Museum (Norges Olympiske Museum)—
The museum, housed in the Olympic ice-hockey arena, gives you the highlights of the town's 1994 glory days. Try the bobsled simulator at the ski jump (60 kr, mid-May–Aug daily 10:00–18:00; Sept–mid-May Tue–Sun 11:00–16:00, closed Mon; Håkon Hall, 15-min walk from train station toward Maihaugen, tel. 61 25 21 00, www.ol.museum.no).

▲▲Maihaugen Open-Air Folk Museum (Friluftsmuseet)—This
idyllic park, full of old farmhouses and pickled slices of folk culture, provides a good introduction to the Gudbrandsdal Valley. Anders Sandvig, a "visionary dentist," started the collection in 1887. The outdoor section has 180 old buildings from the Gudbrandsdal region and a town re-created from the 1920s. While July is busy with crafts in action and people living here from ages ago (à la Williamsburg), other months are pretty dead, with no live crafts and most of the buildings locked up.

The museum's three indoor exhibits (near the turnstile) are excellent. The "We Won the Land" exhibit sweeps you through Norwegian history from the Ice Age to the Space Age. The Gudbrandsdal art section shows village art at its best. And you can walk through Dr. Sandvig's old dental office and the original shops of 40 crafts- and tradespeople such as a hatter, cooper (barrel maker), and bookbinder.

Since English descriptions are scant, you'll need the 50-kr English guidebook or a guided tour to learn much. Free 45-minute guided tours in English go daily (call for times—especially off-season, tel. 61 28 89 00; museum entry-90 kr; mid-May–mid-Sept daily 10:00–17:00; spring and fall Mon–Sat 10:00–16:00, closed Sun; in winter, the park is open but the houses are closed; www.maihaugen.no). Upon arrival, ask about tours, special events, crafts, or music. Maihaugen is a steep 15-minute walk or short bus ride (1/hr) from the Lillehammer train station. While the museum welcomes picnickers and has a simple cafeteria, the town itself (a 10-min walk below the museum), with lots of fun eateries, is better for lunch.

In the Gudbrandsdal Valley

▲**Eidsvoll Manor**—During the Napoleonic period, control of Norway went from Denmark to Sweden. This ruffled the patriotic feathers of Norway's Thomas Jeffersons and Ben Franklins, and on May 17, 1814, Norway's constitution was written and signed in this stately mansion (in the town of Eidsvoll Verk, north of Oslo). While Sweden still ruled, Norway had more autonomy than ever. The mansion is full of elegant furnishings and stirring history (50 kr, May–Aug daily 10:00–17:00, less off-season, tel. 63 95 13 04).

Scenic Drives—Two side-trips give visitors a good dose of the wild beauty of this land. Peer Gynt Veien (a 30-kr toll road) leaves E-6 at Tretten, loops west for 25 miles, and rejoins E-6 at Vinstra. This trip sounds romantic, but it's basically a windy, curvy dirt road over a high, desolate heath and scrub-brush plateau with fine mountain views: it's scenic, but so is E-6. The second scenic side-trip, Peer Gynt Seterveien, is not much better.

SLEEPING

Lillehammer

$$ **Gjestehuset Ersgaard,** with 30 rooms in a peacefully rural setting a mile east of and above Lillehammer, offers those with a car a fine value with a view of the valley (S-390 kr, Sb-490 kr, D-590 kr, Db-690 kr, Db with a view-790 kr, includes breakfast, Nordseterveien 201, tel. 61 25 06 84, fax 61 25 31 09, www.ersgaard.no, oeilande@online.no).

$ **Mary and Inge's Bed and Breakfast** is run from the desk of a modern building constructed to house athletes for the 1994 Olympics (Sb-350 kr, Db-460 kr, Tb-645 kr, Qb-810 kr, includes breakfast, cash only, 3rd floor at Jernbanetorget 2, tel. 61 26 25 66, fax 61 26 25 77, lillehammervandrerhjem@c2i.net).

$ The **GjesteBu** private hostel is another option for cheap beds (bed in 8-bed dorm-100 kr, S-225 kr, D-350 kr and up, apartment with kitchen and bath for 1–2 people-650 kr, 3-bedroom apartment for up to 5 people-1,300 kr, sheets-50 kr, no breakfast, cash only, 3 blocks from TI, Gamleveien 110, tel. & fax 61 25 43 21, ss-bu @online.no).

Kvam, in the Gudbrandsdal Valley

This is a popular vacation valley for Norwegians, and you'll find loads of reasonable small hotels and campgrounds with huts for those who aren't quite campers (*hytter* means "bungalows," *rom* is "private room," and *ledig* means "vacancy"). These huts normally cost about 300 kr and can hold from four to six people. Although they are simple, you'll have a kitchenette and access to a good WC and shower. When available, sheets rent for an extra 60 kr per person. Local TIs can find you rooms. Reservations are generally only

Sleep Code

(6.5 kr = about \$1, country code: 47)
S = Single, **D** = Double/Twin, **T** = Triple, **Q** = Quad,
b = bathroom, **s** = shower. You can assume credit cards are
accepted unless otherwise noted.

To help you sort easily through these listings, I've divided
the rooms into three categories, based on the price for a standard
double room with bath:

\$\$\$ **Higher Priced**—Most rooms 1,000 kr or more.
\$\$ **Moderately Priced**—Most rooms between 500–1,000 kr.
\$ **Lower Priced**—Most rooms 500 kr or less.

necessary in July. Here are a couple listings in the town of Kvam,
located midway between Lillehammer and Lom.

\$\$ Sinclair Vertshuset Motel has an inexpensive cafeteria and
pub but no personality (Sb-590 kr, Db-790 kr, includes breakfast,
tel. 61 29 54 50, fax 61 29 54 51, www.vertshuset-sinclair.no, post
@vertshuset-sinclair.no). The motel was named after a Scotsman
who led a band of adventurers into this valley, attempting to set up
their own Scottish kingdom. They failed. All were kilt.

\$ Kirketeigen Ungdomssenter ("Church Youth Center"), 100
yards away from the Sinclair Vertshuset, welcomes travelers year-
round with camping spots (135 kr per tent or van), cabins with
kitchen and bath (570 kr, up to 6 people), and simple four-bed
rooms (300 kr for 2–4 people with sheets, sheets and blankets rent
for 65 kr, Visa is the only credit card accepted, behind town church,
tel. 61 21 60 90, www.kirketeigen.no).

Jotunheimen Mountains

You can play roller coaster with mountain passes, take rugged
hikes, wind up scenic toll roads, and get up close—nice and icy—to
a huge glacier. The gateway to the mountains is the unassuming
town of Lom.

Lom

While Lom isn't much of a town, its great stave church causes the
closest thing to a tour-bus traffic jam this neck of the Norwegian
woods will ever see. Park by the church; you'll see its dark spire
just over the bridge.

Tourist Information: The TI is across the street from the church (mid-July–mid-Aug Mon–Fri 9:00–21:00, Sat–Sun 10:00–20:00, shorter hours off-season, tel. 61 21 29 90, www.visitlom.com).

SIGHTS AND ACTIVITIES

In Lom

▲▲**Lom Stave Church**—In spite of its more modern renovations, Lom's church (from 1170) is a textbook example of a stave church. These churches are the finest architecture to come out of medieval Norway. Wood was plentiful and cheap, and locals had an expertise with woodworking (from all that boat-building). In 1300, there were 800 stave churches in Norway. After a 14th-century plague, Norway's population dropped and many churches fell into disuse.

By the 19th century, with only 30 stave churches surviving, they became recognized as part of the national heritage, and were protected. A distinguishing feature of the "stave" design is its vertical planks (as opposed to the "laft" horizontal structure of typical log cabins). The sill along the bottom and a thick coat of tar kept the planks from decaying over the centuries. Stave churches were dark, with almost no windows. Even after the Vikings stopped raiding, they ornamented their churches with warlike, evil spirit-fighting dragons reminiscent of their ships.

This church has been extensively remodeled. Inside, look high for the parts from 1170, such as the circle of X-shaped St. Andrew crosses and the Norman arches above them. The apse (behind the altar) is from 1240. Lepers came to the grilled window in the apse for a blessing. When the Reformation hit in 1536, the old paintings were whitewashed over. The transepts, pews, and windows were added in the 17th century. Men sat on the right, women on the left, and prisoners with the sheriff in the caged area in the rear (30 kr, daily mid-June–mid-Aug 9:00–21:00, spring and fall 10:00–16:00, closed winter and during funerals, fine 5-kr leaflet, check out little footbridge over waterfall and peek at the only surviving stave church dragon-head "steeple" in the museum adjacent to the shop in the church parking lot). Small groups can arrange for a tour, even after regular hours, by calling 97 07 53 97.

In the Jotunheimen Mountains

▲▲**Sognefjell**—Norway's highest mountain-crossing (4,600 feet) is a thrilling drive through a cancan line of Northern Europe's tallest

mountains. The highest is Galdhopiggen. In previous centuries, the farmers of Gudbrandsdal took their horse caravans over this difficult mountain pass on their necessary treks to Bergen. Today the road (Route 55) is still narrow, windy, and otherworldly (and usually closed mid-Oct–May). The 10 hairpin turns between Turtagrø and Fortun are white-knuckle exciting. Be sure to stop, get out, look around, and enjoy the lavish views. Treat each turn as if it were your last.

Scenic Drives and Hikes—From the main road near Bøverdal and Røisheim, you have several options springing from three toll roads. The Lom TI has a mountain museum and plenty of maps and good information on hikes in the region.

Spiterstulen: From Røisheim, this 11-mile toll road (60 kr) takes you to the Spiterstulen mountain hotel/lodge (3,600 feet). This is the best destination for serious all-day hikes to Norway's two mightiest mountains, Glittertinden (8,100 feet) and Galdhopiggen (a 4-hr hike up and a 3-hr hike down, doable without a guide).

Juvasshytta: This toll road, starting from Bøverdal, takes you the highest you can drive and the closest you can get to Galdhopiggen by car (6,050 feet). At the end of the 70-kr toll road, there are daily guided six-hour hikes across the glacier to the summit and back (90 kr, 10:00 and 11:30 in the summer, 4 miles each way, hiking shoes a good idea, easiest ascent but very dangerous without a guide). You can sleep in the Juvasshytta lodge (Db-580 kr, D without sheets-400 kr, 175-kr beds in quads, sheets-35 kr, breakfast-80 kr, dinner-175 kr, tel. 61 21 15 50, www.juvasshytta.no).

Leirvassbu: This 11-mile, 30-kr toll road is most scenic for car hikers. It takes you to a lodge (owned by the Elvesæter Hotel people—see page 183) at 4,600 feet with great views and easy walks. A serious (4-hr round-trip) hike goes to the lone peak, Kyrkja (6,660 feet).

Besseggen: This ridge offers an incredible opportunity to hike between two lakes separated by less than five feet of land and a 1,000-foot cliff. To get to the trailhead, drivers detour down road #51 after Otta south to Maurvangen. Turn right to Gjendesheim to park your car. From Gjendesheim, catch the boat to Memurubu. The path starts at the boat dock. Hike along the ridge with a blue lake on one side and a green lake on the other, and keep your balance. The six-hour trail leads back to Gjendesheim. (This is a thrilling but potentially hazardous hike, and it's a major detour: Gjendesheim is about an hour, or 55 miles, from Røisheim.)

▲**Jostedal's Nigardsbreen Glacier Hike**—Jostedal is the most accessible branch of mainland Europe's largest glacier (185 square miles), and the Nigardsbreen Glacier hike offers a good opportunity for a hands-on glacier experience. It's an easy drive up Jostedal from Lustrafjord.

From Gaupne, road #604 dead-ends after 23 miles at a glacier museum. From there, a 20-kr toll road continues two miles to a lake facing the actual tongue of the glacier.

Breheimsenteret, the glacier information center, stands at the entrance to the Nigardsbreen Glacier valley (before the toll road, 1.5 miles past Gjerde). The center boldly charges 50 kr for a relaxing 20-minute slide presentation showing ice climbing and glacier scenery with no words and a small gallery of glacier-related exhibits (daily in summer 9:00–19:00, May–mid-June and mid-Aug–Sept 10:00–17:00, free Internet access, shop, cafeteria, tel. 57 68 32 50).

From the end of the toll road, you can hike or take a special boat (20 kr round-trip, 2/hr, 15 min, mid-June–mid-Sept 10:00–18:00) to a spot just 20 minutes from the glacier. The walk is steep and slippery. Follow the red marks. There are 90-minute guided family-friendly walks of the glacier (100 kr, 50 kr for kids, daily departures 12:00–14:30 depending on demand, minimum age 5, I'd rate them PG-13 myself, you get clamp-on crampons). Tougher glacier hikes are also offered (starting at 210 kr, includes boots and real crampons, daily 10:30 and 13:00, 4 hrs), but you'll need to be at the glacier center nearly two hours early to buy tickets and pick up your gear (book by phone the day before, tel. 57 68 32 50). For information on the glacier, go to www.jostedal.com.

Respect the glacier. It's a powerful river of ice, and fatal accidents are not uncommon. The guided walk is the safest option and plenty exciting. Use the Gaupne TI to confirm your plans (tel. 57 68 15 88). If this is your first glacier, it's worth the time and hike even without the tour. If glaciers don't give you tingles and you're feeling pressed, it's not worth the time.

Sleeping near the Glacier: $$ **Jostedal Hotel** rents 19 cozy rooms—with hardwood floors and fluffy comforters—split between two buildings on a farm, three miles from the Nigardsbreen Visitors Center (Sb-600 kr, Db-750 kr, attached restaurant with outdoor terrace, tel. 57 68 31 19, fax 57 68 31 57, www.jostedalhotel.no, post@jostedalhotel.no, Laila Gjerde).

SLEEPING

(6.5 kr = about $1, country code: 47)
Near Lom
The first three listings are a 15-minute drive up the road from Lom. Røisheim and Elvesæter are hotel road stops in the wild. The youth hostel is in the tiny village of Bøverdal.

$$$ **Røisheim,** in a marvelously remote mountain setting, is a storybook hotel composed of a cluster of centuries-old, sod-roofed

log farmhouses. It's filled with antiques, Norwegian travelers, and the hard work of its owners, Ingrid and Haavard Lunde. Røisheim is a cultural end in itself. Each room is rustic but elegant (Sb-2,100–3,300 kr, Db-2,500–3,300 kr depending on size—most expensive rooms include a fireplace; includes breakfast, packed lunch, and an over-the-top 3-course traditional dinner served at 19:30). Some rooms are in old log huts with low ceilings and heavy beams. Call ahead so they'll be prepared (open mid-May–Sept, 10 miles south of Lom on Sognefjell Road 55 in the Bøver Valley, tel. 61 21 20 31, fax 61 21 21 51, r-drif-a@online.no).

$$ **Elvesæter Hotel** is as Old World romantic as Røisheim, but bigger, cheaper, and less impressed with itself (Sb-650 kr, Db-850 kr, Tb-930 kr, Qb-990 kr, includes breakfast, wonderful 225-kr buffet dinners, strictly non-smoking, swimming pool, open June–mid-Sept, a few minutes farther up Road 55, just past Bøverdalen, tel. 61 21 20 00, fax 61 21 21 01, www.elveseter.no, post @elveseter.no). They also offer apartments with kitchens and all bedding (3–6 people, 740–990 kr without breakfast). The Elvesæter family has done a great job of retaining the historic character of their medieval farm, even though the place is big enough to handle large tour groups. Even if you're not staying here, stop to wander through the public spaces and pick up a flier explaining the towering Sagasøyla column celebrating Norwegian independence. It was built to stand in front of Oslo's parliament building but, because of changing political winds after World War II, was eventually erected here in 1992.

$ **Bøverdalen Youth Hostel** offers cheap but comfortable beds and a far more rugged clientele—real hikers rather than car hikers (105 kr per bed in 4- to 6-bed rooms, D-255 kr, 4-person cabins-460 kr with shower and toilet, 360 kr without, 25 kr extra for non-members, sheets-60 kr, breakfast-60 kr, hot and self-serve meals, closed Oct–late May, in Bøverdal, tel. & fax 61 21 20 64, www.vandrehjem.no, boeverdalen.hostel@vandrerhjem.no). It's in the center of a little community (store, campground, and toll road up to Galdhopiggen area).

$ **Strind Gård,** a rustic 150-year-old farmhouse and a last resort, rents dingy rooms in sod-roofed huts and in the main house (hut D-180 kr, house D-250 kr, apartment for 4–6 with private bath-600 kr, sheets-50 kr, no breakfast, valley views, 2 miles outside Lom on Route 55 toward Sogndal, tel. 61 21 12 37, www.strind-gard.no).

TRANSPORTATION CONNECTIONS

Cars are better, but if you're without wheels: **Oslo to Lillehammer** (13 trains/day, 2.5 hrs), **Lillehammer to Otta** (6 trains/day, 1.5 hrs); a bus meets some trains (confirm schedule at the train station in Oslo) for travelers heading on to **Lom** (2 buses/day, 1 hr) and from **Lom to Sogndal** (2 buses/day, 4 hrs).

Route Tips for Drivers

Use low gears and lots of patience both up (to keep it cool) and down (to save your brakes). Uphill traffic gets the right-of-way, but drivers, up or down, dive for the nearest fat part whenever they meet. Ask backseat drivers not to scream until you've actually been hit or have left the road.

From Oslo to Jotunheimen: It's 2.5 hours from Oslo to Lillehammer and three hours after that to Lom. Wind out of Oslo following signs for E-6 (not to Drammen, but for Stockholm and then to Trondheim). In a few minutes, you're in the wide-open pastoral countryside of eastern Norway. Norway's Constitution Hall is a five-minute detour off E-6, several miles south of Eidsvoll in Eidsvoll Verk (follow the signs to Eidsvoll Bygningen). Then E-6 takes you along Norway's largest lake (Mjøsa), through the town of Hamar, and past more lake scenery into Lillehammer. Signs direct you uphill from downtown Lillehammer to the Maihaugen Open-Air Folk Museum. There's free parking near the pay lot above the entrance. From Lillehammer, signs to E-6/Trondheim take you up the valley of Gudbrandsdal. At Otta, exit for Lom.

BERGEN

Bergen is permanently salted with robust cobbles and a rich sea-trading heritage. Norway's capital in the 12th and 13th centuries, Bergen's wealth and importance came thanks to its membership in the heavyweight medieval trading club of merchant cities called the Hanseatic  League. Bergen still wears her rich maritime heritage proudly.

Famous for lousy weather, Bergen gets an average of 80 inches of rain annually (compared to 30 inches in Oslo). A good year has 60 days of sunshine. With 230,000 people, Bergen has its big-city tension, parking problems, and high prices. But visitors sticking to the old center find it charming.

Enjoy her salty market, then stroll the easy-on-foot old quarter. From downtown Bergen, a funicular zips you up a little mountain for a bird's-eye view of this sailors' town.

Planning Your Time
Bergen can be enjoyed even on the tail end of a day's scenic train ride from Oslo before returning on the overnight train. But that teasing taste will make you wish you had more time. On a three-week tour of Scandinavia, Bergen is worth a whole day. Start that day at the harborfront fish market and spend the rest of the morning in the Bryggen quarter (the 11:00 tour is a must).

Bergen, a geographic dead-end for most travelers, is an efficient place to begin or end your Scandinavian tour. Consider flying "open jaw," departing from or arriving in Bergen.

ORIENTATION

The action is on the waterfront. Nearly everything listed in this chapter is within a few minutes' walk of the fish market (Fisketorvet). The busy Torget (market square and fish market) is at the head of the bay. Facing the sea from here, Bergen's TI is behind you on your left. Its historic Hanseatic quarter (Bryggen) lines the harbor on the right. Hydrofoils from Flåm and Stavanger dock at the harbor on the left. Two blocks from the market square (behind Bryggen), a funicular stands ready to whisk you to the top of Mount Fløyen.

Tourist Information

The TI, filling the historic old Bergen Exchange building, is frescoed with old murals showing local and traditional life. It covers Bergen and western Norway, has information and tickets for tours and concerts, and maintains a daily events board (June–Aug daily 8:30–22:00; May and Sept daily 9:00–20:00; Oct–April Mon–Sat 9:00–16:00, closed Sun; on the harborfront, across from fish market at Vågsallmenningen 1, a 10-min walk from train station, tel. 55 55 20 00, fax 55 55 20 01, www.visitbergen.com). The free *Bergen Guide* lists all sights, hours, and special events and has a fine map. For a 30-kr booking fee, they can help you find a hotel room. The TI changes money. Although its rate is 5 percent worse than the banks, it doesn't charge the usual 15-kr per-check fee for traveler's checks or cash (so it's OK if you're changing less than $100 or stuck with small checks).

Bergen Card: The Bergen Card gives you free use of the city buses and the Mount Fløyen funicular, free admission to most museums, and discounts on some tours, events, and sights—including a 60 percent discount on Troldhaugen/Edvard Grieg's Home (170 kr/24 hrs, 250 kr/48 hrs, sold at TI, train station, and most hotels). While the card doesn't cover the Hanseatic Museum in summer (June–Aug), it may save you money if you'll be using the bus a lot. To stay in a fine hotel *and* get a Bergen Card, consider buying the Bergen Package, which includes accommodations and a Bergen Card (sold at TI; for details, see "Sleeping," page 193).

Arrival in Bergen

By Train or Bus: Bergen's train and bus stations are on Strømgaten, facing a park-rimmed lake. The train station has an office with long hours for booking all your travel in Norway (Mon–Fri 6:45–23:00, Sat 7:30–17:15, Sun 7:30–23:00). There are 24-hour luggage lockers, pay toilets, a Narvesen kiosk, a Bon Appetit sandwich shop, and a coffee shop. (To get to the bus station, follow the covered walkway behind the Narvesen via the Storcenter shopping mall.) Taxis are waiting beyond the exit on your right, behind the luggage lockers.

From the train station, it's a 10-minute walk to the TI: Walk around the lake to the square called Ole Bulls Plass; from here, the wide street called Torgalmenningen leads down to Torget, where you'll find Bergen's famous and fragrant fish market, the waterfront, and the TI. Alternatively, for a longer (15 min), more scenic approach to town from the train station, cross the street (Strømgaten) in front of the station and take Marken, a cobbled street, down to the TI and fish market.

By Plane: The airport bus runs between Bergen's Flesland Airport and downtown Bergen, stopping at the SAS hotel in Bryggen, Hotel Norge, and the bus station at platform 17 (65 kr, 4/hr, 40 min, tel. 177). Taxis take up to four people and cost about 250 kr for the 30-minute ride. SAS info: tel. 81 52 04 00.

Helpful Hints
Laundry: Jarlens Vaskoteque is at Lille Øvregate 17, near Korskirken (2-hr drop-off service for 100 kr, self-service for less, Mon–Fri 10:00–18:00, Wed–Thu until 20:00, Sat 10:00–15:00, closed Sun, tel. 55 32 55 04).

Getting Around Bergen
By Foot and Bus: Most sights can be seen on foot. Buses cost 24 kr per ride or 100 kr for a 48-hour Tourist Ticket (buy from driver). The best buses for a city joyride are #20 and #21 (along the coast) and #11 (into the hills).

By Ferry: The *Beffen,* a little orange ferry, chugs across the harbor every half hour (13 kr, Mon–Fri 7:10–16:15, no weekend runs). This three-minute "poor man's cruise" has great harbor views. The Vågen ferry departs from in front of the fish market for the aquarium (30 kr one-way, 2–3/hr daily May–Aug 10:00–18:00, doesn't run Sept–April).

By Taxi: For a taxi, call 55 99 70 10.

TOURS

▲▲▲**Bryggen Walking Tour**—This is one of Bergen's best activities (80 kr, June–Aug daily at 11:00 and 13:00, 90 min; see page 189).

Attractions Bus—The public bus company, Gaia, runs this hop-on, hop-off bus from mid-June to mid-August. For 75 kr, you can get to various sights and museums, including the Fantoft Stave Church, Troldhaugen, and the aquarium. Buses depart from near the TI at 9:30, 10:30, 11:30, 12:30, 14:00, 15:00, and 16:00 (www.gaiatrafikk.no).

Bus Tours—The TI sells tickets to bus tours (3-hr, 250-kr coach tours depart daily at 10:00 and 14:00 and include Troldhaugen and the Fantoft stave church or Gamle Bergen). There are also full-day tour options from Bergen, including bus/boat tours to nearby Hardanger and Sogne fjords. The TI is packed with brochures describing all the excursions.

Bergen

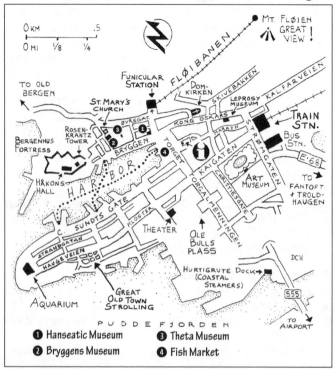

O KM .5
O MI 1/8 1/4

MT. FLØIEN
GREAT!
VIEW!

TO OLD BERGEN

FUNICULAR STATION

FLØIBANEN

DOM-KIRKEN

SKIVEBAKKEN

LEPROSY MUSEUM

KALFARVEIEN

ST. MARY'S CHURCH

ØVRÆGAT.

KONG OSKARS

TRAIN STN.

ROSEN-KRANTZ TOWER

❸
❶
❷

MARKEN

STRØMGATEN

BUS STN.

BERGENHUS FORTRESS

BRYGGEN

TORGET

❹

KAIGATEN

E-68

TO FANTOFT & TROLD-HAUGEN

HÅKONS HALL

HARBOR

ART MUSEUM

CHRISTIESGATE

SUNDTS GATE

KLOSTER

THEATER

TORGALMENNINGEN

OLE BULLS PLASS

DCH

STRANDGATEN

HAUGEVEIEN

HURTIGRUTE DOCK (COASTAL STEAMERS)

555

TO AIRPORT

AQUARIUM

GREAT OLD TOWN STROLLING

P U D D E F J O R D E N

❶ Hanseatic Museum   ❸ Theta Museum
❷ Bryggens Museum   ❹ Fish Market

Harbor Tours—The *White Lady* leaves from the fish market daily at 14:30 for a 60-minute cruise (100 kr) and at 10:00 and 15:30 for four-hour cruises (300 kr, tel. 55 25 90 00).

Tourist Train—This tacky little Bergens-Expressen train departs from in front of the Hanseatic Museum (90 kr, late June–late Aug 10:00–19:00, 2/hr on the half hour, 55 min, with English-language headphone narration).

Local Guides—To hire a local guide, call tel. 55 30 10 60.

SIGHTS AND ACTIVITIES

Bergen's Hanseatic Quarter (Bryggen)

Bergen's old German trading center was called "the German wharf" until World War II, and is now just called "the wharf," or "Bryggen" (BREW-gun). From 1370 to 1754, German merchants controlled Bergen's trade. In 1550, it was a German city of 2,000 workaholic merchants—walled and surrounded by 8,000 Norwegians. Bryggen, which has burned down several times, is now touristy and boutiquey, but still lots of fun. Explore. You'll find plenty of sweater shops, restaurants, planky alleys, leaning old wooden warehouses, atmospheric eating, and two worthwhile museums within a five-minute walk of each other.

▲▲▲**Bryggen Walking Tour**—Local guides take visitors on an excellent 90-minute walk through 900 years of Bergen history via the old Hanseatic town (30 min in Bryggens Museum, 30-min walk through old quarter, and 30 min in Hanseatic Museum). Tours cost 80 kr (10 percent discount with Bergen Card) and leave from the Bryggens Museum (next to the big, modern SAS Hotel). When you consider that the tour price includes entry tickets to the Hanseatic and Bryggens museums and the Hanseatic Assembly Rooms (called Schøtstuene, worthwhile only with a guide), the tour is virtually free (daily at 11:00 and 13:00 June–Aug, re-enter museums with tour ticket for the rest of the day, tel. 55 58 80 10).

▲▲**Hanseatic Museum (Hanseatiske Museum)**—This wonderful little museum is in an atmospheric old merchant house furnished with

dried fish, old ropes, an old oxtail (used for wringing spilled cod-liver oil back into the bucket), sagging steps, and cupboard beds from the early 1700s—one with a medieval pinup girl (45 kr, covered by Bergen Card only Sept–May, daily June–Aug 9:00–17:00, Sept–May 11:00–14:00, good 45-min guided tours, tel. 55 31 41 89, www.hanseatisk.museum.no). Your admission includes entry to the medieval Hanseatic Assembly Rooms (Schøtstuene, separate entrance behind St. Mary's Church).

▲▲**Bryggens Museum**—This modern museum on the archaeological site of the earliest Bergen (1050–1500), with interesting temporary exhibits upstairs, offers adequate English-language information. To understand the exhibits better, you can borrow the museum guidebook, follow the included 30-minute audioguide tour, or take the walking tour—see above (40 kr, May–Aug daily 10:00–17:00, off-season most days 11:00–15:00, tel. 55 58 80 10, www.uib.no/bmu). The museum has an inexpensive cafeteria with soup-and-bread specials.

▲▲**Fish Market (Fisketorvet)**—This famous, bustling market has become touristy but still offers lots of smelly photo fun. Many stands sell pre-made smoked-salmon *(laks)* sandwiches, fish soup, and other snacks ideal for a light lunch (ask the price first). If you want to try Norwegian jerky, pick up a bag of dried cod snacks *(torsk)*. The red meat for sale is minke whale, caught off the coast of northern Norway. Many stands also sell local fruit in season and hand-knit sweaters for decent prices (Mon–Fri 7:00–17:00, Sat until 16:00, closed Sun, shorter hours off-season).

St. Mary's Church (Mariakirken)—Dating from the 12th century, this is Bergen's oldest building and one of Norway's finest churches (10 kr; late May–Aug Mon–Fri 9:30–11:30 & 13:00–16:00, closed Sat–Sun; Sept–late May Tue–Fri 12:00–13:30, closed Sat–Mon; tel. 55 31 59 60). Ask about evening concerts, usually held every Tuesday at 19:30 late June through September.

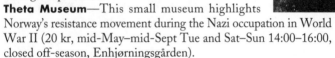

Theta Museum—This small museum highlights Norway's resistance movement during the Nazi occupation in World War II (20 kr, mid-May–mid-Sept Tue and Sat–Sun 14:00–16:00, closed off-season, Enhjørningsgården).

Elsewhere in Bergen

▲**Håkon's Hall/Rosenkrantz Tower**—These reminders of Bergen's medieval importance sit barren and boldly out of place on the harbor just beyond Bryggen. Håkon's Hall, which is the largest secular medieval building in Norway, was a royal residence 700 years ago when Bergen was the political center of Norway. The Rosenkrantz Tower—the keep of a 13th-century castle—is pretty empty but offers a fine harbor view from the rooftop.

Tours, which cover both sights and provide a serious introduction to Bergen's history, start in Håkon's Hall and leave on the hour (50 kr covers hall and tower entries and the tour, daily mid-May–Aug 10:00–16:00, Sept–mid-May 12:00–15:00, 45-min tours each hour, last tour 1 hour before closing, tel. 55 31 60 67). To visit only the tower, it's 25 kr, but you'll have to hitch along with the guided tour (rather than go it alone) due to fire regulations.

▲▲**Fløibanen**—Bergen's popular funicular climbs 1,000 feet to the top of "Mount" Fløyen in eight minutes for the best view of the town, surrounding islands, and fjords all the way to the west coast. The top is a popular picnic or pizza-to-go dinner spot (a Peppe's Pizza is a block away from the base of the lift) and the starting point for many peaceful hikes. Sunsets are great here. And if you need a goofy giant troll to pose with, look no further. It's a pleasant walk back down into Bergen. But to save your knees, get off at the Promsgate stop halfway down, and then wander through the delightful cobbled and shiplap lanes. There are often concerts at the top in the summer; check with the TI (60 kr round-trip, Mon–Fri

7:30–23:00, Sat from 8:00, Sun from 9:00, May–Aug until 24:00, departures each way on the half hour and often on the quarter hour, tel. 55 33 68 00, www.floibanen.no). This funicular is actually used by locals commuting into and out of downtown.

Leprosy Museum (Lepramuseet)—This unique museum is in St. Jørgens Hospital, a leprosarium that goes back to about 1700. Up until the 19th century, as much as 3 percent of Norway's population had leprosy. This hospital—once called "a graveyard for the living"—has a meager exhibit in a thought-provoking shell attached to a 300-year-old church (30 kr, daily mid-June–Aug 11:00–15:00, closed Sept–mid-June, pick up English pamphlet, Kong Oscars Gate 59, tel. 55 96 11 55, www.lepra.no).

▲▲**Wandering**—Bergen is a great strolling town. The harborfront is a fine place to kick back and watch the pigeons mate. Other good areas to explore are over the hill past Klostergate, Marken, Knosesmanet, Ytre Markevei, and the area behind Bryggen. The modern town—especially around Ole Bulls Plass—also has a pleasant ambience. To get away from the crowds, stroll around the artificial lake, Lille Lungegaardsvann.

▲▲**Aquarium (Akvariet)**—Small, but great fun if you like fish, this aquarium claims to be the second-most-visited sight in Norway. A pleasant 20-minute walk from the center, it's wonderfully laid out and explained in English (80 kr, kids-50 kr, May–Sept discount with Bergen Card, Oct–April fully covered by Bergen Card, daily 9:00–19:00, off-season 10:00–18:00; feeding times at 12:00, 15:00, and 18:00 in season; cheery cafeteria with light sandwiches, bus #11, tel. 55 55 71 71, www.akvariet.com). A handy little ferry sails from the fish market to near the aquarium (30 kr, 4/hr, show your boat ticket at aquarium to receive discounted admission price of 65 kr). The lovely park behind the aquarium has views of the sea. The totem pole erected here was a gift from Bergen's sister city in the United States—Seattle.

Swimming—Nordnes Sjøbad, near the aquarium, offers swimmers an outdoor heated pool and a protected area of the sea (25 kr, kids-10 kr, free with Bergen Card, mid-May–Aug Mon–Fri 9:00–19:00, shorter hours Sat–Sun, closed off-season, Nordnesparken 30).

▲**Old Bergen (Gamle Bergen)**—This is a Disney-cute gathering of 40 18th- and 19th-century shops and houses offering a cobbled look at "the old life." It's free to wander through the town and duck into the art galleries and gift shops housed in historic buildings. English tours (60 kr) departing on the hour get you into the 20 or so museum buildings (mid-May–Aug daily 10:00–17:00, closed Sept–mid-May, tel. 55 39 43 04). Take any bus heading west from Bryggen (such as #20, direction: Lonborg) to Gamle Bergen (first stop after the first tunnel).

▲**Bergen Art Museum (Bergen Kunstmuseum)**—If you need to get out of the rain (and enjoyed the National Gallery in Oslo), check out the Rasmus Meyer Collection. This tidy little museum has a good collection by Norwegian painters—Harriet Backer, J.C. Dahl, Christian Krohg, Edvard Munch, and others. Small description sheets in English can be found in each room. The Stenersen Collection next door has some interesting modern art, including Munch and Picasso (50 kr for both galleries, free with Bergen Card, daily 11:00–17:00, closed Mon mid-Sept–mid-May, Rasmus Meyers Allé 3, tel. 55 56 80 00, www.bergenartmuseum.no).

Near Bergen
▲**Fantoft Stave Church**—This huge, preserved-in-tar stave church burned down in 1992. It was rebuilt and reopened in 1997, but it can never be the same. Situated in a quiet forest next to a mysterious stone cross, this replica of a 12th-century wooden church is bigger, though no better, than others covered in this book. But it's worth a look if you're in the neighborhood, even after-hours, for its evocative setting (30 kr, daily mid-May–mid-Sept 10:30–14:00 & 14:30–18:00, no English information, 3 miles south of Bergen on E-39 in Paradis; for public transportation, see next listing).

▲**Edvard Grieg's Home, Troldhaugen**—Norway's greatest composer spent his last 22 years here (1885–1907), soaking up inspirational fjord beauty and composing many of his greatest works. In a romantic Victorian setting, the place is pleasant for anyone and essential for Grieg fans. The house and adjacent museum are full of memories, and his little studio hut near the water makes you want to sit down and modulate (50 kr, 60 percent discount with Bergen Card; May–Sept daily 9:00–18:00; Oct–Nov and mid-Jan–April Mon–Fri 10:00–14:00, Sat–Sun 12:00–16:00; closed Dec–mid-Jan; tel. 55 92 29 93, www.troldhaugen.com).

Ask the TI about concerts in the on-site concert hall (200 kr, 150 kr with Bergen Card, 130 kr on Sat, free shuttle bus from TI if you show concert ticket; concerts scheduled roughly mid-June–mid-Aug Wed at 19:30, Sat at 14:00, and Sun at 19:30; Sept–mid-Nov Sun at 14:00).

Getting to Fantoft and Troldhaugen: The **Attractions Bus** for 75 kr is the easiest, least expensive way to get to Fantoft and Troldhaugen (and avoid excessive walking, runs mid-June–mid-Aug); see "Tours," page 187.

The daily three-hour bus tour promoted by the TI is worthwhile for the informative guide, easy transportation, and doorstep service (250 kr, 10:00 and 14:00).

SHOPPING

Most shops are open Mon–Fri 9:00–16:30, Thu until 19:00, Sat 9:00–15:00, and closed Sun. Many of the tourist shops at the harborfront strip along Bryggen are open daily—even during holidays—until 20:00 or 21:00.

Bryggen is bursting with sweaters, pewter, and trolls. The Husfliden Shop is popular for its handmade Norwegian sweaters and goodies (good variety and quality but expensive, just off the market square at Vågsalmenning 3).

The Galleriet shopping center on Torgallmenningen has six floors of shops, cafés, and restaurants. You'll find a pharmacy, photo shops, clothing, sporting goods, bookstores, and a basement grocery store (Mon–Fri 9:00–20:00, Sat 9:00–18:00, closed Sun).

NIGHTLIFE

Folk Evenings—The **Fana Folklore show** is Bergen's most-advertised folk evening. An old farm hosts this touristy collection of cultural clichés, with food, music, dancing, and colorful costumes. While some think it's too gimmicky and some think it's lots of fun, nobody likes the meager dinner (280 kr includes short bus trip and meal, June–Aug Thu and Fri 19:00–22:30, extra evenings in May and Sept and other days during the season, reservations required, tel. 55 91 52 40 or book at TI or through your hotel, www.fanafolklore.no).

The **Bergen Folklore show** offers a smaller, homier program, featuring a good music-and-dance look at rural and traditional Norway. Performances are downtown in the Hanseatic Assembly Rooms (95-kr tickets sold by TI and at the door, 1 hr, mid-June–late July Tue at 21:00, in Aug also Sun at 21:00, at Schøtsuene, tel. 55 31 20 06).

Concerts—From mid-June through August, you'll find concerts at the restaurant on top of Mount Fløyen, at Domkirken (cathedral), at St. Mary's Church, and other places. Ask the TI for details (tel. 55 55 20 00).

SLEEPING

There are two kinds of demands on the hotel scene in Bergen: Business travelers fill up the fancy hotels outside of summer and weekends, and tourists take the budget places from June through mid-August.

If you want cheap accommodations in summer, reserve ahead. But if you just show up at the TI in summer, unless you're unlucky and hit some convention, you'll get a great deal on a business-class hotel.

Sleep Code

(6.5 kr = about $1, country code: 47)
S = Single, **D** = Double/Twin, **T** = Triple, **Q** = Quad,
b = bathroom, **s** = shower. You can assume credit cards are
accepted unless otherwise noted.

To help you sort easily through these listings, I've divided
the rooms into three categories, based on the price for a standard
double room with bath:

  $$$ **Higher Priced**—Most rooms 1,000 kr or more.
   $$ **Moderately Priced**—Most rooms between 600–1,000 kr.
    $ **Lower Priced**—Most rooms 600 kr or less.

The private homes and hostel-style places listed are inexpensive, central, and well run. If you can handle showers down the hall and cooking your own breakfast in a communal kitchen, several pensions offer rooms with a homey atmosphere and fine locations for half the cost of a hotel room.

Rainbow Hotels

For a description of this popular chain of business-class hotels, see page 146 in Oslo chapter. They offer three kinds of rooms: singles (plenty of these for businesspeople), "combi" twins (slightly smaller rooms with twin beds or "combi" beds—a twin and a sofa bed, only available at Bryggen Orion), and full double rooms. Twin rooms are preferable to combi rooms at the same price. A big buffet breakfast is included.

The Rainbow hotels offer steep discounts if you purchase a 90-kr **Skanplus Hotel Pass** from them (www.rainbow-hotels.no). You'll save nearly 400 kroner per night every day May–September and weekends the rest of the year.

"Weekend" means Fridays and Saturdays. The card also gives you every sixth night free. Listed below are the rack rate/Skanplus rate. Don't pay the rack rate.

  $$$ **Rainbow Hotel Rosenkrantz** is one block behind Bryggen, between the Bryggens Museum and the Fløibanen funicular station (Sb-1,150/660 kr, Db-1,450/840 kr, extra bed-200 kr, 100 kr for children under 12, Rosenkrantzgate 7, tel. 55 30 14 00, fax 55 31 14 76, rosenkrantz@rainbow-hotels.no).

  $$$ **Rainbow Hotel Bristol** is a block off Ole Bulls Plass (Sb-1,150/660 kr, Db-1,400/840 kr, extra bed-200 kr, 100 kr for children under 12, Torgalmenningen 11, tel. 55 55 10 00, fax 55 55 10 01, bristol.bergen@rainbow-hotels.no).

Bergen Hotels and Restaurants

1 Rainbow Hotel Rosenkrantz
2 Rainbow Hotel Bristol
3 Rainbow Hotel Bryggen Orion
4 Hotel Hordaheimen
5 Park Pension
6 Hotel Dreggen
   & Slottskroen Restaurant
7 Hotel Charme
8 Skansen Pensjonat
9 Heskja Rooms
10 Olsnes Rooms
11 Dahl Rooms
12 To Vågenes Rooms
13 Marken Gjestehus
14 Nygård Apartment

15 YMCA
16 To Montana Hostel
17 Bryggeloftet & Stuene,
   Enhjørningen & To Kokker
   Restaurants
18 Vagsbunnen Rest.
   & Kong Oscar's Sausages
19 Kjøttbasaren Food Hall & Egon Rest.
20 Fløien Folkerestaurant
21 Fish Market (Fisketorvet)
22 Lido Cafeteria
23 Zachariasbryggen restaurants
24 Dickens Restaurant
25 Radisson SAS/Hotel
   Norge's Buffet
26 Café Opera

$$ Rainbow Hotel Bryggen Orion is beyond Bryggen near Håkon's Hall (Sb-995/630 kr, Db-1,245/790 kr, extra bed-175 kr, Bradbenken 3, tel. 55 30 87 00, fax 55 32 94 14, bryggenorion @rainbow-hotels.no).

More Hotels and Pensions

$$$ Hotel Hordaheimen, old, prestigious, and central, is just off the harbor. It has sleek and comfy rooms, and is a good value if you can score a discount. It sells a 75-kr **Scan Holiday Pass** offering 20 percent savings on rooms from late June to mid-August (Sb-850–1,150 kr, Db-1,250–1,490 kr, includes breakfast, non-smoking, Sundts Gate 18, tel. 55 33 50 00, fax 55 23 49 50, info@hordaheimen.hl.no).

$$$ Park Pension is classy, comfortable, and in a fine central-but-residential neighborhood. It's tinseled in Old World, lived-in charm (34 rooms, 22 in classy old hotel, 12 in annex across street, Sb-840 kr, Db-1,040 kr, extra bed-250 kr, includes breakfast, winter weekend discounts, Harald Hårfagres Gate 35, tel. 55 54 44 00, fax 55 54 44 44, www.parkhotel.no).

$$ Hotel Dreggen is a nondescript, 31-room place a block from Håkon's Hall at the end of the Bryggen (May–Sept S-450 kr, Sb-750 kr, D-650 kr, Db-950 kr; Oct–April S-390 kr, Sb-590 kr, D-490 kr, Db-690 kr; mention this book to receive these prices in 2005, includes breakfast, non-smoking rooms, elevator, Sandbrugaten 3, tel. 55 31 61 55, fax 55 31 54 23, www.hotel-dreggen.no, post @hotel-dreggen.no).

$$ Hotel Charme is charming, with 20 clean, modern rooms. Located near the lively theater and university areas, it provides a quiet retreat in a mostly residential area (Sb-650 kr, Db-800 kr, larger family room with balcony-1,400 kr, extra bed-100 kr, includes breakfast, Rosenbergsgate 13, tel. 55 90 72 80, fax 55 90 72 81, post @hotel-charme.com).

$$ Skansen Pensjonat, situated a steep but scenic four-minute climb above the entrance to the Fløibanen lift and overlooking the fish market, rents eight rooms and three spacious apartments in an elegant old house (S-350–400 kr, D-550 kr, fancy D on corner with view and balcony-650 kr, includes breakfast, 2 showers on ground floor, sinks in rooms, family room with TV, Db apartments with no breakfast but kitchen-700 kr, 1 parking place, non-smoking). To get there, follow the switchback road behind the Fløibanen station halfway up the hillside (about 3 switchbacks) to Vetrlidsalmenning 29 (tel. 55 31 90 80, fax 55 31 15 27, www.skansen-pensjonat.no, mail@skansen-pensjonat.no, run by Alvær/Skjøtskift family).

Private Homes

These private homes are inexpensive, quite private, and lack a lot of chatty interaction with your hosts. The Heskja and Dahl rooms—far more quiet, homey, and convenient than hostel beds, and for less money when you consider sheet rental—are the best values in town.

$ **Alf and Elisabeth Heskja** rent four non-smoking doubles that share a shower/WC, another WC, and a kitchen in their home, beautifully situated on a steep, cobbled lane called "the most painted street in Bergen" (D-360 kr, reserve in advance, 4 blocks from station at Skivebakken 17, tel. 55 31 30 30, fax 55 31 30 90, mail@skiven.no). From the station, go down Kong Oscars Gate, uphill on D. Krohns Gate, and up the many stairs at the end of the block on the left.

$ The **Olsnes' home,** across the street from the Heskja home, keeps backpackers happy with its cheap, basic rooms and a shared kitchen (Sb-350 kr, D-350 kr, Db-400 kr, extra bed-100 kr, cash only, Skivebakken 24, tel. 55 31 20 44, svolsne@online.no, run by Ylva).

$ **Marit and Hugo Dahl** devote two floors of their fine old house to guests May through September. One floor of the Dahl house has four simple and clean twins and doubles (which share a shower and 2 WCs). The lower floor is a comfy living room and kitchen. Though a 15-minute hike from the station, it's in the middle of fairy-tale old Bergen in a tranquil, cobbled, residential neighborhood a 10-minute walk from the fish market (D-380 kr, cash only, just more than halfway between train station and aquarium at Trangesmauet 14, tel. 55 23 16 69, mobile 93 68 37 93, maritd2@online.no).

$ The **Vågenes family** has four doubles in a large, comfortable house on the edge of town (small apartment with kitchen and bathroom-600 kr, Db with kitchenette-520 kr, extra bed-100 kr, cash only, washing machine available, easy parking, J. L. Mowinckelsvei 95, tel. 55 16 11 01, fax 55 16 00 85). It's 10 minutes from downtown by car or bus #60. Driving (and via bus #60) from downtown, cross Puddefjordsbroen bridge (Road 555), go through the upper tunnel on Road 540, turn left 200 yards later on J. L. Mowinckelsvei, and continue to Helgeplasset street (or Helgeplasset bus stop). It's just past Hagesenter on the right.

Dorms and Hostels

$$ **Marken Gjestehus** is quiet, tidy, well run, and conveniently positioned between the station and the harborfront. Its rooms are spartan but modern and cheery (dorm bed in 6-bed room-165 kr, in 4-bed room-195 kr, S-355 kr, Sb-495 kr, D-470 kr, Db-610 kr, Tb-795 kr, sheets-55 kr, towels-10 kr, breakfast-75 kr, extra bed-125 kr, elevator, kitchen, laundry, open all year, 4th floor at Kong Oscars Gate 45, tel. 55 31 44 04, fax 55 31 60 22, www.marken-gjestehus.com, markengjestehus@smisi.no).

$$ **Nygård Apartment,** a student dorm run by the Marken Gjestehus, is well located, vinyl, plain, clean, and practical. It rents rooms from June through mid-August (S-365 kr, Sb-510 kr, D-530 kr, Db-650 kr, sheets-55 kr, towel-10 kr, extra bed-145 kr, 75-kr

breakfast, kitchenettes, elevator, Nygårdsgate 31, tel. 55 32 72 53, fax 55 31 60 22, www.marken-gjestehus.com).

$ Bergen Vandrerhjem YMCA (IYHF), just off Vågsall-menningen square in front of the TI and across from the fish market, is the best location for the price (bed in 12- to 40-bed dorm-125 kr, shared shower and kitchen, bed in 4- to 6-bed family room with bathroom and kitchen-170 kr, Db with kitchen-600 kr, non-members pay 25 kr extra, sheets-45 kr, breakfast-45 kr, fully open mid-May–mid Sept, fewer beds off-season, Nedre Korskirkeall-menningen 4, tel. 55 60 60 55, http://home.broadpark.no/~ymca).

$ Montana Youth Hostel (IYHF), while one of Europe's best, is high-priced for a hostel and way out of town. Still, the bus con-nections (#31, 15 min from the center) and the facilities—modern rooms, classy living room, no curfew, huge parking lot, and mem-bers' kitchen—are excellent (dorm bed-135 kr mid-May–Aug only, bed in Q-195 kr, bed in Qb-215 kr, bed in D-285 kr, bed in Db-305 kr, S-400 kr, Sb-420 kr, non-members pay 25 kr extra, sheets-55 kr, includes breakfast, singles not available mid-June–mid-Aug, 30 Johan Blydts Vei, tel. 55 20 80 70, fax 55 20 80 75, www.montana.no, montvh@online.no).

EATING

Bergen has numerous choices:

- Restaurants with rustic, woody atmosphere, candlelight, and steep prices (200–300-kr entrées).
- Inexpensive cafeterias, restaurants, and ethnic eateries where you can get quality food at lower prices (75–200 kr) with less atmosphere (except for the ethnic restaurants).
- Chain restaurants that serve pizza, burgers, ribs, and chicken (100–200-kr entrées and pizzas).
- Take-away sandwich shops, bakeries, and cafés for a light bite (30–75 kr). Remember, if you get your food to go, you'll save 12 percent.

In or near Bryggen

The old Hanseatic quarter is lined with restaurants that serve traditional Norse food by candlelight. If you're in the mood for a little Donner or Blitzen, you're in luck. You'll pay a premium to eat at the first three places, but you'll have a memorable meal in a pleasant setting. To ensure getting a table, call in a reservation.

Bryggeloftet & Stuene, one restaurant on two levels, serves seafood and traditional meals (80–150-kr lunches, 150–300-kr dinners). Upstairs feels less stuffy and less touristy (Mon–Sat 11:00–23:30, opens Sun at 13:00, #11 in Bryggen harborfront, consider reserving a view window upstairs, tel. 55 31 06 30). If there's a line downstairs, climb the stairs.

Enhjørningen ("The Unicorn") is *the* place in Bergen for seafood. They offer fine seafood dinners from about 260 kr (nightly from 16:00, look for anatomically correct unicorn on the old wharf facade, try to reserve a window table, tel. 55 32 79 19).

To Kokker, down the alley from Enhjørningen, also serves seafood, along with plenty of meat dishes, in an elegant, old, wooden building (180–240-kr dishes, Mon–Sat 17:00–23:00, closed Sun, tel. 55 32 28 16).

Slottskroen, an inexpensive restaurant at the far end of Bryggen near the Rosenkrantz Tower, serves up 125–200-kr entrées in a clean, homey atmosphere. This is probably your best opportunity to try whale without harpooning your wallet. You can get light meals, soups, and salads for 70–100 kr and sandwiches for 20–50 kr (Mon–Sat 11:00–23:00, Sun 12:00–23:00, Slottsgate 3, tel. 55 32 07 11).

Vagsbunnen Restaurant, a good budget bet, is a hardworking, unpretentious, and family-run place serving good, traditional, candlelit Norwegian meals for 90–200 kr (daily 11:30–23:00, 2 blocks in from fish market at Kong Oscars Gate 5, tel. 55 90 03 94).

Kong Oscar's Pølse Stand, near Kong Oscar Gate, is a sausage stand (open daily until late) selling artery-clogging guilty pleasures. Sausages range in size, price, and flavor—they even have reindeer!

Fløien Folkerestaurant, atop Mount Fløyen, offers meals with a panoramic view. The cheaper cafeteria section has coffee, cake, and sandwiches from 50 kr (daily 11:00–22:00). The restaurant section has decent dinners for about 150 kr (daily 17:00–24:00, tel. 55 32 18 75). From mid-June through late August, have a bite and take in a concert (tickets-160 kr, 195 kr with salad and bread, 120 kr with Bergen Card).

The following two restaurants are chains you'll find throughout Norway. **Egon,** below the Kjøttbasaren food hall (listed below), is a ribs, chicken, and burger kind of place where you can get a substantial meal for 150–200 kr. **Peppe's Pizza,** across the street behind the Hanseatic Museum, has cold beer and great pizzas (medium size for 1–2 people from 150 kr, large for 2–3 people from 250 kr, take-out possible; consider the Moby Dick, with curried shrimp, leeks, and bell peppers). There are four Peppe's in Bergen.

Eating Cheap Facing the Harbor

For a tasty, memorable, and inexpensive meal in Bergen, assemble a seafood picnic at the **fish market (Fisketorvet).** The stalls are bursting with salmon sandwiches, fresh shrimp, fish and chips, and fish cakes (ask for prices first; Mon–Fri 7:00–17:00, Sat until 16:00, closed Sun, shorter hours off-season).

Kjøttbasaren, the restored meat market of 1887, is a food hall with stalls selling picnic supplies or pre-made food to go (Mon–Fri 10:00–17:00, Thu until 18:00, Sat 9:00–16:00, closed Sun).

Zachariasbryggen, a modern restaurant complex, lines a pier at the head of the harbor (on Torget). Ignore the overpriced Italian and Tex-Mex restaurants. Look instead for **Baker Brun,** which makes sandwiches, including wonderful shrimp baguettes, and pastries such as *skillingsbolle*—cinnamon rolls—warm out of the oven (open from 9:00, seating inside or take-away). **Bon Appetit** also sells baguette sandwiches (about 50 kr), plus wraps (40 kr) and ice cream. You'll see Baker Brun and Bon Appetit shops in Bryggen, too.

Lido, overlooking the fish market, serves good, basic food in its upstairs self-service cafeteria (50–100-kr lunches, 100–150-kr dinners, Mon–Sat 10:00–22:00, Sun 13:00–22:00, closes earlier off-season, 2nd floor, Torgallmenningen 1, tel. 55 32 59 12).

From Ole Bulls Plass up to the Theater

Bergen's "in" cafés are stylish, cozy, small, and open very late—great places to experience the local yuppie scene. Around the cinema on Neumannsgate, there are numerous ethnic restaurants, including Italian, Middle Eastern, and Chinese.

The lively **Dickens** serves beautifully presented entrées of fish, chicken, and steak (150–250 kr). The window tables in the atrium are great for people-watching (daily 11:00–24:00, reservations smart, Kong Olav V's Plass 4, tel. 55 36 31 30).

The trendy **Café Opera** is good for pasta and vegetarian dishes with a Middle Eastern flair (100–140-kr dinners, 60–80-kr lunches, daily 11:00–24:00, often live music Fri–Sat, live locals nightly, English newspapers, chess, across from theater, Engen 18, tel. 55 23 03 15).

Radisson SAS/Hotel Norge's Koltbord buffet, on the second floor of Bergen's ritziest hotel, offers a daily all-you-can-eat buffet in the classy Ole Bulls restaurant. You'll find hot dishes, seafood, and desserts (245-kr lunch, Mon–Sat 12:00–16:00, Sun 13:00–16:00, tel. 55 57 30 00). They also do *store koldt bord* evenings (16:30–21:30) for 280 kr.

TRANSPORTATION CONNECTIONS

Bergen is conveniently connected to **Oslo** by plane and train (departing Bergen daily at 7:58, 10:30, 14:58, 15:58, and 23:00, arriving at Oslo 7 scenic hrs later, confirm times at station, 50-kr seat reservation required, book several weeks in advance if traveling mid-July–Aug). From Bergen, you can take the Norway in a Nutshell train/bus/ferry route; for information, see the Norway in a Nutshell chapter. Train info: tel. 55 96 69 00 or 81 50 08 88.

To get to **Stockholm, Copenhagen,** or even **Trondheim,** you'll go via Oslo unless you fly. Before buying a ticket for a long train trip from Bergen, look into cheap flights.

By express boat to Balestrand and Flåm (on Sognefjord): The handy Fylkesbaatane express boat links Bergen with Balestrand (4 hrs) and Flåm (5.5 hrs). For details, see the "Transportation Connections" for Balestrand (page 170).

By bus to Kristiansand: If you're heading to Denmark on the ferry from Kristiansand, catch the Haukeli express bus (departing Bergen at 7:30 daily except Sun). After a nearly two-hour layover in Haukeli, take the bus at 14:40, arriving at 18:50 in Kristiansand in time for the overnight ferry to Denmark (tel. 55 55 90 70, within Bergen dial 177).

By boat to Stavanger: Flaggruten catamarans sail to Stavanger (2–3/day, 4 hrs, 560 kr one-way, 670 kr round-trip; nearly half-price for students, Scanrail/Eurail passholders, or for 1 partner when a couple travels together; tel. 55 23 87 80). From Stavanger, trains run to Kristiansand and Oslo (overnight possible).

By boat to Newcastle, England: Fjordline sails from Bergen to Newcastle, England (Tue–Sun mid-May–mid-Sept, less off-season, tel. 81 53 35 00, www.fjordline.co.uk). The cheapest summer crossing for the 22-hour trip is 850–1,000 kr, depending on the day of the week, for a reclining chair or sleeperette (available early June and late Aug). From late June to early August, those same sleeperettes are 1,000–1,350 kr. Bunks in a four-person cabin cost 265 kr extra per person, and a two-berth inside cabin with a shower and WC is about 600 kr extra per person. Drivers with up to four passengers pay 2,600–3,800 kr (price includes a reclining seat).

By boat to the Arctic: Hurtigruten coastal steamers depart daily (April–Sept at 20:00, Oct–March at 22:30) for the seven-day trip north up the scenic west coast to Kirkenes on the Russian border.

This route was started in 1893 as a postal and cargo delivery service along the west coast of Norway. Still flying the Norwegian postal flag, Hurtigruten delivers mail, people, cars, and cargo from Bergen to Kirkenes. A lifeline for remote areas, the ships call at 34 fishing villages and cities.

For the seven-day trip to Kirkenes, allow $1,245–1,800 per person based on double occupancy (includes 3 meals per day, taxes, and port charges). Prices vary depending on the season (highest June–mid-July), cabin, and type of ship ("Traditional"—oldest, no-frills, least expensive; "Mid-Generation"—moderate and comfortable; "Contemporary"—nice and pricier; and "Millennium"—newest and most luxurious). Shorter trips are possible (e.g., 2 days from Bergen to Trondheim-1,450 kr for deck passage, free sleeping lounge with airplane-deck seats). Deck space and seats are usually available with short or no notice, but cabins should be booked well in advance. Discounts are available off-season (Oct–March). Ship services: 24-hour cafeteria, pay showers, launderette (but not on "Traditional" ships), and optional port excursions ($50–150).

Call Norwegian Coastal Voyage in New York (U.S. tel. 800/323-7436, www.coastalvoyage.com) or in Norway (tel. 81 03 00 00, www.hurtigruten.com). For most travelers, the ride makes a great one-way trip, but a flight south is a logical last leg (rather than returning to Bergen by boat—a 12-day round-trip).

SOUTH NORWAY

Stavanger, Setesdal Valley, and Kristiansand

South Norway is not about must-see sights or jaw-dropping scenery—it's simply pleasant and pretty. Spend a day in the harbor-side town of Stavanger and delve into your Scandinavian roots at the Emigration Center or into the oil industry at the surprisingly inter-esting Petroleum Museum. Window-shop in the old town, cruise the harbor, or hoof it up Pulpit Rock for a fine view.

A series of time-forgotten towns stretch across Setesdal Valley, with sod-roofed cottages and locals who practice fiddles and har-monicas, rose painting, whittling, and gold- and silver-work. The famous Setesdal filigree echoes the rhythmical designs of the Viking era and Middle Ages. Each town has a weekly rotating series of hikes and activities for the regular, stay-put-for-a-week visitor. The upper valley is dead in the summer but enjoys a bustling winter.

In Kristiansand, Norway's answer to a seaside resort, prome-nade along the strand, sample a Scandinavian zoo, or stow away to Denmark.

Planning Your Time

Even on a busy itinerary, Stavanger warrants a day. If you are an avid genealogist, consider two. The port town is connected by boat to Bergen and by train to Kristiansand.

Frankly, without a car, the Setesdal Valley is not worth the trouble. There are no trains in the valley, bus schedules are as sparse as the population, and the sights are best for joyriding. If you're dri-ving in Bergen and want to get back to Denmark, this route is more interesting than repeating Oslo. On a three-week Scandinavian trip, I'd do it in one long day, as follows: 7:00-Leave Bergen, 9:00-Catch Kvanndal ferry to Utne, 10:00-Say goodbye to the last fjord at Odda, 13:00-Lunch in Hovden at the top of Setesdal Valley, 14:00-Frolic south with a few short stops in the valley, 19:00-Arrive in

Kristiansand for dinner. Spend the night and catch the 9:00 boat to Denmark the next morning. (Budget night owls could instead take in a late-night movie in Kristiansand, then catch the 1:15 overnight boat to Denmark, saving on hotel costs.) Kristiansand is not a destination town, but rather a place to pass through, conveniently connecting Norway to Denmark by ferry.

Stavanger

This small city of about 100,000 feels more cosmopolitan than most Norwegian cities. This is thanks in part to the oil industry, with its multinational workers and the money they bring into the city. Known as Norway's festival city, Stavanger hosts several lively events, including jazz (early May), chamber music (mid-Aug), and wooden boats (early June). For details, see www.visitstavanger.com.

ORIENTATION

The most scenic and interesting parts of Stavanger surround its harbor. Here you'll find the Norwegian Emigration Center, lots of shops and restaurants, the indoor fish market, a produce market (Mon–Sat 9:00–16:00, closed Sun), and the TI. The artificial Lake Breiavatnet—bordered by Kongsgaten on the east and Olav V's Gate on the west—separates the train and bus stations from the harbor.

Tourist Information

The helpful staff at the TI can help you plan your time in Stavanger, and give you hiking tips and day-trip information. Pick up a free city guide and map (June–Aug daily 9:00–20:00; Sept–May Mon–Fri 9:00–16:00, Sat 9:00–14:00, closed Sun; Rosenkildetorget 1, tel. 51 85 92 00).

Arrival in Stavanger

By Boat: Express boats from Bergen dock at Fiskepiren. From here, you can take a public bus to the center of town or to the train station. A taxi to a hotel downtown costs 70–80 kr.

By Train and Bus: Stavanger's train and bus stations are a five-minute walk around Lake Breiavatnet to the harbor (train ticket and reservation office Mon–Fri 6:30–20:00, Sat 6:30–16:30, Sun 10:00–20:00). Luggage lockers and Norway-wide train timetables are available at the train station.

By Plane: Stavanger's Sola Airport, about nine miles outside the city, is connected to downtown by the **Flybussen** (60 kr, buy ticket on bus, Mon–Fri 7:45–23:45, 3–4/hr, less Sat–Sun, 30 min). This airport bus shuttles travelers to the bus station (Byterminalen)

Stavanger

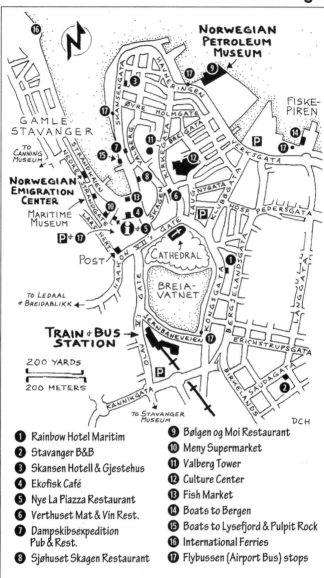

1 Rainbow Hotel Maritim
2 Stavanger B&B
3 Skansen Hotell & Gjestehus
4 Ekofisk Café
5 Nye La Piazza Restaurant
6 Verthuset Mat & Vin Rest.
7 Dampskibsexpedition
   Pub & Rest.
8 Sjøhuset Skagen Restaurant

9 Bølgen og Moi Restaurant
10 Meny Supermarket
11 Valberg Tower
12 Culture Center
13 Fish Market
14 Boats to Bergen
15 Boats to Lysefjord & Pulpit Rock
16 International Ferries
17 Flybussen (Airport Bus) stops

and train station (next to each other), the city center, and the boat terminal (Fiskepiren). To get to the airport from the city center, catch the shuttle at any of these stops.

SIGHTS

▲▲**Norwegian Petroleum Museum (Norskolje Museum)**—This entertaining, informative museum—dedicated to the discovery of oil in Norway's North Sea in 1969 and the industry built up around it— offers something for everyone. It describes how oil was formed, how it's found and produced, and what it's used for. There are interactive exhibits covering everything from the  "History of the Earth" (4.5 billion years displayed on a large overhead globe, showing how our planet has changed—stay for the blast that killed the dinosaurs!), to day-to-day life on an offshore platform, to petroleum products in our lives. Kids love the model drilling platform that they can climb on. The museum's architecture was designed to echo the foundations of the oil industry—bedrock (the stone building), slate and chalk deposits in the sea (slate floor of the main hall), and the rigs (cylindrical platforms). While the museum has its fair share of propaganda, it also has several good exhibits on the environmental toll of drilling and consuming oil (80 kr, June–Aug daily 10:00–19:00, Sept–May Mon–Sat 10:00–16:00, Sun 10:00–18:00, tel. 51 93 93 00, www.norskolje.museum.no). The small museum shop sells various petroleum-based products.

The **Bølgen og Moi** restaurant has an inviting terrace over the water for thirsty museumgoers. They also serve lunch (from 150 kr) and dinner (from 250 kr), with a fantastic view over the harbor (daily 11:00–23:00, reservations recommended for dinner, tel. 51 93 93 51).

▲**Norwegian Emigration Center (Det Norske Utvandrer-senteret Ble)**—This fine museum, in an old warehouse near the wharf where the first boats sailed with emigrants to "Amerika" in 1825, is worth ▲▲▲ for anyone seeking their Norwegian roots. On the second floor, you'll find a study center and library. There are computers (Internet and microfilm) free for use to look up your relatives. The library is lined with shelves of *bygdebøker*—books from farm districts all over Norway, documenting the history of landowners and local families. For 200 kr, the staff will give you a step-by-step consultation. Otherwise, they'll help answer questions and steer you in the right direction for free. The third floor has a small exhibit everyone will enjoy. It tells the story of the first emigrants who left for the United States—why they left, the journey, and what life was like in the New World (library free, 40 kr for the museum, Mon–Fri 9:00–15:00, Tue until 18:00, closed Sat–Sun, tel. 51 53 88 60, www.emigrationcenter.com). If you want to look up relatives, do some homework ahead of time and have at least two or three of the following: family surname, farm name, birth year, emigration year.

Stavanger Museum—This museum actually is five different buildings/museums covered on one ticket: the **Stavanger Museum,** featuring the history of the city and a zoological exhibit (Muségate 16); Stavanger **Sjøfartsmuseum,** the maritime museum (Nedre Strandgate 17–19); **Norsk Hermetikkmuseum,** the Norwegian canning museum (*brisling*—herring—is smoked mid-June–mid-Aug Tue and Thu, Øvre Strandgate 88A); **Ledaal,** a royal residence and manor house (Eiganesveien 45); and **Breidablikk,** a wooden villa from the late 1800s (Eiganesveien 40A). Pick up the handy brochure and buy your ticket from the TI (40 kr; mid-May–mid-June Mon–Fri 11:00–15:00, Sun 11:00–16:00, closed Sat; mid-June–mid-Aug daily 11:00–16:00; mid-Aug–mid-Sept Mon–Thu 11:00–15:00, closed Fri–Sun; mid-Sept–Nov and Jan–mid-May Sun 11:00–16:00, closed Mon–Sat and Dec; www.stavanger.museum.no).

Gamle Stavanger—Stavanger's "old town" centers on Øvre Strandgate, on the west side of the harbor. Wander the narrow, winding back lanes and peek into a workshop or gallery to find ceramics, glass, jewelry, and more (free, shops and galleries open roughly daily 10:00–16:00, coinciding with the arrival of cruise ships).

Stavanger Cathedral (Domkirke)—The cathedral was originally built in 1125 in a Norman style, with basket-handle Romanesque arches. After a fire badly damaged the church in the 13th century, a new chancel was added in the pointy-arched Gothic style. Have a look inside and see where the architecture changes about three-quarters of the way up the aisle (free, June–Aug daily 11:00–19:00; Sept–May Mon and Fri 11:00–16:00, closed Tue–Thu and Sat–Sun).

Day Trips to Lysefjord and Pulpit Rock

The nearby Lysefjord is an easy day trip. Those with more time (and strong legs) can hike up to the top of the 1,800-foot-high Pulpit Rock (Preikestolen). The dramatic 270-square-foot plateau atop the rock gives you a fantastic view of the fjord and surrounding mountains. The TI has brochures for several boat tour companies and sells tickets.

Boat Tour of Lysefjord—Two companies, Rodne and Fjord Tours, offer nearly identical three- to four-hour round-trip excursions from Stavanger to Lysefjord (including a view of Pulpit Rock). Both companies depart from the east side of the harbor, in front of Skansegaten, along Skagenkaien. Buy your ticket on board or at the TI. Rodne is pricier at 290 kr, but offers more cruises (July–mid-Aug daily at 10:30 and 14:30; June and mid-Aug–mid-Sept daily at 12:00; May Wed–Sun at 12:00; tel. 51 89 52 70) than Fjord Tours (270 kr, daily mid-May–Aug at 12:00, tel. 51 53 73 40).

Ferry and Bus to Pulpit Rock—Public transportation to the trail's starting point is a snap—then comes the hard part: the two-hour hike to the top. The total distance is 4.5 miles and the elevation gain is roughly 1,000 feet. Pack a lunch and plenty of water and wear good shoes. Ferries depart from Fiskepiren to Tau (35 kr, 25–40 min, runs late June–Sept Mon–Sat at 8:00 and 9:25, mid-June–mid-Aug also Sun at 8:25, doesn't run Oct–May). In Tau, buses meet the incoming ferries and head to Pulpit Rock cabin—Preikestolhytta (55 kr, 35–40 min, Mon–Sat at 8:35 and 9:40). Return buses from Preikestolhytta depart at 14:50 or 16:25 for Tau and meet with a corresponding ferry. Pick up the helpful leaflet and confirm details at the TI. They can also give you details about more strenuous hikes.

SLEEPING

$$$ **Rainbow Hotel Maritim,** about two blocks from the train station, near the artificial Lake Breiavatnet, can be a good deal for a big-business class hotel. Discounts are possible daily in summer (mid-June–mid-Aug) and weekends the rest of the year with the 90-kr Skanplus Hotel Pass (described on page 146). The cheaper prices in this listing are the Skanplus rates (Sb-1,195/550 kr, Db-1,495/690 kr, includes breakfast, elevator, Kongsgaten 32, tel. 51 85 05 00, fax 51 85 05 01, www.rainbow-hotels.no/maritim).

$$ **Stavanger B&B** is your best home away from home in Stavanger. This large, red house among a sea of white houses has 14 tidy rooms, all with shower, but a toilet down the hall. Waffles, coffee, and friendly chatter are served up every evening at 21:00 (Ss-540 kr, Ds-640 kr, Ts-790 kr, Qs-890 kr, includes breakfast, 10-min walk behind train station in residential neighborhood, Vikedalsgate 1A, tel. 51 56 25 00, fax 51 56 25 01, www.stavangerbedandbreakfast.no, peck@online.no). If you let them know in advance, they can pick up or drop off at the boat dock or station.

Sleep Code

(6.5 kr = about $1, country code: 47)
S = Single, **D** = Double/Twin, **T** = Triple, **Q** = Quad, **b** = bathroom, **s** = shower. All of these places accept credit cards.

To help you sort easily through these listings, I've divided the rooms into three categories, based on the price for a standard double room with bath:

$$$ **Higher Priced**—Most rooms 1,000 kr or more.
$$ **Moderately Priced**—Most rooms between 600–1,000 kr.
$ **Lower Priced**—Most rooms 600 kr or less.

$$ The **Skansen Hotell & Gjestehus** splits 30 rooms between its hotel (newer, more expensive rooms) and guest house (less expensive for essentially the same quality). Most of the rooms are on the street and can be noisy, but you're just off the harbor in a great location (hotel: Sb-760 kr, Db-895 kr; guest house: Sb-660 kr, Db-795 kr; prices about 100 kr less on Fri, Sat, and Sun nights; includes breakfast, non-smoking floors, elevator to most floors, Skansengate 7, tel. 51 93 85 00, fax 51 93 85 01, www.skansenhotel.no, post @skansenhotel.no).

EATING

Casual Dining

Ekofisk, named after Norway's first oil-drilling platform, is a small fish market and café with a few indoor and outdoor tables. You can try fish cakes (a tasty cake made from white fish, cream, herbs, and spices—ask for a sample), fish soup, or *bacalao* (dried, salted cod cooked in a tomato sauce) with salad and bread for 60–80 kr. You'll pay less for take-away, so do like the locals do—picnic on the floating docks in the guest harbor across the street (Mon–Fri 9:00–16:30, Sat 9:00–14:00, closed Sun, across square from TI at Nedre Strandgate 13, tel. 51 52 54 09).

Nye La Piazza, above the TI, has an assortment of pasta and other Italian dishes, including pizza, for 125–200 kr (Mon–Sat 12:00–24:00, Sun 12:00–22:00, Rosenkildettorget, tel. 51 52 02 52).

Verthuset Mat & Vin, in an elegant setting, serves up big portions of traditional Norwegian food (100–150-kr specials are served Mon–Fri 11:30–19:00 and Sun 12:30–18:00) and pricier contemporary fare (200–300 kr, light meals-90–150 kr, open daily, a block behind main drag along harbor at Skagen 10 ved Prostbakken, tel. 51 89 51 12).

Meny is a large supermarket with a good selection and a fine deli for super-picnic shopping (Mon–Fri 10:00–20:00, Sat 10:00–18:00, closed Sun, Nedre Strandgate).

Dining along the Harbor with a View

The harborside street of Skansegata is lined with lively restaurants and pubs—most serving food. Here are a couple options:

N. B. Sorensen's Dampskibsexpedition consists of a lively pub on the first floor (150–200 kr for pasta, fish, meat, and vegetarian dishes) and a fine-dining restaurant on the second floor, with tablecloths, view tables overlooking the harbor, and steep prices (entrées-250–300 kr, Mon–Thu 11:00–24:30, Fri–Sat 11:00–24:00, Sun 13:00–24:00, Skagenkaien 26, tel. 51 84 38 22). The restaurant is named after a company from the 1800s that shipped from this building, among other things, Norwegians to the United States.

Passengers and cargo waited on the first floor, and the manager's office was upstairs. The place is filled with emigrant-era memorabilia.

Sjøhuset Skagen, with a woodsy interior, invites diners to its historic building for lunch or dinner. The building, from the late 1700s, housed a trading company. Today, you can choose from local seafood specialties with an ethnic flair, as well as plenty of meat options (lunch-100–150 kr, dinner-200–250 kr, Mon–Sat 11:00–23:00, Sun 14:00–23:00, Skagenkaien 16, tel. 51 89 51 80).

TRANSPORTATION CONNECTIONS

From Stavanger by train to: Kristiansand (4–6/day, 3 hrs), **Oslo** (3/day, 8 hrs, overnight possible).

By boat to Bergen: Flaggruten catamarans sail between Bergen and Stavanger (2–6/day, 4 hrs, 560 kr one-way, 670 kr round-trip; nearly half-price for students, railpass holders, or for 1 partner when a couple travels together; tel. 55 23 87 80, www.flaggruten.no).

Setesdal Valley

Welcome to the remote—and therefore very traditional—Setesdal Valley. Probably Norway's most authentic cranny, the valley is a mellow montage of sod-roofed water mills, ancient churches, derelict farmhouses, yellowed recipes, and gentle scenery.

The Setesdal Valley joined the modern age with the construction of the valley highway in the 1950s. All along the valley, you'll see the unique two-story storage sheds called *stabburs* (the top floor was used for storing clothes; the bottom, food) and many sod roofs. Even the bus stops have rooftops the local goats love to munch.

In the high country, just over the Sessvatn summit (3,000 feet), you'll see herds of goats and summer farms. If you see an *Ekte Geitost* sign, that means genuine homemade goat cheese is for sale. (It's sold cheaper and in more manageable sizes in grocery stores.) To some, it looks like a decade's accumulation of earwax. I think it's delicious. Remember, *ekte* means all-goat—really strong. The more popular and easier-to-eat regular goat cheese is mixed with cow's-milk cheese.

For more information on the Setesdal Valley, see www.setesdal.com.

SIGHTS

These sights are listed from north to south.

Odda—At the end of the Hardanger Fjord, just past the huge zinc and copper industrial plant, you'll hit the industrial town of Odda (well-stocked **TI** for whole region and beyond, in summer Mon–Fri

Setesdal Valley

10:00–20:00, Sat 9:00–17:00, Sun 11:00–18:00, off-season Mon–Fri 9:00–16:00, tel. 53 64 12 97). Odda brags that Kaiser Wilhelm came here a lot, but he's dead and I'd drive right through. If you want to visit the tongue of a glacier, drive to Buar and hike an hour to Buarbreen. From Odda, drive into the land of boulders. The many mighty waterfalls that line the road seem to have hurled huge rocks (with rooted trees) into the rivers and fields. Stop at the giant double waterfall (on the left, pull out on the right, drive slowly through it if you need a car wash).

Røldal—Continue over Røldalsfjellet and into the valley below, where the old town of Røldal is trying to develop some tourism. Drive straight through. Its old church isn't worth the time or money. Lakes are like frosted mirrors, making desolate huts come in pairs. Haukeliseter, a group of sod-roofed buildings filled with cultural clichés and tour groups, offers pastries, sandwiches, and reasonable hot meals (from 100 kr) in a lakeside setting. Try the traditional *rømmegrøt* porridge.

Haukeligrend—Haukeligrend is a bus/traffic junction, with daily bus service to/from Bergen and to/from Kristiansand (**TI** open daily all year 7:00–22:00, tel. 35 07 03 67).

Hovden—Hovden is a ski resort (2,500 feet high) at the top of the Setesdal Valley, barren in the summer and painfully in need of charm. Locals come here to walk and relax for a week. Good walks offer a chance to see reindeer, moose, arctic fox, and wabbits—so they say. A chairlift sometimes takes sightseers to the top of a nearby peak. Hegni Center, on the lake at the south edge of town, rents canoes (160 kr/day, tel. 37 93 96 62). A super indoor spa/pool complex, the Hovden Badeland, provides a much-needed way to spend an otherwise dreary and drizzly early evening here (145 kr, daily 10:00–19:00 in summer, less off-season, tel. 37 93 93 93). The **TI** is open all year (Mon–Fri 9:00–16:00, summer Sat 10:00–14:00, July also on Sun 12:00–16:00, otherwise closed Sat–Sun, tel. 37 93 96 30, www.hovden.com, post@hovden.com).

Sleeping in Hovden: $ Hovden Fjellstoge is a big, old ski chalet renting Hovden's only cheap beds: bunk-bed doubles for 450 kr, cabins for 550 kr, and dorms (dorm bed-160 kr, 25 kr extra if you're not a hostel member, sheets-70 kr, breakfast-70 kr, tel. 37 93 95 43, www .hovdenfjellstoge.no). Built in 1911, this is the oldest place in town.

▲**Dammar Vatnedalsvatn**—Just south of Hovden is a two-mile side-trip to a 400-foot-high rock-pile dam. Great view, impressive rockery. This is one of the highest dams in Northern Europe. Read the chart. Sit out of the wind a few rows down the rock pile and ponder the vastness of Norwegian wood.

▲**Bykle**—The most interesting folk museum and church in Setesdal are in the teeny town of Bykle. The 17th-century church has two balconies—one for men and one for women (20 kr, mid-June–mid-Aug daily 11:00–17:00, tel. 37 93 85 00).

The **Huldreheimen Museum,** a wonderful little open-air museum, is a typical 800-year-old *seterhouse* used when the cattle spent the summer high in the mountains. Follow the sign up a road to a farm perched above the town, park, then hike a steep 150 yards into Norway's medieval peasant past. You'll get a fine view, six houses filled with old stuff, and a good English brochure (25 kr, late June–mid-Aug daily 11:00–17:00).

Grasbrokke—On the east side of the main road (at the Grasbrokke sign), you'll see an old water mill (1630). A few minutes farther south is a Picnic and WC sign. Exit onto that little road. You'll pass another old water mill with a fragile rotten-log sluice. At the second picnic turnout (just before this roadlet returns to the highway—you'll find a covered picnic table for rainy lunches), turn out and frolic along the river rocks.

Flateland—The **Setesdal Museum** (Rygnestadtunet) offers more of what you saw at Bykle (20 kr, 2 buildings, daily late June and Aug 11:00–17:00, July 10:00–18:00, closed off-season, 1 mile east of the road, tel. 37 93 63 03). Unless you're a glutton for culture, I wouldn't do both.

▲**Valle**—This is Setesdal's prettiest village (but don't tell Bykle). In the center, you'll find fine silver- and gold-work, traditional dinners in the cozy Bergtun Hotel (150–200 kr, summer only), homemade crafts next to the TI, and old-fashioned *lefse* cooking demonstrations (in the small log house by the campground). The fine suspension bridge attracts kids of any age (b-b-b-b-bounce) and anyone interested in a great view over the river to the strange mountains that look like polished, petrified mud slides. European rock climbers, tired of the over-climbed Alps, often entertain spectators with their sport. Is anyone climbing? (**TI** open early June–late Aug Mon–Fri 10:00–17:00, Sat 10:00–14:00, closed Sun; off-season Mon–Fri 7:30–15:00, closed Sat–Sun; tel. 37 93 75 29, valle@setesdal.com.)

Sleeping in Valle: $$ Bergtun Hotel, run by Halvor Kjelleberg, has a folksy, sit-a-spell Setesdal lodge full of traditional furniture, paintings, and carvings in each charming room (D-600 kr, some rooms have bunks, extra bed-125 kr, includes breakfast, open July–mid-Aug, Valle i Setesdal, tel. 37 93 77 20, fax 37 93 77 15). Off-season, **$$ Valle Hotel** answers Bergtun's phone and rents rooms (Db-650 kr, includes breakfast, tel. 37 93 77 00, www.valle-motell.no, motell@online.no).

Nomeland—Sylvartun, the silversmith with the valley's most aggressive publicity department, demonstrates the Setesdal specialty in a 17th-century log cabin and a free little gallery/museum. He also gives a free 30-minute fiddle concert weekdays in July at 13:00. On some Mondays and Thursdays at 14:30, you can see a 30-minute folk-dance show (50 kr, tel. 37 93 63 06).

Grendi—The Ardal Church (1827) has a rune stone in its yard. Three hundred yards south of the church is a 900-year-old oak tree.

Evje—A huge town by Setesdal standards (3,500 people), Evje is famous for its gems and mines. Fancy stones fill the shops here. Rock hounds find the nearby mines fun; for a small fee you can hunt for gems. The **TI** is by Highway 9 in the center of Evje (mid-June–mid-Aug Mon–Fri 8:30–18:00, Sat 8:30–15:00, Sun 10:00–16:00; off-season Mon–Fri 8:30–16:00, closed Sat–Sun; tel. 37 93 14 00). The **Setesdal Mineral Park** is on the main road, two miles south of town (75 kr, June–Aug daily 10:00–16:00).

Kristiansand

This "capital of the south" has 75,000 inhabitants, a pleasant Renaissance grid-plan layout (Posebyen), a famous zoo with Norway's biggest amusement park (6 miles toward Oslo on the main road), a daily bus to Bergen, and lots of big boats going to England and Denmark. It's the closest thing to a beach resort in Norway. Markensgate is the bustling pedestrian market street—a pleasant place for good browsing, shopping, eating, and people-watching. Stroll along the Strand Promenaden (marina) to Christiansholm Fortress.

The **TI** is at Vester Strandgate 32, next to the boat, bus, and train station (Mon–Fri 8:30–18:00, Sat 10:00–18:00, Sun 12:00–18:00; off-season Mon–Fri 8:30–15:30, closed Sat–Sun; tel. 38 12 13 14). The bank at the Color Line terminal opens for each arrival and departure (even the midnight ones). The Fønex Kino cinema complex is within two blocks of the ferry and TI (60–75 kr, 7 screens, showing movies in English, schedules at the entrance).

SLEEPING

(6.5 kr = about $1, country code: 47)
Except for the fine Hotel Sjøgløtt, Kristiansand hotels are expensive and nondescript.

$$$ Rica Hotel Norge is a modern option (rack rates: Sb-1,195, Db 1,295; June–mid-Aug: Sb-890, Db-1,090 kr; weekend rates year-round: Sb-725 kr, Db-925 kr; Dronningensgate 5, tel. 38 17 40 00, fax 38 17 40 01, www.hotel-norge.no, booking@hotel-norge.no).

$$$ Rainbow Hotel Wergeland is inviting for a large chain hotel. It's within earshot of the church bells and busy Kirkegate, but quieter rooms away from the street are available (Sb-895, Db-1,145, about 150 kr less if you buy 90-kr Skanplus Hotel Pass—see page 146, includes breakfast, non-smoking rooms, no elevator, free Internet access, Kirkegate 15, tel. 38 17 20 49, fax 38 02 73 21, www.rainbow-hotels.no/wergeland, post@hotellwergeland.no).

$$ Hotel Sjøgløtt is your best comfy-and-cozy bet. Friendly Helene Ranestad gives this well-worn hotel lots of class (S-350–450 kr, Ss-490 kr, Sb-640 kr, D-660 kr, Ds-690 kr, Db-840 kr, includes breakfast, near harbor on quiet street at Østre Strandgt 25, tel. & fax 38 02 21 20, www.sjoglott.no, sjoglott@sjoglott.no).

EATING

The otherwise uninteresting harbor area has a cluster of wooden buildings called **Fiskebasaren** ("Fish Bazaar"). While the indoor fish market is only open during the day, numerous restaurants (serving fish, among other dishes) provide a nice atmosphere for dinner. Follow Vester Strandgate past the Fønix movie theater to Østre Strandgate, take a right, and follow the signs to Fiskebrygga.

TRANSPORTATION CONNECTIONS

From Kristiansand by train to: Stavanger (4–6/day, 3 hrs), **Oslo** (4/day, 4.5 hrs).

By boat to Hirtshals, Denmark: The Color Line ferry sails from Kristiansand in Norway to Hirtshals in Denmark (daily mid-June-late Aug, departures at about 8:15-regular, 9:00-fast, 13:30-regular,

15:00-fast, 21:45-slow, and 1:15-slowest; 2-4 departures daily other months). Fast boats take 2.5 hours, regular boats take 4.5 hours, and the overnight boat arrives at 7:00. Passengers pay 200-450 kr (July and weekends are most expensive). The car package lets five in a car travel for as low as 950 kr (summer Mon–Thu; weekend departures cost more). Ferries have decent *store koldt bord* buffets, music, duty-free shopping, a desk to process your Norwegian duty-free tax rebates, and a bank.

When you can commit yourself to a firm date, call Color Line to make a reservation. They accept telephone reservations, payable when you get to the dock (long hours daily, Norwegian tel. 81 00 08 11, Danish tel. 99 56 19 77, www.colorline.com). Ask about specials. Students and seniors save about 50 percent. Round-trip fares can be lower than one-way fares.

Take the night boat to save the cost of a hotel. Enjoy an evening in Kristiansand, then sleep (or vomit) as you sail to Denmark. Beds are reasonable (reclining seats euphemistically called "sleeperettes"-50 kr, simple *couchettes*-82 kr, bed in a 4-berth room-164 kr, the cheapest private double with shower-280 kr per person). You owe yourself the comfort of a private room if you're efficient enough to spend this night traveling. I slept so well that I missed the Denmark landing and ended up crossing three times! After chewing me out, the captain said it happens a lot. Set your alarm or spend an extra day at sea.

Route Tips for Drivers

Bergen to Kristiansand via Setesdal Valley (10 hrs): Your first key connection is the Kvanndal–Utne ferry (a 2-hr drive from Bergen, departures hrly 6:00–23:00, tel. 55 23 87 80 to confirm times, reservations not possible or even necessary if you get there 20 min early, breakfast in cafeteria). If you make the 9:00, your day will be more relaxed. Driving comfortably, with no mistakes or traffic, it's two hours from your Bergen hotel to the ferry dock. Leaving Bergen is a bit confusing. Pretend you're going to Oslo on the road to Voss (signs for Nestune, Landås, Nattland). About a half hour out of town, after a long tunnel, leave the Voss road and head for Norheimsund. This road, treacherous for the famed beauty of the Hardanger Fjord it hugs as well as for its skinniness, is faster and safer if you beat the traffic (which you will with this plan).

The ferry drops you in Utne, where a lovely road takes you to Odda and up into the mountains. From Haukeligrend, turn south and wind up to Sessvatn at 3,000 feet. Enter Setesdal Valley. Follow the Otra River downhill for 140 miles south to the major port town of Kristiansand. Skip the secondary routes. As you enter Kristiansand, follow signs for Denmark.

SWEDEN
(Sverige)

Sverige, as it's known in Swedish, takes its name from the Svea tribe that inhabited this vast country more than a thousand years ago. Swedish warriors traveled east in the early Middle Ages, founding Novgorod and Kiev and even serving as royal guards in Constantinople (modern-day Istanbul). During the later Middle Ages, German settlers and traders strongly influenced Sweden's culture and language.

In the 17th century, Sweden was a major European power, with one of the largest naval fleets in Europe and an empire extending around the Baltics, including Finland, parts of Poland, Russia, Germany, and the present-day Baltic countries. But by the early 19th century, Sweden's war-weary empire had shrunk. The country's current borders date from 1809.

During a massive wave of emigration in the mid- to late 19th century, about a third of Sweden's three million people left for the Promised Land—America. Many emigrants were farmers from the southern region of Småland. Images of these poor emigrants were popularized in the movie *The Immigrants,* based on the book trilogy by Vilhelm Moberg.

While other European countries were embroiled in the two World Wars, neutral Sweden grew stronger, building the foundations of its current economy.

Recession hit in the 1990s, but over the last decade, Sweden's economy improved, buoyed by a strong lineup of successful multinational companies. Saab, Volvo, Scania trucks and machinery, Ikea, and Ericsson (the telecommunications giant) are leading the way in manufacturing, design, and technology. A sizable share of Swedish exports come from forest products and mineral industries. Locals still debate the wisdom of their entry into the European Union.

How Big, How Many, How Much

- Sweden is 173,700 square miles (a little bigger than California).
- Population is 9 million (about 50 per square mile).
- 7 Swedish kronor = about $1

Sweden

200 MILES
200 KM
↑ TO ÖSTERSUND
N
FINLAND
NORWAY
MORA
DALARNA
GÄVLE
TURKU
OSLO
UPPSALA
ÅLAND ISLANDS
TO HELSINKI & TALLINN
ARJÄNG
KARLSTAD
STOCKHOLM
GÖTA CANAL
GOTLAND
GÖTEBORG
VISBY
FRED.
OSKARS.
SMÅLAND
VÄXJÖ
ÖLAND
KALMAR
DENMARK
LUND
COPE.
MALMÖ
BALTIC SEA
DCH

Swedes are often stereotyped as socialist, suicidal, and sex-crazed—which could not be further from the truth. Sweden's economic and social welfare programs are based on creating a *folkhemmet*, or "home of the people," for citizens from cradle to grave. As for suicide rates, Sweden actually ranks low here—well behind Japan, Germany, Austria, France, Switzerland, and others. The bad rap stems from the fact that Sweden was one of the first countries to begin recording suicide as a cause of death—back when other countries labeled it as "an accident." Several steamy Swedish films and film stars from the 1950s and 1960s stuck Sweden with the sexpot stereotype, which still reverberates among male tourists. Italians continue to travel up to Sweden looking for those bra-less, loose, and lascivious blondes...about 40 years late. Although rather frank and open about sexuality, Sweden actually ranks nearly last in rates of teenage pregnancy and STDs.

While Sweden is 90 percent Lutheran, less than 5 percent of the population goes to church regularly. Swedes are more likely to find religion in nature, whether relaxing at their summer cottage, hiking in the vast wilderness, or fishing in one of the thousands of lakes or rivers. Sweden is nearly 80 percent wilderness, and modern legislation incorporated an ancient common law called *Allemanns rätt* that guarantees people the right to move freely through Sweden's natural scenery without asking the landowner for permission, as long as they behave responsibly.

At work, Swedes are diligent and focused, but during their free time they are wild, fun-loving, and laid-back. This is most evident in summer, when Swedes take advantage of the long days and warm evenings for festivals such as Midsummer in June and crayfish parties in August. Long vacations allow for holidays in the countryside. Many Swedes have a summer cottage—or know someone who has one—where they spend countless hours soaking up the sun.

Since the 1960s, Sweden (like Denmark and Norway) has accepted many immigrants and refugees from southeastern Europe, the Middle East, and elsewhere. This praiseworthy humanitarian policy has dramatically (and sometimes painfully) diversified a formerly homogenous country. The suburbs of Rinkeby and Tensta are Stockholm's ethnic neighborhoods. Many of the service-industry workers you will meet have come to Sweden from elsewhere.

For great electronic fact sheets on everything in Swedish society from health care to its Sami people, see www.sweden.se.

Most Swedes speak English, but a few Swedish words are helpful. "Hello" is *"Hej"* (hay) and "Goodbye" is *"Hej då"* (hay doh). "Thank you" is *"Tack"* (tahk), which can also double for "Please."

STOCKHOLM

If I had to call one European city home, it could be Stockholm. One third water, one third parks, on the sea, surrounded by woods, bubbling with energy and history, Sweden's stunning capital is green, clean, and underrated.

Crawl through Europe's best-preserved old warship and relax on a canal-boat tour. Browse the cobbles and antique shops of the lantern-lit Old Town and take a spin through Skansen, Europe's first and best open-air folk museum. Marvel at Stockholm's glittering City Hall, modern department stores, and art museums.

While progressive and sleek, Stockholm respects its heritage. In summer, mounted bands parade daily through the heart of town to the Royal Palace, announcing the Changing of the Guard and turning the most dignified tourist into a scampering kid.

Planning Your Time

On a two- to three-week trip through Scandinavia, Stockholm is worth two days. I'd spend them this way:

Day 1: 9:00-Pick up map and Stockholm Card at the TI; 10:00-Catch 90-minute bus tour from Royal Opera House; 12:00-See *Vasa* warship and grab lunch; 14:00-Visit Nordic Museum; 15:00-Tour Skansen Open-Air Museum and ride boat to Nybroplan; 18:30-Take Royal Canal tour (last boat departs earlier Sept–April); 20:00-Enjoy a *smörgåsbord* feast at the Grand Hotel or wander Gamla Stan in search of dinner.

Day 2: 10:00-Take City Hall tour and climb City Hall tower for a fine view; 12:15-Catch the Changing of the Guard at the palace (13:15 on Sun); 13:00-Lunch on Stortorget; 14:00-Tour Royal Palace and Armory and follow my Old Town self-guided walk; 16:00-Browse the modern city center around Kungsträdgården, Sergels Torg, Hötorget market and indoor food hall, and Drottninggatan area.

If you're more interested in sightseeing than in shopping and browsing (or if it's Sept–April, when boat tours end earlier), you could do the canal tour on the second day rather than the first.

ORIENTATION

(area code: 08)
Greater Stockholm's 1.8 million residents live on 14 islands that are woven together by 54 bridges. Visitors need only concern themselves with five islands: **Norrmalm** is downtown, with most of the hotels and shopping areas, and the train-and-bus station. **Gamla Stan** is the old city of winding, lantern-lit streets, antiques shops, and classy, glassy cafés clustered around the Royal Palace. **Södermalm,** aptly called "Stockholm's Brooklyn," is residential and not touristy. **Skeppsholmen** is the small, central, traffic-free park/island with the Museum of Modern Art and two fine youth hostels. The park island of **Djurgården** ("Animal Garden") is Stockholm's wonderful green playground, with many of the city's top sights (bike rentals just over bridge as you enter island).

Stockholm: City of Islands

Tourist Information
Sweden House (Sverige Huset) is Stockholm's official TI (6-block walk from train/bus station at Hamngatan 27, T-bana: Kungsträdgården). Until renovations are finished sometime in 2005, the TI will be in temporary quarters in the basement of Kulturhuset on Sergels Torg. They've got free city maps, pamphlets on everything, and an "excursion shop" for Stockholm Cards (see below), transportation passes, and day-trip and bus-tour information and tickets (June–Aug Mon–Fri 9:00–19:00, Sat 9:00–17:00, Sun 10:00–16:00, less off-season, tel. 08/789-2490, www.stockholmtown.com). *What's on Stockholm* is a free monthly listing the opening times and directions to sights, special events, and much more.

Those arriving by train or bus can get limited tourist information at **Hotellcentralen** (Hotel Center), a branch of the TI whose primary purpose is helping visitors with hotel bookings. It's located in the train station's main hall (May–Aug daily 8:00–20:00; Sept–April Mon–Sat 9:00–18:00, Sun 12:00–16:00; tel. 08/789-2490, fax 08/791-8666). Often clogged with long lines of visitors,

Hotellcentralen may not be worth the long wait. The Sweden House is just a few blocks away and has more space, more staff, and more information. Though excellent free maps are all over town, Hotellcentralen stocks only a 20-kr map. However, they are good at finding discounted business-class hotel rooms (60-kr booking fee, see "Sleeping," page 242).

The **Stockholm Card,** a 24-hour pass for 260 kr, includes all public transit (except harbor shuttle ferry), virtually every sight (70 places), some free or discounted tours, free parking, and a handy sightseeing handbook. An added bonus is the substantial pleasure of doing everything without considering the cost (many of Stockholm's sights are worth the time but not the money). This card pays for itself if you do Skansen, the *Vasa* Museum, and Millesgården. You can stretch it by entering Skansen on your 24th hour. Parents: Up to two children (age 7–17) can share a pass for 100 kr. The Stockholm Card also comes in 48-hour (390 kr for adults, 140 kr for kids) and 72-hour (540 kr for adults, 190 kr for kids) versions. Cards are sold at the Sweden House TI, Hotel Center (in train station), hostels, and some subway stations.

Arrival in Stockholm

By Train or Bus: Stockholm's combined train and bus station is a wonderland of services, shops, exchange desks, and people on the move. The bus section (called Cityterminalen) is up the escalators from the train station's main hall. The station has a T-bana stop and taxi stands, and is just a few blocks away from the TI (see above). If you're sailing to Finland, look for the Viking Line office in the bus terminal.

By Plane: Stockholm's Arlanda Airport is 28 miles north of town (airport info: tel. 08/797-6100, SAS toll-free tel. 077/0-727-727). **Shuttle buses** (Flygbussarna) make the 40-minute trip between the airport and the train/bus station (89 kr, 6/hr, can take longer at rush hour, buy tickets from ticket windows, www.flygbussarna.se). The Arlanda Express **airport train** is twice as fast, but costs twice as much and goes less frequently (180 kr, free with railpass, 4/hr, 20 min, has its own separate platform in station, toll-free tel. 020/222-224). Buy your ticket either at the kiosk next to the train's terminal or from the automatic machine with cash or credit card; you'll pay 40 kr extra if you buy your ticket on board. **Taxis** take about 30–40 minutes (at a fixed rate of about 400 kr, depends on company).

By Boat: For information on Stockholm's cruise-ship terminals, see page 296 for Tallink boats to Tallinn, or page 271 for Viking and Silja boats to Helsinki.

By Car: Only a Swedish meatball would drive his car in Stockholm. Park it and use the public transit. The TI has a *Parking in Stockholm* brochure. Those with the Stockholm Card can park free in a big central garage or at any parking meter for the duration of the ticket (ask for parking card and specifics when buying your Stockholm Card). Those sailing to Finland or Estonia should ask about long-term parking at the terminal when reserving their ticket. Avoid the cheap lot at Ropsten, the subway station near the Silja Line terminal; readers have reported vandalism and theft here. Use a parking garage instead.

Helpful Hints

Telephone: In case of an emergency, dial 112. For operator assistance, call 118-118. Numbers starting with 020 are toll-free. Numbers beginning with 070 and 073 are mobile phones—costing about triple the cost of a regular call. And 077 calls are like 900 numbers in the States—expensive. Kiosks sell cheap international phone cards offering calls to the United States for less than one krona per minute.

Medical Help: For around-the-clock medical advice, call tel. 08/320-100, then press 2. A 24-hour pharmacy is near the train station at Klarabergsgatan 64 (tel. 08/454-8130).

Internet Access: The best deal is in the bus station hall (use coin-op machines to buy reusable tickets, 19 kr/hr, 19-kr minimum, change machine in station, daily until 24:00). Or try in the basement of Kulturhuset on Sergels Torg (40 kr/hr, Tue–Fri 11:00–18:00, Sat–Sun 11:00–16:00, closed Monday, tel. 08/508-31489).

Laundry: Tvättomaten is a rare find in central Stockholm (self-serve-74 kr, same-day full service-160 kr; Mon–Fri 8:30–18:30, Sat 9:30–15:00, closed Sun year-round and Sat July–mid-Aug; across from Gustav Vasa church, Västmannagatan 61 on Odenplan, T-bana: Odenplan, tel. 08/346-480).

Bike Rental: Rent bikes, in-line skates, and boats at Djurgårdsbrons Sjöcafe, next to Djurgårdsbron Bridge near the *Vasa* Museum (bikes-250 kr/day, May–Oct daily 9:00–21:00, closed Nov–April, tel. 08/660-5757).

Getting Around Stockholm

By Bus and Subway (T-bana): Stockholm has a fine bus and subway system, and special passes that take the bite out of the city's cost. It's a spread-out city with several different centers, so most visitors will need public transport at some point (transit info tel. 08/600-1000 and press 8, www.sl.se/english). The subway is easy to figure out, but many sights are better served by bus. The main lines are listed on the map in *What's On Stockholm*. A more detailed system map is posted around town and available free from subway ticket windows and SL info desks in main stations. Ride the subway, or Tunnelbana ("T-bana" for short), just for the futuristic drama of being a human mole, and to

Greater Stockholm

check out the modern public art (tops at Kungsträdgården station).

Buses and the subway work on the same tickets (valid for 1 hour). Use two strips per ride. Single tickets cost 15 kr per strip (buy from driver or turnstile attendant). Strip cards are much cheaper (10 strips for 80 kr, 20 strips for 145 kr, shareable, saves money if you take at least 3 rides). Everything I mention is in the central fare zone, except for the Carl Millesgården (in Zone 2, requires 3 strips from the center) and Drottningholm (Zone 3, requires 4 strips; also accessible by boat—see "Getting to Drottningholm" on page 240.

The **Tourist Card,** which isn't necessary if you're getting the Stockholm Card (above), gives you free use of all public transport and the harbor shuttle ferry (24 hrs/95 kr, 72 hrs/180 kr; 72-hr version covers Gröna Lund amusement park and half-price entry to Skansen; sold at TIs, bigger subway stations, and newsstands).

By Harbor Shuttle Ferry: Throughout the summer, ferries connect Stockholm's two most interesting sightseeing districts. They make the five-minute journey from Nybroplan and Slussen to Djurgården, landing next to the *Vasa* Museum, a 10-minute walk from Skansen (20 kr, ferry covered by Tourist Card but not Stockholm Card, 3/hr, daily 10:00–20:00). While practical, this is also fun and scenic.

By Taxi: To get a taxi quick, call Taxi Stockholm (tel. 08/150-000) or Taxi Kurir (tel. 08/300-000). Minimum charge is 80 kr. Ouch.

TOURS

Hop-on, Hop-off Bus Tour—Like hop-on, hop-off buses throughout Europe, Open Top Tour's topless double-decker bus makes a 90-minute circuit of the city, stopping at the 14 essential places. The commentary, though recorded, is good (180-kr ticket good all day—you can hop off, tour a sight, and catch a later bus; buses run roughly April–Oct, 4/hr, first departure 10:00 from Strömkajen by Grand Hotel, last departure 16:20, tel. 08/161-533). The bus provides a convenient connection to sights from Skansen to City Hall.

Quickie Orientation Bus Tour—Several different city bus tours leave from the Royal Opera House on Gustav Adolfs Torg. City Sightseeing's Stockholm Panorama tour provides a good overview (200 kr, 90 min, mid-April–Oct daily at 10:00, 12:00, and 14:00, more in mid-summer, tel. 08/587-14020, www.citysightseeing.com).

Old Town Walk—City Sightseeing also offers a 90-minute Old Town walk (80 kr, daily July–Aug at 11:30, 13:30, and 15:30, leaves from Mynttorget, tel. 08/587-14020, www.citysightseeing.com).

▲City Boat Tour—For a good floating look at Stockholm and a pleasant break, consider a sightseeing cruise. The handiest are the Stockholm Sightseeing boats leaving from Strömkajen in front of the Grand Hotel (tel. 08/587-14020). You have two choices: short and scenic or long and informative. Both come with a tape-recorded spiel. The short, scenic, 60-minute Royal Canal tour is a joyride through lots of greenery (110 kr, free or discounted with Stockholm Card, departing at :30 past each hour, generally daily May–Aug 10:30–18:30, April and Sept 10:30–15:30, Oct–Dec 10:30–13:30, none Jan–March). The two-hour Under the Bridges tour goes through two locks and under 15 bridges (160 kr, not covered by Stockholm Card, early June–mid-Sept daily 10:00–18:00, departures on the hour). They also do a 2.5-hr archipelago tour (190 kr, departs daily at 9:30 and 13:00 in season).

Bike Tours—John's Bike Tours outfits you with bike and helmet for a guided ride through the city, leaving from the boat office on Strömkajen by the Grand Hotel (daily late June–mid Sept, 3-hr tour for 270 kr leaves at 9:30, 2-hr tour for 190 kr leaves at 14:30, www.johnsbiketours.se).

Local Guides—To hire a private guide, call tel. 08/789-2496 (Mon–Fri 9:00–17:00, closed Sat–Sun) or visit www.guidestockholm .com. The standard rate is about 1,100 kr for a half-day tour.

Stockholm

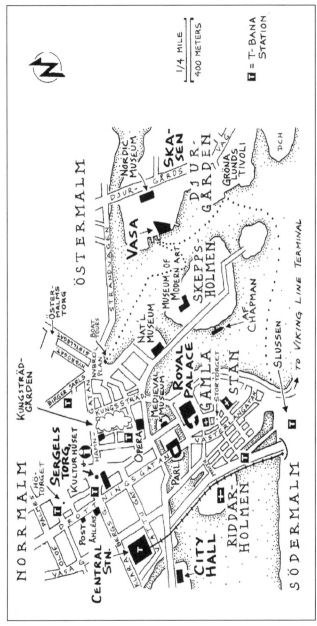

1/4 MILE
400 METERS

🚇 = T-BANA STATION

ÖSTERMALM

NORDIC MUSEUM

SKA-NSEN

DJUR-GÅRDS

DJUR-GÅRDEN

GRÖNA LUNDS TIVOLI

VASA

MUSEUM OF MODERN ART

SKEPPS-HOLMEN

ÖSTER-MALMS TORG

STRANDVÄGEN

NAT'L MUSEUM

BOAT TOURS

AF CHAPMAN

TO VIKING LINE TERMINAL

KUNGSTRÄD-GÅRDEN

NYBROGATAN

SIBYLLEGAT

NYBROPLAN

BIRGER JARLS GATAN

KUNGSTRÄD

MEDIEVAL MUSEUM

ROYAL PALACE

GAMLA STAN

SLUSSEN

VÄSTERLÅNGGATAN

STORTORGET

NORRMALM

PALMES

HÖTORGET

SERGELS TORG

KULTURHUSET

OPERA

PARL

HAMN

GATAN

OLOF

VASA

POST

ÅHLÉNS

KLARA BERGS G.

DROTTNING G.

SVEAVÄGEN

TUNNEL G.

CENTRAL STN.

CITY HALL

RIDDAR-HOLMEN

SÖDERMALM

Stockholm at a Glance

▲▲▲**Skansen** Europe's first, and among its best, open-air folk museums, with more than 150 old homes, churches, shops, and schools. **Hours:** Daily May 10:00–20:00, June–Aug 10:00–22:00, Sept 10:00–17:00, Oct–April 10:00–16:00.

▲▲▲*Vasa* **Museum** Ill-fated 17th-century warship dredged from the sea floor, now the showpiece of an interesting museum. **Hours:** Daily mid-June–mid-Aug 9:30–19:00, off-season 10:00–17:00, winter Wed until 20:00.

▲▲▲**Nordic Museum** Danish Renaissance palace design and five fascinating centuries of traditional Swedish lifestyles. **Hours:** Daily late June–Aug 10:00–17:00, Sept–late June 10:00–16:00.

▲▲▲**Royal Armory** Europe's most spectacular collection of medieval royal armor, in the Royal Palace. **Hours:** June–Aug daily 10:00–17:00, Sept–May Tue–Sun 11:00–17:00, Thu until 20:00, closed Mon.

▲▲**Military Parade and Changing of the Guard** Punchy daily pomp starting at Nybroplan and finishing at Royal Palace outer courtyard. **Hours:** Starts Mon–Sat at 11:45, Sunday at 12:45, mid-May–Sept.

▲▲**City Hall** Gilt mosaic architectural jewel of Stockholm and site of Nobel Prize banquet, with tower offering the city's best views. **Hours:** Tours daily at 10:00 and 12:00, more in summer; tower open May–Sept daily 10:00–16:30, closed Oct–April.

▲▲**Millesgården** Dramatic cliffside museum and grounds featuring works of Sweden's greatest sculptor, Carl Milles. **Hours:** Mid-May–Aug daily 10:00–17:00; Sept–mid-May Thu–Sun 12:00–17:00, closed Mon–Wed.

Self-Guided Walk: Stockholm's Old Town

Stockholm's old island core (Gamla Stan) is charming, fit for a roll of film, and full of antiques shops, street lanterns, painted ceilings, and surprises. Until the 1600s, all of Stockholm fit on Gamla Stan. Stockholm traded with other northern ports such as Amsterdam, Lübeck, and Tallinn. German culture influenced art, building styles, and even the language, turning Old Norse into modern Swedish. With its narrow alleys and stairways, Gamla Stan mixes poorly with cars and modern economies. Today it's been given over to the Royal Palace and to the tourists—sometimes seemingly unaware that most of Stockholm's major attractions are

▲▲Drottningholm Palace Resplendent 17th-century royal residence with a Baroque theater. **Hours:** May–Aug daily 10:00–16:30, Sept daily 12:00–15:30, Oct–April Sat–Sun only 12:00–15:30.

▲▲Archipelago Mostly half-day cruises to Vaxholm and many other small island destinations. **Hours:** Several options per day in summer, some including a meal onboard.

▲Nobel Museum Star-studded tribute to some of the world's most accomplished scientists, artists, economists, and politicians. **Hours:** Mid-May–mid-Sept daily 10:00–18:00, Tue until 20:00; off-season Tue–Sun 11:00–17:00, Tue until 20:00, closed Mon.

▲Royal Palace Museums Complex of Swedish royal museums, the two best of which are the Apartments of State and Royal Treasury. **Hours:** Mid-May–Aug daily 10:00–16:00; Sept–mid-May Tue–Sun 12:00–15:00, closed Mon and for one month in winter (usually Jan).

▲Kungsträdgården Stockholm's lively central square, with life-sized chess games, concerts, and perpetual action. **Hours:** Always open.

▲Sergels Torg Modern square with underground mall. **Hours:** Always open.

▲National Museum of Fine Arts Convenient, crowd-free gallery with work of locals Larsson and Zorn, along with Rembrandt, Rubens, and Impressionists. **Hours:** Tue–Sun 11:00–17:00, Tue until 20:00, closed Mon.

▲Thielska Galleriet Enchanting waterside mansion with works of local artists Larsson, Zorn, and Munch. **Hours:** Mon–Sat 12:00–16:00, Sun 13:00–16:00.

elsewhere—who throng Gamla Stan's main drag, Västerlånggatan.

While you could just happily wander, give this quick ▲▲ walk a try first:

Royal Palace: Start at the base of the esplanade leading up to the palace (bottom of Slottsbacken, palace described on page 233), where a statue of King Gustav III gazes at the palace, built upon the site of Stockholm's first castle. Gustav loved the arts and founded the Royal Dramatic Theater and the Opera in Stockholm. Ironically, he was assassinated at a masquerade ball at the Royal Opera House in 1792, inspiring Verdi's opera *Un Ballo in Maschera*.

Self-Guided Walk: Stockholm's Old Town

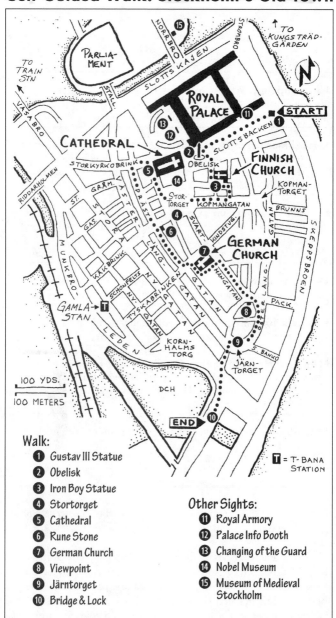

Walk:
1. Gustav III Statue
2. Obelisk
3. Iron Boy Statue
4. Stortorget
5. Cathedral
6. Rune Stone
7. German Church
8. Viewpoint
9. Järntorget
10. Bridge & Lock

Other Sights:
11. Royal Armory
12. Palace Info Booth
13. Changing of the Guard
14. Nobel Museum
15. Museum of Medieval Stockholm

T = T-BANA STATION

Walk up the broad, cobbled boulevard. (There's a fine Sweden bookshop on the left near bottom.) Partway up the hill, stop and scan the harbor. The grand building (across the water) is the National Museum—often mistaken by tourists for the palace. In the distance beyond that is a fine row of buildings—Strandvägen. Until the 1850s this was a slum, but as the city was entering its grand stage, this was cleaned up and replaced by fine apartments, which are some of the city's smartest addresses today. Live here, and you call Bjorn Borg your neighbor. Stockholm's TV tower—back in the 1970s a major attraction—stands tall in the distance. The Viking ship moored closest to you is friendly (a tour boat and restaurant). Turn to the palace facade on your left (finished in 1754, replacing one that burned in 1697). The niches are filled with Swedish big-wigs (literally) from the mid-18th century.

The **obelisk** honors Stockholm's merchant class for its support in a war against Russia (1788). In front of the obelisk are tour buses (their drivers worried about parking cops) and a new sand pit for *boules.* The royal family took a liking to the French game during a Mediterranean vacation, and it's quite popular around town today. Behind the obelisk stands Storkyrkan, Stockholm's cathedral (which we'll visit later in this walk). Opposite the palace (orange building on left) is the Finnish church (Finska Kyrkan), which originated as the royal tennis hall.

Stroll behind the church into the shady churchyard where you'll find the fist-sized *Iron Boy,* the tiniest statue (of about 600) in Stockholm. Old ladies knit caps for him in the winter when it's cold. Some say it honors the orphans who had to transfer cargo from sea ships to lake ships before Stockholm's locks were built. Some people rub his head for good luck (which the orphans didn't have). Others rub his head for wisdom. Continue through the yard, cross Träd-gårdsgatan, go down the tiny lane to Kopmangatan (the medieval merchants' street, now popular with antiques dealers), turn right, and head for Stortorget, the old square.

Stortorget, Stockholm's Oldest Square: The grand building on the right is the Stock Exchange. This building now houses the noble Nobel Museum (described on page 232). Upstairs is the Swedish Academy, which awards the Nobel Prize for literature each year. On the immediate left is the Stockholm Stadsmission (offering the cheapest and best lunch around—see "Eating," page 247), and at #5 is their secondhand shop, affording those who peek in a fine look at the richly decorated ceilings characteristic of the Gamla Stan in the 17th century. The exotic flowers and animals implied that the people who lived or worked here were worldly. The town well is still a popular meeting point. Scan the fine old facades. The square has a notorious history. It was the site of Stockholm's bloodbath of 1520—during a royal power grab, most of the town's aristocracy was beheaded. Rivers of blood were said to have flowed through the streets. Later, this was the location of the town's pillory. At the far end of the square (under the finest gables), turn right and follow Trangsund toward the cathedral.

Cathedral (Storkyrkan): Just before the church, you'll see my favorite phone booth (Rikstelefon) and the gate to the churchyard being guarded by statues of Caution and Hope. Enter the cathedral (20 kr, daily mid-May–mid-Sept 9:00–18:00, until 16:00 off-season; the free and worthwhile English-language flier describes the interior). The interior is cobbled with centuries-old tomb-stones; more than 2,000 people are buried under the church. The tombstone of the Swedish reformer Olaus Petri sits appropriately simple and appropriately located—under the pulpit. The royal pews date from 1684. In front on the left, *Saint George and the Dragon* (1489) is carved of oak and elk horn. To some, this sym-bolizes the Swedes' overcoming the evil Danes. To others, it's more general—inspiring them to take up the struggle against even non-Danish evil. Regardless, it must be the gnarliest dragon's head in all of Europe. Near the exit is a painting that depicts Stockholm in the early 1500s, showing a walled city filling only today's Gamla Stan. It's a 1630 copy of the 1535 original. The fancy door on the left (and the plain one on the right) lead to free WCs. The exit door next to the painting takes you into the kid-friendly church-yard (once the cemetery).

Prästgatan Lane: Back in front of the church, continue down Trangsund. At the next corner, go downhill on Storkyrkobrinken

and take the first left on Prästgatan. Enjoy a quiet wander down this peaceful "Priests' Lane." (Västerlånggatan, the touristy drag, parallels this lane 1 block to the right—you can walk back up on it later.) As you stroll, look for sewage drain spouts (a foot or so off the cobbles—an improvement over the toss-it-out-the-window days, but raw nevertheless), tie bolts (iron bars that bind timber beams together), flaming gold phoenixes under red-crown medallions (telling firefighters this house paid its insurance and could be saved in case of fire), and small coal or wood hatches for fuel delivery back in the good old days.

After two blocks (at Kåkbrinken), a cannon barrel on the corner guards a medieval rune stone. (In case you can't read the old Nordic script, it says: "Torsten and Thorgun erected this stone in memory of their son.")

Continue farther down Prästgatan to Tyska Brinken and turn left. You will see the powerful brick steeple of the German church (Tyska Kyrkan). Its carillon has played four times a day since 1666. Think of the days when German merchants worked here. Wander through the churchyard and out the back. Exit right onto Svartmangatan and follow it to its end at an iron railing overlooking Österlånggatan.

Viewpoint: From this perch, survey the street below to the left and right. Notice how it curves. This marks the old shoreline. In medieval times, piers stretched out like fingers into the harbor. Gradually, as land was reclaimed and developed, these piers were extended, becoming lanes leading to piers farther away. Below you is a cute shop where elves can actually be seen making elves.

Walk right along Österlånggatan to Järntorget—a customs square in medieval times, and home of Sweden's first bank back in 1680 (the yellow building with the bars on the windows). A Konsum supermarket here, open daily, offers picnic fixings. From here, Västerlånggatan—the eating, shopping, and commercial pedestrian mall of Gamla Stan—leads back across the island. You'll be there in a minute, but finish this walk by continuing out of the square (opposite where you entered) down Järntorgsgatan. Walk out into the traffic hell and stop on the bridge above the canal.

This is Stockholm's lock—where boats are raised a yard to sail from the sea into the lake. Nicknamed "the divorce lock," this is where captains and first mates learn to communicate under pressure and the public eye. Survey the view. Opposite Gamla Stan is the island of Södermalm—bohemian, youthful, artsy, and casual—with its popular view elevator. Moored on the saltwater side are the cruise ships, which bring thousands of visitors into town each day through the season. Many of these boats are bound for Finland. The towering white syringe is Gröna Lund's (amusement park) "free-fall" ride. The equestrian statue is Jean Baptiste Bernadotte, the French nobleman invited to establish the current Swedish royal dynasty 200 years ago.

Bus #2 (which heads back downtown) stops just beyond Bernadotte near the waterfront. Better yet, linger longer in Gamla Stan—day or night, a lively place to enjoy. Västerlånggatan, Gamla Stan's main commercial drag, is a festival of distractions that keeps most visitors from seeing the historic charms of Old Town—which you just did. Now you can window-shop and eat (see "Eating," page 247). Or if it's late, get jazzed (see "Nightlife," page 242).

For more sightseeing, consider the other sights in Gamla Stan (see below) or at the Royal Palace (see "Royal Palace," below). If you continue back up Västerlånggatan, you'll pass the parliament building and cross back over onto Norrmalm (where the street becomes Drottninggatan). This puts you back in Stockholm's modern, vibrant new town, with some worthwhile sights (see "Downtown Stockholm," below) and great shopping (see "Shopping," page 241).

SIGHTS

Gamla Stan

The best of Gamla Stan is covered in my self-guided walk, page 226. But here are a few ways to extend your time in the Old Town.

▲**Nobel Museum (Nobelmuseet)**—Opened in 2001 for the 100-year anniversary of the Nobel Prize, this wonderful little museum is thoroughly entertaining and as creative as the  people it celebrates. Portraits of all 700-plus prize winners hang from the ceiling—shuffling around the room like shirts at the dry cleaner's (miss your favorite, and he or she will come around again in 3 hours). Two video rooms run a continuous montage of quick programs (3-min bios of various winners in one, and 5-min films celebrating various intellectual environments—from Cambridge to Parisian cafés—in the other). The Viennese-style Café Satir is the place to get creative with your coffee...and sample the famous Nobel ice cream. And don't miss the lockable hangers—to protect your fancy furry winter coat (50 kr; mid-May–mid-Sept daily 10:00–18:00, Tue until 20:00; off-season Tue–Sun 11:00–17:00, Tue until 20:00, closed Mon; on Stortorget in the center of Gamla Stan a block from the Royal Palace, tel. 08/232-506, www.nobel.se/nobelmuseet). The Swedish Academy, which awards the Nobel Prize for literature each year, is upstairs.

Parliament (Riksdaghuset)—For a firsthand look at Sweden's government, tour its Parliament buildings (free 1-hr tours in English late June–Aug, usually Mon–Fri at 11:00, 12:30, 14:00, and 15:30, enter at Riksgatan 3a, call 08/786-4000 to confirm times). It's also possible to watch the parliament in session.

Museum of Medieval Stockholm (Medeltidsmuseet)—While a bit grade-schoolish, this gives a good look at medieval Stockholm (60 kr, Tue–Sun 11:00–16:00, Wed until 18:00, closed Mon except July–Aug, enter from park in front of Parliament, tel. 08/508-31808). The Strömparterren park, with its café and Carl Milles statue of the *Sun Singer* greeting the day, is a pleasant place for a sightseeing break (but an expensive place for a potty break—use the free WC in the museum).

Royal Palace (Kungliga Slottet)

While the royal family beds down at Drottningholm, this complex in Gamla Stan is still the official royal residence. The palace, in Italian Baroque style, was completed in 1754 after a fire wiped out the earlier palace.

Don't miss the awesome Royal Armory; the Royal Treasury is worth a look; the chapel is nice but no big deal; the Apartments of State are not much as far as palace rooms go; and you can skip Gustav III's Museum of Antiquities and the Museum of Three Crowns. At some point during your Stockholm stay, try to see the Changing of the Guard. The information booth in the semicircular courtyard (at the top, where the guard changes) gives out an explanatory brochure with a map marking the different entrances (main entrance is on the west side—away from the water—but the Royal Armory has a separate entrance). They also have a list of today's guided tours. In peak season, there are up to four different English tours a day—at the top of four successive hours (included in the admission)—allowing you to systematically cover the entire complex. Since the palace is used for state functions, it's sometimes closed to tourists).

▲▲**Military Parade and Changing of the Guard**—Starting at Nybroplan (Mon–Sat at 11:45, Sun at 12:45, mid-May–Sept), Stockholm's daily military parade marches over Norrbro Bridge and up to the Royal Palace's outer courtyard, where the band plays and the guard changes. The performance is fresh and spirited because the soldiers are visiting Stockholm just like you—and it's a chance for boys from all over Sweden in every branch of the service to show their stuff in the big city. You can march with the band or gather at the palace courtyard where the band arrives at about 12:15 (13:15 on Sun). The best place to stand is along the wall in the inner courtyard, near the palace information and ticket office. There are columns with wide pedestals for easy perching, as well as benches that people stand on to view the ceremony—arrive early. Generally, after the barking and goose-stepping formalities, the band shows off for an impressive 40-minute marching concert. While the royal family now lives out of town at Drottningholm, the palace guards are for real. If the guard by the cannon in the semicircular courtyard looks a little lax, try wandering discreetly behind him.

▲▲▲**Royal Armory (Livrustkammaren)**—This oldest museum in Sweden has the most interesting and best-displayed collection of medieval royal armor I've seen anywhere in Europe. The original 17th-century gear includes royal baby wear "from frock to kilt," outfits kings wore when they were killed in battle or assassinated, gowns representing royal fashion through the ages, and five centuries of royal Swedish armor—all wonderfully described in English. An added bonus is a basement lined with royal coaches (including coronation coaches), all well-preserved, richly decorated, and with evocative audioguide coverage (65 kr, June–Aug daily 10:00–17:00; Sept–May Tue–Sun 11:00–17:00, Thu until 20:00, closed Mon; 20-kr audioguide is excellent—romantic couples can share it and crank up the volume; 45-min tours June–Aug Mon–Fri 13:00, Sat–Sun 14:00; entrance at bottom of Slottsbacken at base of palace, tel. 08/519-55544, www.lsh.se/livrustkammaren).

▲**Other Royal Palace Museums**—For the four museums below, you can enter through the main entrance and buy a 110-kr combo-ticket covering them all (otherwise 70 kr apiece; mid-May–Aug daily 10:00–16:00; Sept–mid-May Tue–Sun 12:00–15:00, closed Mon; entirely closed for about a month in winter, usually in Jan; tel. 08/402-6130, www.royalcourt.se).

Apartments of State (Representationsvåningarna): The stately palace exterior encloses 608 rooms (1 more than Britain's Buckingham Palace) of glittering 18th-century Baroque and rococo decor. Clearly the palace of Scandinavia's superpower, it's steeped in royal history. You'll walk the long halls through four sections: the Hall of State (with an exhibit of fancy state awards); the lavish Bernadotte Apartments (some fine rococo interiors and portraits of the Bernadotte dynasty); the State Apartments (with rooms dating to the 1690s); and the Guest Apartments—where visiting heads of state still crash.

Royal Treasury (Skattkammaren): Climbing down into the super-secure vault, you'll see 12 cases filled with fancy crowns, scepters, jeweled robes, and plenty of glittering gold. Nothing is explained, so get the 2-kr flier.

Gustav III's Museum of Antiquities (Gustav IIIs Antik-museum): In the 1700s, Gustav III traveled through Italy and brought home an impressive gallery of classical Roman statues. These are displayed exactly as they were in the 1790s. This was a huge deal if you'd never been out of Sweden (closed Sept–mid-May).

Museum of Three Crowns (Museum Tre Kronor): This shows off bits of the palace from before a devastating 1697 fire. It's basically just more old stuff...interesting only to real history buffs.

Downtown Stockholm

▲**Kungsträdgården**—Five hundred years ago, this "King's Garden Square" was the private kitchen garden of the king—where he grew his cabbage salad. Today, this downtown people-watching center is considered Stockholm's living room. Watch the life-size game of chess and enjoy summer concerts at the bandstand. There's always something going on. Surrounded by the Sweden House, NK department store, the harborfront, and tour boats, it's *the* place to feel Stockholm's pulse (but always ask first: *"Får jag kanna din puls?"*). Kungsträdgården throws huge parties. Restaurant Days is the "taste of Stockholm" festival for a week in early June, when restaurateurs show off and bands entertain all day. The beer flows freely—a rare public spectacle in Sweden. The Swedes even celebrate the Fourth of July here with several days of festival events.

The nearby Kungsträdgården T-bana station is famous as the best art station in town. The man at the turnstile is generally friendly to tourists who ask *snälla rara* (snel-lah rar-rah; pretty please) for permission to nip down the escalator to see the far-out design—proving that Stockholm sits upon a grand ancient civilization.

▲**Sergels Torg**—The heart of modern Stockholm, between Kungsträdgården and the train station, is dominated by a square that

suggests Moscow won the Cold War. The glassy tower was designed by Orrefors. That and everything around you dates from the 1960s and 1970s. There's a huge discussion going on about what to do with the *"Platan"* ("the platter," as it's nicknamed)—so dated...and so convenient for junkies. Enjoy the colorful, bustling underground mall, prowl through Åhléns department store, and dip into the Gallerian mall. In the Kulturhuset, you'll find the temporary home of the TI (until it moves back to Hamngatan sometime in 2005), a library, Internet café, chessboards, art exhibits, and a café with foreign newspapers (Tue–Fri 11:00–18:00, Sat–Sun 11:00–16:00, closed Mon, tel. 08/508-31508, www.kulturhuset.stockholm.se). For more people action, stroll from Sergels Torg up the Drottninggatan pedestrian mall to the Hötorget produce market.

▲▲**City Hall (Stadshuset)**—The Stadshuset is an impressive mix of eight million bricks, 19 million chips of gilt mosaic, and lots of

Stockholm pride. One of Europe's finest public buildings (built in 1923) and site of the annual Nobel Prize banquet, it's particularly enjoyable and worthwhile for its entertaining tours (50 kr, daily at 10:00 and 12:00, more in the summer, 300 yards behind station, bus #3 or #62, tel. 08/5082-9059, www.stockholm.se /stadshuset). Climb the 395-foot-tall tower (an elevator takes you halfway) for the best possible city view (20 kr, May–Sept daily 10:00–16:30, closed Oct–

April). The City Hall's cafeteria serves complete lunches for 65 kr (Mon–Fri 11:00–14:30, closed Sat–Sun).

▲**Orientation Views**—For a bird's-eye perspective on this wonderful urban mix of water, parks, concrete, and people, consider these viewpoints: City Hall's tower (described above; view from tower pictured below); the Kaknäs Tower (at 500 feet, once the tallest building in Scandinavia; 30 kr, daily May–Aug 9:00–22:00, Sept–April 10:00–21:00, restaurant on 28th floor, east of downtown—

take bus #69 from Nybroplan or Sergels Torg, tel. 08/667-2105; view pictured on page 216); the observatory in Skansen; or the Katarina elevator (circa 1930s, ride 130 feet to the top; 5 kr, Mon–Sat 7:30–22:00, Sun 10:00–22:00, near Slussen T-bana stop—walk behind Katarina-vägen toward Fjallgatan for grand city and harbor views).

▲National Museum of Fine Arts—Though mediocre by European standards, this 200-year-old museum is small, central, uncrowded, and user-friendly. Highlights include several Rembrandts, Rubenses, a fine group of Impressionists, works by the popular and good-to-get-to-know local artists Carl Larsson (who frescoed the entrance hall) and Anders Zorn, and a sizable collection of Russian icons. The

museum has recently expanded beyond painting with the "Design 1900–2000" exhibit. This tracks the history of modern design: gracefully engraved glass from the 1920s, works from the Stockholm Exhibition of 1930, industrial design of the 1940s, Scandinavian Design movement of the 1950s, plastic chairs from the 1960s, modern furniture from the 1980s, and the Swedish new simplicity from the 1990s (all thoughtfully described in English). If you'd like a private tour with the former museum director, rent the excellent audioguide (25 kr), which describes the top 13 works (entry-75 kr, Tue–Sun 11:00–17:00, Tue until 20:00, closed Mon, Södra Blasieholmshamnen, T-bana: Kungsträdgården, tel. 08/5195-4310, www.nationalmuseum.se).

Museum of Modern Art (Moderna Museet)—This bright, cheery, and free gallery on Skeppsholmen island is as far-out as can be, with Picasso, Braque, and lots of goofy Dada art (such as *Urinal* and *Goat with Tire*), as well as more contemporary stuff (free except for some temporary exhibitions, fine bookstore, Tue–Wed 10:00–20:00, Thu–Sun 10:00–18:00, closed Mon, walk or take bus #65, tel. 08/5195-5200, www.modernamuseet.se).

Stockholm's Djurgården

Four hundred years ago, Djurgården was the king's hunting ground. Now this entire lush island is Stockholm's fun center, protected as a national park. It still has a smattering of animal life among its biking paths, picnicking local families, art galleries, and various amusements. Of the three great sights on the island, the *Vasa* and Nordic museums are neighbors, and Skansen is a 10-minute walk away (or hop on any bus—they come every couple of minutes).

Stockholm's Djurgården

Getting There: Take bus #47 from the train station and get off at the Nordic Museum (also for the *Vasa*), or continue on to the Skansen stop. In summer, you can also take a ferry from Nybroplan or Slussen (see "Getting Around Stockholm—By Harbor Shuttle Ferry," page 223) or an antique train from Nybroplan (daily in summer, weekends only in spring and fall).

▲▲▲**Skansen**—This is Europe's original open-air folk museum, founded in 1891. It's a huge park gathering more than 150 historic

buildings (homes, churches, shops, and school-houses) transplanted from all corners of Sweden.

Skansen was the first in what became a Europe-wide movement to preserve traditional architecture in open-air museums. Other languages have even borrowed the Swedish term "Skansen" (which originally meant "the Fort") to mean "open-air museum." Today, tourists still explore this Swedish-culture-on-a-lazy-Susan, seeing folk crafts in action and wonderfully furnished old interiors

(lively June–Aug before about 17:00, otherwise pretty dead).

In "Old Stockholm" (top of the escalator), shoemakers, potters, and glassblowers are busy doing their traditional thing in a re-created Old World Stockholm. The glassblowing demonstration here is as good as any you'll see in Sweden's glass country to the south. The rest of Sweden spreads out from Old Stockholm. Northern Swedish culture and architecture is in the north (top of park map) and southern Sweden's in the south (bottom of map).

Consider the 5-kr map or the 50-kr museum guidebook (which comes with the same map). With the book, you'll understand each building you duck into and even learn about the Nordic animals awaiting you in the zoo. Check the live crafts schedule at the infor-

mation stand by the main entrance below the escalator to confirm your Skansen plans. Guides throughout the park are happy to answer your questions—but only if you ask them. The old houses come alive when you take the initiative to get information.

Kids love Skansen, especially its zoo (ride a life-size wooden Dala-horse and stare down a hedgehog, or go on a feeding tour at 14:00), Lill' Skansen (a children's zoo), and mini-train and pony rides.

Cost and Hours: May–Aug 70 kr; Sept–April 30 kr on weekdays, 50 kr on weekends. Open daily May 10:00–20:00, June–Aug 10:00–22:00, Sept 10:00–17:00, Oct–April 10:00–16:00, closed only on Christmas Eve. The historical buildings are open 11:00–17:00, some until 19:00 June–Aug, Oct–April 11:00–15:00 (only a few are open in winter). Tel. 08/578-90005 for recorded info, or tel. 08/442-8000 (www.skansen.se). Gröna Lund, Stockholm's amusement park, is across the street.

Music: Skansen does great music. There's fiddling (June–Aug nightly except Sun at 18:45), folk-dancing (June–Aug at 19:00, also Sun at 14:30 and 16:00), and public dancing to live bands (nightly except Sun from 20:00, call for evening theme—big band, modern, ballroom, folk).

Eating at Skansen: Skansen's main restaurant, **Solliden,** serves a big *smörgåsbord* lunch in a grand blue-and-white room (280 kr, daily 12:00–16:00 in summer). The adjacent **Ekorren** café offers less-expensive self-service lunches with a view (60–70-kr daily specials). The old-time **Stora Gungan Krog,** in Old Stockholm at the top of the escalator, is a cozy inn (80–100-kr indoor or outdoor lunches—meat, fish or veggie—with a salad-and-cracker bar, daily 11:00–17:00, their freshly baked cakes will tempt you). Skansen encourages **picnicking,** with plenty of hot dog stands and benches all over—especially at Bollnästorget, where peacenik local toddlers don't bump on the bumper cars.

Aquarium: Admission to the aquarium is the only thing not covered on your Skansen ticket, but it is included on the Stockholm Card (aquarium entry-65 kr; mid-June–mid-Aug daily 10:00–18:00, July until 20:00; mid-Aug–mid-June Tue–Sun 10:00–16:30, closed Mon; tel. 08/660-1082).

▲▲▲*Vasa* **Museum (Vasamuseet)**—Stockholm turned a titanic flop into one of Europe's great sightseeing attractions. This glamorous but unseaworthy warship—top-heavy with an extra cannon

deck—sank 20 minutes into her 1628 maiden voyage when a breeze caught the sails and blew her over. After 333 years at the bottom of Stockholm's harbor, she rose again from the deep with the help of marine archaeologists. Ironically, this Edsel of the sea is today the best-preserved ship of its age anywhere—housed in a state-of-the-art museum. The masts perched atop the museum's roof—best seen from a distance—show the actual height of the ship.

The 25-minute movie (top of each hour with English subtitles, actually in English at 11:30 and 13:30) tells the fascinating story. Displays are well described in English. Learn about the ship's rules (bread can't be older than 8 years), why it sank (heavy bread?), how it's preserved (the ship, not the bread), and so on.

Cost, Hours, Location: 70 kr, daily mid-June–mid-Aug 9:30–19:00, off-season 10:00–17:00, winter Wed until 20:00, Galärvarvet, Djurgården, tel. 08/519-54800, www.vasamuseet.se. The *Vasa* is on the waterfront immediately behind the stately brick Nordic Museum, a 10-minute walk from Skansen. The museum also has a good café inside.

Tours: For more information, take the free 25-minute English tour (mid-June–late Aug at :30 past each hour from 10:30 on, fewer tours off-season, call for times).

▲▲▲**Nordic Museum (Nordiska Museet)**—Built to look like a Danish Renaissance palace, the museum offers a good peek at 500 years of traditional Swedish lifestyles. It's arguably more informative than Skansen. Take time to let the free and excellent audioguide enliven the exhibits. Carl Milles' huge statue of Gustav Vasa, father of modern Sweden, overlooks the main gallery.

Highlights are spread over four floors. Level 1 (the basement): a fascinating Sami (Lapp) exhibit. Level 2 (where you enter): changing exhibits. Level 3: the *Traditions* exhibit (showing and describing each old-time celebration of the Swedish year with exquisite table settings), folk costumes, and fancy fashions from the 18th through the 20th centuries. Level 4: old furniture and the excellent "Cosy" collection showing Swedish living rooms over the last century.

Cost, Hours, Location: 75 kr, daily late June–Aug 10:00–17:00, Sept–late June 10:00–16:00, Djurgårdsvägen 6–16, at Djurgårdsbron, tel. 08/5195-6000, www.nordiskamuseet.se.

▲**Thielska Galleriet**—If you liked the Larsson and Zorn art in the National Gallery and/or if you're a Munch fan, this charming mansion on the water at the far end of the Djurgården park is worth the trip (50 kr, Mon–Sat 12:00–16:00, Sun 13:00–16:00, bus #69 from train station, tel. 08/662-5884, www.thielska-galleriet.se).

Outer Stockholm

▲▲**Millesgården**—The home and garden of Sweden's greatest sculptor is dramatically situated on a steep slope running down to the water in Stockholm's upper-class suburb of Lidingö. Carl Milles' entertaining and provocative art was influenced by Rodin. The house dates from the 1920s; the extensive grounds have been turned into a museum. There's a classy café and a great picnic spot with views of Stockholm (75 kr, 15-kr English booklet explains art; mid-May–Aug daily 10:00–17:00; Sept–mid-May Thu–Sun 12:00–17:00, closed Mon–Wed; tel. 08/446-7590, www.millesgarden.se). Catch the T-bana to Ropsten, then take bus #202, #204, #205, #206, #207, or #212 to the first stop (Torsvik). It's a five-minute walk from there (follow the signs).

▲▲**Drottningholm Palace**—The queen's 17th-century summer castle and present royal residence has been called "Sweden's Versailles." Touring the palace, you'll see the queen making the point: She's divine and belongs with the gods. Below the clouds are her earthly subjects...and you. But she was a divine monarch on a budget: Test the "marble" doorways. They warm to the touch...painted to look like marble. You'll see three crowns on the Swedish coat of arms, a reminder of Sweden's aspiration to rule Norway and Denmark. The Room of War—with kings, generals, battle scenes, and war trumpet–like candleholders—is from the time (1600–1750) when Sweden was a superpower (60 kr, May–Aug daily 10:00–16:30, Sept daily 12:00–15:30, Oct–April Sat–Sun only 12:00–15:30; call 08/402-6280 to reserve free-with-admission palace tours in English, offered June–Aug usually at 11:00, 12:00, 13:00, and 15:00, fewer off-season; www.royalcourt.se).

The 18th-century **Drottningholm Court Theater** (Drottningholms Slottsteater) somehow survived the ages—complete with its instruments, sound-effects machines, and stage sets. It's one of two such theaters remaining in Europe (the other is in Český Krumlov, Czech Republic). Visit it on a 30-minute guided tour (60 kr, May–Sept English theater tours normally depart half-past each hour, 11:30–16:30, no tours off-season, tel. 08/759-0406). Or check their schedule for the rare opportunity to see perfectly authentic operas (about 25 performances each summer). Tickets for this popular, time-tunnel musical and theatrical experience cost 165–600 kr and go on sale by phone, fax, or mail each March (see www .drottningholmsslottsteater.dtm.se).

Getting to Drottningholm: Reach the palace via a relaxing boat ride (100 kr round-trip, discount with Stockholm Card, 1 hr, from City Hall), or take the T-bana to Brommaplan, where you can catch any 300-series bus to Drottningholm.

▲▲**Archipelago (Skärgården)**—Some of Europe's most scenic islands (24,000 of them!) surround Stockholm. If you cruise to

Finland, you'll get a good dose of this island beauty. Otherwise, consider a half- or full-day trip from downtown Stockholm to the archipelago. Strömma Kanal-bolaget/Cinderella Båtarna ships leave from Nybrokajen, while Waxholmsbolaget ships leave from Strömkajen. It's about 140

kr round-trip to Vaxholm, the most popular destination, but there are many cruises to choose from (some shorter or longer, and some including brunch, lunch, or dinner). The TI has a free archipelago mini-guidebook. For details, see www.waxholmsbolaget.se, www.strommakanalbolaget.com, or www.cinderellabatarna.com.

Spa and Sauna

The **Central-badet spa** lets you enjoy an extensive gym, "bubble-pool," sauna, steam room, and an elegant Art Nouveau pool from 1904 (90 kr, long hours, last entry 20:30, closed Sun in July, ages 18 and up, Drottninggatan 88, 10 min up from Sergels Torg, tel. 08/545-21300). If you won't make it to Finland, enjoy a sauna here (for more info on saunas, see page 286 in Helsinki chapter). The steam room is mixed; the sauna is not. Bring your towel into the sauna—not for modesty, but to separate your body from the bench. Bring two towels into the steam room (one for modesty and the other to sit on). The pool is more for floating than for jumping and splashing. The leafy courtyard restaurant is a relaxing place to enjoy affordable, healthy, light meals.

SHOPPING

Modern design, glass, clogs, and wooden goods are popular targets for shoppers. Drop by the Nordiska Kompaniet (NK, short for "no kronor left," Stockholm's top-end department store), located in an elegant early-20th-century building just across from the Sweden House. The less-classy Gallerian mall is across the street. The Åhléns store, nearby at Sergels Torg, is also less expensive than NK. Designtorget, a store dedicated to contemporary Swedish design, sells the unique work of local designers for a commission (Mon–Fri 10:00–19:00, Sat 10:00–17:00, Sun 11:00–17:00, underneath Sergels Torg—enter from basement level of Kulturhuset). For more on Swedish design, pick up the *2005 Design Guide* flier at the TI (listing smaller stores throughout town with a flair for design). The trendy and exclusive shops (including Orrefors and Kosta) line Biblioteksgatan just off Stureplan. The people's shopping boulevard is Drottninggatan.

Traditionally stores are open weekdays from 10:00 to 18:00, Saturdays until 15:00, and closed on Sundays. Some of the bigger stores (such as NK and Åhléns) are open later on Saturdays and on Sunday afternoons (12:00–17:00).

For a *smörgåsbord* of Scanjunk, visit the Loppmarknaden, Northern Europe's biggest flea market, at the planned suburb of Skärholmen (free entry on weekdays, 15 kr on weekends when it's busiest, Mon–Fri 11:00–18:00, Sat 9:00–15:00, Sun 10:00–15:00, T-bana: Skärholmen and walk across the square, tel. 08/710-0060). Hötorget, the produce market, also hosts a Sunday flea market.

Visit Systembolaget, Sweden's state-run liquor store chain, before it disappears (rumor is that Sweden will soon follow Denmark's lead in liberalizing alcohol sales). For decades, Swedes have not been trusted to browse the wine and booze shelves on their own; only pictures are on display, and you have to order at the counter. One branch is on Gamla Stan at Lilla Nygatan 18, and another is on Norrmalm at Vasagatan 21 (both Mon–Wed 10:00–18:00, Thu–Fri 10:00–19:00, Sat 10:00–15:00, closed Sun).

NIGHTLIFE

Gamla Stan is busy with jazz and nightclubs. The music doesn't start until late, and some clubs don't welcome tourists. For a place with live music and a comfortable mix of locals and tourists, try stompin' at **Stampen** (100-kr cover and 50-kr beers, free blues Mon, music—mainly jazz—at 21:00 Mon–Sat, 2 bands on Fri and Sat, closed Sun, Stora Nygatan 5, tel. 08/205-793, www.stampen.se).

If jazz isn't your style, a nighttime stroll along Gamla Stan's main drag, Västerlånggatan, comes with mellow, picturesque Old World ambience.

SLEEPING

Prices for business-class hotels are significantly lower on weekends and in summer months (see below). When I list two hotel rates, the first is the peak-season rate and the second is the summer/weekend rate.

Peak season for Stockholm's hotels is business time—weeknights outside of summer vacation time. Rates drop by 30–50 percent in the summer (late June–early Aug) or on weekends. Some hotels will discount their rates even further if business is slow.

Even in summer, Stockholm hotels are expensive. It's hard to find a normal hotel double for less than $150. But Stockholm has plenty of money-saving deals for the savvy visitor willing to compromise a bit—ask. Many places keep an odd misfit room (100 kr cheaper than the others) lashed to a bedpost in the attic. Several places have a range of rooms, blurring the distinction between

Sleep Code

(7 kr = about $1, country code: 46, area code: 08)
S = Single, **D** = Double/Twin, **T** = Triple, **Q** = Quad,
b = bathroom, **s** = shower. Unless otherwise noted, all of my listings have non-smoking rooms and elevators, accept credit cards, and include big breakfast buffets. Everyone speaks English.

To help you sort easily through these listings, I've divided the rooms into three categories, based on the price for a standard double room with bath during high season:

$$$ **Higher Priced**—Most rooms more than 1,600 kr.
$$ **Moderately Priced**—Most rooms between 800–1,600 kr.
$ **Lower Priced**—Most rooms 800 kr or less.

"hotel" and "hostel." Hotels here are so expensive that money-conscious travelers are often willing to share a bathroom—a respectable option in clean and wholesome Stockholm.

There are other budget options. Plenty of people offer private accommodations ($100 doubles). Stockholm's hostels are among Europe's best, offering good beds in simple but interesting places for about $20–30 per bed. Each has helpful English-speaking staff, pleasant family rooms, and good facilities. Hostelling is cheap only when you're a member, provide your own sheets, and picnic for breakfast.

Through a program called **Stockholm à la Carte,** you can reserve off-peak (weekend and summer) rooms and get a Stockholm à la Carte card thrown in for free. This includes free public transportation, and sightseeing discounts almost as good as the Stockholm Card (though not including the *Vasa* Museum). You can sign up for Stockholm à la Carte by phone or online (tel. 08/663-0080, www.destination-stockholm.com).

In the listings below, when two rates are listed for a hotel, the first is the peak-season rate and the second is the summer/weekend rate.

In Downtown Norrmalm, near the Train Station

$$$ Freys Hotel is Scan-mod, with 118 rooms on a quiet pedestrian street just a few doors from the train station (Sb-1,595/895 kr, Db-1,790/1,290 kr, Bryggargatan 12, tel. 08/5062-1300, fax 08/5062-1313, www.freyshotels.com, freys@freyshotels.com).

$$$ Central Hotel, right across from the train station, is futuristic, with small, plush rooms and tight security (Sb-1,550/850 kr, Db-1,775/1,150 kr, extra bed-300 kr, garage-275 kr/day, Vasagatan 38, tel. 08/5662-0800, fax 08/247-573, www.profilhotels.se).

Stockholm Hotels

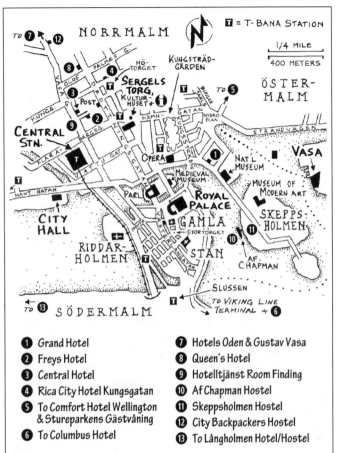

❶ Grand Hotel
❷ Freys Hotel
❸ Central Hotel
❹ Rica City Hotel Kungsgatan
❺ To Comfort Hotel Wellington & Stureparkens Gästvåning
❻ To Columbus Hotel
❼ Hotels Oden & Gustav Vasa
❽ Queen's Hotel
❾ Hotelltjänst Room Finding
❿ Af Chapman Hostel
⓫ Skeppsholmen Hostel
⓬ City Backpackers Hostel
⓭ To Långholmen Hotel/Hostel

$$$ Rica City Hotel Kungsgatan, central but characterless, fills the top floors of a downsized department store with 270 rooms. You'll save money by taking a room with no windows (Sb-1,650/920 kr, windowless Sb-1,195/720 kr, Db-1,900/1,320 kr, windowless Db-1,445/990 kr, Kungsgatan 47, tel. 08/723-7220, fax 08/723-7299, www.rica.se).

$$ Queen's Hotel, a 10-minute walk from the station on a fine pedestrian street, is a bit rough around the edges but has a great location. The 32 rooms, scattered throughout an old apartment building, vary widely in amenities (18 with private shower and toilet, 6 with private shower but shared toilet, 8 with no private facilities)—so be clear about what you reserved (S-750 kr, Ss-795 kr, Sb-995/895 kr, D-795 kr, Ds-850 kr, Db-1,100/995 kr, better Db 1,490/1,350 kr, extra bed-300 kr, Drottninggatan 71A, tel. 08/249-460, fax 08/217-620, www.queenshotel.se, queenshotel@queenshotel.se).

$ City Backpackers is very central—just a quarter-mile from the station—and open year-round. It's enthusiastically run, with 85 beds and plenty of creativity (bunk in 8-bed room-180 kr, in quad-220 kr, bunkbed D-490 kr, sheets-50 kr, free coffee and tea but no breakfast, laundry-50 kr, free Internet access, sauna, lockers, kitchen, shoes-off policy, Upplandsgatan 2A, tel. 08/206-920, fax 08/100-464, www.citybackpackers.se, info@citybackpackers.se).

On Norrmalm, in Quieter Residential Areas

These options are in stately, elegant neighborhoods of five- and six-story turn-of-the-century apartment buildings. All are too far to walk from the station with luggage, but still in easy reach of downtown sights and close to T-bana stops.

$$$ Comfort Hotel Wellington, two blocks off in-love-with-life Östermalmstorg, is modern, bright, and a little sterile, with hardwood floors, 60 ample rooms, and a friendly welcome (prices with this book for 2005: Sb-1,516/1,095/890 kr, Db-1,876/1,395/1,190 kr, 3rd price valid for summer and weekends only with purchase of 100-kr Nordic Hotel Pass, every 5th night free, sauna, old-fashioned English bar, T-bana: Östermalmstorg and walk towards big church, Storgatan 6, tel. 08/667-0910, fax 08/667-1254, www.wellington.se, info.wellington@comfort.choicehotels.se).

$$ Hotel Oden, a recently renovated 140-room place with all the comforts, is three T-bana stops from the train station (Sb-1,095/770 kr, Db-1,360/950 kr, extra bed-150 kr, sauna, free Internet, free coffee and tea in the evening, T-bana: Odenplan, exit in direction of Västmannagatan, Karlbergsvägen 24, tel. 08/457-9700, fax 08/457-9710, www.hoteloden.se).

$$ Stureparkens Gästvåning, carefully run by Jan Lönnberg, is one floor of an apartment building converted into nine bright, clean, quiet, and thoughtfully appointed rooms. Only two rooms have private bath (S-520 kr, D-895 kr, Db-995 kr, sprawling Db apartment-1,500 kr, extra bed-175 kr, kitchen, T-bana: Stadion, across from Stureparken at Sturegatan 58, take elevator to 4th floor, tel. 08/662-7230, fax 08/661-5713, www.stureparkens.nu, info@stureparkens.nu).

$$ Hotel Gustav Vasa is an old hotel with 42 rooms on several floors of a late-19th-century apartment building (S-595/395 kr, Sb-995/595 kr, Db-1,260/795 kr, T-bana: Odenplan, Västmannagatan 61, tel. 08/343-801, fax 08/307-372, www.gvh.se).

$ Bed and Breakfast is a tiny, woody, and easygoing independent hostel renting 36 cheap beds (190–210 kr per bunk in 4- to 10-bed rooms, tiny windowless S-375 kr, tiny windowless bunkbed D-500 kr, includes breakfast, sheets-45 kr, kitchen, laundry, Internet access, across the street from T-bana: Rådmansgatan, just off Sveavägen at

Rehnsgatan 21, tel. & fax 08/152-838, www.hostelbedandbreakfast
.com). From June to August, they also rent bunks in the nearby "Hole
in the Ground," a 40-bed hall, for 125 kr a night.

On Gamla Stan and Skeppsholmen

These options are in the midst of sightseeing, a short bus or taxi ride
from the train station.

$$$ **Rica City Hotel Gamla Stan** offers Old World elegance in
the heart of Gamla Stan (a 5-min walk from Gamla Stan T-bana
station). Its 51 rooms are filled with chandeliers and hardwood floors
(Sb-1,695/1,050, Db-1,945/1,590, Lilla Nygatan 25, tel. 08/723-
7250, fax 08/723-7259, www.rica.se, info.gamlastan@rica.se).

$$$ **Lady Hamilton Hotel** is an expensive, elegant place shoe-
horned into Gamla Stan on a quiet street a block below the Catholic
cathedral and Royal Palace. The centuries-old building has 34 plush
rooms and is filled with thoughtful touches and antique furniture (Sb-
1,990–2,190/1,050–1,250 kr, Db-2,390–2,690/1,750–1,950 kr, Tb-
2,890–3,090/2,250 kr, sauna, Storkyrkobrinken 5, tel. 08/5064-0100,
fax 08/5064-0110, www.lady-hamilton.se, info@lady-hamilton.se).

$ *Af Chapman* **Hostel (IYHF),** Europe's most famous youth
hostel, is a 100-year-old cutter ship permanently moored to
Skeppsholmen island. It's open all year and has 140 beds in two- to
10-bed staterooms (lockout daily 11:00–15:00). The reception is at
Skeppsholmen Hostel (see below). The ship is due for a major year-
long renovation, so you might find it closed.

$ **Skeppsholmen Hostel (IYHF),** just ashore from the *Af
Chapman,* has better facilities and smaller rooms (160 beds in 2- to
6-bed rooms plus one 17-bed dorm, no lockout during day; rates
for both hostels: bunk in 3- to 10-bed room-230 kr, in 17-bed
dorm-185 kr, D-510 kr, 45 kr less for hostel members, sheets-60
kr, breakfast-70 kr, laundry service, STF Vandrarhem Af Chapman,
Skeppsholmen, bus #65 from station or walk about 20 min, tel. 08/
463-2266, fax 08/611-7155, www.stfchapman.com, info@chapman
.stfturist.se).

On or near Södermalm

Södermalm is residential and hip, with Stockholm's best café and
bar scene. You'll need to take the bus or T-bana to get here from
the train station.

$$ **Columbus Hotel,** in a 19th-century building that formerly
housed a brewery, a jail, and a hospital, has 69 quiet rooms in the
heart of Södermalm. Half of its rooms (1st and 2nd floors) have pri-
vate facilities. Third-floor rooms have facilities down the hall (S-695
kr, Sb-1,250/950 kr, D-895 kr, Db-1,550/1,250 kr, T-1,095 kr, no
elevator, T-bana: Medborgarplatsen, or bus #53 from train station
to Renstiernas Gata, then a 5-min walk to Tjärhovsgatan 11,

tel. 08/5031-1200, fax 08/5031-1201, www.columbus.se, columbus
@columbus.se).

$$ Långholmen Hotel/Hostel (IYHF) is on Långholmen, a
small island off of Södermalm that was transformed in the 1980s
from Stockholm's main prison into a lovely park. Rooms are con-
verted cells in the old prison building. You can choose between
hostel- and hotel-standard rooms at many different price levels
(hostel rooms: dorm bed-240 kr, D-585 kr, Db-675 kr, Q-1,020 kr,
Qb-1,060 kr, 45-kr discount for hostel members, sheets-55 kr,
breakfast-75 kr; hotel rooms: small Sb-995/695 kr, larger Sb-
1,195/855 kr, Db-1,495/1,155 kr, extra bed-215 kr, includes break-
fasts; laundry room, kitchen, cafeteria, free parking, on-site
swimming, T-bana: Hornstull, then walk 10 min down and cross
small bridge to Långholmen island, tel. 08/720-8500, fax 08/720-
8575, www.langholmen.com).

Rooms in Private Homes

Stockholm's private rooms can be a deal in high season if you want
to have an at-home experience. During hotels' weekend/summer
discount periods, private rooms don't save you much over a hotel.
Be sure to get the front-door security code when you call, as there's
no intercom. Contact **Hotelltjänst**, a B&B booking agency (S-400
kr, Sb-600 kr, D-600 kr, Db-800 kr, cash only, no breakfast, 2-
night minimum, fully furnished apartments also available,
Nybrogatan 44, near train station, tel. 08/104-437, fax 08/213-716,
www.hotelltjanst.com).

EATING

To save money, eat your main meal at lunch and look for 75-kr daily
special plates *(dagens rätt)* at cafés and restaurants. Most museums
have handy cafés. Picnics are a great option—especially for dinner,
when restaurant prices are highest.

In Gamla Stan

Any restaurant in Gamla Stan will serve you a weekday lunch special
for about 75 kr: main dish, small salad, bread, and free tap water.
Choose from Swedish, Asian, or Italian. Several popular places are
right on Stortorget, the main square. Järntorget, at the far end, is
another fun tables-in-the-square scene (and has a small Konsum
supermarket for picnic shopping). Touristy places line Väster-
långgatan (and are worth scouting out). You'll find more romantic
places hiding on side lanes. Here are my favorites (for locations, see
the map on next page).

   Grillska Huset is a cheap and handy cafeteria run by
Stadsmissionen, a charitable organization for the poor. On the old

Gamla Stan Hotels and Restaurants

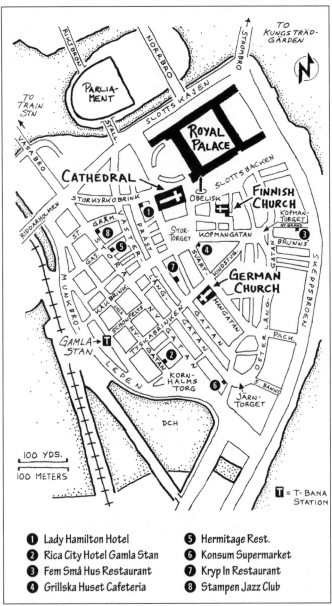

1 Lady Hamilton Hotel
2 Rica City Hotel Gamla Stan
3 Fem Små Hus Restaurant
4 Grillska Huset Cafeteria
5 Hermitage Rest.
6 Konsum Supermarket
7 Kryp In Restaurant
8 Stampen Jazz Club

square with great indoor and outdoor seating, fine daily specials (listed in Swedish only), a hearty salad bar, and a staff committed to helping others, you can feed the hungry (that's you) and help house the homeless at the same time. Lines can get long (the 75-kr daily special—available Mon–Fri 11:00–14:00—gets you a hot plate, salad bar, and coffee; restaurant serves daily 11:00–18:00, 65-kr salad bar closes at 14:00, Stortorget 3, tel. 08/787-8605).

Hermitage Restaurant serves tasty vegetarian food. Their daily special (only 65 kr, or 80 kr after 16:00 and on weekends) buys a hot plate, salad, bread, and coffee (Mon–Sat 11:00–21:00, Sun 12:00–20:00, Stora Nygatan 11, tel. 08/411-9500).

Kryp In, a small, cozy restaurant tucked into a peaceful lane, has a stylish hardwood and candlelit interior and great sidewalk seating. They serve delicious modern Swedish cuisine with a 330-kr three-course dinner (Mon–Fri 17:00–23:00, Sat 12:30–23:00, Sun 13:00–22:00, Prästgatan 17, tel. 08/208-841).

Fem Små Hus is an even fancier splurge, with candles leading you into a 16th-century cellar (375- and 450-kr 3-course meals, daily 17:00–24:00, Nygränd 10, tel. 08/108-775, www.femsmahus.se).

Royal *Smörgåsbord* at the Grand Hotel

To stuff yourself with all the traditional Swedish specialties (a dozen kinds of herring, salmon, reindeer, meatballs, lingonberries, and shrimp, followed by a fine table of cheeses and desserts) with a super harbor view, consider splurging for Stockholm's best *smörgåsbord* at the Grand Hotel's dressy **Grand Veranda Restaurant.** The Grand Hotel, where royal guests and Nobel Prize winners stay, faces the harbor across from the palace (350 kr, tap water is free, other drinks extra, nightly 18:00–22:00, Sat–Sun also 13:00–16:00, May–Sept also Mon–Fri 12:00–15:00, reservations necessary, Södra Blasieholmshamnen 8, tel. 08/679-3586).

On Norrmalm

At the Royal Opera House: The Operakällaren, one of Stockholm's most exclusive restaurants, runs a little "hip pocket" restaurant called **Backfickan** on the side, specializing in traditional Swedish quality cooking at reasonable prices. It's ideal for someone eating out alone or for anyone wanting an early dinner (as they serve daily specials from 11:30 all the way up to 20:00). Sit inside with classy locals at the bar or at tiny side tables, or—in good weather—grab a table on the sidewalk. Choose from three different daily specials (about 130–140 kr) or pay about 150 kr for plates from their regular menu (closed Sun, on the inland side of Royal Opera House, tel. 08/665-800).

At or near Hötorget: Hötorget ("Hay Market") now feeds people instead of horses. This vibrant outdoor produce market, just two blocks from Sergels Torg, is a fun place to picnic-shop. The outdoor market closes at 18:00, and many merchants put their unsold produce on the push list (earlier closing and more desperate merchants on Sat). **Kungshallen,** an indoor food court across the street from Hötorget, has 14 mostly chain restaurants, ranging from Chinese and pizza to Mexican. **Hötorgshallen,** next to Hötorget (in the basement under the modern cinema complex), is a colorful indoor food market with an old-fashioned bustle, plenty of exotic and ethnic edibles, and—in the tradition of food markets all over Europe—some great little eateries. The best is **Kajsas Fisk Restaurang,** hiding behind the fish stalls. Owner Monica dishes out delicious fish soup to little Olivers who can hardly believe they're getting...more. For 70 kr, you get a big bowl of her hearty soup (includes 1 refill), plus a simple salad, crackers, butter, and water. They also do 70–85-kr daily fish specials (Mon–Fri 11:00–18:00, Sat 11:00–15:00, closed Sun, Hötorgshallen 3, tel. 08/207-262).

Near Sergels Torg: **Åhléns** department store has a Hemköp supermarket in the basement (Mon–Fri 8:00–21:00, Sat–Sun 10:00–21:00) and two fine cafeterias upstairs with 79-kr daily specials—Swedish on the second floor (Mon–Sat 10:00–17:00, Sun 11:00–17:00) and Italian on the fourth floor (Mon–Fri 11:00–19:00, Sat 11:00–18:00, Sun 11:00–17:00).

In Östermalm: The **Saluhall,** on Östermalmstorg square (near the recommended Comfort Hotel Wellington), is a great old-time indoor market with plenty of fun eateries (Mon–Fri 9:30–18:00, Sat 9:30–14:00, closed Sun). Next door, the **Örtagården** vegetarian restaurant serves a 75-kr buffet weekdays until 17:00, and a larger 125-kr buffet evenings and weekends (Mon–Fri 11:00–21:30, Sat–Sun 12:00–20:30, Nybrogatan 31, tel. 08/662-1728).

At the Train Station: When all else fails, the late-hours convenience store downstairs in the train station is picnic-friendly, with basic groceries and ready-made sandwiches (Mon–Fri 6:30–23:00, Sat–Sun 9:00–23:00).

TRANSPORTATION CONNECTIONS

Reservations are required on long and express trains (international desk at the station ticket office). Railpass-holders pay about 150 kr for first-class seat reservations to Copenhagen and Oslo (60 kr for second class). To avoid lines at the station, make reservations at travel agencies or by calling 0771/757-575, using your credit card, and picking your ticket up from a machine at the station. Train info: tel. 0771/757-575 (toll-free in Sweden) or 46-8/696-7540 (from outside Sweden).

From Stockholm by train to: Uppsala (2–3/hr, 40 min), **Kalmar** (12/day, 5–6 hrs), **Copenhagen** (10/day, 5 hrs, overnight service 23:00–7:00 requires change in Malmö, all trains stop at

Copenhagen airport before terminating at central station), **Oslo** (2/day departing about 7:00 and 17:00, 5 hrs).

By bus to: Copenhagen (7/day, 8.5 hrs, 500 kr), **Oslo** (8/day, 7.5 hrs, 400 kr). Buses take longer than trains, but have more predictable pricing, shorter ticket lines, and student discounts. The main operators are Swebus (www.swebusexpress.se), Säfflebussen (www.safflebussen.se), and Eurolines (www.eurolinestravel.com).

By boat to: Helsinki and Tallinn (daily/nightly boats, 17 hrs, see Helsinki and Tallinn chapters), **Turku** (daily/nightly boats, 11 hrs). The boat companies run shuttle buses to each departure from the station—check for details when you buy your ticket.

Route Tips for Drivers

Stockholm to Oslo: It's a 4.75-hour drive from Stockholm to Oslo. **Arjang,** just before the Norwegian border, is worth a stop if you don't make it to Oslo. The Arjang TI books rooms (tel. 0573/14136). Hotel Karl XII is cheap if anyone's home (Sveavägen 22, near marketplace, tel. 0573/10156, fax 0573/711-426).

At the border, change money at the little TI kiosk (on right side, Mon–Fri 8:00–21:00, Sat–Sun 9:00–21:00, less on winter weekends, fair rates, standard 75 kr traveler's-check fee, tel. 47/6981-1857 or 0573/29130). Pick up the Oslo map and *What's on in Oslo*, and consider buying your Oslo Card here.

The freeway zips you into downtown Oslo. Follow E-18 signs to Sentrum, then Sentral Stasjon (train station) and Paleet P (a central parking garage). If your hotel is near the station, don't take the Sentrum O exit; instead, follow the sign for Paleet P.

Near Stockholm:
Uppsala and Sigtuna

These two charming towns offer the handiest side-trips from Stockholm.

Uppsala

Uppsala is a compact city with a cathedral and university that win Sweden's "oldest/largest/tallest" awards. If you're not traveling anywhere else in Sweden other than Stockholm, Uppsala makes a pleasant day trip. But if you're short on time, Uppsala is not worth sacrificing time in Stockholm. If you visit, allow the better part of a day, including the train from Stockholm.

ORIENTATION

The sights of historic Uppsala, along with its 30,000 university students, cluster around the university and cathedral. Just over the river near the train station is the bustling shopping zone.

Tourist Information: The TI is near the cathedral just along the river (Mon–Fri 10:00–18:00, Sat 10:00–15:00, Sun 12:00–16:00, closed Sun off-season, tel. 018/727-4800, fax 018/132-895, http://res.till.uppland.nu). Pick up their free, entertaining, and helpful *Tourist in Uppsala* brochure.

SIGHTS

▲▲**Uppsala Cathedral**—One of Scandinavia's largest, most historic cathedrals, it has a breathtaking interior, the tomb of King Gustav Vasa, and twin 400-foot spires. Ask about a guided tour (usually late June–mid-Sept Mon–Sat 14:00). Otherwise, push the English button for a tape-recorded introduction in the narthex opposite the TI table (daily 8:00–18:00).

University—Scandinavia's first university was founded here in 1477. Linnaeus and Celsius are two famous grads. Several of the old buildings are open, including the library (see below). The anatomy theater in the Gustavianum is thought-provoking. Its only show was a human dissection.

Carolina Rediviva—Uppsala University's library is home to the 4th-century Silver Bible (*Codex Argenteus* in Latin), named not for its cover but for its silver-ink writing in the extinct Gothic language (20 kr, mid-May–mid-Sept Mon–Fri 9:00–17:00, mid-June–mid-Aug until 20:00, Sat 10:00–17:00, Sun 11:00–16:00).

Gamla Uppsala—The pagan, illiterate ancestors of today's Swedish people lived, worshiped, and were buried here in the 6th century. The site, which gives historians goosebumps even on a sunny day, includes nine large burial mounds circled by a walking path with English descriptions. The Visitors Center features items found in the mounds (50 kr, daily May–Aug 11:00–17:00, less off-season, guided tours available in summer; bus #2, #20, #24, or #54 from Storatorget, Uppsala's main square; tel. 018/239-300). Adjacent to the burial site is the Gamla Uppsala Cathedral (free, daily April–Sept 9:00–18:00, Oct–March 9:00–16:00).

More Sights—**Uppland Museum,** a city history museum with prehistoric bits and folk-art scraps, is on the river by the waterfall (30 kr, Tue–Sun 12:00–17:00, closed Mon). Near the Carl Linnaeus Botanical Garden and Museum, the 16th-century **Uppsala Castle** on the hill runs slice-of-castle-life tours (60 kr, daily June–late Aug at 13:00 and 15:00, tel. 018/727-2485).

EATING

The university district abounds with inexpensive eateries. Try **Kung Kral** for great food; ask about a five-shot sampler of schnapps (St. Persgatan 4, tel. 018/125-090). **Colour Kitchen** on the main shopping street has a tasty lunch special (St. Persgatan 7). Along the river, there are several cafés and restaurants with outdoor seating. You can pack a picnic and enjoy one of Uppsala's parks or join the locals down on the boardwalk along the river, below St. Olov's Bridge. For picnic fixings, try Åhléns department store's grocery, **Hemköp,** on the ground level on Storatorget.

Sigtuna

Between Stockholm and Uppsala, you pass Sigtuna. Possibly Sweden's cutest town, Sigtuna is fluff. You'll see a medieval lane lined with colorful wooden tourist shops, TI, café, romantic park, lakeside promenade, old church, and rune stones. The **TI** has maps of town and can help you get oriented (tel. 08/5948-0650). If it's sunny, Sigtuna is worth a browse and an ice cream cone, but little more. It's one hour from Stockholm (2 trains/hr to Marsdal, then bus #570 or #575).

SOUTH SWEDEN
Växjö and Kalmar

Outside of Stockholm, Småland is the most interesting region in Sweden. This Swedish province is famous for its forests, lakes, great glass, and the many immigrants it sent to the United States. More Americans came from this area than any other part of Scandinavia, and the emigration center in Växjö tells the story well. Between Växjö and Kalmar is Glass Country, a 70-mile stretch of forest sparkling with glassworks—which welcome guests to tour and shop. Historic Kalmar has a rare Old World ambience and the most magnificent medieval castle in Scandinavia. From Kalmar, you can cross one of Europe's longest bridges to hike through the Stonehenge-like mysteries of the strange island of Öland.

Planning Your Time

By train, on a three-week Scandinavian trip, I'd skip this area in favor of the direct, high-speed train from Copenhagen to Stockholm, or the night train from Malmö (just over the Øresund Bridge from Copenhagen) to Stockholm. Side-trips from Stockholm to Helsinki and Tallinn merit more time than this part of Sweden does. If you're driving, the sights described below make that same trip an interesting way to spend a couple of days. While I'm not so hot on the Swedish countryside (OK, blame my Norwegian heritage), you can't see only Stockholm and say you've seen Sweden. Visiting Kalmar gives you the best possible dose of small-town and countryside Sweden. (I find Lund and Malmö, both popular side-trips from Copenhagen, relatively dull. And I'm not old or sedate enough to find a sleepy boat trip along the much-loved Göta Canal appealing.) Drivers can spend three days getting from Copenhagen to Stockholm this way:

Day 1: Leave Copenhagen after breakfast, drive over the bridge to Sweden, tour Växjö's House of Emigrants, drive into

South Sweden

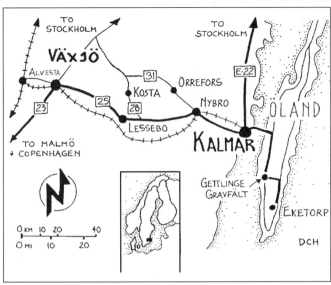

Glass Country, tour Kosta glassworks, and arrive in Kalmar in time for dinner.

Day 2: Spend the day in Kalmar touring the castle and Läns Museum, and browsing through its people-friendly old center.

Day 3: 8:00-Begin five-hour drive north along the coast to Stockholm, 10:30-Break in Västervik, 12:00-Stop in Söderköping for picnic lunch and a walk along the Göta Canal, 13:30-Continue drive north, 16:00-Arrive in Stockholm and possibly catch the night boat to Helsinki.

Thinking ahead to your Helsinki cruise: Boat tickets may be cheaper (especially Sun–Wed off-season) and your drive to Oslo more reasonable (allowing you to get an earlier start) if you do the Helsinki excursion immediately after Kalmar, before seeing Stockholm.

Växjö

A pleasant but dull town of 75,000, Växjö (VEK-fwuh) is in the center of Småland. The town is compact, with the train station, town square, two important museums, and the TI all within two blocks of each other. Växjö has a pedestrian-friendly center. An enjoyable three-mile path encircles its nearby lake. Train travelers not interested in glass can make this a convenient three-hour stopover en route to Kalmar. A farmers' market enlivens the otherwise too-big main square on Wednesday and Saturday mornings.

Tourist Information

The TI is at the train station (mid-June–Aug Mon–Fri 9:30–18:00, Sat–Sun 10:00–14:00, open Sun in July–mid-Aug only; Sept–mid-June Mon–Fri 9:30–16:30, closed Sat–Sun, tel. 0470/41410, www.turism.vaxjo.se).

SIGHTS AND ACTIVITIES

▲▲**House of Emigrants (Utvandrarnas Hus)**—This tidy brick box is a user-friendly archive filled with letters home to the old country, ships' registers, and Minnesotans pondering their roots. A large percentage of the 1.3 million Swedes who moved to the United States came from this neck of the Swedish woods. If you have Swedish roots, this place is really exciting. Even if you don't, this small exhibit is an interesting stop. In 1900, Chicago was the second-largest Swedish town in the world. Back then, one in six Swedes lived in the United States. The "Dream of America" exhibit tells the story of the "American Fever" that burned from the 1850s to the 1920s (40 kr, June–Aug Mon–Fri 9:00–18:00, Sat–Sun 11:00–16:00; Sept–May Mon–Fri 9:00–16:00, Sat–Sun 11:00–16:00, tel. 0470/20120). The emigration festival, three days around the second Sunday in August, is a real hoot, as thousands of Minnesotans storm Växjö.

Upstairs is an excellent library and research center. You're welcome to take a peek. Interview an American Swede at work. Roots-seekers (10,000 a year from the U.S.) are welcome, encouraged to write well in advance for research form and information (Box 201, S-35104, Växjö), and advised to bring whatever information they have—such as ship names and birth dates. (The research center is open on the same dates and days as the museum, but is closed weekends, 150 kr/half day, 200 kr/day, www.swemi.nu).

The Liv Ullmann movie about the emigration, *The Emigrants,* and its sequel, *The New Land,* make for great pretrip viewing.

▲**Swedish Glass and Smålands Museum**—This instructive museum offers a good look at the glass industry, plus exhibits on local forestry and prehistory, and a fine traditional costume display on the top floor (40 kr, Mon–Fri 10:00–17:00, Sat–Sun 11:00–17:00, closed Mon off-season, uphill from House of Emigrants, www.smalandsmuseum.se).

Domkyrka—Växjö's proud church (dedicated to the 11th-century English missionary St. Sigfrid) features some fine sacred art—in glass, of course. The thoughtfully written 15-kr brochure describes it well. The church offers concerts many Thursday evenings in July and August at 20:00 (50 kr).

Linneparken—This peaceful park, located behind the cathedral, is dedicated to the great Swedish botanist Carl von Linné (a.k.a. Carolus Linnaeus). It has an arboretum, lots of well-categorized perennials, and a children's playground.

Swimming—From the House of Emigrants you can see the town's modern lakeside swimming hall *(Simhall)*, a five-minute walk away (45 kr including sauna; extra if you want to tan, use the exercise room, or rent a towel or locker; call for open-swim hours, tel. 0470/41204).

SLEEPING

Hotels generally charge less on Fridays and Saturdays and from late June through early August. When I list two hotel rates, the first is the peak-season rate and the second is the summer/weekend rate. For a 50-kr fee, the TI can find private rooms for about 150 kr per person (plus 40 kr for breakfast).

$$$ Elite Stadshotell, in the town center, is a big, modern, business-class hotel with all the comforts (Sb-1,095/695 kr, Db-1,495/995 kr, summer and weekend rates can stretch during slow times, a block in front of train station at Kungsgatan 6, tel. 0470/13400, fax 0470/44837, www.elite.se).

$$ Hotel Esplanad, a quiet, comfortable, and well-worn hotel run by Birgit, is three blocks from the town center (S-475/350 kr, Sb-650/425 kr, D-575/450 kr, Db-750/650 kr, low rates include Fri nights, N. Esplanaden #21A, tel. 0470/22580, fax 0470/26226). From the train station, walk five blocks up Kungsgatan and turn left on N. Esplanaden. From the freeway, follow Centrum signs into town. At the Royal Corner Hotel, turn left; 200 yards later, at the first light, turn right onto N. Esplanaden.

$$ Hotell Värend is similarly well-worn, close to the center, and inexpensive (24 rooms, Sb-690/450 kr, Db-790/650 kr, Tb-890/750

Sleep Code

(7 kr = about $1, country code: 46, area code: 0470)
S = Single, **D** = Double/Twin, **T** = Triple, **Q** = Quad, **b** = bathroom, **s** = shower. All of these hotels accept credit cards and include breakfast.

To help you sort easily through these listings, I've divided the rooms into three categories, based on the price for a standard double room with bath during high season:

$$$ **Higher Priced**—Most rooms 1,000 kr or more.
$$ **Moderately Priced**—Most rooms between 600–1,000 kr.
$ **Lower Priced**—Most rooms 600 kr or less.

kr, non-smoking rooms, elevator, a block past N. Esplanaden at Kung-gatan 27, tel. 0470/776-700, fax 0470/36261, www.hotellvarend.se, info@hotellvarend.se).

$ *Hostel:* Växjö's fine hostel is on a lake two miles out of town (D-310 kr, 155-kr beds in 2- to 4-bed rooms, non-members welcome for 45 kr extra, breakfast-50 kr, reservations required in summer, office open daily 8:00–10:00 & 17:00–20:00, STF Vandrarhem Evedal-IYHF, tel. 0470/63070, fax 0470/63216). Take bus #1C from the TI to the last stop (summer only, last ride 16:15, first ride 9:15, so hitch a ride into Växjö with a fellow hosteler).

EATING

After-hours Växjö has precious little charm. You might consider dining out. These splurges are recommended by locals: **Lager Lunden** (180-kr meals, at Statt Hotel), **PM** (100–200-kr meals, friendly service and good modern-European cuisine in bistro ambience popular with discerning yuppies, Mon–Sat 11:30–23:00, closed Sun, across from theater at Storgatan 24, tel. 0470/700-444), and **Spisen** (70-kr lunch specials, 100–200-kr dinners, traditional Swedish, across from station, tel. 0470/12300). The restaurant in **Hotell Teaterparken** has light meals for about 90 kr. **Fiskepiren** is the choice for seafood lovers (Båtmanstorget 1, tel. 0470/15656).

TRANSPORTATION CONNECTIONS

From Växjö by train to: Copenhagen (6/day, 2.5 hrs, reservations required on some trains), **Stockholm** (1/hr, 3.5 hrs, change in Alvesta, reservations required), **Kalmar** (11/day, 70 min). Train info: tel. 0771/757-575 (toll-free in Sweden) or 46-8/696-7540 (from outside Sweden). Though there are buses from Växjö to Kosta and a bus to Glass Country from Växjö, the glassworks aren't worth the time and trouble unless you have a car. Instead, take a careful look at the glass exhibit in the Växjö museum and train straight to Kalmar.

BETWEEN VÄXJÖ AND KALMAR

Lessebo Paper Mill (Handpappersbruk)—The town of Lessebo has a 300-year-old paper mill that's kept working for visitors to see. If you've never seen handmade paper produced, this mill is worth a visit. Get the English-language brochure (free, Mon–Fri 7:00–18:00, Sat 10:00–16:00, closed Sun, less outside of summer; English tours at 9:30, 10:30, 13:00, and 14:15 in summer; the mill makes paper 7:00–11:30 & 12:30–15:00, otherwise it's open but dead, tel. 0478/47691). By car,

Lessebo is an easy stop between Växjö and Kosta. Just after the Kosta turnoff, you'll see a black-and-white Handpappersbruk sign.

▲▲**Kingdom of Crystal**—This is Sweden's Glass Country. Frankly, these glassworks cause so much excitement because of the relative rarity of anything else thrilling in Sweden, outside of greater Stockholm. The helpful Glasriket *Kingdom of Crystal* brochure (available at any TI) describes the many glassworks that welcome the public with tours and demonstrations. It's an ever-changing scene. Kosta and Orrefors are the most famous places to visit. The Glasriket Pass (95 kr, good for discounts on tours, special events, and exhibitions) is worthwhile only if you're visiting several glass houses or plan on joining one of the special "Hyttsill" dinners at the glass school (for details, see www.glasriket.se).

Kosta boasts the oldest of the *glasbruks,* dating back to 1742. Today, the glassworks are a thriving tourist and shopping center (open year-round Mon–Fri 9:00–19:00, Sat–Sun 10:00–17:00, actual glassblowing is seen only Mon–Fri but not from 10:00–11:00, tel. 0478/34500, www.kostaboda.se). Tours start in the historic and glass exhibition rooms, then go to the actual blowing room, where guides are constantly narrating the ongoing work. Tours are free in summer, but off-season you must call in advance to reserve a guided tour in English for an extra fee. You can visit the exhibition hall, blowing room, and—of course—the shop for free all year.

Making great strides toward getting the lead out, Kosta's crystal is already 80 percent lead-free. Visitors show the most enthusiasm in the shopping hall, where crystal "seconds" (with tiny bubbles or sets that don't quite match) and discontinued models are sold at good prices. This is duty-free shopping, and they'll happily mail your purchases home. Kosta is a well-signposted 15-minute drive from Lessebo. In town, follow signs for Glasbruk.

Orrefors has the most famous of the several renowned glassworks in Glass Country. Its glassworks are the standard big-bus tour stop with regular 30-minute tours (offered hourly, tel. 0481/34195 to confirm tour times). Most visitors just observe the work from platforms (glassblowing action Mon–Fri 9:00–15:00 except during the 10:30–11:00 lunch break; longer hours in July: Mon–Fri 10:00–16:00, Sat 10:00–16:00, Sun 12:00–16:00). Like Kosta, their shop sells nearly perfect crystal seconds at deep discounts (Mon–Fri 9:00–18:00, Sat 10:00–16:00, Sun 11:00–16:00; www.orrefors.se). Don't miss the dazzling museum (open same hours as shop)

Transjö Glashytta offers a much different experience. Set up in an old converted farm just 10 minutes south of Kosta, this tiny glassworks does expensive but fine art pieces (tel. 0478/50700 for hours and specifics).

Kalmar

Kalmar feels formerly strategic and important. In its day, the town was called "the gateway to Sweden"—back when the Sweden/Denmark border was just a few miles to the south. Today it's a bustling small city of 60,000, with 7,000 students in its University and Maritime Academy. It's also the gateway to the holiday island of Öland. Kalmar's salty old center, fine castle, and busy waterfront give it a wistful sailor's charm. The town is great on foot or by bike.

History students remember Kalmar as the place where the treaty establishing the Kalmar Union was signed. This 1397 "three crowns" treaty united Norway, Sweden, and Denmark and created a huge kingdom—impressive for its day, as most of Europe was fragmented and bickering. But the union, which was dominated by Denmark, lasted only about a hundred years. When Gustav Vasa came to power in 1523, it was dissolved.

ORIENTATION

Tourist Information

The TI has helpful brochures and maps of town, which will provide you with more information than the staff. They are located in a modern building on the harbor, 200 yards from the train station (late June–early Aug Mon–Fri 9:00–21:00, Sat–Sun 10:00–17:00; early June and late Aug Mon–Fri 9:00–19:00, Sat–Sun 10:00–16:00; off-season closes Mon–Fri at 17:00 and closed Sat–Sun; free Internet access—limit 15 min, tel. 0480/417-720, fax 0480/417-720). The building is the Maritime Academy for the University. It's built to look like a ship, and its bridge simulator inside is used for training future sailors.

Get the handy town map and city guide, and confirm your sightseeing plans. The TI sells a 30-kr brochure, *A Walk around Kalmar*, outlining the town's historical sights, the Old Town, park, and castle. Guided tours in English (50 kr) leave from the TI at 18:00 on Wednesdays in July.

Bike Rental: Kalmar, with its cheery lanes, surrounding parks, and brisk harborfront, makes for happy biking. Team Sportia, a big sport shop near the station, rents fine bikes for 100 kr per day (Mon–Fri 10:00–18:00, Sat 10:00–15:00, closed Sun; leaving station, turn left on Stationsgatan and walk 300 yards to roundabout; tel. 0480/21244). Frimurare Hotellet rents bikes to its guests (30 kr, see "Sleeping," page 263). The TI's *Vasa Stigen* flier outlines a pleasant bike/hike past the castle and around the Stensö Peninsula.

Arrival in Kalmar

Arriving by train couldn't be easier. Get a reservation for your departure at the station (lockers available). The main, modern area of town (Kvarnholmen) is dead ahead; bikes are to your left; the TI to your right; and the castle behind you.

SIGHTS

▲▲**Kalmar Castle (Kalmar Slott)**—This moated castle is one of Europe's great medieval experiences. The stark exterior, cuddled by a lush park, houses a fine Renaissance palace interior, which is the work of King Gustav Vasa and his sons.

Approaching the castle, you'll walk up steps made of Catholic gravestones into faded but grand halls alive with Swedish history. The fine architectural details were mostly painted onto the walls—a necessary cost-saving measure in relatively poor Northern Europe. The elaborately furnished rooms are entertainingly explained in English (70 kr, 60 kr in April–May and Sept; daily April–May and Sept 10:00–16:00, June–Aug 10:00–17:00, July 10:00–18:00; Oct–March open only Sat–Sun 11:00–16:00 on second weekend of month; tel. 0480/451-491). English tours are worthwhile for the goofy medieval antics of Sweden's kings (free, 45 min, offered daily June–mid-Aug—call for times). Check out the eerie exhibit on the women's prison; find the book with English-language descriptions. Walk around the ramparts. The castle lawn cries out for a picnic.

▲**Krusenstiernska Gården**—This early-19th-century middle-class home is lovingly cluttered with old family photos, toys, and Gustavian-style furniture. A helpful English leaflet gives a room-by-room inventory. The garden, with its breezy café selling traditional homemade cakes, is also a treat (25 kr, garden open May–Aug Mon–Fri 10:00–18:00, Sat–Sun 12:00–16:00; museum tourable June–Aug only with guide, at the top of the hour Mon–Fri 13:00–17:00, Sat–Sun 13:00–16:00, closed off-season; 200 yards in front of castle at St. Dammgatan 11, tel. 0480/411-552).

Between this house, the castle, and the station is Kalmar's Gamla Stan (Old Town), a toy village of well-painted wooden homes, tidy yards, and perfect fences.

▲**Kalmar Town**—The Kvarnholmen area of Kalmar is more interesting than its grid plan. Stroll the Storgatan spine to the main square, Stortorget, and the biggest Baroque church in Sweden—built in the 17th century in a grand style befitting a European power. The area beyond Östra Vallgatan (the old eastern wall of the city) has a pleasant park, small swimming beach, and the last remaining *Klapphus* in Kalmar. In the mid-1800s, there were four of these small, wooden buildings—used for washing laundry—at the seaside.

Today the *Klapphus* is still used for washing rugs and carpets—take a peek inside and see if anyone is at work. The quieter lanes and Lilla Torget street have fine old wooden homes. The surviving ramparts mark the old harbor line. The 20th-century extension is filled with parked cars and a modern shopping center.

▲▲**Kalmar County (Läns) Museum**—The second floor of this museum displays the impressive salvaged wreck of the royal ship *Kronan*, which sank nearby in 1676. Lots of interesting soggy bits and rusted pieces giving a here's-the-buried-treasure thrill are well described in English. (For maximum info, borrow the *Kronan* English booklet.) While the actual ship has yet to be recovered, this museum gives a much more intimate look at life at sea than Stockholm's grander *Vasa* Museum. See the excellent 12-minute film (to avoid a delay, request an English-language showing as you enter). The third floor is worth a quick look for its Jenny Nystrom exhibit (an early-1900s Kalmar artist who gained fame for her cute Christmas decorations featuring elves and pixies), a little old-time Kalmar city-life exhibit, and a cozy cafeteria (daily, same hours as museum). From the harborfront museum's door, you can see the distant half of the long bridge leading to the island of Öland (50 kr, mid-June–mid-Aug daily 10:00–18:00; mid-Aug–mid-June Mon–Fri 10:00–16:00, Sat–Sun 11:00–16:00, tel. 0480/451-300).

Maritime History Museum (Sjöfartsmuseum)—This humble little three-room exhibit behind the Läns Museum is a jumble of model boats, charts, and paraphernalia interesting only to sailors who speak Swedish (25 kr, mid-June–mid-Sept Mon–Fri 11:00–16:00, Sat–Sun 12:00–16:00, Sun only in off-season 12:00–16:00, Södra Långgatan 81, tel. 0480/15875).

▲**Island of Öland**—Until recently, this was Europe's longest bridge (free, 3.7 miles), connecting Öland with Kalmar and the mainland. The island, 90 miles long and only eight miles wide, is a pleasant local resort known for its birds, windmills, flowers, beaches, and prehistoric sights. Sweden's king and queen have their summer home on Öland. Public transportation is miserable, and the island is worthwhile only if you have a car and three extra hours. A 60-mile circle south of the bridge will give you a good dose of the island's windy rural charm.

Gettlinge Gravfält (just off the road about 10 miles up from the south tip) is a wonderfully situated, boat-shaped, Iron Age graveyard littered with monoliths and overseen by a couple of creaky old windmills. It offers a commanding view of the windy and mostly treeless island.

Farther south is the **Eketorp Prehistoric Fort,** a very reconstructed 5th-century stone fort that, as Iron Age forts go, is fairly interesting. Several evocative huts and buildings are filled with what someone imagines may have been the style back then, and the huge rock fort is surrounded by strange, runty, piglike creatures—common in gardens 1,500 years ago. A sign reads: "For your convenience and pleasure, don't leave your children alone with the animals" (50 kr, daily 10:00–17:00, until 18:00 late-June–Aug, free English tours usually daily July–Aug at 13:15, tel. 0485/662-000).

SLEEPING

(7 kr = about $1, country code: 46, area code: 0480)
The TI can nearly always find you a room in a private home (300 kr per double, 40 kr per person for sheets, 50-kr fee per booking, no breakfast). They can also get you special last-minute discounts on fancy hotels.

$$$ **Frimurare Hotellet** fills a grand old building overlooking a fine square. While quite large, it has soul and is warmly run by Marianne, her daughter Linda, and a disarmingly friendly staff. Rich public areas, broad hardwood halls, chandeliers, and pilasters give it a neoclassical elegance. Rooms have been thoughtfully renovated and provide modern comfort (Sb-940 kr, Db-1,160 kr; mid-June–mid-Aug and Fri–Sun: Sb-650 kr, Db-875 kr; includes breakfast, family rooms, non-smoking rooms, free sauna, bike rental-30 kr/day, 50 yards in front of train station facing square at Larmtorget 2, tel. 0480/15230, fax 0480/85887, www.frimurarehotellet.gs2.com).

$$$ **Scandic Stadshotellet** is a 1,500-kr place with an affordable summer price (Fri, Sat, and late June–mid-Aug: Sb/Db-950 kr, includes breakfast, non-smoking rooms, central at Stortorget 14, tel. 0480/496-900, fax 0480/496-910, stadshotelletkalmar@scandic-hotels.com).

$$ **Kalmar Lågprishotell Svanen,** an IYHF hotel a 15-minute walk or short bus ride from the center in the Ängö neighborhood, offers more comfort and than its adjoining hostel (listed directly below). Its double rooms have separate beds, although they have one double-bedded room for 795 kr. Single and double rooms without bath all have toilets in the rooms (S-500 kr, Sb-575–755 kr, D-595 kr, Db-695 kr, includes sheets and breakfast, STF Vandrarhem, Rappegatan 1, tel. 0480/25560, fax 0480/88293, www.hotellsvanen .se). You'll see a blue-and-white hotel sign and a hostel symbol at the edge of town on Ängöleden Street, a mile from the train station. Catch bus #402 at the station to Ängöleden (2/hr, 5 min, 15 kr, pay driver). They rent canoes for exploring the small bays around Kalmar (90 kr/half day, 150 kr/day).

$ The **IYHF hostel,** adjacent to the Hotel Svanen (above), has two- to six-bed rooms, laundry, TV, and sauna (195 kr per bed, sheets-50 kr, non-members pay 45 kr extra, breakfast-60 kr, reservations recommended, reception open daily 7:30–21:00, 1 mile from station; same contact information as Hotel Svanen, above).

Kalmar

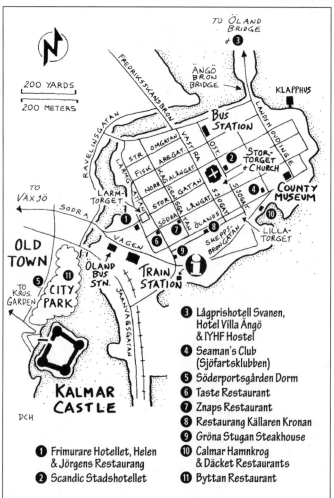

3 Lågprishotell Svanen,
Hotel Villa Ängö
& IYHF Hostel

4 Seaman's Club
(Sjöfartsklubben)

5 Söderportsgården Dorm

6 Taste Restaurant

7 Znaps Restaurant

8 Restaurang Källaren Kronan

9 Gröna Stugan Steakhouse

10 Calmar Hamnkrog
& Däcket Restaurants

11 Byttan Restaurant

1 Frimurare Hotellet, Helen
& Jörgens Restaurang

2 Scandic Stadshotellet

$ The **Seaman's Club (Sjöfartsklubben)** opens its ship-shape
little dorm to tourists June through mid-August. This historic home,
built as a girls' school in 1820, now houses student sailors during the
school year. With harbor views and a lazy garden, this has by far the
best cheap beds in Kalmar (13 rooms, S-225 kr, D-335 kr, T-425 kr,
Q-500 kr, sheets-40 kr, no breakfast, kitchen privileges, lively
common room, reception open same hours as TI, Ölandsgatan 45,
on the corner of Proviantgatan and Ölandsgatan near the Läns
Museum, tel. 0480/10810).

$ Söderportsgården, a university dorm that welcomes tourists mid-June through mid-August, is idyllically located next to a park, facing the castle (35 simple yet classy rooms, 2 to a flat sharing a bathroom and kitchen, S-395 kr, D-595 kr, T-950 kr, includes sheets and breakfast, Slottsvägen 1, tel. & fax 0480/12501, www .soderportsgarden.se).

$ Hotel Villa Ängö, a few blocks beyond the hostel, is a big, old house with a peaceful garden on the water and nine homey ground-floor rooms (S-395 kr, Sb-450 kr, D-550 kr, Db-600 kr, includes breakfast in summer, basement sauna, Bagensgatan 20, tel. 0480/85415). Catch bus #402 at the station to Ängöleden and the hostel listed above; from there, it's a three-block walk. The management lets the place virtually run itself, leaving the door open and the key waiting for you in the door.

EATING

Kalmar has a surprising number of good dining options for a small city. For lunch, look for *dagens rätt,* the "blue-plate special" for 60–70 kr. You can choose from among three or four hot dishes, including salad, bread, and usually coffee and a soft drink. Order and pay at the cashier and take a seat. Dine before 18:00 to take advantage of dinner specials for about 100 kr. In the summertime, you'll often find dinner specials all evening for 90–120 kr.

In the Old Center

I'd stroll the two busy cross streets, Storgatan and Kaggensgatan, to survey the many competitive places—both ethnic and Swedish. **Taste** is just off the town square and offers a delightfully light and modern interior and cuisine to match (Södra Långgatan 5, tel. 0480/15565). **Znaps** is popular for sushi and nouveau Swedish cuisine (Kaggensgatan 1, 0480/20703).

Elegant Dining: Restaurang Källaren Kronan is a candlelit cellar restaurant with classy stone arches. They serve fine old-time Swedish dishes as well as modern cuisine (entrées 170–225 kr, 2- and 3-course *menus* available, Mon–Fri 11:30–14:00 & 18:00–23:00, Sat 11:30–23:00, Sun 13:00–21:00, Ölandsgatan 7, tel. 0480/411-400). **Helen & Jörgens Restaurang,** a local favorite, has a modern bistro ambience and elegant food. They offer a colorful multi-course tasting menu (300–500 kr). Most dishes can be ordered à la carte as well for about 200 kr (daily for dinner 18:00–22:00, open mid-Aug–mid-June only for lunch 11:00–14:00, next to Frimurare Hotellet on Larmtorget, reservations smart, tel. 0480/28830).

On the Modern Harborfront

Gröna Stugan Steakhouse, a small, green building *(Gröna Stugan)* between the train station and the modern harborfront shopping area, offers tasty steak dinners (as well as fish) for 150–200 kr in a casual setting popular with locals. It's on the corner of Skeppsbrogatan and Larmgatan, across from the guest harbor (Mon–Sat 16:00–23:00, Sun 16:00–22:00, reservations recommended, tel. 0480/15858). For dressy harborview dining, consider **Calmar Hamnkrog** (200–250-kr dinners, daily 11:30–14:00 & 18:00–22:00, call ahead to reserve window seats, Skeppsbrogatan 30, tel. 0480/411-020). For a more casual and less expensive meal from the same kitchen with the same harbor views, consider **Däcket,** where the chalkboard shows its special offerings (125-kr dinners, Mon–Sat 18:00–23:00, closed Sun, indoor or outdoor seating).

Near the Castle

There are cafeterias in the castle and directly in front of the castle at **Söderportsgården.** For classier dining (or just a coffee break) in the city park with a view of the castle, consider the venerable **Byttan Restaurant** (70-kr lunch special Mon–Fri 11:30–14:00, more expensive dinners; open Mon–Fri 11:30–22:00, Sat 12:00–23:00, Sun 13:00–17:00, closed off-season Sat–Sun; you'll pass it as you walk to the castle, tel. 0480/16360).

TRANSPORTATION CONNECTIONS

From Kalmar by train to: Växjö (9/day, 70 min, reservation not required), **Stockholm** (10/day, 4.5–5.5 hrs, normally a transfer in Alvesta, reservation mandatory), **Copenhagen** (9/day, 3.5 hrs, usually change in Alvesta, reservation required on some trains).

Route Tips for Drivers

Copenhagen to Sweden: See "Route Tips for Drivers" at the end of the Copenhagen chapter.

Växjö to Kalmar: This is a 70-mile joy—light traffic with endless forest and lake scenery punctuated by numerous glassworks. The TI's free *Kingdom of Crystal* map lists them all and is your best navigational tool. For glass, leave Växjö on the road to Kalmar. The driving time between Växjö and Kosta is 45 minutes; between Kosta and Kalmar, 45 minutes.

Kalmar to Stockholm: Leaving Kalmar, follow E-22 Lindsdal and Nörrköping signs. The Kalmar–Stockholm drive is 230 miles and takes 5 hours. Sweden did a cheap widening job, paving the shoulders of the old two-lane road to get 3.8 lanes. Still, traffic is polite and sparse. There's little to see, so stock the pantry, set the compass on north, and home in on Stockholm.

Make two pleasant stops along the way. **Västervik** is 90 miles north of Kalmar, with an 18th-century core of wooden houses (3 miles off the highway, Centrum signs lead you to the harbor). Park on the waterfront near the great little smoked-fish market (Mon–Sat).

Söderköping is just right for a lunch on the **Göta Canal** stop. Stay on E-22 past where you'd think you'd exit for the town center, then turn right at the Kanalbåtarna/Slussen. Look for the Kanal P signs leading to a handy canalside parking lot. From there, walk along the canal into the action.

Sweden's famous Göta Canal consists of 109 miles of canals cutting the country in half, with 58 locks *(slussen)* working up to a summit of 300 feet. It was built 150 years ago, with more than seven million 12-hour man-days (60,000 men working about 22 years) at a low ebb in the country's self-esteem—to show her industrial might. Today it's a lazy three- or four-day tour, which shows Sweden's zest for good living. Take just a peek at the Göta Canal over lunch, in the medieval town of Söderköping.

The TI on Söderköping's Rådhustorget (a square about a block off the canal) has good town and Stockholm maps, a walking brochure, and canal information. On the canal is the Kanalbutiquen, a yachters' laundry (40 kr, wash and dry, open daily), shower, shop, and WC, with idyllic picnic grounds just over the lock. From the lock, stairs lead up to the Utsiktsplats pavilion (commanding view).

From Söderköping, E-22 takes you to Nörrköping. Follow E-4 signs through Nörrköping, past a handy rest stop, and into Stockholm. The Centrum is clearly marked. (Viking's ferry terminal for Helsinki is in Södermalm; Silja's is northeast of town in Ropsten—see ferry terminal info in beginning of Helsinki chapter, page 274.)

FINLAND
(Suomi)

From medieval times to 1809, Finland was ruled by Sweden. City fires have left little standing from this period, but Finland still has a substantial Swedish minority, bilingual street signs, and close cultural ties to Sweden.

In 1809, Sweden lost Finland to Russia. Under the next century of relatively benign Russian rule, Finland began to industrialize, and Helsinki grew into a fine and elegant city. Still, at the beginning of the 1900s, the rest of Finland was mostly dirt-poor and agricultural, and its people were eagerly emigrating to northern Minnesota. (Read Toivo Pekkanen's *My Childhood* to learn about the life of a Finnish peasant in the early 1900s.)

In 1917, Finland and the Baltic states won their independence from Russia, and enjoyed two decades of peace...until the secret Nazi–Soviet pact of August 1939 assigned them to the Soviet sphere of influence. When Russia invaded, only Finland resisted successfully, its white-camouflaged ski troops winning the Winter War against the Soviet Union in 1939–1940 and holding off the Russians in the Continuation War from 1941–1944.

After World War II, Finland was made to suffer for having fought against one of the Allied Powers. The Finns were forced to cede Karelia (eastern Finland) to the U.S.S.R., to accept Soviet naval bases on Finnish territory, and to pay huge reparations to the Soviet government. Still, Finland's bold, trend-setting modern design and architecture blossomed, and it built up successful timber, paper, and electronics industries. All through the Cold War, Finland teetered between the West and the Soviet Union, trying to be part of Western Europe's strong economy while treading lightly and making nice with her giant neighbor to the east. The collapse of the Soviet Union has done to Finland what a good long sauna might do to you.

When the menace of Moscow vanished, so did about 20 percent of Finland's trade. After a few years of adjustment, Finland is

---

How Big, How Many, How Much

- Finland is 130,600 square miles (almost the size of Montana).
- Population is 5.2 million (40 per square mile).
- €1 (euro) = about $1.20

Finland

on an upswing now. Many Finns used to move to Sweden (where they are the biggest immigrant group), looking for better jobs in Stockholm. Some still nurse an inferiority complex, thinking of themselves as poor cousins to the Swedes. But now, Finland is the most technologically advanced country in Europe. Home to the giant mobile-phone company Nokia, Finland has more mobile-phone numbers than fixed ones, and more Web sites per capita than any other European country. Finns are counting on their membership in the European Union and the euro zone to cement the strength of their economy.

We think of Finland as Scandinavian, but it's better to call it "Nordic." Technically, the Scandinavian countries are Denmark, Sweden, and Norway—all constitutional monarchies with closely related languages. Add Iceland, Finland, and maybe Estonia—former Danish or Swedish colonies that speak separate languages—and you have the "Nordic countries." Iceland, Finland, and Estonia are republics, not monarchies. In 1906, Finnish women were the first in Europe to vote, and today 40 percent of the Finnish parliament—and the Finnish president—is female.

Finland is known as a nation of few words, and Finns value silence, yet are easily approachable. Tourists are not considered a headache to the locals, as they are in places like Paris and Munich. Compared to Sweden or Denmark, Finland has not attracted many immigrants, and few of the service workers you will deal with come from elsewhere.

Finnish

Finnish is a difficult-to-learn Finno-Ugric language originating east of Russia's Ural Mountains; it's related in Europe only to Estonian (closely) and Hungarian (distantly). Finland is officially bilingual, and 6 percent of the country's population speaks Swedish as a first language. You'll notice that Helsinki is called *Helsingfors* in Swedish. Helsinki's street signs list places in both Finnish and Swedish. Nearly every educated young person speaks effortless English—the language barrier is just a road turtle.

The only essential word needed for a quick visit is *kiitos* (KEY-toes)—that's "thank you," and locals love to hear it. *Kippis* (keep-peace) is what you say before you down a shot of Finnish vodka or cloudberry liqueur *(lakka)*.

HELSINKI

The next best thing to being in Helsinki is getting there. Europe's most enjoyable cruise, from Stockholm to Helsinki, starts with dramatic archipelago scenery, a setting sun, and a royal *smörgåsbord* dinner. Dance until you drop and sauna until you drip. Budget travel rarely feels this hedonistic. Sixteen hours after you depart, it's "Hello, Helsinki."

The Cruise from Stockholm to Helsinki

Two fine and fiercely competitive lines, Viking and Silja, connect the capitals of Sweden and Finland. Each line offers state-of-the-art ships with luxurious *smörgåsbord* meals, reasonable cabins, plenty of entertainment (discos, saunas, gambling), and enough duty-free shopping to sink a ship. Of the two, Viking has the reputation as the party boat. Silja is considered more elegant (but still has its share of sometimes irritating and noisy passengers).

The Pepsi and Coke of the Scandinavian cruise industry vie to outdo each other with bigger and fancier boats. The ships are big—at 56,000 tons, nearly 200 yards long, and with 2,700 beds, they're the largest (and cheapest) luxury hotels in Scandinavia. Many other shipping lines buy their boats used from Viking and Silja.

Which line is best? You could count showers and compare *smörgåsbords,* but both lines go overboard to win the loyalty of the nine million duty free–crazy Swedes and Finns who make the trip each year. If you have a Eurailpass, take Silja, which offers you free passage in its cheapest, under-the-car-deck quads (or, if you want nicer digs, it covers the cost of transportation, leaving you to pay only for your cabin; reserve ahead, trip costs one flexi-day). Scanrail passholders get 50 percent off the cost of passage on both Silja and Viking (does not use up a flexi-day). Viking has an older, less luxurious fleet, but caters better to low-budget travelers, selling cheap

Sailing the Baltic Sea

ekonomi cabins (shower down the hall) and allowing passengers to pay for deck passage only and sleep for free on chairs, sofas, and under the stars or stairs. Both lines give modest student and senior discounts.

Cruise Schedules

Both lines sail nightly from Stockholm and Helsinki. In both directions, the boats leave at about 17:00 and arrive the next morning at about 9:30. Both companies also sail daily between Stockholm and Turku, Finland.

Scenery: During the first few hours out of Stockholm, your ship passes through the *skärgården* (archipelago). The third hour features the most exotic island scenery—tiny islets with cute red huts and happy people. I'd have dinner at the first sitting (shortly after departure) and be on deck for sunset.

Time Change: Finland is one hour ahead of Sweden. Sailing from Stockholm to Helsinki, operate on Swedish time until you're ready to go to bed, then reset your watch. Morning schedules are Finnish time (and vice versa when you return). The cruise-schedule flier in English makes this clear (pick it up as you board).

Cost

Fares vary by season and by day of the week. Mid-June to mid-August is most crowded and expensive (with prices the same

Helsinki Harbor

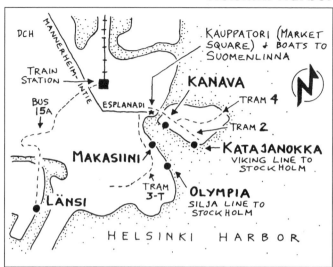

regardless of day). During the off-season, Friday prices are about double the regular fare; try to avoid travel on a Friday.

In summer, a one-way ticket per person for the cheapest bed that has a private bath (in a below-sea-level, under-car-deck "C" quad) costs about €60. Couples will pay a total of about €180–200 for the cheapest double room (with bath) that's above the car deck. Fares drop about 25 percent off-season for departures Sunday through Wednesday. Each ship offers a whale of a *smörgåsbord* dinner for an extra €22–26 and a big breakfast for €8. Reserving your meals in advance knocks about 10 percent off the cost and the hassle of hustling for a reservation after you board. Try to reserve a specific table in advance, too (window seats go fast).

Round-trip cruise fares (across and back on successive nights, leaving you access to your bedroom throughout the day) generally cost little more than a one-way trip. In peak season, couples can share a double cabin round-trip for about €210–250. The drawback is that this leaves you with only a few hours on land. But you can get the round-trip fare on non-successive nights if you book a hotel through the cruise line for every intervening night—if it fits your schedule, this is a good deal (especially on Thursday departures off-season).

The fares are cheap because locals sail to shop and drink duty- and tax-free. It's a huge operation—mostly for locals. The boats are filled with about 40 percent Finns, 55 percent Swedes, and 5 percent cruisers from other countries. Last year, the average passenger spent as much on booze and duty-free items as for the boat fare. The boats now make a midnight stop in the Åland Islands—a part of Finland that's exempt from European Union membership—to preserve the international nature of the trip and maintain the duty-free status.

Reservations

Call the cruise line directly in Scandinavia to reserve your crossing. *For summer or weekend sailings, reserve well in advance.* The Swedish reservations numbers are tel. 46-8/222-140 (Silja) and tel. 46-8/452-4000 (Viking). In Helsinki, call 358-9/18041 (Silja) or 358-9/12351 (Viking). You can pay by credit card and pick up your ticket at the terminal (1 hr before departure). Operators speak English. Any travel agent in Scandinavia can sell you a ticket (with a small booking fee). Neither line allows Internet bookings.

Web sites: Visit Viking at www.vikingline.fi or Silja at www.silja.fi for the most up-to-date timetable information.

Terminals

Locations: In Stockholm, Viking Line ships moor at Stadsgården on Södermalm. To get there from Stockholm's bus station, take Viking's shuttle bus (30 kr) to the dock or public bus #53 to the Londonviadukten stop.

Silja Line's harbor is northeast of the center in Ropsten. Catch the Silja shuttle bus (25 kr) from the bus station.

In Helsinki, both lines are perfectly central, on opposite sides of the main harbor, a 10-minute walk from the center. See the Helsinki map on page 280 for details.

Terminal Buildings: These are well organized, with cafés, lockers, tourist information desks, lounges, and phones. Remember, 2,000 passengers come and go with each boat. Customs is a snap. Boats open 90 minutes before departure. You must be on board 20 minutes before departure.

Parking: Both lines offer safe and handy parking in Stockholm. Ask for details when you reserve your ticket.

Onboard Services

Meals: While ships have cheap, fast cafeterias as well as classy, romantic restaurants, they are famous for their *smörgåsbord* dinners. Board the ship hungry. Dinner is self-serve in two sittings, one at about 18:00, the other a couple hours later. Pay for both the dinner buffet (€22–26) and breakfast buffet (€8) when you buy your ticket (this saves you 10 percent). If you board without a reservation, go to the restaurant and make one. Make sure to reserve your table, not just your meal; window seats are highly sought after. Pick up the *How to Eat a* Smörgåsbord brochure. The key is to take small portions and pace yourself. The price includes free beer, wine, soft drinks, and coffee. Of course, you can also bring a picnic and eat it on deck.

Sauna: Each ship has a sauna. This costs about €5 extra. Reserve a time upon boarding. Saunas on Silja are half price or even free in the morning (for those with a cabin towel). Silja also offers massage on board from 15:00 to 22:00, for an extra fee. Reserve immediately upon boarding.

Banking: Ships take euros and Swedish kronor, and virtually any vendor or shop also accepts credit cards. Each boat has a handy exchange desk on board with acceptable rates. None of the boats has an ATM, but all terminals have ATMs and exchange windows.

Tourist Info on Board: Boats generally offer racks of *Stockholm* or *Helsinki This Week* magazines. Grab a copy for some practical bedtime reading.

Options

Tallinn: You can visit Tallinn as a day trip from Helsinki, or Helsinki as a day trip from Tallinn, or you can make a triangle trip: Stockholm–Helsinki–Tallinn–Stockholm or vice versa. See the Tallinn chapter for details on the Helsinki–Tallinn and Stockholm–Tallinn crossings.

Turku: Both Viking and Silja also sail from Stockholm to Turku in Finland, a shorter crossing. Turku is two hours from Helsinki by bus or train. The boats are usually smaller, with less cruise-ship excitement.

Helsinki

Helsinki is the only European capital with no medieval past. In 1746, Sweden built a huge fortress on an island outside its harbor. The town of Helsinki was founded to supply the fortress. After taking over Finland in 1809, the Russians decided to move its capital and university closer to St. Petersburg—from Turku to Helsinki. They hired a young German architect, Carl Ludwig Engel, to design new public buildings for Helsinki and told him to use St. Petersburg as a model. This is why the oldest parts of Helsinki (around Market Square and Senate Square) feel so Russian—stone buildings in yellow and blue pastels with white trim and columns. Hollywood used Helsinki for the films *Gorky Park* and *Dr. Zhivago,* since filming in Russia was not possible.

Though the city was part of the Russian Empire in the 19th century, most of its residents were still Swedes, and Swedish was the language of business and culture. In the mid-1800s, Finland began to industrialize. The Swedish upper class in Helsinki expanded the city, bringing in the railroad and surrounding the old Russian-inspired core with neighborhoods of four- and five-story apartment buildings, including some Art Nouveau masterpieces.

Meanwhile, Finns moved from the countryside to Helsinki to take jobs as industrial laborers. The Finnish language slowly acquired equal status with Swedish, and eventually Finnish speakers became a majority in Helsinki.

Since downtown Helsinki didn't exist until the 1800s, it was more consciously designed and laid out than other European capitals. Europe's most neoclassical city, with its many architectural overleafs, turns guests into fans of architecture and urban planning. Katajanokka, Kruununhaka, and Eira are good walking neighborhoods for architecture buffs.

Helsinki can be windy and cold, but it's worth the chill.

Planning Your Time

On a three-week trip through Scandinavia, Helsinki is worth at least the time between two successive nights on the cruise ship—about seven hours.

Start with the two-hour Hello Helsinki bus tour that meets the boat at the dock. Then take the self-guided walking tour through the compact city center from the harbor—enjoying Helsinki's ruddy harborfront market and getting goose bumps in the churches—to the National Museum of Finland. In the afternoon, dive into Finnish culture in the open-air folk museum or take a boat tour of the harbor. Enjoy a cup of coffee at Café Kappeli before reboarding. Sail away while sampling another *smörgåsbord* dinner.

ORIENTATION

(Helsinki's area code: 09; from outside Finland: 358-9)
Helsinki's natural gateway is its harbor, where ships from Stockholm and Tallinn dock. At the top of the harbor is Market Square (where vendors sell the catch of the day, produce, and plenty of crafts and souvenirs). Nearby are two towering, can't-miss-them landmarks: the white Lutheran Cathedral and the brick Russian Orthodox cathedral.

From the harbor, the city sprawls uphill. The best shopping and people-watching are along Helsinki's main artery, the Esplanade, which begins at Market Square and heads up towards the train sta-

tion (TI on right a half block up from harbor). Near the station, the Esplanade veers north and becomes the broad, bustling Mannerheimintie. For a do-it-yourself orientation to town along this route, see my "Self-Guided Walk: Welcome to Helsinki," page 281.

Tourist Information

The TI is a half block inland from Market Square, on the right just past the fountain, at the corner of Unioninkatu and Pohjoisesplanadi (May–Sept Mon–Fri 9:00–20:00, Sat–Sun 9:00–18:00; Oct–April Mon–Fri 9:00–18:00, Sat–Sun 10:00–16:00, tel. 09/169-3757, fax 09/169-3839, www.hel.fi/english, then click on "Tourism"). The TI is friendly, helpful, and stocked with free brochures. Pick up the city map, the public-transit map, *Helsinki on Foot* (6 well-described walking tours with maps), the monthly *Helsinki This Week* magazine (lists sights, hours, and events), and *City* magazine (good, opinionated restaurant listings, geared for the younger crowd). Ask for the brochure on the scenic #3T tram and go over your sightseeing plans.

Helsinki Expert, a private service that works with the tourist office, sells ferry tickets and transport passes and makes hotel bookings. They have one branch in the train station hall, and another occupying the back desks in the TI. They always know what wild bargains are available, like luxury-hotel clearance deals that cost only €20 more than the cheapies. There's a €5 fee for walk-in hotel reservations (e-mail and phone reservations are free), and ferry bookings cost €7 (branch in TI office open June–Aug Mon–Fri 9:00–19:00, Sat–Sun 9:00–17:00; Sept–May Mon–Fri 9:00–17:00, Sat 10:00–16:00, closed Sun, tel. 09/2288-1500, fax 09/2288-1599; branch in train station office open June–Aug Mon–Fri 9:00–19:00, Sat–Sun 10:00–18:00; Sept–May Mon–Fri 9:00–18:00, Sat 9:00–17:00, closed Sun, tel. 09/2288-1400, fax 09/2288-1499, www .helsinkiexpert.fi, hotel@helsinkiexpert.fi).

If you're planning a lot of sightseeing in Helsinki, the **Helsinki Card** can be a good deal (24 hrs/€25, 48 hrs/€35, 72 hrs/€45). It includes free entry to sights; free use of buses, trams, and the ferry to Suomenlinna; an orientation bus tour—normally €20—for €8; and a 96-page booklet (sold at Helsinki Expert, TI, most hotels, and ferry ports, www.helsinkicard.com).

Arrival in Helsinki

By Ferry: Helsinki has five ferry terminals *(terminaali)*—see map on page 280. The Olympia and Makasiini terminals are on the west side (to the left as you face inland) of the main harbor. The Katajanokka and Kanava terminals are on the east side (right) of the main harbor. Most Silja Line boats use the Olympia terminal; most Viking boats use the Katajanokka terminal. The Kanava and Makasiini terminals are mostly for fast boats to Tallinn. The Länsi terminal, in Helsinki's western harbor, is for large car ferries to Tallinn. It's connected to Elielinaukio (the square on the western side of the train station) by bus #15A (€2, 2–4/hr, 15-min trip).

By Train and Bus: The train station, an architectural landmark, is at the top of the Esplanade, a 15-minute walk from Market

Square. Local buses leave from both sides of the building, trams stop out front, and the subway runs underneath. The long-distance bus station is two blocks away, on the other side of Mannerheimintie; it's in the process of being reconstructed and moved underground.

By Plane: To get between the airport and downtown Helsinki, take the Finnair bus (€4.90, downtown terminus is platform 30 at Elielinaukio on west side of train station, 3/hr, 35-min trip) or public bus #615 (€3.40, downtown terminus is platform #10 at Rautatientori on east side of train station, 2–4/hr, 45-min trip, also stops at Hakaniemi). Or take the Yellow Line door-to-door shared van service (€20 for 1–2 people, €22 for 3–4 people, tel. 09/106-464, www.airporttaxi.fi). Cabs run €25–32.

Helpful Hints

Time: Finland and Estonia are one hour ahead of Sweden and the rest of Scandinavia.

Money: Euro collectors, take note: Finland is not minting many one- and two-cent coins, since all cash transactions are rounded to the nearest five cents.

Internet Access: Many cafés have a computer or two. The Cable Book Library, a branch of the Helsinki City Library, has free half-hour slots on its terminals, but you have to sign up in advance (inside big post office building on Mannerheimintie, near the train station).

Getting Around Helsinki

In compact Helsinki, you won't need to use public transportation as much as in Stockholm.

By Bus and Tram: With the public-transit route map (available at the TI) and a little mental elbow grease, the buses and trams are easy, giving you Helsinki by the tail. Tickets are good for an hour of travel (€2 from automatic vending machines at larger stops, or from driver). The Tourist Ticket (€5.40 for 24 hrs of unlimited travel) pays if you take three or more rides; longer versions are also available (72 hrs/€10.80, 120 hrs/€16.20). A 24-hour Family Ticket is  available for up to two adults and four children traveling together (€8, a good value even for just 2 adults). Purchase the Tourist and Family Tickets from vending machines, from the HKL Service Point under the train station, or at the TI. The single subway line uses the same tickets but is not useful for most visitors.

Tram #3T makes the rounds of most of the town's major sights in an hour (either buy a single ticket—good for 1 hour—and stay on the tram for the circuit, or get the Tourist or Family Ticket, allowing you to hop off to tour a sight, then catch a later tram). Tram #3 runs in a confusing but convenient figure-eight route around town; tram #3B follows the same route in the opposite direction. The TI promotes tram #3T as a self-guided tour and has a helpful explanatory brochure (available at TI but not on board). Bus #24 goes farther afield, to the Sibelius Monument and the open-air museum (departs from the end of the Esplanade, in front of the Svenska Theater). Each of these gives you a cheap, go-anytime, once-over-lightly, self-guided tour. In summer, the antique red Pub Tram makes a 60-minute circle through the city while its passengers get looped on the beer for sale on board (€8, 3/hr, leaves on the hour mid-May–mid-Aug Wed–Sat 14:00–20:00 from in front of Fennia building, Mikonkatu 17, across from train-station tower).

By Bike: Helsinki is copying Copenhagen's lead and offering free bikes for anyone to borrow. From May to September, 300 blue-and-green bikes are scattered at 26 points throughout the city center. Pay a small deposit fee (about €2) when you pick up the bike; the deposit is returned at whatever point you drop it off. These bikes are popular, and it can be hard to find an available one.

You can rent a more comfortable bike at Greenbike (€10/day, €15/24 hrs, Mannerheimintie 13, behind Kiasma museum and across from Parliament House, in the low building below street level, tel. 09/8502-2850).

TOURS

▲▲▲**Orientation Bus Tour**—A fast, very good 90-minute introductory tour with a live multilingual guide leaves daily from both the Silja and Viking terminals shortly after the ships pull in from Stockholm. A similar tour (with headphone commentary and nice sound effects) departs daily from the corner of Fabianinkatu and the Esplanade a block from the TI (daily on the hour in summer 10:00–14:00, in winter at 11:00 only; either tour costs €20, slightly cheaper if purchased on the ship, discounted to €8 with Helsinki Card, can book by phone at tel. 09/2288-1600, www.helsinkiexpert.fi). These give a good overview with a look at all the important buildings, from the newly remodeled Olympic Stadium to Embassy Row, and 10-minute stops at the Sibelius Monument and the Church in the Rock (Temppeliaukio). You'll learn strange facts, such as how they took down the highest steeple in town during World War II so that the Soviet bombers flying in from Estonia couldn't see their target.

▲**Harbor Tours**—Several boat companies struggle for your attention along Market Square, offering 90-minute, €15 cruises around the waterfront nearly hourly from 10:00 to 18:00. The narration is slow moving—often tape-recorded and in as many as four languages. But if the weather's good and you're looking for

Helsinki

1 Hotel Anna
2 Martta Hotelli
3 Hotel Arthur
4 Lord Hotel
5 Scandic Grand Marina
6 Hotel Cumulus Kaisaniemi
7 Hotelli Finn
8 Hotel Skatta & Eurohostel
9 Academica Summer Hostel
10 Erottajanpuisto Hostel

11 Olympic Stadium Hostel
12 Café Kappeli
13 Strindberg & Papa Giovanni's
   Restaurants
14 Sundmanns Restaurant
15 Lasipalatsi Restaurant
16 Kynsilaukka Garlic Restaurant
17 Konstan Mölja Restaurant
18 Lappi Restaurant
19 Hariton Restaurant

something one step above a snooze in the park...then all aboard.
Local Guide—To hire a private guide, call 09/2288-1222.

Self-Guided Walk: Welcome to Helsinki

Start at the obelisk in the center of **Market Square,** the harborfront market. This is the **Czarina's Stone,** with its double-headed eagle of imperial Russia. This was the first public monument in Helsinki, designed by Carl Engel and erected in 1835 to celebrate the visit by Czar Nicholas and Czarina Alexandra. Step over the chain and climb to the top step for a clockwise spin tour: The big red **Viking ship** and white **Silja ship** are each floating hotels for those making the 36-hour Stockholm–Helsinki round-trip. The brown-and-tan brick building is the old market hall. A number of harbor cruise boats vie for your business. The trees mark the beginning of Helsinki's grand promenade, the Esplanade. Hiding in the leaves is the venerable iron-and-glass Café Kappeli. The yellow building across from the trees is the TI. From there, a string of neoclassical buildings face the harbor. The blue-and-white building is the **City Hall** (designed by Engel in 1833 to be a hotel). The Lutheran Cathedral is hidden from view behind this building. Next is the **Swedish Embassy** (flying the blue-and-yellow Swedish flag and designed to look like Stockholm's Royal Palace). Then comes the **Supreme Court** and, in the far corner, Finland's **Presidential Palace.** Standing proud, and reminding Helsinki of the behemoth to the east, is the Russian Orthodox **Uspenski Cathedral.**

Explore the colorful **produce market**—with more souvenirs and crafts than fruits and veggies (Mon–Fri 6:30–18:00, Sat 6:30–16:00, summer only Sun 10:00–16:00). Then, with your back to the water, walk left. The fountain features the symbol of Helsinki, the "Daughter of the Baltic." Across the street on the right, you'll see the **TI.** Next door to the TI is the delightful **Jugendsalen,** built in Art Nouveau style in 1904, originally as the lobby of a bank. It's now a city information office for locals. Though not a TI, the Jugendsalen does have brochures on Helsinki in a calm environment, plus temporary art and history exhibits (Mon–Fri 9:00–16:00, Sun 11:00–17:00, closed Sat, Pohjoisesplanadi 19).

Make a one-block detour up Unioninkatu to the neoclassical **Senate Square** and **Lutheran Cathedral** (see page 283). You'll pass the Schroder Sport Shop, with a great selection of popular Finnish-made Rapala fishing lures—ideal for the fisherfolk on your gift list.

In the park across the street from the TI is my favorite café in Northern Europe, **Café Kappeli.** When you've got some time, dip into this old-fashioned gazebo-like oasis of coffee, pastry, and relaxation. In the 19th century, it was a popular hangout for local intellectuals and artists. Today the café offers romantic tourists waiting for their ship a great €2-cup-of-coffee memory.

Helsinki at a Glance

▲▲▲Temppeliaukio Church Awe-inspiring, copper-topped 1969 "Church in the Rock." **Hours:** Mon–Fri 10:00–20:00, Sat 10:00–18:00, Sun 12:00–13:45 & 15:15–17:45, closed Tue 13:00–14:00.

▲▲Lutheran Cathedral Green-domed, 19th-century neoclassical masterpiece. **Hours:** Mon–Sat 9:00–18:00, Sun12:00–18:00, June–Aug 9:00–24:00.

▲▲Uspenski Cathedral Russian Orthodoxy's most prodigious display in Western Europe. **Hours:** Mon–Sat 9:30–16:00, Sun 12:00–15:00, Oct–April closed on Mon and Sat at 14:00.

▲▲National Museum of Finland The scoop on Finland, featuring folk costumes, an armory, czars, and thrones; the prehistory exhibit is best. **Hours:** Tue–Sun 11:00–18:00, until 20:00 Tue–Wed, closed Mon.

▲Senate Square Consummate neoclassical square, with Lutheran Cathedral. **Hours:** Square always open.

▲Sibelius Monument Stainless-steel sculptural tribute to Finland's greatest composer. **Hours:** Always open.

▲Flea Market Jumble sale with good grazing for organic foodies. **Hours:** Mon–Fri 8:00–14:00, in summer Mon–Sat 8:00–15:00 and some Sun 10:00–16:00.

▲Seurasaari Open-Air Folk Museum Island museum with 100 historic buildings from Finland's farthest corners. **Hours:** June–Aug daily 11:00–17:00, Wed until 19:00; late May and early Sept Mon–Fri 9:00–15:00, Sat–Sun 11:00–17:00.

▲Suomenlinna Park in Helsinki's harbor sprinkled with history, toy, and military museums. **Hours:** Generally daily May–Sept daily 10:00–17:00, shorter hours off-season.

Finlandia Hall Hometown architect Alvar Aalto's finest building in Finland. **Hours:** Mon–Fri 9:00–16:00, June–Aug also Sat–Sun 9:00–16:00.

Kiasma Modern-art museum. **Hours:** Tue 9:00–17:00, Wed–Sun 10:00–20:30, closed Mon.

Behind Café Kappeli stretches the **Esplanade**—Helsinki's top shopping boulevard, sandwiching a park in the middle (another Engel design from the 1830s). The north side (with the TI) is interesting for window-shopping, people-watching, and sun-worshipping. You'll pass several stores specializing in Finnish design. Farther up on the right, at #39, is the huge Academic Bookstore (Akateeminen Kirjakauppa), designed by Alvar Aalto, with an extensive map and travel section, periodicals, English books, and Café Aalto (bookstore and café open Mon–Fri 9:00–21:00, Sat 9:00–18:00, closed Sun, less in winter). Finally you'll come to the prestigious Stockmann's department store—Finland's Harrods. This biggest, best, and oldest store in town has a fine selection of local design (Mon–Fri 9:00–21:00, Sat 9:00–18:00, closed Sun, Aleksanterinkatu 52B, www.stockmann.fi). Just beyond is the main intersection in town: the Esplanade and Mannerheimintie. Nearby you'll see the famous *Three Blacksmiths* statue. (Locals say, "If a virgin walks by, they'll strike the anvil." It doesn't work. I tried.)

Two blocks to the right, through a busy shopping center, is the harsh (but serene) architecture of the central **train station** (by Eliel Saarinen, 1916). The four people on the facade symbolize the peasant farmers with lamps coming into the Finnish capital. Wander around inside. If you need a break, pop into the Pullman Bar (inside the main entrance, to the right and up one floor) for a local beer (*Lapin Kulta* or *Koff*), a quick bite, and free Internet access. Continuing past the post office and the statue, return to Mannerheimintie, which leads to the large white **Finlandia Hall,** another Aalto masterpiece. Though not open to individuals, it often features guided tours in summer (see page 285). Across the street is the excellent little **National Museum of Finland** (looks like a church; see page 285), and a few blocks behind that is the sit-down-and-wipe-a-tear beautiful rock church, **Temppeliaukio** (see next page). Sit. Enjoy the music. It's a wonderful place to end this walk. Welcome to Helsinki.

If you want to continue on to the **Sibelius Monument,** in a lovely park setting (see page 285), take bus #24 (direction Seurasaari) from nearby Arkadiankatu street. (The same ticket is good for your return trip.) Ride to the end of the line—the bridge to Seurasaari Island and Finland's open-air folk museum. From there, bus #24 returns to the top of the Esplanade.

SIGHTS

Central Helsinki

▲**Senate Square**—Once a town square with a church and City Hall, this square's original buildings were burned in 1808 during Swedish/Russian fighting. Later, after Finland became a grand duchy of the Russian Empire, the czar sent in architect Carl Engel (a German who had lived and worked in St. Petersburg) to give the place some neo-class. The result: the finest neoclassical square in Europe. Survey it from the top of the Lutheran Cathedral steps. The Senate building is on your left. The small, blue, stone building with the slanted mansard roof in the far-left corner, from 1757, is one of just two pre-Russian-conquest buildings remaining in Helsinki. On the right is the university building (36,000 students, 60 percent women). Russian czar Alexander II, popular because he gave Finland more autonomy in 1853, is honored by the statue in the square. The huge staircase leading up to the cathedral is a popular meeting (and tanning) point in Helsinki. Café Engel (facing the cathedral at Aleksanterinkatu 26) is a fine place for a light lunch or cake and coffee. The city history museum is around the corner at Sofiankatu 4, with thorough descriptions in English (€3, free on Thu, open Mon–Fri 9:00–17:00, Sat–Sun 11:00–17:00, www .hel.fi/kaumuseo).

▲▲Lutheran Cathedral—With its prominent green dome and the 12 apostles overlooking the city and harbor, this church is Carl Engel's masterpiece. Finished in 1854, the interior is pure architectural truth. Open a pew gate and sit—surrounded by the saints of Protestantism—to savor neoclassical nirvana (Mon–Sat 9:00–18:00, Sun 12:00–18:00, June–Aug 9:00–24:00, on Senate Square).

▲▲Uspenski Cathedral—This Russian Orthodox cathedral, built in 1868 when Finland belonged to Russia, hovers above Market Square and faces the Lutheran Cathedral as Russian culture faces Europe's. The inside is a fine icon experience (Mon–Sat 9:30–16:00, Sun 12:00–15:00, Oct–April closes on Mon and Sat at 14:00, Kanavakatu 1).

▲▲▲Temppeliaukio Church—Another great piece of church architecture (from 1969), this "Church in the Rock" was blasted out of solid rock and capped with a copper-and-sky-light dome. It's normally filled with live or recorded music and awestruck visitors. Grab a pew. Gawk upward at a 13-mile-long coil of copper ribbon. Look at the bull's-eye and ponder God. Forget your camera. Just sit in the middle, ignore the crowds, and be thankful for peace—under your feet is an air-raid shelter that can accommodate 6,000 people (Mon–Fri 10:00–20:00, Sat 10:00–18:00, Sun 12:00–13:45 & 15:15–17:45 unless there's a church event or concert, closed Tue 13:00–14:00, Lutherinkatu 3). You can attend the English-language Lutheran service (Sun at 14:00, tel. 09/494-698) or one of many concerts.

▲**Sibelius Monument**—Six hundred stainless-steel pipes—built on solid rock as is so much of Finland—shimmer in a park to honor Finland's greatest composer, Jean Sibelius. The artist was forced to add the composer's face to silence the critics of her otherwise abstract work. Bus #24 stops here (20 min until the next bus, or catch a quick glimpse on the left from the bus) on its way to the open-air folk museum. The #3T tram, which runs more frequently, stops a few blocks away.

▲▲**National Museum of Finland (Suomen Kansallismuseo)**—This pleasant, easy-to-handle collection (covering Finland's story from A to Z, with good English descriptions) is in a grand building designed by three of Finland's greatest early architects in the early 1900s. The neoclassical furniture, folk costumes, armory, and portraits of Russia's last czars around an impressive throne are interesting, but the highlight is the "Prehistory of Finland" exhibit, Finland's largest permanent archaeological collection. Following the clear English-language descriptions, you'll learn how Stone, Bronze, and Iron Age tribes of Finland lived (€5.50, free Tue 17:30–20:00, open Tue–Sun 11:00–18:00, until 20:00 Tue–Wed, closed Mon, ask about tours, Mannerheimintie 34, tel. 09/4050-9544, www.kansallismuseo.fi). The museum café, with a tranquil outdoor courtyard, has light meals and Finnish treats such as lingonberry juice and reindeer quiche.

Finlandia Hall (Finlandia-Talo)—Alvar Aalto's most famous building in his native Finland means little to the non-architect without a tour (€6, many days at 14:00 in summer, 30 min, call ahead to reserve; hall open Mon–Fri 9:00–16:00, June–Aug also Sat–Sun 9:00-16:00, Mannerheimintie 13e, tel. 09/402-421, www.finlandia.hel.fi).

Kiasma—Finland's museum of contemporary art, designed by American architect Steven Holl, doesn't have a permanent collection, but you can ask at the TI or check online to find out what's showing (€5.50, Tue 9:00–17:00, Wed–Sun 10:00–20:30, closed Mon, Mannerheiminaukio 2, near train station, www.kiasma.fi).

▲**Flea Market**—If you brake for garage sales, the Hietalahti Market, Finland's biggest flea market, is worth the 15-minute walk from the harbor or a short ride on tram #6 from Mannerheimintie (Mon–Fri 8:00–14:00, in summer Mon–Sat 8:00–15:00 and some Sun 10:00–16:00). Wander through the big brick market hall (specializing in organic food) for a coffee or snack. In the distance, notice the shipyard—birthplace of many of the world's luxury cruise ships.

Concerts—Concerts in churches are heavenly. Ask at the TI and keep an eye out for posters. The Kallio Church has a magnificent new organ.

Sauna

Finland's vaporized fountain of youth is the sauna—Scandinavia's answer to support hose and face-lifts. A traditional sauna is a wood-paneled room with wooden benches and a wood-fired stove topped with rocks. The stove is heated blistering hot. Undress entirely before going in. Lay your towel on the bench, and sit or lie on it (for hygienic reasons). Ladle water from the bucket onto the rocks to make steam. Choose a higher bench for hotter temperatures. Let yourself work up a sweat, then just before bursting, go outside to the shower for a Niagara of liquid ice. Suddenly your shower stall becomes a Cape Canaveral launch pad, as your body scatters to every corner of the universe. A moment later you're back together and can re-enter the cooker and repeat as necessary. Only rarely will you feel so good.

Your hostel, hotel, or the ship you came to Finland on may have a sauna. Ask them when they heat it, and whether it's semi-public (separate men's and women's hours, pay per person) or for private use (book and pay for a 45- to 60-minute time slot, and save money by bringing a group of friends, either mixed or same-sex). Public saunas are a dying breed these days, but Helsinki has a fine traditional wood-heated one, **Kotiharjun Sauna** (€6.50, Tue–Fri 14:00–20:00, Sat 13:00–19:00, closed Sun–Mon, Harjutorinkatu 1, by Sörnäinen subway stop, tel. 09/753-1535). The best way to experience a sauna is in the countryside at a Finnish friend's summer house. The Finnish Sauna Society's informative English Web site details the history of saunas and sweat baths (www.sauna.fi).

Outer Helsinki

A week-long car trip up through the Finnish lakes and forests to Mikkeli and Savonlinna would be relaxing, but you can actually enjoy Finland's green-trees-and-blue-water scenery without leaving Helsinki. Here are two great ways to get out and go for a walk on a sunny summer day.

▲**Seurasaari Open-Air Folk Museum**—Inspired by Stockholm's Skansen, also on a lovely island on the edge of town, this is a collection of 100 historic buildings from every corner of Finland. It's wonderfully furnished and gives rushed visitors an opportunity to sample the far reaches of Finland without leaving the capital city. The €1.20 map or the €6 guidebook provide needed information if you're not taking a tour. (The park is free, €2.50 to enter 1 building, €5 to enter all, June–Aug daily 11:00–17:00, Wed until 19:00; late May and early Sept Mon–Fri 9:00–15:00, Sat–Sun 11:00–17:00; tel. 09/4050-9660, www.seurasaari.fi.) Call the museum to ask about free English tours (June–Aug, most days at 11:30 and 15:30). Off-season, when the buildings are closed, the place is empty and not worth the trouble. To reach the museum, ride bus #24 (from the top of the Esplanade, 3/hr) to the end (note departure times for your return) and walk across the quaint footbridge.

For a €2 bottomless cup of coffee and great homemade cakes in a homey setting, visit the Tomtebo café with the sprawling front yard at the mainland end of the bridge to Seurasaari (June–Aug daily 11:00–17:00, closed off-season). In summer, they host folk-dance exhibitions (€8, June–Aug Wed at 19:00, Sun at 17:00, call for information, tel. 09/484-511 or 09/484-234).

▲Suomenlinna—The island guarding Helsinki's harbor was fortified by Sweden in the 1740s. It's now a popular park with several museums and a Visitors Center about five minutes on foot from the boat dock (May–Aug daily 10:00–18:00, Sept–April Tue–Sun 11:00–16:00, mostly closed late Dec–early Jan, tel. 09/684-1880, www.suomenlinna.fi). You and your imagination get free run of the fortifications and dungeon-like chambers. Consider a tour (€6, covered by Helsinki Card, 60-min tours in English daily June–Aug at 11:00 and 14:00). Pick up a free Suomenlinna mini-newspaper at the Helsinki TI or at the Visitors Center—a handy map is inside (otherwise map costs €2).

The museums include Suomenlinna Museum (€5, history of the fortress and a multivision show, located in Inventory Chambers, with TI), Doll and Toy Museum (€5, daily May–Aug only, weekends only mid-Sept–Oct), a WWII submarine (€3.50, or €5 combo-ticket covers military museums), and two military museums (€3.50 apiece, or €5 combo-ticket for both plus submarine). Museum hours vary but are roughly May through September daily 10:00 to 17:00 (weekends only for the museums open in spring and fall).

To get to Suomenlinna, catch a ferry from Market Square. Walk past the higher-priced excursion boats to the public HKL ferry (€4 round-trip, same tickets as buses and trams, free with Helsinki and Tourist Cards, 15-min trip, 3–4/hr in summer, nearly hourly in winter).

Near Helsinki

Porvoo, the second-oldest town in Finland, has wooden architecture that dates from the Swedish colonial period. This coastal town can be reached from Helsinki by bus (1 hr) or by excursion boat from Market Square.

Turku, the historic capital of Finland, is a two-hour bus or train ride from Helsinki. Overall, Turku is a pale shadow of Helsinki, and there is little reason to make a special trip. It does have a handicraft museum in a cluster of wooden houses (the only part of town to survive a devastating fire in the early 1800s), an old castle, a fine Gothic cathedral, and a market square. Viking and Silja boats sail from Turku to Stockholm every morning and evening (at about

9:00 and 21:00; the cheaper fare saves enough to pay for the trip from Helsinki to Turku, and the ferry companies can sometimes arrange discounted bus or train tickets).

Naantali, a cute, commercial, well-preserved medieval town with a quaint harbor, is an easy bus ride from Turku (4/hr, 20 min). If you've seen or will see Sigtuna (near Stockholm), Naantali offers little. Porvoo may be for you.

SHOPPING

The harborfront **Market Square** is packed not only with fishmongers and producers, but also with stands selling tacky Finnish souvenirs and more refined crafts (Mon–Fri 6:30–18:00, Sat 6:30–16:00, summer only Sun 10:00–16:00). Sniff the stacks of trivets, made from cross-sections of juniper twigs—an ideal, fragrant, easy-to-pack gift for the folks back home (they smell even nicer when you set something hot on them).

The best shopping street in Helsinki is the delightful **Esplanade.** The enormous, sprawling Stockmann's department store is a joy to browse (Mon–Fri 9:00–21:00, Sat 9:00–18:00, closed Sun, Aleksanterinkatu 52B, www.stockmann.fi), but the entire street is lined with other, smaller stores ideal for window-shopping. Keep an eye out for sleek Scan-design gifts. Consider the purses, scarves, clothes, and fabrics by the well-known Finnish designer Marimekko (sold in several shops along the Esplanade, www.marimekko.fi). Bookworms enjoy the impressive Academic Bookstore just before Stockmann's (Esplanade 39).

NIGHTLIFE

While it's easy to make friends in a bar, anything alcoholic is expensive. For the latest on hot nightspots, read the English insert of *City* magazine that lists the "best" of everything in Helsinki. For cheap fun, Suomenlinna park and Hietaranta beach are where the local kids hang out (and even skinny-dip) at 22:00 or 23:00. This city is one of Europe's safest after dark.

SLEEPING

Standard hotel doubles' rack rates start at about €100. But you rarely need to pay this much. You have four basic money-saving options: modest but comfortable smaller hotels, discounted big-hotel rooms in summer and on weekends, unusually nice hostels, and a student dorm that turns into a great summer hotel. Also remember that

Sleep Code

(€1 = about $1.20, country code: 358, area code: 09)
S = Single, **D** = Double/Twin, **T** = Triple, **Q** = Quad,
b = bathroom, **s** = shower.

To help you sort easily through these listings, I've divided the rooms into three categories, based on the full (non-weekend) price for a standard double room with bath:

$$$ **Higher Priced**—Most rooms €100 or more.
 $$ **Moderately Priced**—Most rooms between €60–100.
  $ **Lower Priced**—Most rooms €60 or less.

some of the cheapest beds in Helsinki are on the cruise ships to Stockholm.

Most large Helsinki hotels have a two-tiered pricing system: discounts on Friday and Saturday nights, and higher rack rates the rest of the week. From late June to early August, you get the weekend discount every day of the week. A few hotels extend the weekend discount to Sunday nights as well. When two prices are listed, the first is for weeknights, the second for weekends.

All places listed have elevators and accept credit cards. Unless otherwise noted, breakfast is included. Make sure to book ahead for the first half of August 2005, when Helsinki will host the World Athletic Championships.

Helsinki Expert's hotel booking service, with branches at the TI and the train station, can reserve you a hotel bed for a €5 fee and always knows where the best deals are (see page 277).

Hotels

All of these hotels are central—within walking distance of the train station, harbor, or both.

$$$ Hotel Anna, plush and very central, is warm, friendly, and well run as a fundraiser for the Finnish Free Church (64 rooms, Sb-€110, superior Sb-€125, Db-€150, superior Db-€165, family suite-€195, extra bed-€15, no summer/weekend discounts, 10 percent discount with this book in 2005 except Aug 1–15, non-smoking rooms, elevator, 4 blocks south of the top of the Esplanade, a half-mile from the Makasiini and Olympia terminals, Annankatu 1, tel. 09/616-621, fax 09/602-664, www.hotelanna.fi, info@hotelanna.fi).

$$$ MarttaHotelli, in the same neighborhood, is in a modern building entered through an archway. Less luxurious but a good value, it's owned and run by the Finnish home economics foundation (44 rooms, Sb-€98/€75, small head-to-toe twin Db-€120/€85, full Db-€136/€95, suite-€150/€130, Tb-€145/€100, weekend rates also valid Sun night, non-smoking rooms, sauna, Uudenmaankatu 24, tel. 09/618-7400, fax 09/618-7401, www.marttahotelli.fi).

$$$ **Hotel Arthur,** a five-minute walk from the train station on a quiet street, is hardwood, sleek, basic, and friendly but with big-hotel service (144 rooms, S-€50/€35, Sb-€94/€73, D-€66/€59, Db-€114/€92, nicer Db-€125/€108, extra bed-€20, weekend rates also valid Sun night, non-smoking rooms, Vuorikatu 19, tel. 09/173-441, fax 09/626-880, www.hotelarthur.fi).

$$ **Hotelli Finn** is wonderfully central, stowed quietly on the sixth floor of an office building, with 27 simple, comfy rooms a block beyond the top of the Esplanade. Eighteen of its rooms have full private facilities, while nine have sinks and toilets but share a shower (S-€55, Sb-€65, D-€65, Db-€80, Tb-€97, Qb-€115, small breakfast served in room-€6, Kalevankatu 3B, tel. 09/684-4360, fax 09/6844-3610, www.hotellifinn.fi, hotelli.finn@kolumbus.fi).

$$ **Hotel Skatta** is an old sailors' hotel (from May–Oct, it's still half-booked by Nordic Jet Line for their staff). It's a bit institutional but clean, well run, and just two blocks from the Katajanokka ferry terminal (23 rooms, Sb-€65, Db-€80, extra bed-€10, breakfast-€5, all Db are twins, great gym and sauna in basement for guests—fun if you're looking for a sailor, free Internet access, call well in advance, Linnankatu 3, tel. 09/659-233, fax 09/631-352, www.hotelskatta.com).

Expensive Hotels with Great Weekend Deals

On Friday and Saturday nights and from late June to early August, even Helsinki's more expensive hotels have great deals on doubles.

$$$ **Lord Hotel,** big and modern behind a striking Art Nouveau facade, discounts its €175 doubles to €96 (also on Sun nights; Sb-€145/€90, Lönnrotinkatu 29, tel. 09/615-815, fax 09/680-1315, www.lordhotel.fi).

$$$ **Scandic Grand Marina,** a four-star hotel right between the Katajanokka and Kanava terminals, discounts its €225 doubles to €110 (Katajanokanlaituri 7, tel. 09/16661, fax 09/664-764, www.scandic-hotels.com, grandmarina@scandic-hotels.com).

$$$ **Hotel Cumulus Kaisaniemi** is big and without soul, but right near the train station (Sb-€143/€87, Db-€169/€109, ask for quieter room on back side, Kaisaniemenkatu 7, tel. 09/172-881, fax 09/605-379, www.cumulus.fi, kaisaniemi.cumulus@restel.fi).

Hostels

Helsinki's hostels are unusually comfortable. Eurohostel and Academica are more like budget hotels than hostels. If you'd like an island setting, there's also a hostel on Suomenlinna (www.leirikoulut.com).

$ **Eurohostel** is a wonderful modern hostel 200 yards from the Katajanokka ferry terminal or a 10-minute walk from Market Square (255 beds, S-€36.50, D-€44, T-€66, Q with up to 3 kids under 15-€54, shared twins or triples-€22/person, includes sheets, breakfast-€6, free morning sauna, evening sauna-€5, €2.50 discount for hostel members, private lockable closets, handy tram #4 stop around the corner, Linnankatu 9, tel. 09/622-0470, fax 09/655-044, www.eurohostel.fi). It's packed with facilities, including a laundry room, a members' kitchen with unique refrigerated safety-deposit boxes for your caviar and beer, Internet access, a restaurant, and plenty of good budget-travel information. While generally fully booked in advance, they often release no-show beds at 18:00.

$$ Academica Summer Hostel is a university dorm used as a hostel from June through August. Finnish university students have it good—rooms are hotel-quality with private bath, though all doubles have twin beds. It's a 10-minute walk from the train station; from the harbor, take tram #3T to the Kauppakorkeakoulut stop (250 rooms, Sb-€40–55, Db-€60–75, Tb-€75, Qb-€85; prices include sheets, breakfast, morning sauna, and swimming pool; beds in shared rooms-€16–22 plus €6 for breakfast and €5 if you need sheets; €2.50 discount for hostel members, Hietaniemenkatu 14, between Mechelininkatu and Runeberginkatu, tel. 09/1311-4334, fax 09/441-201, www.hostelacademica.fi, hostelacademica@hyy.fi).

$ Erottajanpuisto is a small, friendly, slightly ramshackle hostel with a great location on the third floor of a 19th-century apartment building in the center of town (15 rooms with 2–8 beds, dorm bed-€22.50, S-€46, D-€60, T-€78, Q-€100, includes sheets, €2.50 discount for hostel members, breakfast-€5, Uudenmaankatu 9, tel. 09/642-169, fax 09/680-2757, www.erottajanpuisto.com, info @erottajanpuisto.com).

$ Olympic Stadium Hostel (Stadionin Retkeilymaja) is big, crowded, impersonal, and a last resort (€15 per bed in 9- or 12-bed rooms, €2.50 discount for hostel members, paper sheets-€3, cotton sheets-€5, breakfast-€5.30, tel. 09/477-8480). Take tram #3T or #7A from downtown or bus #617 from the airport.

EATING

Helsinki is filled with restaurants serving everything from traditional Finnish and Russian food to nouveau cuisine in modern, bright interiors. Restaurants are a good value for lunch. Finnish companies get a tax break if they distribute lunch coupons (worth about €8) to their employees. It's no surprise that most downtown Helsinki restaurants offer weekday lunch specials that cost exactly the value of the coupon. For a cheap dinner, consider visiting the supermarket and making a picnic. A few restaurants close for lunch during the summer.

Cafés and restaurants line the sunny north side of the Esplanade. **Strindberg,** at the corner of Mikonkatu, is worth a stop.

Downstairs is an elegant cafeteria with outdoor and indoor tables great for people-watching, sandwiches and salads for €6–8, and coffee, drinks, and desserts (Sun–Thu 9:00–22:00, Fri–Sat 9:00–24:00). Follow the back staircase to the posh restaurant upstairs. The lounge, popular with the after-work office crowd, is filled with comfy sofas where you can munch appetizers and have a cocktail. The modern yet cozy restaurant has huge entrées for €15–22 with fish, meat, pasta, and vegetarian options. Many tables overlook the Esplanade (Mon 11:00–23:00, Tue–Fri 11:00–24:00, Sat 12:00–24:00, closed Sun, reservations smart—a must for a window seat, Pohjoisesplanadi 33, tel. 09/681-2030).

Lasipalatsi consists of a trendy upstairs restaurant and cheaper downstairs café on Mannerheimintie right between the bus and train stations. The café offers soup, salad bar, bread, and coffee for €7.50 at lunch, plus €4 sandwiches and €4 cakes (Mon–Fri 7:30–23:30, Sat–Sun 9:00–23:30). The restaurant offers soups and salads for €7–15 and main dishes for €15–27 (Mon–Fri 11:00–24:00, Sat from 12:00, Sun 18:00–23:00, across from Sokos department store and post office at Mannerheimintie 22-24, tel. 09/612-6700).

Konstan Möljä is a homey, family-run restaurant serving country Finnish cooking (Karelian), hearty soup, and home-baked bread. It's decorated with old photos and lumberjack mementos (à la carte main dishes-€15–20, €8 lunch buffet 11:00–14:30, good-value €12 dinner buffet starts at 16:00, open Mon–Fri 11:00–22:00, Sat 14:00–22:00, closed Sun, Hietalahdenkatu 14, 2 blocks behind flea market at the end of Bulevardi, walk or take tram #6 from Mannerheimintie, tel. 09/694-7504).

Kynsilaukka Garlic Restaurant is the spot for garlic lovers. They serve everything from pork to salmon dishes, each cooked up with copious amounts of garlic. Wash it all down with a garlic beer—although they serve regular beer as well (main dishes-€14–19, Mon–Fri 11:00–23:00, Sat–Sun 13:00–23:00, Fredrikinkatu 22, tel.09/651-939).

The harborside **Sundmanns**—a venerable, expensive restaurant for fine dining—overlooks the red-brick indoor market. They serve modern as well as traditional Finnish cuisine in a fancy setting with crisp, white tablecloths and candlelight (main dishes-€30–35, fixed-price *menus*-€65–75, Mon–Fri 11:00–14:30 & 17:00–24:00, Sat 18:00–24:00, closed Sun, Eteläranta 16, tel. 09/622-6410).

Ethnic Eateries

Lapland Cuisine: At **Lappi Restaurant,** you lash your reindeer to the hitchin' post and travel north for dinner. The friendly staff serves tasty Sami dishes in a snug and very woody atmosphere (€15–35 dinner plates, Mon–Fri 17:00–24:00, Sat–Sun 13:00–24:00, mid-Aug–mid-June also Mon–Fri 12:00–17:00, reserve to eat after 19:00, off Bulevardi at Annankatu 22, tel. 09/645-550).

Russian Cuisine: Hariton is a small, inviting place with a traditional Russian ambience and better Russian cooking than you're likely to find in Russia (€8 lunch specials until 14:00, €17–22 dinner plates, Mon–Fri 11:30–24:00, Sat–Sun 13:00–22:00, a block off mid-Esplanade from the statue, Kasarmikatu 44, tel. 09/622-1717). From mid-June through August, lunch is served in Hariton's **Volga Bar,** a summer beer garden in the courtyard (enter around the corner through the archway on Rikhardinkatu, look for big wooden cow).

Italian Cuisine: Papá Giovanni's, in the thriving World Trade Center building, is popular with young locals for €9–13 pastas and €16–23 main dishes (Mon–Fri 11:00–24:00, Sat 12:00–24:00, Sun 15:00–23:00, Keskuskatu 7, enter building between Stockmann's and train station, fancy pasta upstairs, cheaper pizza downstairs, tel. 0800-97272).

Picnics

For picnics or a quick, light meal, graze the colorful stalls at the harbor and the neighboring red-brick **indoor market** (with a delightfully out-of-place little sushi bar inside). At the **harborside market,** you'll find local "tent" cafés (meaty pasties, traditional sweets, café), fast-food stalls, and delicious fresh fish (cooked if you like), explosive little red berries, and sweet carrots.

In **supermarkets,** buy the semi-flat bread (available dark or light) that Finns love—every slice is a heel. Finnish liquid yogurt is also a treat (sold in liter cartons). Karelian pasties (filled with rice or mashed potatoes) make a good snack. There are several supermarkets in the center, including one underneath the Stockmann's department store (Aleksanterinkatu 52B) and a big one at Lönnrotinkatu and Annankatu (Mon–Fri 8:00–21:00, Sat 8:00–18:00, June–Aug only Sun 12:00–21:00).

TRANSPORTATION CONNECTIONS

From Helsinki, it's easy to get to **Turku** (about 2 hrs) or **St. Petersburg, Russia** by either bus or train. To St. Petersburg, the bus is slower and cheaper (4/day, 8 hrs, about €45–50, less for students) than the train (2/day, 6 hrs, about €70, no student discount). Travelers to Russia need a visa and should not wait until Helsinki to plan their trip. For train info, visit www.vr.fi/heo/eng. For bus information in English, visit www.expressbus.com.

By boat: To **Stockholm,** Silja and Viking lines sail nightly. (See beginning of this chapter for details.) To **Tallinn,** ferries and (in summer only) fast boats travel the 50 miles many times a day. (See the Tallinn chapter for details.) See "Arrival in Helsinki," page 277, for terminal locations.

ESTONIA
(Eesti)

Estonians are related to the Finns and have a history similar to Finland's—first Swedish domination, then Russian (1710–1918), and finally independence after World War I. In 1940, Estonians were at least as affluent and as advanced as the Finns. But they could not manage to preserve their independence from Soviet expansion in World War II. As a result, Estonia sank into a 50-year communist twilight from which it is still emerging. In 2004, Estonia took a significant step forward by joining the European Union.

One problematic legacy of the Soviet experience is Estonia's huge Russian population. Most Estonian Russians' parents and grandparents were brought to Estonia in the 1950s and 1960s to work in now-defunct factories in Tallinn and in the northeastern cities. Twenty-five percent of Estonia's population is now Russian. Making Russians feel at home in Estonia while at the same time building a distinctly Estonian culture and identity has been one of independent Estonia's biggest challenges. Estonia will always face both west across the Baltic and east into the Russian hinterlands.

EU membership seems like a natural next step to many Estonians. They already think of themselves as part of the Nordic world. Language, history, religion, and twice-hourly ferry departures connect Finns and Estonians. It's only 50 miles between Helsinki and Tallinn, and an overnight boat ride to Stockholm. Finns visit Tallinn to eat, drink, and shop more cheaply than at home. While some Estonians resent how Tallinn becomes a Finnish nightclub on summer weekends, most people on both sides are happy to have friendly new neighbors.

Younger Estonians speak English—it's the first choice these days at school. Estonian is similar to Finnish, and equally difficult.

How Big, How Many, How Much

- Estonia is 17,500 square miles (about the size of New Hampshire and Vermont together).
- Population is 1,340,000 (77 per square mile).
- 12 krooni = about $1

Estonia

Two useful phrases to know are *"Tänan"* (TAN-on; "Thank you") and *"Terviseks!"* (TEAR-vee-sex; "Cheers!"). The deeper you go beyond the touristy zones, the more you see that Russian is still Estonia's main second language. If you know some Russian, use it. It's the mother tongue of more than 40 percent of Tallinners.

 # TALLINN

Stepping off the boat in Tallinn, you feel that you've traveled farther culturally than you have throughout the rest of Scandinavia. Tallinn's Nordic Lutheran culture and language connect it with Stockholm and Helsinki, but two centuries in Russia and 45 years in the Soviet Union have blended in a distinctly Russian flavor. Like Prague and Kraków, Tallinn has modernized at an astounding rate since the fall of the Soviet Union in 1991, while preserving the Old World ambience of its walled town center. Colorfully painted medieval houses share cobbled lanes with blocky, communist-style buildings...and with happy Estonians, relieved to be free once again.

If you're pondering a cultural detour on your Scandinavian vacation, Tallinn and Helsinki are the logical choices—both are quite different from the "core" Scandinavian countries, and both are easily reached on a night cruise from Stockholm. Tallinn is much cheaper than Helsinki, with great restaurants and good shopping. It's also more challenging. Why not give yourself an extra day and do both as a triangular side-trip from Stockholm?

Sailing from Stockholm to Tallinn

Tallink's ships leave Stockholm at 17:30 every evening and arrive in Tallinn at 10:30 or 11:00 the next morning. Return trips follow the same schedule. All times are local; Tallinn is an hour ahead of Stockholm.

Tallink has two ships. The *Victoria* is new (built in 2004) and just as nice as the Stockholm–Helsinki boats; the *Regina Baltica* is an older, less luxurious ship with cheaper fares. If luxury is important to you, check the schedule online (www.tallink.ee/en.html) and time your trip to go on the *Victoria*.

Fares are highest on Friday nights and from July 1 to August 15; they're lowest on Sunday through Wednesday nights the rest of the year. Thursday and Saturday prices are in the middle. I've given high (Fri)/low (Sun–Wed) prices here in Swedish currency (7 kronor = about $1). A one-way berth in a four-person cabin with a private bath costs 365/220 kronor on the *Regina Baltica*, 545/370 kr on the *Victoria*. Round-trip prices cost a little more: 455/280 kr on the *Regina Baltica*, 680/460 kr on the *Victoria*. The two legs of a round-trip don't have to be on successive days (unlike the Stockholm–Helsinki ferries), and the price depends on both the outbound and return days of the week.

Breakfast is 79 kr, and the *smörgåsbord* dinner is 195 kr. Reserve your meal (and even, if possible, your table) when you buy your ticket. The boats have exchange offices with acceptable rates for your leftover cash.

Depending on where you're leaving from, reserve by calling either the Stockholm reservations line at tel. 46-8/666-6001 or the Estonian booking number at tel. 372/640-9808. Unfortunately, they cannot take your credit-card number over the phone; they'll send you a form to mail or fax back. Pick up your tickets at the port on the day of departure. Online booking is possible only in Swedish and for entire cabins (www.tallink.se).

In Stockholm, Tallink ships leave from the Frihamnen harbor. To get from downtown Stockholm to Frihamnen harbor, take the shuttle bus from the main station (25kr, leaves at about 15:00 and 15:50), or take public bus #1 from Kungsgatan to the end of the line (30 kr, 3–6/hr, 25-min trip). In Tallinn, the ships dock at Terminal D.

Speeding between Helsinki and Tallinn

From April to October, **fast boats** link Helsinki and Tallinn (2/hr, 90–100 min, first departure about 7:00, last about 21:30). Four different companies compete. You can reserve in advance by phone, or buy tickets from a travel agency (such as the Helsinki Expert office in the TI—see below), but it's rarely necessary. Fast-boat trips may be canceled in stormy weather.

Fares run €20–40 one-way (evening departures from Helsinki and morning departures from Tallinn are cheapest). Round-trips start at about €30 if you come back with the same company. Linda Line, which uses small hydrofoils, is the fastest (only 90 min). The Tallink, Nordic Jet, and Silja fast ferries take cars and tolerate bad weather the best.

Big **car ferries** also run year-round between Helsinki and Tallinn (7/day, 3.5 hrs, cheaper at €15–18 one-way, €23 round-trip, student and senior discounts) and come with great *smörgåsbord*

Helsinki/Tallinn Connections

Company	Ship Type	Helsinki Terminal	Helsinki Phone #
Tallink	Ferries and fast boats	Länsi	09/228-311
Linda Line	Fast boats	Makasiini	09/668-9700
Nordic Jet Line	Fast boats	Kanava	09/681-770
Silja	Fast boats	Makasiini	09/180-4555
Eckerö Line	Ferries	Länsi	09/228-8544
Viking	Ferries	Katajanokka	09/12351
Sea Wind	Ferries	Olympia	02/210-2800

buffets (€15–18 extra). Foot passengers prefer the Sea Wind or Viking ferries, which depart from central Helsinki. The Tallink and Eckerö Line ferries use Helsinki's Länsi terminal (no problem for drivers, but the bus ride to the terminal for foot passengers takes time and adds €2 to the one-way cost).

The helpful **Helsinki Expert** desk in the Helsinki TI sells tickets (€7 fee per booking) and posts a sheet clearly explaining departures, time in Tallinn, and costs. The TI in Tallinn posts a list but does not sell tickets. The chart in this chapter lists the names, ship types, phone numbers, terminals, and Web sites for the main ferry operators. Respective Web sites have all the latest, and most allow online booking. Tallinn and Helsinki each have five different ferry terminals—make sure you know which one your boat leaves from (for descriptions of Helsinki's terminals, see page 277; for Tallinn, see "Arrival in Tallinn," below).

If the jet boat isn't fast enough, Copterline makes hourly **helicopter** trips from Helsinki to Tallinn in 18 minutes (€79–179 plus poorly advertised €9 "reservation fee"; cheaper last-minute and special fares sometimes available, end-of-day trips are cheapest, takes off from Hernesaari in Helsinki and Linnahall roof in Tallinn, Helsinki tel. 09/3505-2198, Tallinn tel. 610-1818, www.copterline.com).

Helsinki Expert (see above) also sells day-trip **tours to Tallinn** that give you fast round-trip boat crossings, transfers, a three-hour bus and walking tour, lunch, and an hour or so to wander and shop (€139, departing daily April–Oct at 10:00, returning 21:30). But Tallinn is accessible enough for most travelers to do it on their own—it's cheaper and more fun to just buy boat tickets and follow my "Self-Guided Walk," below.

Company	Tallinn Terminal	Tallinn Phone #	Web site
Tallink	Ferries: A; Fast boats: D	640-9808	www.tallink.ee, www.tallink.se
Linda Line	Linnahall	699-9333	www.lindaline.ee
Nordic Jet Line	C	613-7000	www-eng.njl.fi
Silja	D	611-6661	www.silja.fi
Eckerö Line	B	631-8606	www.eckeroline.fi
Viking	A	666-3966	www.vikingline.fi
Sea Wind	D	611-6699	www.seawind.fi

Tallinn

Among Nordic medieval cities, there's none nearly as well preserved as Tallinn. Its mostly intact city wall includes 26 watchtowers, each topped by a pointy red roof. Baroque and choral music ring out in its old Lutheran churches. Tallinn has more restaurants, cafés, and surprises than any other city in this book—and the fun is affordable on nearly any budget.

Tallinn is busy cleaning up the mess left by the communist experiment. New shops, restaurants, and hotels are bursting out of old buildings. The city changes so fast, even locals can't keep up. The Old Town is getting a lot of tourist traffic now, so smart shopping is wise. You can cut restaurant bills in half by seeking out places frequented by locals.

Tallinn was a medieval stronghold of the Baltic trading world. In the 19th and early 20th centuries, Tallinn expanded beyond its walls. Architects circled the Old Town, putting up broad streets of public buildings, low Scandinavian-style apartment buildings, and single-family wooden houses. After 1945, Soviet planners ringed this with stands of now-crumbling concrete high-rises where many of Tallinn's Russian immigrants settled.

Fairly small and modest, Tallinn doesn't knock your socks off, but its Old Town is a great package of pleasing towers, ramparts, facades, churches, shops, and people-watching. It's a secure, stable detour for those who want to spice their Scandinavian travels with an ex-Soviet twist.

Planning Your Time

On a three-week tour of Scandinavia, Tallinn is worth a day. Get oriented with either the official walking tour or my "Self-Guided Walk" (see both below). Check concert schedules if you'll be around for the evening.

Day-Trippers: Whether arriving from Helsinki or Stockholm, hit the ground running by following my "Self-Guided Walk" right from the ferry terminal. Enjoy the best restaurant you can afford in the Old Town for lunch. And spend the afternoon shopping and browsing (or out at the open-air museum, if you're into folk history). Remember to bring a jacket (it can be cold even on sunny summer days).

ORIENTATION

(12 Estonian krooni = about $1)

Virtually everything of interest to tourists is in Tallinn's walled Old Town, an easy 15-minute walk from the ferry terminals where most visitors land (see "Arrival in Tallinn," below). The Old Town is divided into two parts (historically, two separate towns): the upper town—called Toompea, with the castle—and the lower town, with the Town Hall Square. Each part is surrounded by a remarkably intact medieval wall, and another wall separates them. The best shopping drag, Viru, is at the east end of the lower town (towards the landmark Soviet-style Hotel Viru).

Splurge for taxis until you know the lay of the land. On arrival, find the Town Hall Square (Raekoja Plats), in the heart of the medieval lower town. The TI and nearly everything of sightseeing and edible interest is nearby.

Tourist Information

Tallinn's English-speaking TI has maps, concert listings, *Tallinn This Week,* and free brochures (Mon–Fri 9:00–20:00, Sat–Sun 10:00–18:00, closes 1–2 hrs earlier off-season, 1 block off Town Hall Square at Kullassepa 4, tel. 645-7777, www.tourism.tallinn.ee, turismiinfo@tallinnlv.ee).

Tallinn in Your Pocket is the best city guidebook on Tallinn (35 kr, on sale all over town, on ships, and at TI). It has complete restaurant, hotel, and sights listings that go far beyond what's listed in this book, plus a rare Old Town map listing all of the streets. (For pretrip planning, see www.inyourpocket.com).

The **Tallinn Card,** sold at the TI, airport, ports, and big hotels, gives you free use of public transport and entry to museums (6 hrs/90 kr, 24 hrs/250 kr, 48 hrs/300 kr, 72 hrs/350 kr, includes good info booklet). From the 24-hour level up, it also includes the 2.5-hour bus and walking tour (see "Tours," below).

Arrival in Tallinn

By Boat: If you have no luggage, just walk into the center of town (15 min; could follow my "Self-Guided Walk," below). With luggage, it's best to grab a cab (expect about 50 kr to hotels in the center; see taxi advice under "Getting Around Tallinn," below). Trams #1 and #2 stop near the port area, as do buses.

Tallinn has four terminals lettered A through D, and a fifth terminal called Linnahall. Terminals A, B, and C are clustered together; Terminal D is 10 minutes' walk to the east; and the Linnahall terminal is 10 minutes' walk to the west. Find out which terminal you're leaving from so that you don't miss your return boat. Each terminal offers baggage storage.

By Plane: The airport is close to town (www.tallinn-airport.ee). A taxi to the Old Town should cost about 70 kr. Public bus #2 runs into town (single tickets cost 10 kr from kiosks, 15 kr from driver).

Helpful Hints

Currency Exchange: About 12 Estonian krooni (kr) equal $1. The kroon rises and falls with the euro (15.65 krooni = €1). ATMs are everywhere, including the ferry terminals and airport. Credit cards are widely accepted. Euros are rarely accepted, and if they are, don't expect a good exchange rate. Plenty of exchange offices compete to change your leftover Swedish kronor and euros. Banks usually have the best rates.

Telephones: If you're calling Estonia from another country, dial the international access code of the country you're calling from (European countries-00, U.S./Canada-011), then dial Estonia's country code (372), then the local number. To call from Estonia to the United States or Canada, dial 00-1-area code-local number. Estonian phone numbers are seven digits with no area codes. Tallinn numbers begin with 6, and mobile phones (more expensive to call) begin with 5. Phone cards are sold at kiosks around town.

Internet Access: The Neo Internet café at Väike-Karja 10 is open 24 hours daily and charges 35 kr per hour (50 kr/2 hrs, 100 kr/up to 10 hrs). The top floor at the Kaubamaja department store charges a straight 35 kr per hour (daily 9:00–21:00).

Bookstore: Apollo, at Viru 23, has a fine selection of English books, plus an upstairs café with expensive Internet access (60 kr/hr, Mon–Fri 10:00–20:00, Sat 10:00–18:00, Sun 11:00–16:00).

Laundry: Pesumaja will do your laundry for you for 55 kr per load; come before noon if you want same-day service (Mon–Fri 8:00–20:00, Sat–Sun 11:00–19:00, Pärnu Maantee 48, across from Kosmos stop of tram lines #3 or #4, or walk 10 min from Vabaduse Väljak).

Getting Around Tallinn

Cabs are cheap and handy. Locals never hail taxis on the street, and rarely use taxi stands—and neither should you. Call for a taxi, or ask a friendly local with a mobile phone to call for you. Tulika Takso is the most reliable and honest taxi company (white cars with a black-and-yellow logo, can pay with credit card, tel. 612-0000, or tel. 1200 from mobile phones, www.tulikatakso.ee). Most taxis have a minimum charge of about 45 kr. Cabs at taxi stands are allowed to add a "waiting charge" to the fare (another good reason to order by phone). The cabbies who hang out at tourist stops, have run-down looking cars, or offer strip-club brochures are likely into creative income augmentation.

Tallinn has regular buses, trolley buses (with overhead wires), and trams (on rails). Kiosks by bus stops sell 10-kr tickets (valid for buses, trolleys, and trams) that you punch in the machines on board. They also sell packets of 10 tickets for 70 kr. Drivers sell tickets as well, but for 15 kr. Some express and private buses (like the ones from the port) cost extra. The Tallinn Card includes public transport (see "Tourist Information," above).

TOURS

With a Guide

Old Town Walking Tour—I thoroughly enjoyed this 90-minute tour (100 kr, daily June–Aug at 11:30, 14:00, and 16:00, in English and Finnish, departs at corner of Toompea and Komandandi near Alexander Nevsky Cathedral and ends at Town Hall Square, more info at TI).

Bus and Walking Tour—This 2.5-hour tour of Tallinn leaves from the ferry port's Terminal A (200 kr, covered by Tallinn Card—except 6-hr version of card, in English and Finnish, daily departures at 10:00, 12:30, and 14:30, leaves 30 min later from Hotel Viru).

Self-Guided Walk: Tallinn's Old Town

This walk, worth ▲▲▲, explores the "two towns" of Tallinn. The city once consisted of two feuding medieval towns separated by a wall. The upper town—filling the hill called Toompea—was the seat of government ruling Estonia. The lower town was an autonomous Hanseatic trading center filled with German, Danish, and Swedish merchants who imported Estonians to do their menial labor.

Two steep, narrow streets—the "Long Leg" and the "Short Leg"—connect Toompea and the lower town. This walk explores both towns, going up the short leg and down the long leg. From the ferry terminal, start with #1 (and allow approximately 75 min for this 1.5-mile walk). If starting from the Town Hall Square, begin at #2 (and figure on an hour for the 1-mile walk).

Tallinn

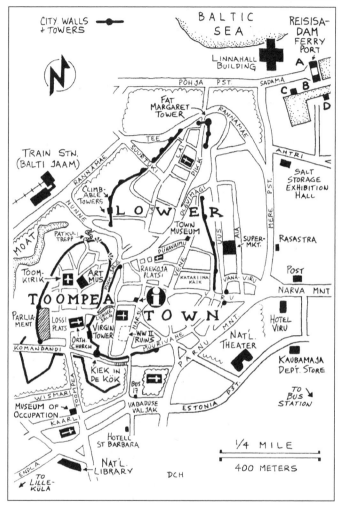

City Walls & Towers
N
BALTIC SEA
REISISADAM FERRY PORT
LINNAHALL BUILDING
A
C B
D
PÕHJA P.ST. SADAMA
FAT MARGARET TOWER
RANNAMÄE
TEE
SUURTÜKI
LAI
PIKK
AHTRI
SALT STORAGE EXHIBITION HALL
TRAIN STN. (BALTI JAAM)
RANNAMÄE
CLIMBABLE TOWERS
NUNNE
L O W E R
OLEVIMÄGI
MERE P.ST.
MOAT
PATKULI TREPP
TOWN MUSEUM
VENE
UUS
AIA
SUPER-MKT.
RASASTRA
TOOMKIRIK
ART MUS
PÜHAVAIMU
RAEKOJA PLATSI
KATARIINA KÄIK
VANA-VIRU
POST
PARLIAMENT
LOSSI PLATS
LÜHIKE JALG
HARJU
VIRU
NARVA MNT.
T O O M P E A
VIRGIN TOWER
ORTH. CHURCH
WW II RUINS
MÜÜRIVAHE
T O W N
MNT.
HOTEL VIRU
NAT'L. THEATER
KOMANDANDI
PIKK JALG
KIEK IN DE KÖK
BUS 17
PÄRNU P.ST.
KAUBAMAJA DEPT. STORE
TO BUS STATION
WISMARI
MUSEUM OF OCCUPATION
TOOMPEA
KAARLI
VABADUSE VALJAK
ESTONIA
¼ MILE
400 METERS
ENDLA
TO LILLE-KÜLA
HOTEL ST BARBARA
NAT'L. LIBRARY
DCH

1. Ferry Terminal to the Town Hall Square: From the terminal, hike toward the tall tapering spire, go through a small park, and enter the Old Town through the archway by the squat Fat Margaret Tower (containing the Maritime Museum—in medieval times, the sea came all the way to here). Head up Pikk street. Pikk, the medieval merchants' main drag leading from the harbor up into town, is lined with

interesting buildings—many were warehouses complete with cranes on the gables. After #14, turn left, where a small lane leads into...

2. Town Hall Square (Raekoja Plats): A marketplace through the centuries, this is the starting point for Old Town explorations.

Once the scene of bad people chained to pillories for public humiliation and knights showing off in chivalrous tournaments, today it's full of Finns sipping cheap beer, children singing on the bandstand, and clever little bike-taxis (TI a block up the street across the square). The 15th-century Town Hall dominates the square; climbing the tower earns a commanding view (25 kr, Tue–Sun 11:00–18:00, closed Mon). The cancan of fine old buildings with their proud weathervanes is a reminder that this was the center of the autonomous lower town, a merchant city of Hanseatic traders. The pharmacy (across from #12 in the corner, open to visitors) dates from 1422 and claims—as do many—to be Europe's oldest. Facing the Town Hall, head right up Dunkri street one block to the well.

3. The Wheel Well: The well is named for the "high-tech" wheel, a marvel that made fetching water easier. Most of Old Town's buildings are truly old, dating from the 15th- and 16th-century boom-time. Decrepit before the 1991 fall of the USSR, Tallinn is being revitalized with the help of Western investments. Several recommended restaurants are within a few cobbles of here (see "Eating," page 314). Head uphill 50 yards (passing carefully between the Harley-Davidson biker bar and the Hedonism Bar) to...

4. St. Nicholas' (Niguliste) Church: This church served German merchants and knights living in this neighborhood 500 years ago. The Russians bombed it in World War II. In one terrible night, on March 9, 1944, half of Tallinn was destroyed. The area around this church—once a charming district, dense with medieval buildings—was flattened. Beyond the church, some ruins remain.

From the church, turn right and climb the steep, cobbled, Lühike Jalg (Short Leg Lane). Passing through the gate, notice the original oak door, one of two gates through the wall separating the two cities. Circle left of the Russian church to the garden overlooking the wall.

5. Danish King's Garden: The imposing wall once had 46 towers. The big round tower ahead is nicknamed "Kiek in de Kök" (Peek in the Kitchen). It was so tall, peek is exactly what guards could do. (It's now a museum; see "Sights," page 307.) You're standing in the Danish King's Garden. Tallinn is famous among Danes as the birthplace of their flag. (According to legend, the Danes were losing a battle here. Suddenly a white cross fell from heaven and landed in a pool of blood. The Danes were inspired and went on to win. To this day, their flag is a white cross on a red background.) Walk toward the pink palace and look at the Russian Orthodox church.

6. Russian Cathedral and Toompea Castle: The Alexander Nevsky Cathedral was built here in 1900 over the grave of a legendary Estonian hero. It was a crass attempt to flex Russian cultural muscles during a period of Estonian national revival. Step inside for a whiff of Russian Orthodoxy; more than a quarter of all Estonians are ethnic Russians. Cross the street to that pink palace—an 18th-century addition that Russia built into the Toompea Castle. Today, it's the Estonian Parliament building, flying the Estonian flag.

It's the flag of both the first (1918–1940) and second (1991–present) Estonian Republics. Notice the Estonian seal: three lions for three great battles in Estonian history, and oak leaves for strength and stubbornness. Rather than eat their Wheaties, ancient pagan Estonians, who believed spirits lived in oak trees, would walk through forests of oak. Step left around the palace into the park to see the...

7. Tall Herman Tower: This tallest tower of the castle wall is a powerful symbol here. For 50 years, while Estonian flags were hidden in cellars, the Soviet flag flew from Tall Herman. In 1987, as the USSR was unraveling, the Estonians proudly and defiantly replaced the red Soviet flag with their own black, white, and blue flag.

In 1988, 400,000 patriots—imagine...a third of all Estonians—gathered at the festival song grounds outside Tallinn to sing national songs. In 1989, the people of Latvia, Lithuania, and Estonia held hands to make "the Baltic Chain." This human chain stretched 360 miles from Tallinn to Vilnius in Lithuania. Finally, in 1991, Estonia declared its freedom.

8. Walking to the Dome Church: Backtrack and go uphill, passing the Russian church on your right. Climb Toom-Kooli to the Dome Church (Toomkirik). Estonia is primarily Lutheran, but few Tallinners go to church. Most churches double as concert venues or museums. Enter Toomkirik (Tue–Sun 9:00–17:00, closed Mon). It's a textbook example of simple Northern European Gothic. Once the church of Tallinn's wealthy, it's littered with unique medieval coats of arms, each representing a rich merchant family and carved by local masters—the smaller the coat of arms, the older the family. In keeping with Lutheran tradition, the floor is paved with tombstones. Leaving the church, turn left. Pass the slanted tree and the big green Estonian Art Museum (Eesti Kunsti Klassika) on your right, and go down cobbled Rahukohtu lane, where barely a glimpse of the ramshackle 1980s survives. Local businesses are moving their offices here and sprucing up the neighborhood. Pass under the yellow Patkuli Vaateplats arch and belly up to the grand viewpoint.

9. Patkuli Viewpoint: Survey the scene. On the far left, the neoclassical facade of the executive branch of Estonia's government enjoys the view. Below you, a bit of the old moat survives. In the distance ferries shuttle to and from Helsinki (just 50 miles away). Beyond the lower town's medieval wall and towers stands the green spire of St. Olav's Church, once 98 feet taller and—locals claim—the world's tallest tower in 1492 (climb the 234 stairs for 30 kr, daily 10:00–14:00). Beyond that is the 985-foot-tall TV tower (famously fast Japanese elevators zip visitors to a café for grand views). During Soviet domination, Finnish TV was responsible for giving Estonians their only look at Western lifestyles. Imagine: In the 1980s, locals had never seen a banana or pineapple—except on TV.

Go back through the arch, turn left down the narrowest lane in town (driver's ed teachers say, "Go through here and make the turn without scratching, and you deserve your license"), turn right without scratching, take the first left, and pass through the trees to another viewpoint.

10. Lower Town Viewpoint: Ahead is the Church of the Holy Ghost, the youngest of the medieval churches in town; the spire to

its right is the 16th-century town hall spire. On the far right is the tower of St. Nicholas' Church. Visually trace Pikk street, Tallinn's historic main drag, which leads from Toompea down the hill (below you from right to left), through the gate tower, past the Church of the Holy Ghost (and the Town Hall Square), and out to the harbor. Four skyscrapers mark the start of the modern world. The nearest is Hotel Viru, in Soviet times the biggest hotel in the Baltics, and infamous as a clunky, dingy slumber mill. This walk ends there.

11. Descending to the Lower Town and Church of the Holy Ghost: From the viewpoint, go out and left down Kohtu, past the European Commission at #10 (Estonia joined the EU in 2004) and the Finnish Embassy (on left). Back at the Dome Church, the slanted tree points the way, left down Piiskopi (Bishop's Street). At the onion domes, turn left again and follow the old wall down Pikk Jalg (Long Leg Street) into the lower town. At the bottom, under the tower gate, veer right, following Pikk (Long Street) a couple of blocks to the Church of the Holy Ghost.

12. Maiasmokk, Great Guild Hall, and Church of the Holy Ghost: Pikk, home to the big-shot merchants, feels Germanic because it was. The Great Guild Hall—the epitome of wealth, with its wide and therefore highly taxed front—has a charming little museum (worth 10 kr and 10 min, good English descriptions, Thu–Tue 10:00–18:00, closed Wed, Pikk 17, tel. 641-1630). It faces the famous Maiasmokk coffee shop. Maiasmokk (which means "sweet tooth") was the sweetest place in town during Soviet days. It's still great for a cheap coffee-and-pastry break (Pikk 16, see "Eating," page 314). Architecture fans detour down Pikk for several fanciful facades (#18 is boldly Art Nouveau, and check out the colorful and eclectic facade across the street). The Church of the Holy Ghost, sporting a medieval clock from 1633, is worth a visit for its altarpiece and general historic murkiness (Pühavaimu 2, tel. 644-1487). From the church, the tiny Saiakang lane (meaning "white bread"—bread, cakes, and pies have been sold here since medieval times) leads back to the Town Hall Square.

13. Town Hall Square to Hotel Viru: Cross through the square (left of the Town Hall's tower) and go downhill (passing the kitschy medieval Olde Hansa Restaurant, with its bonneted waitresses and merry men). Continue straight down Viru street to Hotel Viru (the blocky white skyscraper in the distance). Viru street—Tallinn's best collection of boutiques and its busiest shopping street—is a hit with Finns on shopping trips. Just past the strange and modern wood/glass/stone mall, Müürivahe street leads left along the old wall. This is a colorful and tempting gauntlet of women selling handmade knitwear (although anything with images and bright colors is likely machine-made). Beyond the sweaters, Katarina Käik, a lane with top-notch local artisan shops, leads left. Back on Viru, the golden arches lead to the medieval arches that mark the end of old Tallinn. Outside the gates (at Viru 23), an arch leads into the Bastion Gardens, a tangle of antique, quilt, and sweater shops that delight shoppers. Opposite Viru 23, above the flower stalls on a piece of old bastion known as the Kissing Hill, notice the pavilion. Legend says any maiden sitting here is waiting for a kiss. From there, a flower market ushers you out to Hotel Viru and the real world.

SIGHTS

In or near the Old Town

Tallinn has dozens of small museums, most suitable only for specialized tastes (complete listings in *Tallinn in Your Pocket*). These are the only three I'd bother with.

▲▲**Kiek in de Kök**—The "Peek in the Kitchen" tower, now a museum, mixes medieval cannons and charts left over from the Livonian wars (floors 3–5) with modern photography exhibits (floors

1, 2, and 6, 15 kr, good English descriptions, Tue–Fri 10:30–18:00, Sat–Sun 11:00–16:30, closed Mon, tel. 644-6686).

▲▲**Tallinn City Museum (Tallinna Linnamuuseum)**—This museum features Tallinn history from 1200 to the 1950s, fully described in English. It's especially strong on the late 19th and early 20th centuries (25 kr, Wed–Mon 10:30–17:30, closed Tue, Vene 17, at corner of Pühavaimu, tel. 644-6553).

▲▲**Museum of Occupation (Okupatsioonide Muuseum)**— Newly opened with funding from a wealthy Estonian-American, this compact museum tells the history of Estonia under Nazi and Soviet occupation from 1939 to 1991. It's organized around seven TV monitors screening documentary films in English and Estonian, each focusing on a different time period. In the basement by the WCs is a collection of Soviet-era statues of communist leaders (10 kr, Tue–Sun 11:00–18:00, closed Mon, Toompea 8, at corner of Kaarli Pst., tel. 668-0250, www.okupatsioon.ee).

Away from the Center

▲**Kadriorg**—This seaside park and summer residence, a 10-minute tram ride from Tallinn, was built by Peter the Great for Czarina Catherine after Russia took over Tallinn in 1710. Occupying Peter's palace, the **Foreign Art Museum** (Väliskuunsti Muuseum) has a very modest Russian and Western European collection in a pretty building with pleasant gardens out back (45 kr, Tue–Sun 10:00–17:00, closed Mon, tel. 606-6400). The mansion on the far side of the gardens is the local White House (although it's pink)—home of Estonia's president. The park, which runs down to the sea to the north, is delightful for a stroll or picnic. Trams #1 and #3 take 10 minutes to go east from the center of Tallinn to Kadriorg, the end of the line (where the tram makes a U-turn).

▲**Open-Air Museum (Vabaõhumuuseum)**—As in every Nordic country, Estonians salvaged farm buildings, windmills, and an old church from rural areas and transported them to Rocca al Mare, a parklike setting just outside of town. The park's Kolu tavern serves traditional dishes (28 kr, May–Sept daily 10:00–18:00, grounds stay open until 20:00, Oct–April buildings closed but grounds and tavern open daily 10:00–17:00, take bus #21 or trolley #6 from the center, www.evm.ee).

SHOPPING

With so many Scandinavian tourists coming to Tallinn, Old Town is full of trinkets, but it's possible to find quality stuff. For sweaters and woolens, go to the stalls under the wall on Müürivahe (near the corner of Viru, described in "Self-Guided Walk," above). Wooden trivets and butter knives are a good value here.

Diele Gallerii sells good postcards and displays work by Estonian artists; look for prints by Navitrolla (Vanaturu Kael 3, just below the Town Hall Square). **Katariina Käik,** a small alley off Müürivahe street, has several handicraft stores and workshops selling pieces that make nice souvenirs. The **Bogapott** ceramics store, with its small café, is worth a look (Pikk Jalg 9, on the way up to Toompea). For jewelry by local artists, check out **A Galerii** at Hobusepea 8. More shops in Tallinn stay open on Sundays than in Sweden or Finland (it's the legacy of Soviet atheism).

ENTERTAINMENT

Music

Tallinn has a dense schedule of Baroque, Renaissance, and choral music performances, especially during the annual Old Town Days in early June (June 2–5 in 2005). Choral singing became a symbol of the struggle for Estonian independence after the first Estonian Song Festival in 1869 (still held every 5 years—next one in 2009). Even outside of festival times, you'll find performances in Tallinn's churches and concert halls (advertised on posters around town). Tickets are usually available at the door. Hortus Musicus is one of Estonia's best classical ensembles.

Estonia's three best modern choral composers and arrangers are Arvo Pärt, Veljo Tormis, and Erkki-Sven Tüür. Other Estonian groups have also put out a lot of good CDs. Check out the record shop in the Kaubamaja department store (daily 9:00–21:00, behind Hotel Viru).

SLEEPING

Tallinn has a great choice of hotels. There are some bargains, even in the Old Town, but even more if you're willing to stay a short walk or bus ride away. Summer is high season (Tallinn has more leisure than business travelers), so prices often drop from about November to April. Use a taxi to get to your hotel when you arrive, and then figure out the public transport later.

In the Old Town

$$$ **Hotel St. Petersbourg,** small and elegant with 27 eclectic Art Deco rooms, is a very classy place in the Old Town. You'll find plush public spaces and over-the-top services at top-end prices (Sb-3,400–3,950 kr, Db-4,000–4,550 kr, less Dec–April, suites and fancier rooms, children under 12 free, elevator, includes sauna, a block off

Sleep Code

(12 kr = about $1, country code: 372)
S = Single, **D** = Double/Twin, **T** = Triple, **Q** = Quad,
b = bathroom, **s** = shower. Credit cards are accepted and breakfast
is included unless otherwise noted.

To help you sort easily through these listings, I've divided
the rooms into three categories, based on the full price for a
standard double room with bath:

   $$$ **Higher Priced**—Most rooms 1,400 kr or more.
   $$ **Moderately Priced**—Most rooms between 800–1,400 kr.
   $ **Lower Priced**—Most rooms 800 kr or less.

Town Hall Square at Rataskaevu 7, tel. 628-6500, fax 628-6565,
www.schlossle-hotels.com, stpetersbourg@schlossle-hotels.com). If
you're loaded, sleep at the same company's even more luxurious
Schlössle Hotel, the best address in town (standard Db starts at over
€300, same Web site).

$$$ Domina City Hotel, central and upscale, has 68 rooms
divided into two classes; the more expensive ones allow a free trip to
the sauna (Sb-1,800–2,100 kr, Db 2,100–2,400 kr, check online for
discounts, elevator, expensive Internet access but cheap Internet café
is around the corner, Vana-Posti 11/13, tel. 681-3900, fax 681-
3901, www.dominahotels.ee, city@domina.ee).

$$$ Taanilinna Hotel, near the Viru shopping street, has 20
comfortable, fully-equipped rooms in a boxy building (Sb-1,500 kr,
Db-1,790 kr, cheaper top-floor twin Db-1,270 kr, extra bed-380 kr,
Uus 6, tel. 640-6700, fax 646-4306, www.taanilinna.ee).

$$ Meriton Old Town Hotel, a good value, is at the tip of the
Old Town not far from the ferry terminals. Most of its doubles have
twin beds (41 rooms, Sb-750 kr, Db-900–1,200 kr, non-smoking,
elevator, free Internet access, Lai 49, tel. 614-1300, fax 614-1311,
www.meritonhotels.com, oldtown@meritonhotels.com).

$ Villa Hortensia, in a courtyard tucked away from the Vene
shopping street, has six cozy rooms for rent above a small café and
chocolate shop. Three twin-bedded rooms and one double-bedded
room have a kitchenette and sleeping loft. A fifth "deluxe" room
comes with a double bed and small balcony. A sixth room—really
an apartment—is on two floors, with kitchenette, mini-balcony, a
double bed upstairs and a fold-out sofa-bed in the living room. This
is a great choice for a home-away-from-home in the heart of the
Old Town (Sb-600 kr, deluxe Sb-900 kr, Db-800 kr, deluxe Db-
1,200 kr, apartment-2,000 kr, reserve well in advance, 50 yards off
the corner of Vene and Viru streets at Vene 6, look for archway and

Tallinn Hotels and Restaurants

1 Hotel St. Petersbourg
2 Villa Hortensia & Chocolaterie
3 Olematu Rüütel Rooms
4 To Hotel G9 & Restaurant Tallinna Eesti Maja
5 Hostel Vana Tom
6 Domina City Hotel
7 Taanilinna Hotel
8 To Meriton Old Town Hotel
9 To Hotell St. Barbara
10 Rasastra B&B Res. Agency & Peetri Pizza
11 To Valge Villa, Hotell Nepi & Tihase B&B
12 Von Krahli Baar & Vanaema Juures Restaurant
13 Kloostri Ait Pub
14 Beer House Pub & Kuldse Notsu Kõrts Restaurant
15 Peppersack & Olde Hansa Restaurants
16 Le Bonaparte Restaurant & Hell Hunt Pub
17 Maiasmokk Café & Pastries
18 Pizza Americana
19 Kaubamaja Department Store
20 Patkuli Viewpoint
21 Lower Town Viewpoint

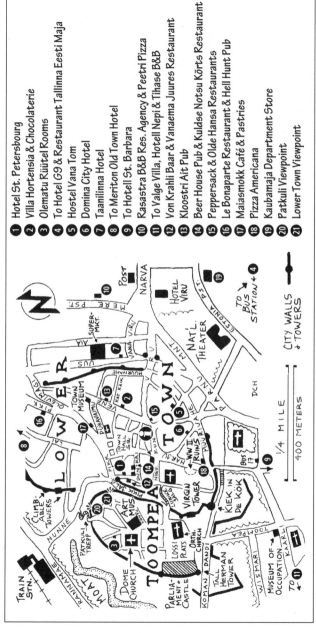

Chocolaterie signs, tel. 504-6113, jaan.parn@mail.ee, Jaan Pärn).

$ Olematu Rüütel ("The Nonexistent Knight"), a quiet, out-of-the-way restaurant on Toompea, rents three sleek, comfy, but basic rooms. One room has a private bathroom, and the other two rooms share a bathroom. Call well in advance—especially in summer—for the only inexpensive rooms in Toompea (D-650 kr, Db-800 kr, extra bed-80 kr, breakfast-30 kr, sauna-300 kr/hr, Kiriku Põik 4a, tel. 631-3827, fax 631-3826, www.hot.ee/olematuryytel, nonexistent@hot.ee).

$ Hostel Vana Tom, centrally located two blocks off the Town Hall Square, is a modern, well-run hostel with 60 beds (15-bed triple-bunk rooms-235 kr/bunk; simple, sinkless, but sleepable D-595 kr; T-830 kr, Q-1,065 kr, showers down the hall, discounts for hostel members, includes breakfast, Väike-Karja 1, tel. 631-3252, www.hostel.ee). Try to ignore the harmless little Striptiis Bar upstairs.

Just Outside the Old Town

$$$ Hotell St. Barbara is a business hotel on a quiet street two blocks south of Vabaduse Väljak and the Old Town, in a 19th-century stone building with high ceilings (53 rooms, Sb-1,510 kr, Db-1,610 kr, Roosikrantsi 2A, tel. 640-7600, fax 640-7440, www.scandic-hotels.com, stbarbara@scandic-hotels.com).

$ Hotell G9 is a fine value, with 23 rooms on the third floor of a large nondescript building on the other side of Hotel Viru from the Old Town. All but three rooms have twin beds (Sb-550–650 kr, Db-670–750 kr, extra bed-180 kr, no breakfast, Gonsiori 9; set back from street at intersection of Maneeži, Gonsiori, and Reimann streets; tel. 626-7100, fax 626-7102, www.hotelg9.ee, hotelg9@hot.ee).

Near the Ferry Terminals

If you're cruising in, these two places are almost too convenient—right next to Terminals A/B/C and D, respectively, but without any Old Town character.

$$ Express Hotel is a few steps from Terminals A, B, and C and also close to the Linnahall terminal. It's a modern Motel 6–type place—cheery, great prices, and plenty comfortable. Each of the well-designed 166 rooms is the same (Sb or Db-1,017 kr, extra bed-350 kr, children under 16 sleep free, non-smoking rooms, elevator, free Internet access, Sadama 1, tel. 667-8700, fax 667-8800, www.revalhotels.com, expresstallinn@revalhotels.com).

$$ Saku Rock Bed & Beer Hotel is right across from Terminal D. Named after and sponsored by Estonia's largest brewery, you get a free beer on check-in, and the bedside lamps are converted beer cans; otherwise, it's a normal hotel with 113 identical rooms (Sb/Db-986 kr, extra bed-350 kr, check online for lower rates, Sadama 25A, tel. 680-6600, fax 680-6601, www.sakurockhotel.ee).

In Lilleküla

Lilleküla is a quiet, green, peaceful residential area of single-family houses, small Soviet-era apartment blocks, and barking dogs. For a clearer understanding of Estonian life, stay here. You'll save money without sacrificing comfort. The downside: It's a 10- to 15-minute, 10-kr bus ride into the center (take a cab your first time out). To get to Lilleküla by bus from the center, go to Vabaduse Väljak (see Tallinn overview map, page 303) and board bus #17, or take bus #17a from the stop across the square from Palace Hotel (runs roughly every 20 min, can also board by Estonia Theater).

$$ **Valge Villa** ("White Villa"), a homey guest house in a great garden run by Anne and Andres Vahtra and their family, does everything right and is worth the high-for-a-guest-house price. Its 10 rooms are spacious and well furnished (Sb-700 kr, Db-880 kr, small suite-990 kr, larger suite-1,170 kr, suite-apartments-1,600 kr, extra bed-300 kr, 10 percent off when booked online, kids under 12 stay free in same room, every 5th night free, bikes-225 kr/day, sauna-300 kr, laundry service-120 kr; take bus #17 or #17a to Räägu stop, or trolley #2, #3, or #4 to Tedre stop; Kännu 26/2, between Rästa and Räägu streets, tel. & fax 654-2302, www.white-villa.com).

$ **Hotell Nepi** is a small, less-eager place with comfy public areas and 10 well-worn but serviceable rooms (Sb-490 kr, Db-590–690 kr, breakfast-50 kr, Nepi 10, take bus #17 or #17a to Koolimaja stop, or bus #23 or #23a to Ööbiku stop and walk 300 yards, tel. 655-1665, fax 655-1664, www.nepihotell.ee, nepihotell @nepihotell.ee, Tõnis SE).

$ At **Tihase B&B**, young, English-speaking Ivo Roosi rents two funky double-bedded spare rooms in his bachelor pad, along with a cottage with a private bath and a sauna out back. Complete with a garden and tabby cat, this is your best real-people experience. It's a Scandinavian-style red wooden house with white trim (S-400 kr, D-500 kr, Db-700 kr, 100 kr less off-season, cash only, sauna-250 kr, take bus #17 or #17a to Hauka stop, Tihase 6A, tel. 683-1775, mobile 511-9541, www.tihase.ee, tihase@tihase.ee). Ivo does one-day countryside car tours tailored to your interests (from 500 kr), and can pick you up at the ferry terminal or airport for an extra fee.

Rooms in Private Homes

$ The **Rasastra** agency, run by English-speaking Ms. Urve Susi, coordinates a network of families around town (and throughout the Baltics) who rent out spare rooms and apartments. Expect to be shown your room and be mostly left alone by your host. In fact, many families actually move to their country cottages (where they work their gardens) and leave you alone with their flats (S-260 kr, D-480 kr, T-650 kr; apartments with sitting room, bedroom, kitchen, and private bathroom are 800 kr; breakfast-30 kr, all located in city center). The office, which has an array of TI booklets and maps, is at Mere Puiestee 4, near Hotel Viru; follow the signs up the stairs (daily 9:30–18:00, tel. & fax 661-6291, www.bedbreakfast.ee, rasastra@online.ee).

EATING

Unlike those in Helsinki or Stockholm, restaurants in Tallinn are cheap, plentiful, and usually good. Visiting Scandinavians gorge themselves on inexpensive food. Few restaurants have non-smoking sections. Most accept credit cards. Your bill doesn't include a service charge—if service is good, round up to no more than 10 percent of your total bill.

A few years ago it was hard to find authentic local cuisine, but now it seems Estonian food is trendy—a hot and hearty Northern mixture of meat, potatoes, root vegetables, mushrooms, bread, and soup. Pea soup is a local specialty. A typical pub snack is Estonian garlic bread *(küüslauguleivad)*—deep-fried strips of dark rye bread smothered in garlic and served with a dipping sauce. Estonia's Saku beer is good, cheap, and on tap at most eateries. Try the nutty, full-bodied Tume variety.

Pubs in the Old Town

Young Estonians eat well and affordably at pubs. Soup, a main dish, and a beer will run you about 100 kr ($8). At lunch on weekdays, look for the *päeva praad* (dish of the day—meat, veggies, and a starch) for only 35–40 kr. *Tallinn in Your Pocket* lists the latest places to go. In some pubs, you go to the bar to look at the menu, order, and pay. Then you find a table, and they'll bring your food out when it's ready.

Kloostri Ait is cheery, with a loyal local crowd, occasional live music, a fireplace, and a fun, no-stress menu: tasty 25–35-kr soups, fine 65–100-kr main dishes, and *hõõgvein* (mulled wine) in the winter (daily 12:00–24:00, Vene 14, next to Dominican cloister, tel. 641-8374).

Von Krahli Baar serves hearty Estonian grub—such as potato pancakes *(torud)* stuffed with mushroom or shrimp (50 kr, half-portion-35 kr)—in a dark, beer-stained bar or a peaceful little courtyard (daily 12:00–23:00, Rataskaevu 10/12, a block uphill from Town Hall Square, near Wheel Well, tel. 626-9096).

Hell Hunt ("The Gentle Wolf") attracts a mixed expat and local crowd with its good food (soups-35–45 kr, main dishes-55–75 kr, daily 12:00–02:00, Pikk 39, tel. 681-8333).

The Beer House, two doors up from Town Hall Square, is a microbrewery serving light meals (including pizza) among shiny copper vats or outside on wooden picnic tables (40–50-kr lunch plates, 60–130-kr main dishes, Sun–Thu 9:00–24:00, Fri–Sat 9:00–02:00, Dunkri 5, tel. 627-6520).

Dining in the Old Town

The Old Town is full of restaurants packed with atmosphere and traditionally dressed servers. Dine under medieval arches, in candlelit restaurants, or at tables outside in good weather. Most offer stick-to-your-ribs Estonian fare as well as more modern options.

Vanaema Juures ("Grandma's Place"), a small cellar restaurant, serves homey, candlelit, traditional Estonian meals, such as pork roast with sauerkraut and juniper berries. Soups cost 40 kr, entrées run 110–160 kr, and dinner reservations are strongly advised. This is your best bet for local cuisine (Mon–Sat 12:00–22:00, Sun 12:00–18:00, Rataskaevu 10, tel. 626-9080).

Kuldse Notsu Kõrts ("The Golden Piggy") is touristy and rustic, decorated with country-style antiques and Estonian proverbs painted on the walls (ask for a translation). They dish up soups for 60 kr and plenty of pork and traditional Estonian dishes for 140–200 kr (daily 12:00–24:00, a half-block up from Town Hall Square, Dunkri 8, tel. 628-6567).

Medieval Cuisine: Two restaurants just below the Town Hall Square specialize in re-creating medieval food (from the days before the arrival of the potato and tomato from the New World). **Olde Hansa** fills three creaky old floors and outdoor tables with tourists, candle wax, and scurrying medieval waitresses—but has gotten quite expensive, with most main dishes approaching 200 kr (live music on the 2nd floor, daily 11:00–24:00, a belch below Town Hall Square at Vana turg 1, reserve by phone or online, tel. 627-9020, www.oldehansa.ee). **Peppersack,** across the street, has a grand dining room, with stained glass and wooden beams, as well as a more casual and quiet "grill" downstairs. The menu is for meat lovers, with medieval names for the 140–250-kr dishes (daily 12:00–23:00, reservations advised, Viru tänav 2, tel. 646-6900, www.peppersack.ee). The casual café to the left of the main entrance offers coffee and light meals.

Russian Food: Troika, through a hallway off Town Hall Square, has *bliny* pancakes for 64–96 kr, *pelmeni* dumplings for 49–82 kr, and main dishes for 100–160 kr (daily 10:00–23:00, Raekoja Plats 15, tel. 627-6245, www.troika.ee).

Upscale French: Le Bonaparte serves tasty non-Estonian food. The main dishes are primarily French and range 180–310 kr. The classy dining room has painted wooden beams, as well as a wine cellar with tables. Reservations are smart (Mon–Sat 12:00–15:00 & 19:00–24:00, closed Sun, Pikk 45, tel. 646-4444, www.bonaparte.ee). The more casual café in front serves quiche, pastries, and coffee (Mon–Sat 8:00–22:00, Sun 10:00–18:00).

More Eateries

Tallinna Eesti Maja ("Tallinn Estonian House"), worth seeking out, serves good traditional Estonian food, including a 75-kr weekday lunch buffet (buffet Mon–Fri 11:00–15:00, main dishes-100–150 kr, open daily 11:00–23:00, outside Old Town, behind Hotel Viru, at Lauteri 1 by the corner of Rävala Puiestee, downstairs, tel. 645-5252, www.eestimaja.ee).

Maiasmokk ("Sweet Tooth") café and pastry shop, founded in 1864, is the grande dame of Tallinn cafés—ideal for dessert or breakfast. Back in the Soviet days, this was the place for a good pastry. Point to what you want at the pastry counter, or sit down for breakfast or coffee on the other side of the shop. Everything's very cheap (Mon–Sat 8:00–19:00, Sun 10:00–18:00, Pikk 16, across from church with old clock).

The **Chocolaterie** at Vene 6 has scrumptious fresh pralines, sandwiches, coffee, and a lovely courtyard.

For pizza and pasta, there's **Pizza Americana** in the Old Town at Müürivahe 2 or Pikk 1/3, and the cheaper **Peetri Pizza** at Mere Pst. 6.

Supermarkets: The **Rimi** supermarket at Aia 7 is on the edge of the Old Town, a few blocks from Hotel Viru (daily 8:00–22:00). Another supermarket is in the basement of the big shopping center directly behind Hotel Viru.

TRANSPORTATION CONNECTIONS

The bus is usually the best way to travel by land from Tallinn. The bus station *(autobussijaam)* is a few stops outside the center on trams #2 and #4.

From Tallinn to: Riga (6 buses/day, 6 hrs, no train option), **Vilnius** (2 buses/day, 10 hrs), **St. Petersburg** (5 buses/day, 9 hrs), **Moscow** (fly or take the overnight train). For the latest bus and train schedules, consult *Tallinn in Your Pocket.*

APPENDIX

Let's Talk Telephones

This is a primer on telephoning in Europe. For more information on Scandinavia, see "Telephones" in the Introduction.

Making Calls within a European Country: About half of all European countries use area codes (like we do); the other half uses a direct-dial system without area codes.

To make calls within a country that uses a direct-dial system (Denmark, Norway, Estonia, Belgium, the Czech Republic, France, Italy, Portugal, Spain, and Switzerland), you dial the same number whether you're calling across the country or across the street.

In countries that use area codes (such as Finland, Sweden, Austria, Britain, Germany, Ireland, and the Netherlands), you dial the local number when calling within a city, and you add the area code if calling long-distance within the country.

Making International Calls: You always start with the international access code (011 if you're calling from America or Canada, or 00 from Europe), then dial the country code of the country you're calling (see chart below).

What you dial next depends on the phone system of the country you're calling. If the country uses area codes, drop the initial 0 of the area code, then dial the rest of the number.

Countries that use direct-dial systems (no area codes) vary in how they're accessed internationally by phone. For instance, if you're making an international call to Denmark, Norway, Estonia, the Czech Republic, Italy, Portugal, or Spain, simply dial the international access code, country code, and phone number. But if you're calling Belgium, France, or Switzerland, drop the initial 0 of the phone number.

European Calling Chart

Just smile and dial, using this key:
AC = Area Code, LN = Local Number.

European Country	Calling long distance within ...	Calling from the U.S.A./ Canada to ...	Calling from a European country to ...
Austria	AC + LN	011 + 43 + AC (without the initial zero) + LN	00 + 43 + AC (without the initial zero) + LN
Belgium	LN	011 + 32 + LN (without initial zero)	00 + 32 + LN (without initial zero)
Britain	AC + LN	011 + 44 + AC (without initial zero) + LN	00 + 44 + AC (without initial zero) + LN
Czech Republic	LN	011 + 420 + LN	00 + 420 + LN
Denmark	LN	011 + 45 + LN	00 + 45 + LN
Estonia	LN	011 + 372 + LN	00 + 372 + LN
Finland	AC + LN	011 + 358 + AC (without initial zero) + LN	00 + 358 + AC (without initial zero) + LN
France	LN	011 + 33 + LN (without initial zero)	00 + 33 + LN (without initial zero)
Germany	AC + LN	011 + 49 + AC (without initial zero) + LN	00 + 49 + AC (without initial zero) + LN
Gibraltar	LN	011 + 350 + LN	00 + 350 + LN From Spain: 9567 + LN
Greece	LN	011 + 30 + LN	00 + 30 + LN

European Country	Calling long distance within…	Calling from the U.S.A./ Canada to…	Calling from a European country to…
Ireland	AC + LN	011 + 353 + AC (without initial zero) + LN	00 + 353 + AC (without initial zero) + LN
Italy	LN	011 + 39 + LN	00 + 39 + LN
Morocco	LN	011 + 212 + LN (without initial zero)	00 + 212 + LN (without initial zero)
Netherlands	AC + LN	011 + 31 + AC (without initial zero) + LN	00 + 31 + AC (without initial zero) + LN
Norway	LN	011 + 47 + LN	00 + 47 + LN
Portugal	LN	011 + 351 + LN	00 + 351 + LN
Spain	LN	011 + 34 + LN	00 + 34 + LN
Sweden	AC + LN	011 + 46 + AC (without initial zero) + LN	00 + 46 + AC (without initial zero) + LN
Switzerland	LN	011 + 41 + LN (without initial zero)	00 + 41 + LN (without initial zero)
Turkey	AC (if no initial zero is included, add one) + LN	011 + 90 + AC (without initial zero) + LN	00 + 90 + AC (without initial zero) + LN

- The instructions above apply whether you're calling a fixed phone or mobile phone.

- The international access codes (the first numbers you dial when making an international call) are 011 if you're calling from the U.S.A./Canada, or 00 if you're calling from anywhere in Europe.

- To call the U.S.A. or Canada from Europe, dial 00, then 1 (the country code for the U.S.A. and Canada), then the area code and number. In short, 00 + 1 + AC + LN = Hi, Mom!

Country Codes

After you've dialed the international access code (011 if you're calling from America or Canada, or 00 from Europe), dial the code of the country you're calling.

Austria—43	Ireland—353
Belgium—32	Italy—39
Britain—44	Morocco—212
Canada—1	Netherlands—31
Croatia—385	Norway—47
Czech Rep.—420	Poland—48
Denmark—45	Portugal—351
Estonia—372	Slovenia—386
Finland—358	Spain—34
France—33	Sweden—46
Germany—49	Switzerland—41
Gibraltar—350	Turkey—90
Greece—30	U.S.A.—1

U.S. Embassies

If you lose your passport, here's who to contact:
Denmark: tel. 35 55 31 44, Dag Hammarskjölds Allé 24, Copenhagen, www.usembassy.dk
Estonia: tel. 668-8100, Kentmanni 20, Tallinn, www.usemb.ee
Finland: tel. 09/616-25701, Itainen Puistotie 14b, Helsinki, www.usembassy.fi
Norway: tel. 22 44 85 50, ext. 8941/8715, Drammensveien 18, Oslo, www.usa.no
Sweden: tel. 08/783-5375, Dag Hammarskjölds Vag 31, Stockholm, www.usis.usemb.se

Festivals and Public Holidays in 2005

Here's a partial list of holidays and festivals in Scandinavia. Many event dates hadn't been set at the time this book went to print. For more information, contact the Scandinavian National Tourist Office in the United States (P.O. Box 4649, Grand Central Station, New York, NY 10163, tel. 212/885-9700, fax 212/885-9710, www.goscandinavia.com, info@goscandinavia.com) and check these Web sites: www.visitdenmark.com, www.visitnorway.com, www.visit-sweden.com, www.finland-tourism.com, www.whatsonwhen.com, and www.festivals.com.

Location	Time of Year	Festival
Odense, *Denmark*	Jan (second half)	Winter Jazz Festival
Lillehammer, *Norway*	Mid-Feb (theater, music)	Winter Arts Festival

2 0 0 5

JANUARY

S	M	T	W	T	F	S
						1
2	3	4	5	6	7	8
9	10	11	12	13	14	15
16	17	18	19	20	21	22
23/30	24/31	25	26	27	28	29

FEBRUARY

S	M	T	W	T	F	S
		1	2	3	4	5
6	7	8	9	10	11	12
13	14	15	16	17	18	19
20	21	22	23	24	25	26
27	28					

MARCH

S	M	T	W	T	F	S
		1	2	3	4	5
6	7	8	9	10	11	12
13	14	15	16	17	18	19
20	21	22	23	24	25	26
27	28	29	30	31		

APRIL

S	M	T	W	T	F	S
					1	2
3	4	5	6	7	8	9
10	11	12	13	14	15	16
17	18	19	20	21	22	23
24	25	26	27	28	29	30

MAY

S	M	T	W	T	F	S
1	2	3	4	5	6	7
8	9	10	11	12	13	14
15	16	17	18	19	20	21
22	23	24	25	26	27	28
29	30	31				

JUNE

S	M	T	W	T	F	S
			1	2	3	4
5	6	7	8	9	10	11
12	13	14	15	16	17	18
19	20	21	22	23	24	25
26	27	28	29	30		

JULY

S	M	T	W	T	F	S
					1	2
3	4	5	6	7	8	9
10	11	12	13	14	15	16
17	18	19	20	21	22	23
24/31	25	26	27	28	29	30

AUGUST

S	M	T	W	T	F	S
	1	2	3	4	5	6
7	8	9	10	11	12	13
14	15	16	17	18	19	20
21	22	23	24	25	26	27
28	29	30	31			

SEPTEMBER

S	M	T	W	T	F	S
				1	2	3
4	5	6	7	8	9	10
11	12	13	14	15	16	17
18	19	20	21	22	23	24
25	26	27	28	29	30	

OCTOBER

S	M	T	W	T	F	S
						1
2	3	4	5	6	7	8
9	10	11	12	13	14	15
16	17	18	19	20	21	22
23/30	24/31	25	26	27	28	29

NOVEMBER

S	M	T	W	T	F	S
		1	2	3	4	5
6	7	8	9	10	11	12
13	14	15	16	17	18	19
20	21	22	23	24	25	26
27	28	29	30			

DECEMBER

S	M	T	W	T	F	S
				1	2	3
4	5	6	7	8	9	10
11	12	13	14	15	16	17
18	19	20	21	22	23	24
25	26	27	28	29	30	31

Location	Date	Event
Bergen, *Norway*	April 1	Hat Festival (spring festival)
Bergen, *Norway*	Before Easter	Easter Festival (theater, concerts)
Denmark	April 2	200th anniversary of H. C. Andersen's birthday
Bergen, *Norway*	End of April	Ole Blues and Maritime Festivals
Sweden	April 30	Walpurgis Night (bonfires, choirs)
Scandinavia	May 1	May Day (parades, some closures)
Stavanger, *Norway*	Early May	Jazz Festival
Oslo, *Norway*	May 15	St. Hallvard's Day (theater, concerts)

Denmark	May 16	Common Prayers Day (businesses closed)
Copenhagen, *Denmark*	Mid-May	Flower Festival
Norway	May 17	Constitution Day (parades, closures)
Norway	End of May	International Festival (theater, music, dance)
Copenhagen, *Denmark*	End of May	Swinging Jazz Festival
Bergen, *Norway*	End of May	Dragon Boat Festival (Chinese boat races)
Tallinn, *Estonia*	June 2–5	Old Town Days (music)
Denmark	June 5	Constitution Day (businesses closed)
Sweden	June 6	National Day (parades)
Stockholm, *Sweden*	Week in early June	Restaurant Days
Stockholm, *Sweden*	June 6	Archipelago Boat Day (steamboat parade)
Oslo, *Norway*	Early June	Norwegian Wood Festival (rock music)
Stavanger, *Norway*	Early June	Wooden Boats Festival
Oslo, *Norway*	Mid-June	Medieval Festival
Bergen, *Norway*	Mid-June–Mid-Aug	Floien Concert Festival (classical music)
Scandinavia	Solstice	Midsummer Eve (celebration, bonfires)
Odense, *Denmark*	Late June–Aug	Hans Christian Andersen Festival
Roskilde, *Denmark*	Late June–July	Roskilde Festival (music, theater)
Copenhagen, *Denmark*	July 1–10	Copenhagen Jazz Festival
Stockholm, *Sweden*	July 4	Fourth of July festivities
Århus, *Denmark*	Mid–Late July	International Jazz Festival
Bergen, *Norway*	Late July	Cutty Sark Tall Ship Race

Stockholm, *Sweden*	Early Aug	Water Festival (10 days)
Växjö, *Sweden*	Mid-Aug	Emigration Festival (3 days)
Oslo, *Norway*	Mid-Aug	Jazz Festival
Stavanger, *Norway*	Mid-Aug	Chamber Music Festival
Oslo, *Norway*	Late Aug	Seafood Festival
Oslo, *Norway*	Late Aug	Chamber Music Festival
Bergen, *Norway*	Late Aug	International Chamber Music Festival
Helsinki, *Finland*	Late Aug–Sept	Helsinki Festival (music, theater)
Århus, *Denmark*	Early Sept	Festival Week (music, dance, theater)
Odense, *Denmark*	Late Sept	Folk Festival
Bergen, *Norway*	Oct 1	Rain Festival (raincoat and umbrella parade)
Bergen, *Norway*	Early Oct–Nov	Art Festival (jazz, dance)
Oslo, *Norway*	Early–Mid-Oct	Contemporary Music Festival
Lillehammer, *Norway*	Mid-Oct	Jazz Festival
Copenhagen, *Denmark*	Early Nov	Autumn Jazz Festival
Copenhagen, *Denmark*	Mid-Nov–Dec 23	Christmas Fair (Tivoli Gardens)
Finland	Dec 6	Independence Day (candlelit windows)
Sweden	Dec 13	Lucia Day (festival of lights)
Scandinavia	Dec 25	Christmas

Climate

First line, average daily low temperature; second line, average daily high; third line, days of no rain.

	J	F	M	A	M	J	J	A	S	O	N	D
DENMARK • Copenhagen												
	29°	28°	31°	37°	45°	51°	56°	56°	51°	44°	38°	33°
	37°	37°	42°	51°	60°	66°	70°	69°	64°	55°	46°	41°
	14	15	19	18	20	18	17	16	14	14	11	12
ESTONIA • Tallinn												
	14º	12º	19º	32º	41º	50º	54º	52º	48º	39º	30º	19º
	25º	25º	32º	45º	57º	66º	68º	66º	59º	50º	37º	30º
	12	12	18	19	19	20	18	16	14	14	12	12
FINLAND • Helsinki												
	17°	15°	20°	30°	40°	49°	55°	53°	46°	37°	30°	23°
	26°	25°	32°	44°	56°	66°	71°	68°	59°	47°	37°	31°
	11	10	17	17	19	17	17	16	16	13	11	11
NORWAY • Oslo												
	19º	19º	25º	34º	43º	50º	55º	53º	46º	38º	31º	25º
	28º	30º	39º	50º	61º	68º	72º	70º	60º	48º	38º	32º
	16	16	22	19	21	17	16	17	16	17	14	14
SWEDEN • Stockholm												
	26º	25º	29º	37º	45º	53º	57º	56º	50º	43º	37º	32º
	30º	30º	37º	47º	58º	67º	71º	68º	60º	49º	40º	35º
	15	14	21	19	20	17	18	17	16	16	14	14

Metric Conversion (approximate)

1 inch = 25 millimeters

1 foot = 0.3 meter

1 yard = 0.9 meter

1 mile = 1.6 kilometers

1 centimeter = 0.4 inch

1 meter = 39.4 inches

1 kilometer = .62 mile

32 degrees F = 0 degrees C

82 degrees F = about 28 degrees C

1 ounce = 28 grams

1 kilogram = 2.2 pounds

1 quart = 0.95 liter

1 square yard = 0.8 square meter

1 acre = 0.4 hectare

Temperature Conversion: Fahrenheit and Celsius

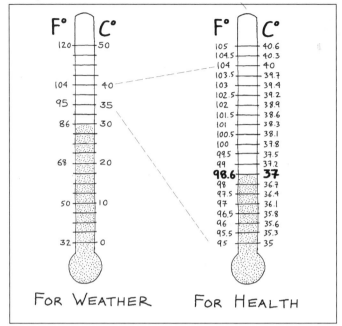

For Weather   For Health

Numbers and Stumblers

- Europeans write a few of their numbers differently than we do. 1 = 𝟣 , 4 = 𝟦 , 7 = 𝟽 . Learn the difference or miss your train.
- In Europe, dates appear as day/month/year, so Christmas is 25/12/05.
- Commas are decimal points and decimals commas. A dollar and a half is $1,50, and there are 5.280 feet in a mile.
- When pointing, use your whole hand, palm down.
- When counting with fingers, start with your thumb. If you hold up your first finger to request one item, you'll probably get two.
- What Americans call the second floor of a building is the first floor in Europe.
- Europeans keep the left "lane" open for passing on escalators and moving sidewalks. Keep to the right.

Making Your Hotel Reservation

Most hotel managers know basic "hotel English." Faxing or e-mailing are the preferred methods for reserving a room. They're more accurate than telephoning and much faster than writing a letter. Use this handy form for your fax or find it online at www.ricksteves.com/reservation. Photocopy and fax away.

One-Page Fax

To: _____ @ _____
             hotel   **fax**

From: _____@ _____
             name   **fax**

Today's date: _____/_____ /_____
                  day   month   year

Dear Hotel _____ ,
Please make this reservation for me:

Name: _____

Total # of people:_____ # of rooms: _____ # of nights: _____

Arriving: _____ /_____/_____   My time of arrival (24-hr clock): _____
          day month year   (I will telephone if I will be late)

Departing: ____ /____/____
           day month year

Room(s): Single _____ Double ____ Twin _____Triple ____ Quad_____

With: Toilet _____ Shower _____Bath _____ Sink only _____

Special needs: View____ Quiet ____ Cheapest ____ Ground Floor ____

Please fax, mail, or e-mail confirmation of my reservation, along with the type of room reserved and the price. Please also inform me of your cancellation policy. After I hear from you, I will quickly send my credit-card information as a deposit to hold the room. Thank you.

_____
Signature

_____
Name

_____
Address

_____
City   **State**   **Zip Code   Country**

_____
E-mail Address

INDEX

RESEARCHER

SONJA GROSET

Sonja Groset, whose immigrant parents are from Sweden and Norway, loves returning to her Scandinavian roots each summer, whether to spend time with relatives or to run the Stockholm Marathon. She's worked for Rick Steves for eight years—researching guidebooks, leading tours, and designing Web pages for www.ricksteves.com.

Start your trip at
www.ricksteves.com

Rick Steves' website is packed with over 3,000 pages of timely travel information. It's also your gateway to getting FREE monthly travel news from Rick — and more!

Free Monthly European Travel News

Fresh articles on Europe's most interesting destinations and happenings. Rick will even send you an e-mail every month (often direct from Europe) with his latest discoveries!

Timely Travel Tips

Rick Steves' best money-and-stress-saving tips on trip planning, packing, transportation, hotels, health, safety, finances, hurdling the language barrier…and more.

Travelers' Graffiti Wall

Candid advice and opinions from thousands of travelers on everything listed above, plus whatever topics are hot at the moment (discount flights, packing tips, scams…you name it).

Rick's Annual Guide to European Railpasses

The clearest, most comprehensive guide to the confusing array of railpass options out there, and how to choo-choose the railpass that best fits your itinerary and budget. Then you can order your railpass (and get a bunch of great freebies) online from us!

Great Gear at the Rick Steves Travel Store

Enjoy bargains on Rick's guidebooks, planning maps and TV series DVDs—and on his custom-designed carry-on bags, wheeled bags, day bags and light-packing accessories.

Rick Steves Tours

Every year more than 5,000 lucky travelers explore Europe on a Rick Steves tour. Learn more about our 26 different one-to-three-week itineraries, read uncensored feedback from our tour alums, and sign up for your dream trip online!

Rick on TV

Read the scripts and see video clips from the popular Rick Steves' Europe TV series, and get an inside look at Rick's 13 newest shows.

Respect for Your Privacy

Ordering online from us is secure. When you buy something from us, join a tour, or subscribe to Rick's free monthly travel news e-mails, we promise to never share your name, information, or e-mail address with anyone else. You won't be spammed!

Have fun raising your Travel I.Q. at
www.ricksteves.com

Travel smart...carry on!

*T*he latest generation of Rick Steves' carry-on travel bags is easily the best—benefiting from two decades of on-the-road attention to what really matters: maximum quality and strength; practical, flexible features; and no unnecessary frills. You won't find a better value anywhere!

Convertible, expandable, and carry-on-size:

Rick Steves' Back Door Bag $99

This is the same bag that Rick Steves lives out of for three months every summer. It's made of rugged water-resistant 1000 denier Cordura nylon, and best of all, it converts easily from a smart-looking suitcase to a handy backpack with comfortably-curved shoulder straps and a padded waistbelt.

This roomy, versatile 9" x 21" x 14" bag has a large 2600 cubic-inch main compartment, plus three outside pockets (small, medium and huge) that are perfect for often-used items. And the cinch-tight compression straps will keep your load compact and close to your back—not sagging like a sack of potatoes.

Wishing you had even more room to bring home souvenirs? Pull open the full-perimeter expando-zipper and its capacity jumps from 2600 to 3000 cubic inches. When you want to use it as a suitcase or check it as luggage (required when "expanded"), the straps and belt hide away in a zippered compartment in the back.

Attention travelers under 5'4" tall: This bag also comes in an inch-shorter version, for a compact-friendlier fit between the waistbelt and shoulder straps.

Convenient, durable, and carry-on-size:

Rick Steves' Wheeled Bag $119

At 9" x 21" x 14" our sturdy Rick Steves' Wheeled Bag is rucksack-soft in front, but the rest is lined with a hard ABS-lexan shell to give maximum protection to your belongings. We've spared no expense on moving parts, splurging on an extra-long button-release handle and big, tough inline skate wheels for easy rolling on rough surfaces.

This bag is not convertible! Our research tells us that travelers who've bought convertible wheeled bags never put them on their backs anyway, so we've eliminated the extra weight and expense.

Rick Steves' Wheeled Bag has exactly the same three-outside-pocket configuration as our Back Door Bag, plus a handy "add-a-bag" strap and full lining.

Our Back Door Bags and Wheeled Bags come in black, navy, blue spruce, evergreen and merlot.

For great deals on a wide selection of travel goodies, begin your next trip at the Rick Steves Travel Store!

Visit the Rick Steves Travel Store at
www.ricksteves.com

Rick Steves

COUNTRY GUIDES 2005

France
Germany & Austria
Great Britain
Ireland
Italy
Portugal
Scandinavia
Spain
Switzerland

CITY GUIDES 2005

Amsterdam, Bruges & Brussels
Florence & Tuscany
London
Paris
Prague & The Czech Republic
Provence & The French Riviera
Rome
Venice

BEST OF GUIDES

Best European City Walks & Museums
Best of Eastern Europe
Best of Europe

More *Savvy*. More *Surprising*. More *Fun*.

PHRASE BOOKS & DICTIONARIES

French
French, Italian & German
German
Italian
Portuguese
Spanish

MORE EUROPE FROM RICK STEVES

Easy Access Europe
Europe 101
Europe Through the Back Door
Postcards from Europe

DVD
RICK STEVES' EUROPE

Rick Steves' Europe All Thirty
    Shows 2000–2003
Britain & Ireland
Exotic Europe
Germany, The Swiss Alps
    & Travel Skills
Italy

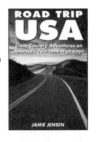

For a complete list of Rick Steves' guidebooks, see page 8.

Thanks to my wife, Anne, for making home my favorite travel destination. Thanks also to Thor, Hanne, Geir, Hege, and Kari-Anne, our Norwegian family. In loving memory of Berit Kristiansen, whose house was my house for 20 years of Norwegian travel.

Avalon Travel Publishing
1400 65th Street, Suite 250
Emeryville, CA 94608
Avalon Travel Publishing is an Imprint of Avalon Publishing Group, Inc.

Text © 2005, 2003, 2002, 2001, 2000 by Rick Steves.
Cover © 2005 by Avalon Travel Publishing, Inc. All rights reserved.
Maps © 2005 by Europe Through the Back Door.

Printed in the USA by Worzalla. Second printing September 2005.
ISBN 1-56691-684-4 • ISSN 1084-7206

For the latest on Rick's lectures, guidebooks, tours, and public television series, contact Europe Through the Back Door, Box 2009, Edmonds, WA 98020, 425/771-8303, fax 425/771-0833, www.ricksteves.com, rick@ricksteves.com.

Europe Through the Back Door Managing Editor: Risa Laib
ETBD Editors: Cameron Hewitt, Jennifer Hauseman
Avalon Travel Publishing Editor and Series Manager: Roxanna Font
Avalon Travel Publishing Project Editor: Patrick Collins
Copy Editor: Matthew Reed Baker
Indexer: Stephen Callahan
Production & Typesetting: Patrick David Barber
Research Assistance: Sonja Groset, Ian Watson
Interior Design: Amber Pirker, Jane Musser, Laura Mazer
Cover Design: Kari Gim, Laura Mazer
Maps and Graphics: David C. Hoerlein, Zoey Platt, Lauren Mills, Rhonda Pelikan, Mike Morgenfeld
Photography: Cameron Hewitt, Sonja Groset, Rick Steves
Front Matter Color Photos: p. i, Copenhagen, Denmark, © Rick Steves; p. iv, Helsinki, Finland, © Lee Foster
Cover Photos: front image, Christmas market at the town square in Gamla Stan, Stockholm, Sweden © Jason Lindsey; back image, Aurlandsfjord, Norway © Stone/Getty
Avalon Travel Publishing Graphics Coordinator: Deborah Dutcher